The Ultimate Guide to Informed Wearable Technology

A hands-on approach for creating wearables from prototype to purpose using Arduino systems

Christine Farion

BIRMINGHAM—MUMBAI

The Ultimate Guide to Informed Wearable Technology

Group Product Manager: Rahul Nair

Publishing Product Manager: Surbhi Suman

Senior Editor: Tanya D'cruz

Content Development Editor: Nihar Kapadia

Technical Editor: Arjun Varma

Copy Editor: Safis Editing

Project Manager: Prajakta Naik

Proofreader: Safis Editing

Indexer: Sejal Dsilva

Production Designer: Shyam Sundar Korumilli

Marketing Coordinator: Nimisha Dua

First published: October 2022

Production reference: 2191022

Published by Packt Publishing Ltd.
Livery Place
35 Livery Street
Birmingham
B3 2PB, UK.

ISBN 978-1-80323-059-7

www.packt.com

This book is dedicated to the makers, creators, curious minds, and the network of people who support and encourage others to be a part of this community.

– Christine Farion

Contributors

About the author

Christine Farion is a post-graduate lecturer at the Glasgow School of Art for M.Design Innovation and Interaction Design. Holding a PhD in Smart objects in the domain of Forgetfulness, Christine has been involved in teaching computing, programming, electronics, and prototyping for over 15 years. Previously, she created interactive installations internationally and did research and support for a visual impairment charity. Her interests are memory, accessibility, and physical computing. Currently researching and creating wearable technologies, her focus is on the way we experience our environment and interact with others. This involves interaction to improve our quality of life, interpersonal communication, and community well-being.

Thank you to my family who encouraged, supported, and helped me in this journey, especially Fergus for inspiration, support, and bottomless coffees. I am motivated by my boys, Samuel, Zak, and Jasper, and by enthusiastic students who make my learning journey rewarding. Also, thanks to Mr Mousseau, an inspirational teacher, and Uncle John, who introduced me to the first computer I used. Lastly, thanks to Adafruit, creators, makers, and the curious everywhere.

About the reviewers

Berit Greinke works as a junior professor in Wearable Computing at Berlin University of the Arts and Einstein Center Digital Future. Her research focuses on engineering design methods and fabrication techniques for electronic textiles, combining crafts with novel manufacturing technologies.

She received an MA in Design for Textile Futures from Central Saint Martins College of Art and Design in 2009, and gained a PhD at the Doctoral Training Centre for Media and Arts Technology at Queen Mary University of London in 2017. She has previously worked as a researcher and post-doc at Design Research Lab at Berlin University of the Arts, and at the German Research Center for Artificial Intelligence.

Pollie Barden is a researcher and technologist with a focus on social and accessibility issues. She has worked with the Arduino platform and wearable technology since 2006. She has conducted Arduino workshops with people ranging from children to senior citizens. She has taught at universities in the US and UK in product, interaction, and game design. She currently works in corporate industry, conducting user experience research to create digital experiences that solve real problems and benefit real people in their everyday lives. Pollie has presented her research, games, and artwork at conferences, museums, and exhibitions across the globe.

We learn and grow as researchers, creators, and technologists through our communities. Special thanks to Tom Igoe, who first introduced me to Arduino, and Despina Papadopoulos for introducing me to the world of wearables. I am deeply indebted to the generosity of the Arduino communities and the people who have worked with and supported me throughout my technology and research journey. It was a joy to work on Christine Farion's amazing book.

Table of Contents

3

Exploring e-textile Toolkits: LilyPad, Flora, Circuit Playground, and More   83

4

Implementing Arduino Code Using Gemma M0 and Circuit Playground   109

Part 2: Creating Sewable Circuits That Sense and React Using Arduino and ESP32

5

Working with Sensors: All About Inputs!   137

6

Exploring Reactions Through Outputs   179

7

Moving Forward with Circuit Design Using ESP32   223

Part 3: Learning to Prototype, Build, and Wear a Hyper-Body System

8

9

10

Soldering and Sewing to Complete Your Project   329

Part 4: Getting the Taste of Designing Your Own Culture-Driven Wearable and Beyond

11

Innovating, with a Human-Centered Design Process   363

12

Designing for Forgetfulness: A Case Study of Message Bag   385

13

Implementing the Best Solutions for Creating Your Own Wearable   411

14

Delving into Best Practices and the Future of Wearable Technology   441

Appendix

Answers and Additional Information   475

Preface

What are informed wearables and why should you care about them? Throughout this book, you'll discover how wearables are changing lives. There are many fun, entertaining, and charming aspects to wearable devices. However, they can also be used in a way that can improve quality of life. This is the concept behind *informed* wearable technology. We will use Design Innovation techniques to learn how to discover the real needs of people. We will also learn how we can truly have an effect on and improve people's lives.

Wearable circuits add interaction and purpose to clothing and items. Products are emerging from research fields into the industry and consumer realms. In recent years, e-textile components, compatible with Arduino, have appeared. These can be used to create socially driven on-body devices. Using Arduino and ESP32-based boards (and more), we can build wearables with purpose.

Reading this book will enable you to understand and implement creative, sewable circuits in your wearable tech projects. These soft circuits can be built for medical, social, safety, entertainment, and sporting fields, to name a few. Your skills will be enhanced through physical computing, bringing your ideas to life.

The Ultimate Guide to Informed Wearable Technology is a comprehensive introduction for those who are beginners to e-textiles and the Arduino platform that will have you up to speed and wearing circuits in no time. You will learn skills to bring your circuits to life, completing projects that you can use. By the end of the book, you will have the knowledge to start your own projects from scratch and the confidence to build and wear them. Let's explore and create a future of informed wearable tech!

> **Disclaimer**
> All the projects developed in this book are for educational and prototyping purposes only. We advise all activities to be done with precaution and appropriate safety measures where needed. Soldering, sewing, using conductive textiles, and connecting electronics require attention and care, therefore, we strongly advise following the instructions given in the book with precaution or under guidance, if needed. The author or Packt cannot be held responsible for any damages in the form of physical/monetary loss, or any kind of loss occurred as a result of building projects that are presented in this book

Who this book is for

This book is for electronics engineers, embedded system engineers/designers, R&D engineers, and developers who are beginners in the wearable tech domain, as well as makers and hobbyists who have an interest in creative computing.

The book will be also useful for artists, creatives, teachers, students, and researchers studying interaction design, physical computing, technology, art, and fashion.

A basic knowledge of wearable technology is not required to work with the content of the book. However, having knowledge of Arduino-based systems may help you to follow the exercises in the book. References will be provided for those new to these systems.

What this book covers

Chapter 1, Introduction to the World of Wearables, looks at the context of wearables and their evolution. We will explore past projects and the application of wearables in a variety of different domains, for medical, safety, entertainment, and fitness purposes. Understanding the definitions and constraints of the tools we have will help us develop interesting and useful wearable tech. We take a look at current research – for example, how designers and engineers are creating medical devices worn on-body to collect essential information for health care. How did we go from research to creating assistive devices for visually impaired people? Do we need to be aware of ethical considerations and privacy when designing for and with people? This chapter will help to inspire you and make you think about ethical considerations for your wearables.

Chapter 2, Understanding and Building Electronic Sewable Circuits, introduces you to electronic circuit basics. We start at the beginning, understanding electricity, and move through to using switches in a circuit. Once the basics are covered, we will build some electronic circuits with LEDs for practice. Understanding these basics will set you up for applying your electronics skills to a sewable circuit. We will use conductive materials and conductive thread, alongside other alternative materials, to understand the introductory concepts and make working circuits in fabrics. We will use conductive materials to create switches and buttons, creating simple and fun projects! You will learn through doing. This will be the foundation for your continued learning.

Chapter 3, Exploring e-textile Toolkits: LilyPad, Flora, Circuit Playground, and More, focuses on learning about e-textile toolkits. You will create starter circuits that you can build upon. We begin by exploring LilyPad components, and then Flora and Circuit Playground. You'll create circuits to see how e-textile toolkits can kick-start your projects. This is followed by exploring the range of Gemma, Flora, Circuit Playground, and other exciting e-textile boards. We will also examine their differences and why you might choose one board over another. Once you have a grasp of these boards and their capabilities, we can begin sewing some electronic circuits. This will lead to using the Arduino IDE to program interactive elements into your designs.

Chapter 4, Implementing Arduino Code Using Gemma M0 and Circuit Playground, focuses on learning by building a practical application with a Gemma M0 or Circuit Playground if you want to expand the capabilities of your circuit. We will explore flex sensors and discover how they have been used in research. You'll learn more about the Arduino IDE, which we'll use to program your wearable. This will be followed by a test of our circuits. You'll add flexibility to your wearable with an off-the-shelf flex sensor or one you've made. We finish the chapter by hooking up and programming a Gemma M0 with Flex and a Servo motor!

Chapter 5, Working with Sensors: All about Inputs!, examines what sensors can be added to our projects, what protocols we use to add them to our circuits, and how we can use the data they provide. Most of the wearables we create will sense something – our touch, the sound, the light, and so on. For example, we might use a temperature sensor to collect temperature data and, when the temperature reaches a programmed level, provide heat or cooling to the body. We will also look at some alternative ways to use a sensor. Also, you will have the knowledge needed to use the protocols (SPI and I²C) to connect sensors to our Arduino-based boards. You'll also be able to use and install a library in the Arduino IDE to add functionality to code.

Chapter 6, Exploring Reactions Through Outputs, explores outputs. Getting a response through and with our wearable is exciting! The world of outputs and actuators can help us to do that. This chapter describes the outputs that bring your projects to life. We experiment with light, from LEDs to NeoPixels and more. Displays can also tell us a lot, so we look at OLEDs, TFTs, and other displays for our wearables. We will also learn about sound, movement, and temperature. In this chapter, you will learn about the outputs that can add huge value to a wearable. Defining the types of outputs and why they are useful is followed by putting them into practice and creating circuits that react to the inputs they receive. By the end of this chapter, you will know about a range of outputs that you can add to your own wearable designs and be able to code your circuit board to react, displaying visual effects, auditory properties, and haptic response.

Chapter 7, Moving Forward with Circuit Design Using ESP32, delves deeper into circuit design, using alternative microcontrollers. These are circuit boards that aren't specifically "sewable," but we can use them for wearables. Looking at the ESP32, a powerful and adaptive microcontroller board, using it will add more interactivity to our sewable circuits. We will prepare the Arduino IDE so that we can program it, and we will write a first sketch. Then, we will advance our knowledge by connecting it to Wi-Fi. We will then work through several activities, including making a touch-activated wearable as a mental health and well-being exploration. This will collect current data from a website through an API. Lastly, you'll understand what an API is, how we connect to one, and how we can update information with it. You'll have completed another wearable item too!

Chapter 8, Learning How to Prototype and Make Electronics Wearable, looks at prototyping, which is essential for all your circuits. In this chapter, you will learn the theory behind prototyping. We will understand the advantages of prototyping in different ways to get different outcomes. These methods will contribute to creating informed wearables that are functional and desirable for the people we are designing for. We will look at the **Houde and Hill model**, as well as **Quick and Dirty** methods of prototyping. You'll see examples created during prototyping sessions. By the end of this chapter, you will understand how to progress rapid prototypes by choosing materials, fabrics, and items that are suitable and appropriate for the informed wearables you make.

Chapter 9, Designing and Prototyping Your Own Hyper-Body System, focuses on designing and building low-fidelity and proof-of-concept prototypes for your hyper-body system, using suitable components and microcontrollers. This chapter will help you to choose appropriate components for your purpose and test your circuits. These are essential skills to create working wearables and fashion tech pieces.

In this chapter, you will be consolidating the knowledge you've acquired in previous chapters to create a wearable technology project that is ambitious and exciting. We will learn about hyper-body systems and how to design a hyper-body system. Then, we'll do some project planning and jump into an ambitious wearable using the **Internet of Things (IoT)**. By the end of this chapter, you will have your circuit ready for sewing into a wearable.

Chapter 10, Soldering and Sewing to Complete Your Project, looks at soldering and other sewing techniques to complete your hyper-body system. This chapter teaches you the basics of soldering to help you to make your circuit more durable and permanent through sewing and soldering the parts. We finish by exploring other ways we can make our circuits more durable and permanent. These skills will help you to move your projects from a low-fidelity prototype to a high-fidelity prototype – and ready for wearing.

Chapter 11, Innovating with a Human-Centered Design Process, explores the Design Innovation process, which can be used to create relevant and socially conscious wearables that can highlight blind spots in the way we think. Through the human-centered design process, we look to seek depth and meaning through the interactions we create, using insights from listening to people. This chapter looks at understanding human-centered design and explains steps we can take and repeat in our own projects and designs.

Chapter 12, Designing for Forgetfulness: A Case Study of Message Bag, looks at the case study of Message Bag to understand the Design Innovation development in practice. Message Bag is a purpose-built object-based memory aid that emerged as a result of investigating forgetfulness and speaking with people. Creating a wearable through understanding the context of a chosen topic and focusing on a need is how we can design an **informed wearable**. These wearables' purpose, specifically to make something better for a person or group of people, is at the forefront of their design.

Chapter 13, Implementing the Best Solutions for Creating Your Own Wearable, continues your wearable journey, through Message Bag. As we work through the iterations of Message Bag, it will provide you with a complete skillset to create your own wearables. In this chapter, you will look at making decisions for iterations in an early prototype version of a wearable, and we will upcycle and complete the Message Bag prototype we started in the previous chapter. We'll also sneak a peek at even more potential upgrades that we don't have to implement, but it's important to learn to push and iterate your designs. You will have come full circle in your journey and created a wearable near-body system with iterations, soldered and sewn it into place, and created plans for your own wearable design.

Chapter 14, Delving into Best Practices and the Future of Wearable Technology, examines the steps we need to take to help find solutions for common errors or issues that can happen when we prototype. We will look at a few handy tips to help us with our wearable journey, as well as understand how to set up our circuits so that they last. We will also have a look at batteries and power solutions, as well as troubleshooting and some of the common ways you can take a step-by-step approach to solve a problem. We finish up with a look at the future and what the world of wearables may hold. What are scientists, technologists, engineers, and designers exploring in these intersections? In this chapter, you will consolidate your learning by discovering tips and tricks to help you continue your wearable practice.

Chapter 15, Appendix: Answers and Additional Information, has useful links for your wearable practice as well as some recommended suppliers. There are also answers to review questions that have been asked throughout the book.

To get the most out of this book

To work through the activities presented in this book, you do not need to have any prior knowledge of wearables or wearable systems. It is assumed that you are starting from a beginner level and the book will take you through example exercises to help you progress. There will be links for further reading and reference. Having some knowledge of Arduino-based systems would be beneficial though not necessary.

You will need a version of Arduino installed on your computer. Activities detailed are demonstrated with Arduino 2.0, but the code works for previous versions of Arduino. All code examples have been tested on both Windows and macOS.

Software/hardware covered in the book	Operating system requirements
Arduino IDE	Windows, macOS, or Linux
Arduino-based microcontroller boards: Flora, Gemma M0, Circuit Playground, ESP32, QTPy ESP32, and QTPy SAMD	Windows, macOS, or Linux
Various hardware inputs and outputs that are suitable for Arduino-based systems, typically with 3.3V or 5V power	Windows, macOS, or Linux

If you are using the digital version of this book, we advise you to type the code yourself or access the code from the book's GitHub repository (a link is available in the next section). Doing so will help you avoid any potential errors related to the copying and pasting of code.

Download the example code files

You can download the example code files for this book from GitHub at `https://github.com/cmoz/Ultimate`. If there's an update to the code, it will be updated in the GitHub repository.

We also have other code bundles from our rich catalog of books and videos available at `https://github.com/PacktPublishing/`. Check them out!

Download the color images

We also provide a PDF file that has color images of the screenshots and diagrams used in this book. You can download it here: `https://packt.link/tMmo3`.

Conventions used

There are a number of text conventions used throughout this book.

`Code in text`: Indicates code words in text, database table names, folder names, filenames, file extensions, pathnames, dummy URLs, user input, and Twitter handles. Here is an example: "In the `setup()` section of code, we can see after initializing the Serial Monitor there is an `#if` defined section."

A block of code is set as follows:

```
int heatPin = 8;

void setup() {
pinMode(heatPin, OUTPUT);
digitalWrite(heatPin, HIGH);
}
```

When we wish to draw your attention to a particular part of a code block, the relevant lines or items are set in bold:

```
void setup() {
  Serial.begin(115200);
#if defined(NEOPIXEL_POWER)
  pinMode(NEOPIXEL_POWER, OUTPUT);
  digitalWrite(NEOPIXEL_POWER, HIGH);
#endif
```

Bold: Indicates a new term, an important word, or words that you see onscreen. For instance, words in menus or dialog boxes appear in **bold**. Here is an example: "**Upload the code** to your QT Py."

> **Tips or Important Notes**
> Appear like this.

Get in touch

Feedback from our readers is always welcome.

General feedback: If you have questions about any aspect of this book, email us at `customercare@packtpub.com` and mention the book title in the subject of your message.

Errata: Although we have taken every care to ensure the accuracy of our content, mistakes do happen. If you have found a mistake in this book, we would be grateful if you would report this to us. Please visit `www.packtpub.com/support/errata` and fill in the form.

Piracy: If you come across any illegal copies of our works in any form on the internet, we would be grateful if you would provide us with the location address or website name. Please contact us at copyright@packt.com with a link to the material.

If you are interested in becoming an author: If there is a topic that you have expertise in and you are interested in either writing or contributing to a book, please visit authors.packtpub.com.

Share Your Thoughts

Once you've read *The Ultimate Guide to Informed Wearable Technology*, we'd love to hear your thoughts! Scan the QR code below to go straight to the Amazon review page for this book and share your feedback.

https://packt.link/r/1803230592

Your review is important to us and the tech community and will help us make sure we're delivering excellent quality content.

Download a free PDF copy of this book

Thanks for purchasing this book!

Do you like to read on the go but are unable to carry your print books everywhere? Is your eBook purchase not compatible with the device of your choice?

Don't worry, now with every Packt book you get a DRM-free PDF version of that book at no cost.

Read anywhere, any place, on any device. Search, copy, and paste code from your favorite technical books directly into your application.

The perks don't stop there, you can get exclusive access to discounts, newsletters, and great free content in your inbox daily

Follow these simple steps to get the benefits:

1. Scan the QR code or visit the link below

https://packt.link/free-ebook/9781803230597

2. Submit your proof of purchase
3. That's it! We'll send your free PDF and other benefits to your email directly

Part 1:
Getting Started with Wearable Technology and Simple Circuits

In this part, you'll get started by understanding electronics. You'll build basic electronic circuits and learn about e-textile toolkits. Using those toolkits, you'll create simple circuits to consolidate your electronic skills.

This part of the book comprises the following chapters:

- *Chapter 1, Introduction to the World of Wearables*
- *Chapter 2, Understanding and Building Electronic Sewable Circuits*
- *Chapter 3, Exploring e-textile Toolkits: LilyPad, Flora, Circuit Playground, and More*
- *Chapter 4, Implementing Arduino Code Using Gemma M0 and Circuit Playground*

1

Introduction to the World of Wearables

Wearables are expanding into all facets of society. The industry around this field is growing and many companies have specialist workshops, prototyping spaces, and research and development facilities. The call for meaningful wearables now includes partners in medical, sports, safety, and many other sectors. There is a pressing need for adapting skillsets to include prototyping abilities, and a keen understanding of the process to create successful wearables. This involves integrating electronics into garments, understanding what wearables are, and how their unique properties can be incorporated. All these factors help us build a picture of new and exciting ways to create wearable technologies that will improve people's daily lives.

In this chapter, you will learn about the context of wearables and their evolution. This will provide a launchpad for understanding exciting new e-textile and prototyping tools. We will explore past projects and the application of wearables in a variety of different domains, including medical, safety, improving quality of life, or fitness purposes. We'll also discuss ethical considerations, which are an essential part of the process of wearable development. Understanding the definitions and constraints of the tools we have will help us develop interesting and useful wearable tech.

We will also look at current research; what are scientists, technologists, engineers, and designers exploring at these intersections? Also, what ethical considerations do we need to be aware of when designing for and with people?

In this chapter, we are going to cover the following main topics:

- What are wearables?
- Terminology, applications, and constraints
- Exciting ideas, concepts, and projects to motivate
- What does the research tell us?
- Cultural and ethical considerations

Let's explore the history of wearables. This is only a small cross-section of what has been developed. Having a foundation in their history will build your appreciation and excitement for the field. As we progress through the artifacts, ask yourself how they can be modified, developed further, and explored in other ways. How can you adapt designs for different parts of the body? How can you push wearables further and for what purpose?

In this section, we will cover the following topics:

- Wearables definition

- When were wearables created?

- Informed wearables

Wearables definition

The definition of wearables can vary based on the field and application. Most definitions include *a continuously worn device*. Typically, augmenting humans for memory, communication, or a physical improvement is an aspect of a wearable. Wearables are seen *as portable computing power, worn on or near the body*. A wearable is in our personal space. It can be controlled by the person wearing it. I, often, interchange the term wearables with **wearable technology** or **wearable computing**. Also, because this field is very different from the traditional programming-only computer field, it can be described as a part of the **physical computing** field. This can include smart clothes or textiles, body-worn devices, and interactive accessories. The term encompasses a broad range of devices, and the definition grows and shifts as new technologies and techniques are created. It's exciting!

Generally, for this book, the wearables you will be making will use the human body in some way. This could be to communicate with or support the technology in question. Typically, wearables have the following properties:

- Garment/material/accessory on or 'near body'

- Embedded electronics

- A power source

- Inputs/outputs of some description

Inputs and outputs will be discussed in detail later in this book as they are essential for our designs. For now, we will say that input is a way to receive data or information in our system. The output is a way of relaying that information or responding in a way to that data. Often, wearables are used to gather data from the wearer, which can provide information or connect to services. Improvements in batteries, miniaturization of components, and new ways to create textiles, garments, and accessories have contributed to their popularity. Though, I'm sure when most people hear the word "wearable" they think of a watch. That's okay, but that's not the full story. So, although we will discuss watch-style devices, we will look at many other interesting wearables. There is so much more to the incredible products and services that companies, makers, and researchers are creating.

When were wearables created?

There are a considerable number of valuable resources online that follow a historical timeline of wearables, so I won't cover it all here. One example is `https://www.media.mit.edu/wearables/lizzy/timeline.html`. A recent paper (2021) that also focuses on connected devices is available online at `https://reader.elsevier.com/reader/sd/pii/S1389128621001651`. I wanted to touch on some interesting thoughts and items to shake up your thinking and consideration when planning your wearables. Remember, we can use the term loosely and adapt it to the projects we are making.

One of the earliest considered wearable "computers" is considered the Chinese Abacus. This small ring has moving parts so that a person can perform calculations on their finger. There are seven rods, with seven beads on each rod. It is considered to have been created and used in the 17th century. The beads are too small to be used with fingers, so a small pin is used to move them. Since the pins that were used were worn in ladies' hair, could this have potentially been for them? This isn't strictly a wearable, in that it doesn't have computing power or a programmable aspect, but we should consider the idea of making jewelry out of an abacus, an item that's not worn and whose purpose is for calculating and combining those two aspects. Around 1907, the first wearable camera was created by the pioneer Julius Neubronner. This was for pigeon photography (an aerial photography technique). It was activated by a timing mechanism that activated the shutter. The camera was strapped to a pigeon!

In the 1960s, a computerized timing device was created to help mathematicians Edward O. Thorp and Claude Shannon win a game of roulette. A timer was hidden in the base of a shoe, under the insole, and another was hidden in a pack of cigarettes. It was designed to predict the motion of the roulette wheel. This was done using microswitches that indicated the speed of the roulette wheel. Musical tones would indicate a section of the wheel to bet on. The wearer had a miniature speaker in their ear to hear the tones that were produced.

July 1, 1979, was a day for portable music. This is when Sony created the Sony Walkman TPS-L2 (`https://www.sony.com/ja/pressroom/pict_data/p_audio/1979_tpsl2.html`):

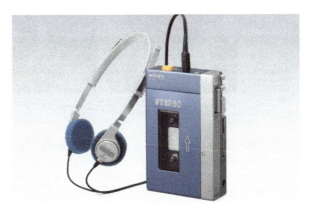

Figure 1.1 – Sony Walkman

The founder of Sony, *Masaru Ibuka*, was searching for a way to listen to music in a portable way so that he could take music on flights with him. Prototypes were made and the Walkman was born. Over 400 million Walkman players, in all their forms, have been sold over time. Their designs became slimmer, sports versions were made, and other improvements were made to their power so that their batteries could be recharged.

You may have come across the Casio calculator watch that was launched in the 1980s, known as the C-80. This was a success and Casio followed up in 1984 with the Databank Telememo CD-40. The sales from these in the first 5 years was around six million units. *Figure 1.2* shows an advertisement from Casio for the calculator watch in the 1980s.

Another original piece of smartwatch technology was the 1988 Seiko WristMac, after which came the Timex Datalink in 1994. This was co-developed with *Bill Gates* (Microsoft) and had a playable Invasion video game on it. *Figure 1.2* shows model 150 with a steel bracelet in PC-communication mode. The Datalink was worn by astronauts during Expedition 16. It had wrist applications that they used as part of their explorations and for sending data for analysis.

A Wearable Wireless Webcam was developed in December 1994 by *Steve Mann*, a Canadian researcher. In 1998, Steve Mann invented, designed, and built the world's first Linux wristwatch, which he presented at IEEE 2000. This is shown on the cover of Linux Magazine in *Figure 1.2*. This prototype was launched by IBM, with wireless connectivity. Steve Mann is considered one of the *fathers of wearable computing*, and you can read more about his decades of experience designing and wearing wearable computers at `https://spectrum.ieee.org/steve-mann-my-augmediated-life`:

Figure 1.2 – Left to right: an advert for the C-80 Casio watch, the Timex Datalink, and Linux Magazine

Today, you can buy a fully programmable LilyGo watch that incorporates an **ESP32** chip – we will be using that chip (not the watch) in *Chapter 7*, *Moving Forward with Circuit Design Using ESP32*.

Lastly, it's worth mentioning the crowdfunding hit, **Pebble**. This smartwatch supported both Android Wear and Apple Watch operating systems. Samsung Galaxy Gear was available in 2013, while Apple Watch was available in 2015.

However, in 2015, Pebble set a record with over 78,000 backers and raised over $20 million with their Kickstarter campaign. Part of this popularity was due to its battery life of 7 days, compared to the Apple Watch's, which was around 18 hours. Also, the price point for Pebble was $99 compared to $349 for Apple Watch.

Informed wearables

What about wearables that can make a real difference in someone's life? Informed wearables look to those around us to find inspiration and where there is a genuine need. Important contributions to wearable history were developed for hearing impaired and/or visually impaired people.

Hearing impairment

Hearables, the first electronic hearing aid, was created in 1898. Miller Reese Hutchison designed a hearing aid that used an electric current to amplify weak signals. It wasn't until around 1913 that the first commercially manufactured hearing aids came to market. Beltone Electronics created the eyeglasses hearing aid in 1960 and started the trend of combining a way to conceal hearing aids. Danavox, a hearing aid solution company `http://www.danavoxhearingaids.com/legacy/`, as shown in *Figure 1.3*, created radio-style hearing aids that looked like radios and could be carried around:

Figure 1.3 – Eyeglass hearing aid

Following those developments, in the 1990s, an all-digital hearing aid was made. The 1990s also saw creativity emerge. These became more of a jewelry item. In 2021, deaf model Chella Man, in collaboration with Private Policy New York, created beautiful gold-plated ear cuffs that could accentuate a hearing device or cochlear implants. He explained, "*I always found myself brainstorming ways to reclaim the machinery that had become a part of me.*"

By 2010, Bluetooth-enabled devices started to surface, which allowed for big changes to be made in the hearing aid field. There are even apps that can connect to an iPhone for a specially designed hearing aid. The **Made for iPhone (MFi)** hearing device connects via Bluetooth and allows a person to control volume, audio presets, and other options.

Visual impairment

In 1977, a camera-to-tactile vest was created for visually impaired people by C.C. Collins (1977). Images were converted into a 1,024-point 10-inch square tactile grid that was on a vest, as shown in the vest's schematic:

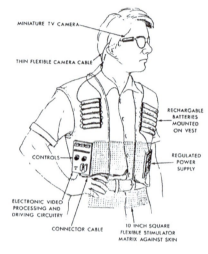

Figure 1.4 – Tactile vest

An updated version (2014) of a vest-style prototype is the **Eyeronman** device. This vibrates as it senses the environment and its obstacles and conveys that information to the wearer to help them navigate:

Figure 1.5 – Eyeronman vest (credit: Tactile Navigation Tools)

One of the medical advisors for the project, Dr J.R. Rizzo, said, "*I want to build a tool that can actually get [visually impaired] people to walk around crowded environments without assistance.*" They see this vest being used in other contexts too, such as for firefighters, police, and soldiers, who may have impaired vision from smoke, night use, explosions, and more.

Other advances

Other important wearables were created as far back as 1977 and include an early model of a heart rate monitor that was created by Polar Electro. This was a monitoring box with a set of electrode leads. These were attached to the chest. It was used as a training aid for the Finnish National Cross Country Ski team.

Between 1991 and 1997, at the MIT Media Lab, Rosalind Picard (Picard, R., Healey, J., 1997), along with students Steve Mann (Mann, S., 1997) and Jennifer Healey, researched data collection from Smart Clothes. These clothes monitored physiological data (Mann, S., 1996) from the wearer. The 1990s was also a time when wearables started to become commercial. Around 1997, BodyMedia commercially made wearable sensors (since acquired by Jawbone). These wearables were designed to help track and monitor for health-specific purposes. This allowed people to be proactive in monitoring their health.

These past inventions, prototypes, and investigations helped set the important and exciting foundations for the world of wearables as we see it today. This is not an exhaustive list but will help you glimpse into the areas you can research further.

With our whirlwind tour of wearable history complete, let's look at some of the current work and research in the wearable technology field.

Current work in the field

What wearable technologies exist that you know about or have? Let's look at recent innovations and the important role wearables play in our lives. We will learn about the current work in the field by covering the following topics:

- The traditional role of clothing
- Headsets and eyeglasses
- Current wearable markets

From around 1995 onwards, artists, researchers, and creators began questioning the traditional role of clothing. To redefine the role, Kipöz (2007) looked at clothing as a *hyper-medium* in risk society. Clothing was redesigned to provoke thought and discussion. Hyper-medium looks to incorporate functionality and contemporary aesthetics. Distinct areas of creation involve protection against disaster, which is the idea of protecting against the unfriendliness of the world around us. Lucy Orta's wearable shelters were conceptualized for disaster victims, homeless people, and similar.

These garment structures became places of comfort and seclusion to meet the need for privacy and personal space. Part of the goal was to also provoke discussions regarding homelessness, place, and space. Another area of concern is the environment itself. A Metropolis Jacket with an anti-smog mask was created in 1998 to help combat the negative environmental impacts on people.

A very exciting vision (*Figure 1.6*) for the adaptability to use this sensor directly on the body to allow movement and comfort is ElectroDermis. As stated by Eric Markvicka, Guanyun Wange, et al., in 2019, *"ElectroDermis is a fabrication system that simplifies the creation of wearable electronics that are comfortable, elastic, and fully untethered."* They recognized that *"wearable electronics require structural conformity, must be comfortable for the wearer, and should be soft, elastic, and aesthetically appealing. We envision a future where electronics can be temporarily attached to the body (like bandages or party masks), but in functional and aesthetically pleasing ways"*:

Figure 1.6 – ElectroDermis (photo credit: Morphing Matter Lab, Carnegie Mellon University)

One of the world's smallest wearables fits on a fingernail and measures UV wavelengths, as shown in *Figure 1.7*. It interacts wirelessly with a mobile phone. Its primary use is to reduce skin cancer frequency. *"We hope people with information about their UV exposure will develop healthier habits when out in the sun,"* Xu said. *"UV light is ubiquitous and carcinogenic. Skin cancer is the most common type of cancer worldwide. Right now, people don't know how much UV light they are getting. This device helps you maintain an awareness and for skin cancer survivors, could also keep their dermatologists informed."* It was developed by Northwestern Medicine and Northwestern's McCormick School of Engineering scientists. One version of it, which looks like a small wearable pin that you can clip onto your nail, is commercially available:

Figure 1.7 – UV nail sensor (photo credit: Drs. June K. Robinson and
John Rogers, Northwestern University, Chicago, IL)

Headsets and glasses are also prototyped often for wearable computing. Around 1980, Steve Mann developed a series of headsets that included embedded cameras and microphones. These recorded daily activities and were cumbersome in their design due to the available technology.

The 1990s saw collaborations with *Thad Starner* and *Steve Mann*, which led to what is seen as modern-wearable computing. Typically, in the 1990s, interdisciplinary explorations began happening in research projects. Some of the research fields allowed for a more interdisciplinary approach, including design, computer science, management, fashion, electronic engineering, computer engineering, and human-computer interaction fields.

Eyeglasses contribute to what is considered an **augmented human** by using lenses to correct vision. An augmented human can be described as an enhancement that's made by making a natural or technological alteration to the human body. Typically, this can be to enhance performance in some way or to add to our capabilities. Eyeglasses have been a focus for wearables since the 1990s. Most notably, a lot of this work, 10 years in the making, culminated in Google Glass being sold in 2015. Glass had privacy issues and there was a backlash against its use. Since 2015, Glass has only been available as Enterprise and not for public purchase.

However, Solos cycling smart glasses help cyclists keep their eyes on the road. This was a successful Kickstarter campaign in 2017 and is now commercially available. Solos provides important running and cycling metrics such as pace, heart rate, and power without someone having to take their eyes off the road. This was initially started as a project for the US Olympic cycling team.

Another product that was created with eyeglasses in mind was OrCam MyEye. This is a device that takes all these features further, as shown in *Figure 1.8*. It was designed for people with vision loss and various eye conditions, including reading fatigue or reading difficulties. OrCam has a camera that interprets a wearer's visual information.

An example of such information could be when you're reading a menu – it can read out, audibly to an in-ear headphone the menu items. It can also recognize faces, colors, products, money, barcodes, and similar:

Figure 1.8 – OrCam MyEye (left) and Pocket Sky (right)

It consists of a magnetically mounted device (for eyeglasses) that works in real time without any need for a smartphone or other device. At the time of writing, it costs around £4,000 to purchase, which makes it a very specialist item, as is common for many assistive technologies unfortunately. However, it is an item that could benefit a lot of people.

There are also Everysight Raptor and Ray-Ban Stories, which allow you to record videos and take photos. Lastly, there's Amazon Echo Frames. However, it doesn't use augmented reality – it's used for playing Alexa feedback. This allows you to control your devices, play music, and similar.

Pocket Sky (*Figure 1.8 right*) acts like sunlight when not enough natural light is available. This version of the eyeglasses wearable activates and keeps a person's sleep-wake rhythm in balance. A lack of daylight in winter can make you tired. Pocket Sky aims to lift your mood and ease seasonal blues.

When you think of wearables, what springs to mind? If you talk with someone about a "wearable," what devices are they talking about?

Some of the successes in these technologies show that there's a great understanding of the craftsmanship and ability to use hardware, alongside knowledge of materials and textiles. This knowledge creates a great combination of skills.

As your journey through this book progresses, you'll learn about the hardware, the sensors, the code, and how to connect it all. You'll also learn about important textile and fabric knowledge. This can be the difference in creating a truly usable wearable prototype.

Taking it further

If you've enjoyed learning about some of the current work in the field, you can look up more wondrous and futuristic designs through the work of Anouk Wipprecht, Pauline van Dongen, Iris Van Herpen, Suzanne Lee, Helen Storey, and Hussein Chalayan. These creators design within intersections of fashion, science, technology, and art to create stunning designs that offer a playful and critical look at how the human body can be transformed.

Now, let's look at the intriguing work that's being done in textile electronics. We'll learn about embroidery, smart fabrics, and the sensors that are used in wearables. This will help us consider materials, fabrics, and textiles in our designs in this field.

Electronic textiles

We have just learned about some of the current work in the field of wearables. This section introduces the ideas and uses of smart materials and concepts to consider when you are creating a wearable. Smart textiles, also known as smart fabrics, include computational functionality. They provide benefits to the wearer.

They often have sensors embedded within them. Electronic textiles have a lot more capabilities than traditional materials.

There are two categories for this field:

- Textiles with components and electronics added, such as **light-emitting diodes** (LEDs), screens, batteries, and similar
- Textiles with the electronics integrated directly

Some electronic textiles are used for communication or energy conduction and have sensors built into them to collect data from the wearer. Some are for aesthetic purposes, while others are for performance. Lights can be added to clothing for a variety of aesthetic purposes. Performance-enhancing garments are typically used by athletes and in the military.

In 1995, *Harry Wainwright* invented the first machine that could insert fiber-optics into fabrics. You can read more about his research online at `https://www.hleewainwright.com/`. He has pioneered electronically enhanced apparel and modern e-textiles. Following that, in 1997, *Selbach Machinery* was the first to produce a CNC machine that automatically implanted fiber optics into any flexible material.

Some fabrics can help regulate the temperature of the body, and we will look at these types of sensors in *Chapter 5, Working with Sensors: All About Inputs!*, but they can also react to vibrations or sound. An example would be an astronaut's space suit, which could have lights, sensors, and properties to heat and cool the astronaut or protect them from radiation. This would be a fun project – that is, to make a space suit-style wearable!

There is a desire to have **seamless integration** with fabric and electronics and this is where the field excels. Sewing or embroidery techniques can be used to directly add electrical components.

According to Hughes-Riley, Dias, and Cork (2018), **first-generation** e-textiles are about devices or components/electronics being affixed to textiles. **Second-generation** e-textiles are all about knitted fabrics and similar that can be used in conductive circuits as functional fabrics. Finally, **third-generation** e-textiles consist of conductive elements integrated into a textile. *Figure 1.9* shows this as an LED yarn.

For textile electronics, the sensors might be embedded into a garment or fabric, or in what can be termed third-generation e-textiles, which means that the garment is the sensor. The Hughes-Riley, Dias, and Cork, (2018) definitions can be read in the context of their research. The following is a link to the paper as a PDF: `http://irep.ntu.ac.uk/id/eprint/33789/1/11263_Hughes-Riley.pdf`.

Figure 1.9 – Examples of each generation of electronic textiles (this image has been reproduced under a Creative Commons Attribution (CC BY) license (http://creativecommons.org/licenses/by/4.0/))

Other seamless integration examples include pressure or strain sensors. Sensors can be used for interesting ideas, such as CuteCircuit's Hug Shirt, where a person can send an electronic hug through sensors in the garment. The hug is sent through actuators.

Smart textiles can be knitted, woven, or have steel/metal fibers embedded. They can be made from conductive threads, yarns, copper (or other material) sheets, conductive metal cores, or metallic meshes and coated with silver to make them respond to the environment or wearer. It is a field that is undergoing experimentation and innovation to study the functions these textiles can take. These garments often need treating so that they can be worn in all weather conditions. Factors such as temperature and other weather conditions need to be considered. For day-to-day wearables, they often have pieces that you can detach so that you can wash them safely. This is something you may want to consider.

Also, the use of smart fabrics has seen enhancements in the field of sports and performance environments. Tennis players today use smart fabrics that allow the garments to record data from the performer. This can include temperature, sweat, and muscle movement. Such data can enhance performance. Data can be collected through sensors and "biometric capture," which will provide information about the wearer's body position or movement, and how their data compares to others. Gestures can be captured and used to analyze performance and endurance.

The development of biotextiles, nanotechnology, techno-fashion, interactive garments, and intelligent fashion allows for experimentation and communication possibilities. People that wear underwear while they sleep can monitor sleep quality through a small pod tucked into the garment. Other uses include remote healthcare, self-heating clothing, and in the industry for employee health.

Uses for electronic textiles

Electronic textiles can be used for many purposes in different fields. Let's look at some of them:

- Health monitoring, which can include heart rate, temperature, movement, and posture
- Sports use and training

- Position tracking for people, teams, the military, and similar

- Monitoring fatigue, potentially for driving and pilots

- Fashionable items

- Sensory perception, music, and similar uses

Lastly, textiles allow us to consider input forms such as **touch**, **pressure**, and **movement** in alternative ways. The wearer can use presses allowing sensors or fabrics to be near the body. This intimacy makes it a unique consideration.

These uses of textiles can even offer limited, or no direct input, from the user, quietly collecting information as the wearer goes about their normal day.

Challenge

Spend a little time sketching out some ideas. What uses do you think are important? What types of textiles would you use and wear? Sketches could be for different locations on the body.

With that, we've learned about textile electronics and the advances in the field. You should now understand their uses and how they allow for innovative forms of input in our wearables. Now, let's look at some of the terminology, applications, and constraints that you will face when designing wearable projects.

Terminology, applications, and constraints

It is important to know the terms you'll come across in this exciting field. This section will help define some of the terms and will also help you generate your project ideas through understanding the various applications and their constraints. Let's start with the terminology.

Terminology

This section defines the context for the words that will be used throughout this book. This will give you background information about when they are referred to in this book.

Wearable computing

Wearable computing can be on the body or near bodily items, such as clothing, typically with sensors and outputs. This can be to extend our natural abilities, augment them, or highlight them. It could enable us to communicate with others or track ourselves. The following is an example of an augmented bag:

Figure 1.10 – Wearable computing example, C Farion

Electronic circuits that have processing power that can read input sensor data and output that data in another form are common in most wearable computing. Often, the garment is continuously worn and will have power needs.

The bag in the preceding figure helps a person to remember what objects they have packed. It has computing power to react to sensors and input and also provides output.

Embedded technology

Technology can be placed into garments or fabrics and used in some way to create wearable technology. This can be as simple as circuitry that carries current and performs some actions. Technology that can be embedded into the human body is often called **biohacks**.

Prototyping

We will explore this in more detail in *Chapter 8, Learning How to Prototype and Make Electronics Wearable*, but here, our objective is to create something before it is market-ready. This can take many different forms and many iterations to make it work in the way we want it to. This can be done with 3D printing, paper, fabrics, or anything we have to hand. Generally, we use less expensive materials to prototype:

Figure 1.11 – Prototyping example

The preceding figure shows a watch concept made with foam board and lights, with some electronics embedded. The first prototype they made (my Interaction Design students) was just with the foamboard, which is also a good example of prototyping.

Electronic prototyping

This is similar to prototyping, but we use electronic components to create circuits for testing. Here, we connect wires and components to see if they are working and correctly inputting or reacting. This is part of electronic prototyping, so you will be prototyping throughout this book. Generally, we use less expensive components to prototype. *Figure 1.12* shows an example:

Figure 1.12 – Electronic prototyping

Once these less expensive components and the circuit configuration have been established, we can start to swap out components for more durable ones.

Interactivity

The term **interactivity** has many definitions and meanings. In this book, we will use it to describe a button circuit, for example, where pressing that button requires interaction. A person, environment, or sensor that has some type of action and reaction is interactive. Also, when thinking in a wider sense, creating two gloves that connect to people, or wearable items that need to be touched, stroked, or moved in some way, creates interactivity that often enhances a device's use. Interacting with people or our environment often generates interesting uses:

Figure 1.13 – Anouk Wipprecht, Heartbeat Dress featuring Keenyah Hill, and (right) synapse for Intel

A stunning example of electronic textile technology that combines 3D printed parts is Anouk Wipprecht's work, as shown in *Figure 1.13*. It has an extraordinary appearance. The Heartbeat Dress monitors the wearer's heartbeat and displays the rhythms in a central pendant. This dress was a collaboration with crystal maker *SWAROVSKI* (`https://www.linkedin.com/company/swarovski/`), researching **Wearable Emotions**.

Other work by Anouk that combines fashion and robotics can be viewed online on her website at `http://www.anoukwipprecht.nl/`. There are many videos that I recommend watching to get a feel for these pieces.

Applications

What are the possible applications and fields that we can design wearables for? This section will provide a list that you can reference when starting new projects.

What types of subject areas do you want to design your wearable for? What inspiration is there? The following diagram shows some of the fields, functions, and constraints of wearables. This will act as a handy reminder when we are developing our projects:

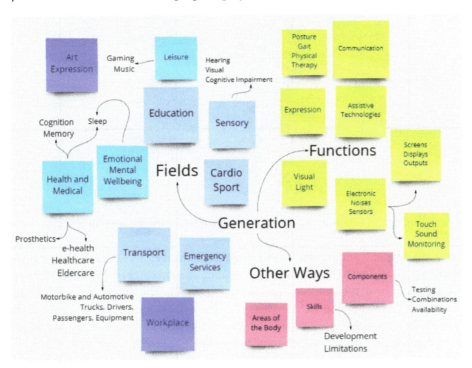

Figure 1.14 – Applications for wearables

Another way we can launch project ideas is to look at specific areas on the body that we may want to design for – especially during the prototyping phase when we are learning new skills. It helps to have some inspiration, and the following figure shows the body location possibilities we have for our designs:

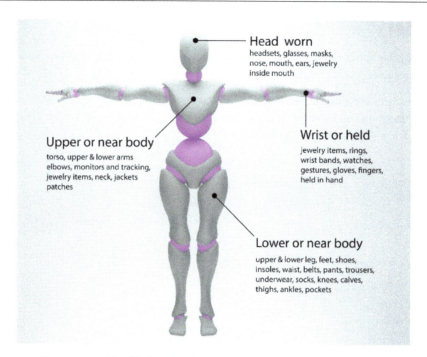

Figure 1.15 – Possible locations (character: https://www.mixamo.com/)

Being aware of the possible locations for using a wearable garment or accessory can be helpful when you are generating ideas. I often refer to this type of guide as a refresher to think through new and exciting ideas that can be developed into a prototype that I can iterate. Hopefully, you have an idea of the different domains to develop for, as well as places on or near the body. Combining these two points of information can help you launch a project idea. Now, let's look at the constraints and what we need to be aware of when designing wearable technology.

Constraints

There can sometimes be constraints when we are planning and designing wearables. The following diagram shows the constraints that we should be aware of when we are designing wearable technology. How many of these factors will affect your designs?

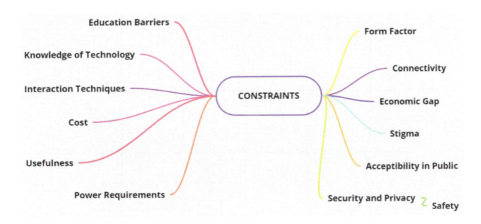

Figure 1.16 – Constraints

With that, we've looked at some common definitions that will be used throughout this book. We also learned about the possible fields where we may make wearables, what their functions might be, and what constraints to be aware of.

This will help you when you're planning your projects and provide subject inspiration when you are unsure where to start. Now, let's look ahead to exciting ideas, concepts, and projects to motivate.

Exciting ideas, concepts, and projects to motivate

So far, we've looked at the history of, and what is current in, the wearable world. What about when devices become smaller, making them easily portable, lowering their energy needs, and smarter? Here are a few projects and products to help you to feel inspired when thinking about your wearable designs.

Extension of the body

The body is a dynamic system, and we can create enhancements for this dynamic system when we augment it with our wearable technology. We can look to extend the body and use our senses to create new and unusual relationships with our surroundings.

We can explore these technologies to understand how our bodies interact within spaces or with each other. The body can be extended through mechanical, gestural, and sensory qualities. These shifts in our perspective can help us acquire new ways of thinking and developing body-technology systems. What can we design to enhance our gestural engagement with the environment around us?

What if we had smart sneakers to analyze how you walk or smart gloves to help your golf swing? The *Under Armour Flow Velociti Wind* will track your running and try to improve it. There are gloves that read grip pressure to provide audio and visual feedback to help your golf game. The *Movano ring* provides you with sensor data for your heart rate, temperature, and more to help you get a better night's sleep.

Pedro Lopes is researching electrical muscle stimulation, as shown in *Figure 1.17*, through components and sensors. More of his research can be found online at `http://plopes.org/`:

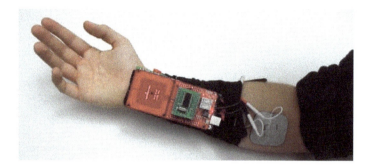

Figure 1.17 – Pedro Lopes: Electrical Muscle Stimulation

Electrical muscle stimulation is used to nudge a person into certain hand gestures. This can be a squeeze, drop, shake, and so on:

Figure 1.18 – External spine with a touch-sensitive ribcage (left) and Bertolt Meyer (right)

Researchers in Canada have designed prosthetic musical instruments. *Figure 1.18* shows an external spine with a touch-sensitive rib cage. It creates music in response to body gestures. Photo credit: Vanessa Yaremchuk. Instrument conception and design are credited to Joseph Malloch and Ian Hattwick of the **Input Devices and Music Interaction Lab** (**IDMIL**) at McGill University. See `http://www-new.idmil.org/` for more information.

Musician Bertolt Meyer (*Figure 1.18*) has a prosthetic arm and uses it to control his synthesizer and music using his mind. He plugs it directly into the synth to control the music by thinking about it.

The *Ivy health tracker*, is a bracelet that monitors your heart rate, respiratory rate, cardiac coherence, and physical and mental activity. It has a non-typical form factor, which is why it's included here. It is designed for women's health, and they are currently working on a device for post-natal depression.

The *Viscero ECG Vest* (Design Partners, 2021) Ireland-based Design Partners is a wearable ECG device that looks like the iconic plain white t-shirt shown in *Figure 1.19*. Designed to do away with the current large, uncomfortable monitors, Viscero is a white vest you wear underneath your clothing. Viscero is as easy to use as wearing a t-shirt.

The body-hugging vest comes with dry electrodes integrated into the t-shirt's design. These are placed in specific areas to accurately capture medical data, while the data itself is sent to a compact smart wearable device that attaches to the side of the t-shirt, right above the pocket:

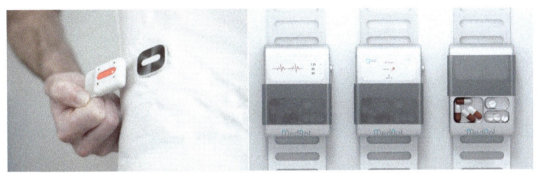

Figure 1.19 – Viscero ECG device (left) and MedBot concept (right)

The *MedBot* smartwatch concept was designed by Batyrkhan Bayaliev (permission and photo: `https://www.behance.net/bayalievbaae07`) as a health wearable, as shown in *Figure 1.19*. The smartwatch is equipped with a blood pressure sensor that will take readings when required and can also be utilized as a way to monitor additional health metrics.

The device also features storage space inside for a person's medication and will remind them when it's time to take their next dose. It also reminds users when it's time to take their pills. This explores the intersection of health and smart technology. This is currently a concept design.

1989, in the era of Nintendo-mania, toymaker giant *Mattel* unleashed a bold technological experiment to an eager public known as the Nintendo Power Glove, as shown here:

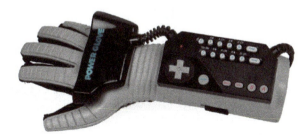

Figure 1.20 – Power Glove (photograph by Evan-Amos-Own work, Public Domain, https://commons.wikimedia.org/w/index.php?curid=16915852)

This was the first video game controller that could use hand gestures. However, the product was a critical failure, with terrible gameplay. Three decades later, dedicated fans continue to repurpose the Power Glove for art pieces, hacking projects, electronic music, and more. Although not "current," it is certainly a great start to making a wearable design.

Meta unveiled a prototype haptic feedback glove as a prototype, as shown in *Figure 1.21*. It is planned to be put into production and has 15 actuators that have contact with skin. These actuators deliver physical sensations through stiffening, loosening, and fabricating resistance:

Figure 1.21 – Meta haptic VR glove, Meta Reality Labs (left) and Wire Sensing glove (right) (Photo Credit: Purdue University/Rebecca McElhoe)

This allows you to feel VR objects. Another glove concept is one where the fingertips of a wireless voltage detection glove illuminate when the wearer's hand approaches a live cable. The gloves are powered wirelessly through a flexible, silk-based coil sewn on the textile and are laundry resistant.

There are even gloves that help with fruit picking. Rafael V. Aroca et al. (2013) propose a system of using gloves for non-typical applications. The gloves have sensors on them and by pointing or touching the fruit, it can analyze and measure their attributes.

Now that we've looked at some of the other ways wearables are being used and made, you may want to look at *Jennifer Crupi's* work for inspiration: `https://www.jennifercrupi.com/work`. She is a metalsmith who creates objects that fit the body in an unusual way.

What does the research tell us?

Researchers in the field of wearable technology follow many types of research practices. When you start to plan and develop your wearables, you will find that you may choose a path that works for you. You may want to learn about **qualitative** methods. This involves collecting first-hand (primary research) data – the stories and the feelings and thoughts to create improved versions of what we are developing. I'm often asked the following by students when I teach about technology and designing for people:

- How do I know what the right design is?
- How can I design something they need?
- When we make something, how do I know if people will use it?

And so on… My answer is typically the same – we get these answers from speaking to people. We don't know the answers, we don't have the perspective of everyone who may use what we make, and we want to understand why someone has a particular need – even if they don't know it yet. All these questions, and many more, can be answered by speaking with people. As Jakob Nielsen, co-founder of Nielson Norman Group, states, "*Pay attention to what users do, not what they say.*" We will discuss ways to do this and how to use engagement tools in *Chapter 11, Innovating with a Human-Centered Design Process*.

As you design your wearables, keep in mind that qualitative data will give you the stories that you need to be able to develop with success. Along the way, you may follow an ethnographic (Gobo, G., Marciniak, L.T., 2011) approach. Primarily, this involves studying people, their behaviors, their social interactions, and similar.

As Hillman Curtis states, "*The goal of a designer is to listen, observe, understand, sympathize, empathize, synthesize, and glean insights that enable him or her to make the invisible visible.*"

This is typically done in their environment, where they study people in context. It is a great way to begin to understand the people you want to design for. This way, you can begin to understand their story, goals, and context.

Using research methods to acquire knowledge

Fieldwork, or field studies, is a generic term for you going into "the field" – the environment where the people you are designing for are located. These studies are not done in a lab or in unnatural settings.

I have also used "in-the-wild" studies to describe some of the research I have done. This is when a participant uses the wearable as part of their daily routine. You may or may not be present for this:

- **Non-participant observation**: You observe people from a distance, without interacting with them. This allows you to gain information and not disturb how people will act naturally in their environment.

- **Participant observation**: This involves you establishing a relationship with the person or people you are observing. You typically stay for a set period in their natural environment. Here, you can interact with them and participate in their everyday habits.

- **Passive observation**: Generally, this method involves shadowing the people you are concerned with. You won't interact with them or interfere in their normal interactions. Documentation is important and can involve video, photography, note-taking, audio recording, and drawings. This method allows you to focus on them fully and maintain your outsider perspective. Also, even though you are not interacting with them directly, often, people are still very conscious or aware of your presence, so their behavior may be altered. This can also depend on what you are observing. It might take several visits or a long time observing to lessen this happening.

- **Interviews**: Interviews are a great follow-on from observation. Speaking to people after observing them can provide additional insights. It provides information about what they are doing and why they are doing it and fills in details on aspects that you weren't able to fully capture or observe. It may offer you more insights if you can interview them in the same location where the observation took place.

- **Auto-ethnographic approach**: For certain wearable items you make, you may want to be the person testing them. It could be that you have a need for the wearable you are making. If so, you can follow an auto-ethnographic approach. This is a research method and methodology that uses the researcher's personal experience as data to describe, analyze, and understand cultural experience (C Ellis, TE Adams, AP Bochner, 2011). When I followed this method, I took huge amounts of field notes. I'll cover this more in *Chapter 11, Innovating with a Human-Centered Design Process*.

- **Research diaries**: A research diary is a great way to protect the work you do in the field. You don't want to forget everything you've been observing or listening to. If I challenge you to tell me what you said in an earlier conversation, you will rarely remember the majority of what was said. It's only until you use a diary of some description that you can begin to form an accurate picture of what happened – not your interpretation of it. Whether they are called diaries, log books, journals, field notes, or lab books, some version of this type of "external memory" has been used by researchers in many disciplines to record their daily observations in the field (Altrichter, H. and Holly, M.L., 2005).

What can people tell us?

These research methods can be very useful for designing wearable technology. This is not an exhaustive list, and I would recommend that you follow up on these concepts. Speaking to people is one of the best ways to answer your questions and set you on your developing journey. Instead of asking what the research tells us, we may ask, *what can people tell us?*

When using these methods and others, it is especially important to follow and be aware of the ethical and cultural considerations. This brings us to the next section.

Cultural and ethical considerations

Various ethical and cultural considerations can affect our designs in two main ways. The wearable design itself has issues that need to be considered, but the way we research and test our wearables may have considerations too. You'll find that this section asks a lot of questions – it is designed to provoke thought and reflection. The issues that will be raised are meant to be thought-provoking and help you reflect on your wearable designs. Let's explore this further so that you have a guide when developing your projects.

In this section, we will cover the following topics:

- Considerations when designing wearable technology
- Ethical considerations in research and testing

Let's get started.

Considerations when designing wearable technology

As we have just learned, wearables can be found in healthcare, part of our daily routines, and often used 24 hours a day. They are often small in size and have sensors that collect data about us or our environment. There can be privacy concerns for people using these devices. To address this, we need to understand what the potential challenges are and how these challenges are seen by the wearer.

Data sharing brings benefits to us – if it didn't, we wouldn't use the devices. But alongside that, there are privacy challenges. Do we feel under surveillance? Culturally, these issues are felt in different ways. Does society in the UK, for example, which has surveillance cameras in many public locations feel more at ease with this aspect? Do cultures or locations with no cameras feel more invaded in their privacy? Are there threats if we use these devices? What are the risks? These are all important topics to consider.

There have been news articles reporting on Apple Tags being used to track people and cars *without* their knowledge – so much so that Apple has issued an app for Android users as well so that they can be alerted if they are being tracked. Does the convenience of using technologies outweigh any concerns we have?

We must consider that most people carry around a mobile phone. These typically track our usage in different ways, and even our locations. So, is there something specific about wearables that concerns people? Is it about a limited understanding of how or when personal data is used or stored? Surveillance concerns were raised with so much objection to Google Glass that the project is no longer available for public purchase. Has the immediate/constant use of cameras on some wearables altered people's perceptions?

What factors do we need to consider when designing wearable technology? How do the cultural aspects of different societies alter how we design for them?

Data security

- Is data collected? If so, where, and how is it stored? Processed? For what length of time is the data held? Who has access and control to it? Is it shared?

- Is some data more sensitive than others? Personal? Medical? Confidential?

Data recorded

- What data is captured? Audio? Video? Sensors? Are they unaware of this being recorded?

- Do we need to be aware of location data and consequences for wearers? Is the location live? Delayed? What are the implications of accessing location data?

- Can the data be deleted? Accessed by the wearer easily? Is it published? Will or can this be opened to criminal abuse?

Privacy

- Is privacy compromised in any way when using the wearable? Whose privacy? The wearer? The environment?

- Does it affect those around or with the wearer?

- Is privacy compromised by using this wearable?

Primarily, there is a concern if a user has granted permission to use their data but that it is then used by a third party. People fear their devices being hacked and manipulated. As an example, Google Glass posed issues for people because it was recording the users but also the environment and those around them. You could be in any location, including ones that would require privacy, and it could be recording without the knowledge of the other people around you. Additionally, the data was stored on Google's servers. In theory, this meant anyone at Google also had access to it.

Zhao, Zheng, and Pedro Lopes, computer science professors at the **University of Chicago** (**UChicago**), created a prototype wearable device that blocks microphones in the vicinity from eavesdropping on conversations:

Figure 1.22 – Bracelet of Silence (Photograph Heather Zheng)

With 24 speakers that emitted ultrasonic signals, it stops the Amazon Echo and similar devices from recording conversations. You can read more about the project at `http://sandlab.cs.uchicago.edu/jammer/` and follow the reference to the research paper at the end of this chapter.

Our physical location of where we live may also impact our use and understanding of wearables. For example, the EU has legal frameworks on privacy and personal data protection. When designing our wearables, we must consider the person using them and what the society they are a part of will feel if it is used there. Will they still be welcomed? Or will they become untrusted? Digital addiction and digital distraction can also play a part in acceptability.

There can be tension between the constant gestures we must make while using a wearable in the company of others. If family members or friends are not supportive, would this make a difference in what wearables can be used? Understanding these issues and the social context of the wearer will increase the wearable's use. It will increase acceptance and satisfaction. Some devices for people with dementia or memory loss issues are associated with the stigma of wearing them, so there is a low use rate, even if the technology could be helpful.

Also, consider if the device is environmentally friendly. What are the waste concerns? Recycling? How is the device created? Are the materials sourced ethically? These questions are too big for one chapter as there are so many considerations and impacts we can look at on the surface. When we design, we should look for ways to be conscious of our impact when designing wearables. An article by Lee, J., Kim, D., Ryoo, H. Y., and Shin, B. S. (2016) describes wearables in terms of their value for a human-oriented experience, but those issues can also be resolved from a sustainability standpoint. Their article defines, "*sustainable wearables is discussed in the context of improving the quality of individual life, social impact, and social public interest.*" When creating our wearables, we should consider, as discussed in the article, that "*Successful and sustainable wearables will lead to positive changes for both individuals and societies overall.*" This article is available online at `https://www.mdpi.com/2071-1050/8/5/466/pdf`.

Recycling and disposing of wearables and e-textiles is also a concern for the wearable community. Both makers and wearers should be concerned with the ability to repair items, dispose of them in an environmentally friendly way, and use biodegradable materials for embedding electronics. Alternative materials such as mycelium – a root type of structure of fungus found in soil – have properties such as heat and thermal resistance, which can be used in wearables. It is currently being used for fashion as it can be made to look like leather, but I've also seen examples of it being used to make furniture and other items. Vasquez, E. S. L., & Vega, K. (2019) describe in their paper about creating "*…sustainability in the prototyping process by producing wearables that make use of biodegradable material for embedding electronics.*"

My colleagues and I have been experimenting with alternative materials too. Recycling and repurposing is a great way to think through environmental considerations. This includes using secondhand clothing, recycled cardboard, or recycling electronics. We've also experimented with recycling cardboard and putting it into molds to form the shapes we want to embed electronics. There are many materials we can reuse; we are currently recycling bubble wrap as a textile.

Energy and power sources should also be a consideration when you develop your wearables. Will you provide or build a solar panel into your device, for example? If not, how will the energy be renewed?

Lastly, there are cost considerations. Is the wearable exclusive and price prohibitive? Or is there access to all? If it is of medical importance, who will pay?

These issues and concerns should be addressed during the development of the wearable, and we will look at this in detail in *Chapter 8, Learning How to Prototype and Make Electronics Wearable.*

Ethical considerations in research and testing

As discussed earlier, there are many research methods we can use to get great results about the wearables we make. But what are the ethical considerations if we are speaking with people to understand the wearable we are making?

This book doesn't focus on research specifically, so this is a guide for you to be aware of if you do test your wearables. Considerations include the following:

- Informed consent
- Voluntary participation
- Potential for harm
- Confidentiality
- Anonymity
- Results communication

It is also important to consider honesty, integrity, and objectivity. You may be designing something for a sensitive topic or purpose, so it is especially important then. You will find that if you create a participant information sheet, for example, the participants may be more willing and trusting to give you feedback on your wearable. This is a letter that details what you are trying to achieve, what the wearable's purpose is, how you are doing it, and details of how they can contact you. It may also contain information about what they will need to do if they participate, as well as the benefits of participating. Coupled with the information sheet, there is usually a participant consent form. This is an agreement that the person you are speaking with will understand what is expected of them and what they can expect of you. It indicates that they are participating of their own free will and understand that they can quit at any time for any reason.

Many examples of **information sheets** and **consent forms** are available online. Not all of them are good, so be sure to look at a few examples before deciding which to use.

Summary

In this chapter, we discussed the context of wearables and their evolution. We explored the exciting applications of wearables in a variety of different domains, including for medical, safety, improving quality of life, and fitness purposes.

We learned about the current research, including what scientists, technologists, engineers, artists, and designers are exploring in these intersections. These impressive innovations can inspire us to keep learning and develop what we dream of. We looked at the benefits that wearables can bring to people with physical or sensory disabilities, visual or hearing impairments, and other mobility or cognitive issues. We also had a quick look at what research can tell us, and the methods we can use to create wearables *with purpose*. Finally, we gained an awareness of what ethical and privacy considerations we should take into account when designing for and with people. I hope this chapter helped give you the foundation and excitement to inspire you and help you think through ethical considerations when designing wearable technologies.

In *Chapter 2, Understanding and Building Electronic Sewable Circuits*, we are going to get up and running with our first electronic circuits. We will start by learning the basics of electronics. Then, we will create essential circuits with conductive threads. After that, we will learn why and how to use a multimeter, how to make switches and buttons, and lastly, how to soft circuits. All of this will prepare you for the wide world of wearables!

References

You may wish to explore the resources that have been used in this chapter. There are also annual conferences with great research outputs. Established in 1997, **International Symposium on Wearables Computers (ISWC)** is a great start. Look out for MIT, Georgia Tech, ACM CHI Conference on Human Factors in Computing Systems, and others. The content ranges from sensors, new hardware, new applications, and new methods for wearable computers. The following are some other resources you may find useful:

Electrodermis: More information is available at `https://www.morphingmatter.cs.cmu.edu/projects/electrodermis`, where additional images and discussions of their prototyping and electronics usage are provided.

Hughes-Riley, T., Dias, T., & Cork, C. (2018). *A historical review of the development of electronic textiles. Fibers, 6(2), 34.* Available at `https://www.mdpi.com/2079-6439/6/2/34/pdf`.

Martin T, Healey J (2007) 2006's wearable computing advances and fashions. *IEEE Pervasive Computing 6(1):14-6.*

Card, Stuart K.; Thomas P. Moran; Allen Newell (July 1980). *The keystroke-level model for user performance time with interactive systems. Communications of the ACM. 23 (7): 396–410.* DOI: 10.1145/358886.358895.

Ometov, A., Shubina, V., Klus, L., Skibińska, J., Saafi, S., Pascacio, P., ... & Lohan, E. S. (2021). *A survey on wearable technology: History, state-of-the-art, and current challenges. Computer Networks, 193, 108074.*

Carlisle, James H. (June 1976). *Evaluating the impact of office automation on top management communication. Proceedings of the June 7–10, 1976, National Computer Conference and Exposition. pp. 611–616.* DOI: 10.1145/1499799.1499885.

Weiser, M. (1999). *The computer for the 21st century. ACM SIGMOBILE mobile computing and communications review, 3(3), 3-11.*

Nieuwdorp, E. (2007). *The pervasive discourse. Computers in Entertainment. 5 (2): 13.* DOI: 10.1145/1279540.1279553

Greenfield, Adam (2006). *Everyware: The Dawning Age of Ubiquitous Computing. New Riders. Pp. 11–12.* ISBN 978-0-321-38401-0.

Licklider, J. C. (1960). *Man-computer symbiosis. IRE transactions on human factors in electronics, (1), 4-11.*

Amft O, Lauffer M, Ossevoort S, Macaluso F, Lukowicz P, Troster G (2004). *Design of the QBIC wearable computing platform.* In: Proceedings *15th IEEE international conference on application-specific systems, architectures and processors, 2004. 2004 Sep 27 (pp 398–410). IEEE.*

Picard, Rosalind; Healey, Jennifer (December 1997). *Affective Wearables. Personal Technologies. 1 (4): 231–240.* DOI: 10.1007/BF01682026

Mann, Steve (March 1997). *Smart Clothes. Personal Technologies. 1 (1): 21–27.* DOI: 10.1007/BF01317885

Mann, S. (1996). *Smart clothing: The shift to wearable computing. Communications of the ACM, 39(8), 23-24.*

C. C. Collins, *Tactile Television - Mechanical and Electrical Image Projection, in IEEE Transactions on Man-Machine Systems, vol. 11, no. 1, pp. 65-71, March 1970.* DOI: 10.1109/TMMS.1970.299964.

C.C. Collins, L.A. Scadden, and A.B. Alden, *Mobile Studies with a Tactile Imaging Device, Fourth Conference on Systems & Devices for the Disabled, 1–3 June 1977, Seattle WA.*

Picard, Rosalind; Healey, Jennifer (December 1997). *Affective Wearables. Personal Technologies. 1 (4): 231–240.* DOI: 10.1007/BF01682026

de Medeiros, M. S., Goswami, D., Chanci, D., Moreno, C., & Martinez, R. V. (2021). *Washable, breathable, and stretchable e-textiles wirelessly powered by omniphobic silk-based coils. Nano Energy, 87, 106155.*

Yuxin Chen, Huiying Li, Shan-Yuan Teng, Steven Nagels, Zhijing Li, Pedro Lopes, Ben Y. Zhao, Haitao Zheng, *Wearable Microphone Jamming, Proceedings of ACM CHI Conference on Human Factors in Computing Systems (CHI), Honolulu, HI, April 2020.* Available at `https://sandlab.cs.uchicago.edu/jammer/`.

Gobo, G. and Marciniak, L.T., 2011. *Ethnography. Qualitative research, 3(1), pp.15-36.*

Brewer, J., 2000. *Ethnography. McGraw-Hill Education (UK).*

Gobo, G., 2008. *Doing ethnography. Sage.*

Ellis, C., Adams, T.E. and Bochner, A.P., 2011. *Autoethnography: an overview. Historical social research/Historische sozialforschung, pp.273-290.*

Chang, H., 2016. *Autoethnography as method (Vol. 1). Routledge.*

Altrichter, H. and Holly, M.L., 2005. *Research diaries. Research methods in the social sciences, pp.24-32.*

Hui Zheng and Vivian Genaro Motti, 2018. *Assisting Students with Intellectual and Developmental Disabilities in Inclusive Education with Smartwatches.* Proceedings of the *2018 CHI Conference on Human Factors in Computing Systems. Association for Computing Machinery, New York, NY, USA, Paper 350, 1–12*. DOI: https://doi.org/10.1145/3173574.3173924.

Eric Markvicka, Guanyun Wang, Yi-Chin Lee, Gierad Laput, Carmel Majidi, and Lining Yao, 2019. *ElectroDermis: Fully Untethered, Stretchable, and Highly-Customizable Electronic Bandages.* Proceedings of the *2019 CHI Conference on Human Factors in Computing Systems. Association for Computing Machinery, New York, NY, USA, Paper 632, 1–10*. DOI: https://doi.org/10.1145/3290605.3300862.

Lee, J., Kim, D., Ryoo, H. Y., & Shin, B. S. (2016*). Sustainable wearables: Wearable technology for enhancing the quality of human life. Sustainability, 8(5), 466*. Available to download online from https://www.mdpi.com/2071-1050/8/5/466/pdf.

Vasquez, E. S. L., & Vega, K. (2019, September). *Myco-accessories: sustainable wearables with biodegradable materials.* In Proceedings of the *23rd International Symposium on Wearable Computers (pp. 306-311).* https://dl.acm.org/doi/pdf/10.1145/3341163.3346938.

Review questions

Answer the following questions to test your knowledge of this chapter:

1. What device or technology would you consider as *augmented human*?
2. What are some typical qualities that a wearable has?
3. Think about some of the intersections that wearables cross for collaborative and interesting outcomes. Who would you collaborate with?
4. How can informed wearables be designed and what is their focus?
5. Where on the body can wearables be made for?
6. How do ethical considerations affect our designs and the research for testing our designs?
7. Sketch your ideas about materials, textiles, functions, or purposes that inspire you.

2

Understanding and Building Electronic Sewable Circuits

Now that we have looked at the history, current work, and ethics of making and testing wearables, it's time to jump into the electricity basics. Understanding and making electronic circuits is important for your wearable journey. We will work through the principles of electricity. Recognizing the principles will help you to follow along with the activities in this book, and it will also help you to plan and make your own wearables.

In this chapter, you will learn the first steps of understanding electricity and then using switches in a circuit. Once the basics have been covered, you will build electronic circuits with **Light Emitting Diodes (LEDs)**. This foundation will set you up with the nuts and bolts of your new skills so that you can apply them to a sewable circuit. Also, we will learn how to use a multimeter and why this is an important tool when working with electricity.

By the end of this chapter, we will get hands-on with some practical examples. To put it all into practice, you will use conductive materials and conductive thread, alongside other materials. You will make working circuits in fabrics. Learning through doing will become the foundation for your continued journey.

In this chapter, we're going to cover the following main topics:

- Understanding electricity
- Using a multimeter
- Electronic circuits
- Soft circuits
- Switches and buttons

Technical requirements

This chapter will have a practical element where you can try building the circuits that are in the book. The best way to learn is by doing. These are the recommended items for the circuits. Note that for easier sourcing, *all of these items* can be purchased in a single kit, including the technology and fabrics, with additional items for future chapters (not including the multimeter) from `https://www.tinkertailor.tech/product-page/busy-new-bee`:

- Various LEDs, a 5 mm through-hole, and sewable LEDs.

- 220 Ohm (also noted as Ω) /330 Ohm resistors.

- A 3V battery (CR2032), which is also called a coin cell.

- Crocodile clips; 5 or 10 is a good number.

- A breadboard; you can use half sizes or full sizes.

- Hookup wire:

  This is measured in gauges, for instance, around **22AWG solid core** will make prototyping easier for these circuits; 1 meter will be enough. When using a hookup wire for a breadboard, a single-core wire maintains its shape well and is easy to push through the breadboard holes. For wearables, we often use stranded wire, which is a lot more flexible because it is made up of several "strands" of wire. This can be more difficult to push into a breadboard. Usually, you will need to hold the strands together and twist them to form a more solid end.

- The Adafruit Beginner LED Sewing Kit (ID:1285) can be found at `https://www.adafruit.com/product/1285#tutorialsstarter`. It contains the following items:

  - 2-ply conductive thread

  - 2 x sewable battery holder for CR2032

  - LEDs

  - 5 mm sewable metal snaps

  - Sewing needles

- Material/fabric: You can upcycle clothes or use soft acrylic felt. Alternatively, denim is a good first choice. We are looking for a fabric with some bend but that is thick enough to be held into place easily to sew.

- Conductive fabric: This could be a silver-, steel-, or copper-based fabric, along with various conductive items (optional).

- Multimeter.

If you are new to sewing, you might find a threader more useful. This makes threading our needles a lot easier to do. When using conductive fabrics, this is especially true as the thread can be more difficult to thread. Now that we have our items ready to use, we'll get started with learning about the basics of working with electricity. We're working with low voltages, so most of our components and circuit boards will only ever use 5V or 3.3V. We are learning about electricity using low voltages, don't ever attempt to use mains electricity without the proper learning required.

Understanding electricity

Let's start with electricity basics to begin our journey of making wearables. We will cover the following:

- What is a circuit?
- Resistance
- Voltage
- Current

The preceding list highlights three main properties that we need to understand to build our circuits: resistance, voltage, and current.

These three properties connect and have a relationship called **Ohm's Law**. It's important that we understand these properties to help us build and fix our circuits. Also, when you have finished the exercises in the book, you will have the confidence and skills to create your own projects. Let's explore them in detail, starting with circuits.

What is a circuit?

A circuit has a start point and an endpoint with an electronic component in between. It forms a loop. This allows electricity to flow. Between the start point and the endpoint, there can be many other connections. Circuits can consist of components such as resistors, sensors, motors, and more. We will begin with a few components and work up to using a few sensors and outputs.

For electricity to flow, we must use conductors, which are items that allow the current to pass through them. Insulators will stop the flow. Common **conductors** include metals, water, human skin, and plants.

Common **insulators**, which stop the flow of electricity, are plastic, rubber, dry wood, and glass. *Figure 2.1* shows a closed loop that moves the electricity from one point to another. It is a schematic diagram that is used to show the electrical representation of this circuit. It also shows a simple circuit with the current flow from positive to negative. In this diagram, you can see the power symbol on the left-hand side. Electricity will flow out the top, on the + positive side, and follow through the resistor. Then, it will flow through the LED, which will light up, and then the complete circuit returns to the power symbol, on the ground side, -:

Figure 2.1 – Schematic of an LED circuit (left-hand side) and the LED circuit (right-hand side)

In the *Using a multimeter* section, we will take a closer look at how we can determine whether an item is a conductor or an insulator.

Note that a schematic drawing is representative of all the components needed and how they are connected. It is not how they are physically located on a circuit. The physical circuit has a battery and an LED. A diode is a component that conducts electric current only in one direction.

> **What's a Short Circuit?**
>
> A short circuit happens if you connect power and ground directly. If you complete a circuit with no components in between, a short will happen. This will burn out your power source quickly and cause damage, so be careful. Be aware of anything in your circuit becoming too hot. Turn off the power immediately.

Why is a circuit important? When we make our wearables, we use circuit boards to control the inputs/outputs:

Figure 2.2 – Printed circuit boards (PCBs)

A circuit connects the boards to our components by turning them on or sending and receiving data. If we connect the electronics correctly, we can control them.

Once we learn how to connect our circuits, we can program them, so this is the first step. A **printed circuit board (PCB)** has components connected with metal traces. See *Figure 2.2*, which shows some examples of PCB boards. As an insulator, it does not conduct electricity.

The conductive material between components carries the electricity in a loop to make the circuit. This will be the same as when we use wires to complete our circuit. The PCB is part of the development process journey. When making a wearable project, we often go from prototyping on a breadboard, to creating a soft circuit, then make it more durable by bringing it to a perfboard or protoboard for soldering (perforated or prototype), and lastly, to PCB.

Open circuit

If you don't connect all the parts, this can result in an open circuit. If your wires are not connected, then the circuit just won't work.

If your circuit isn't working, it is a good idea to check that all your connections are connected where they should be. Sometimes, a wire has come loose or become broken, and this will be the reason why it isn't working. Sometimes, components flicker when they shouldn't, so if you see a flicker, look through your wires in case you have an open circuit. In *Figure 2.3*, we can see the vibration motor has a ground wire that has come off. That's why it isn't working:

Figure 2.3 – An open circuit

Checking through your connections can easily and quickly fix an obvious error. It's always worth looking over your circuits if things aren't behaving as they should.

> **Circuits Not Working?**
>
> An open circuit can happen in our sewable circuits. Threads can easily break or rub against other conductors or insulators, altering our intentions for the circuit. So, always check your threads.

Let's take a closer look at the three terms you will come across for your circuits: resistance, voltage, and current.

Resistance – Ω

Resistance restricts the electrical flow or charge in the circuit. This is measured in Ohms, Ω, and the symbol is R. Resistance is very important for our circuits. If there is too much resistance, the components won't work because not enough electricity is getting to them, for example, an LED won't light up. However, if we have little or no resistance, then the component will burn out. If that happens, you won't be able to use it again.

We can see this visually when using different resistors. Using different values for resistors will alter the brightness of the LED – less resistance will allow more power and the light will be brighter. A resistor can be used in either direction.

Voltage – V

Voltage is the potential flow, measured in a unit called a Volt. The symbol is V. The source of electricity has two sides: positive and negative. Voltage flows from the start of the circuit or the highest electrical potential, positive +, which is power, to the endpoint, ground -. Common ground is known as zero Volts, with no electrical potential. The voltage is the difference in electricity between any two points on the circuit. In our wearable circuits, we will have a positive voltage of 5V or 3.3V and a negative voltage of 0V. It is very important to always check the component you are using and what its maximum voltage is.

Many of the components we use need 3.3V, so they will need to be connected to a similar power source. We will cover this in greater detail later.

Current – I

Current is the amount of electrical flow in our circuit. As described in Ohm's law, current has the symbol of I. This is the rate at which the charge is flowing. It is measured in **Ampere**, or **amp** for short. The unit symbol is A. For our circuits, you might also see it as **milliamps** (mA). You will also see **milliamp Hours** (mAh), which is a measure of the current delivery capacity of a battery.

Remember! Red = Power and Black = Ground

For positive (power) connections, I use the convention of red wires. I use black for negative (ground). Many people follow this same convention. It makes it easier to find errors in our circuit, as we can quickly identify where our power and ground are coming from.

Now we can put the formula together using resistance, voltage, and current using Ohm's law to calculate values.

Ohm's law

Ohm's law tells us that voltage (*V*) is equal to current (*I*) times resistance (*R*):

V = I x R

The equation can be rearranged to work out what the values are for your circuit. So, we can use *I = V / R* or *R = V / I*. We can use Ohm's law to calculate the resistance of the circuit. For example, if you want to know the right voltage for powering an LED, we can use *V=IR*.

Activity 2.1 – creating a simple circuit

The simplest circuit we can create is an LED with a battery. *Figure 2.4* shows the schematic for a simple circuit. A power source and an LED form a complete circuit. Because the battery is only 3V, we don't need to use a resistor. If we do use a resistor, we can light the LED for longer. All we need to do is hold a coin cell battery between the legs of the LED (*Figure 2.4*). Because we are hitting the highest threshold of voltage an LED can take without burning out, we are limiting the lifespan of the LED. Think of it as burning the LED at full power. To extend its life, we use resistors to drop the voltage so that the LED will light and burn for longer. You could add a second or third LED to lower the brightness too.

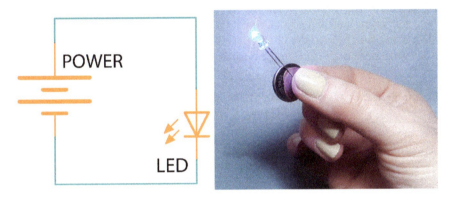

Figure 2.4 – The schematic for the simple circuit (left-hand side) and an LED circuit (right-hand side)

This is also a quick way to check the polarity of your battery. Usually, I keep a coin cell with or near my LEDs as it's such a handy way to check. This is because you need to hold the positive leg (the longer leg) of your LED to the positive side of your battery. The negative leg (the shorter leg) of your LED needs to be touching the negative side of your battery:

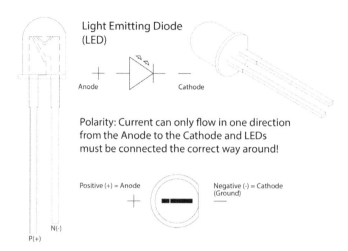

Figure 2.5 – LED polarity

> **Quick Tip**
>
> A tip for figuring out LED polarity is that the **long** leg is the **positive** leg. If you've cut the LED legs and you aren't sure, look at the small rim of the LED: it has one flat side. This flat side is the negative leg. Also, you can hold the LED up to a light and look inside it. There are two pieces of metal. The smaller one connects to the positive leg.

Generally, in a single circuit, we can light an LED with a 3V battery:

1 LED	2 LEDS	3 LEDs	4 LEDs	5 LEDS
10 hours	5 hours	3.3 hours	2.5 hours	2 hours

Table 2.1 – How long the LED will be lit for

We've had a look through the information to understand electricity, and we are gaining an understanding of resistance, voltage, and current. To see what's happening beneath the surface and learn more about current and electricity, let's look at how to use a multimeter.

This is an essential tool for creating wearables. Using a multimeter is important because we can fix broken circuits, work out resistance, and check what materials are conductive.

Using a multimeter

We can use a **multimeter** to measure resistance, voltage, and current. It's a great way to see what's going on in our circuit. Using a multimeter, we can check our connections and find breaks in the circuit; it tells us when something is broken. Multimeters, as shown in *Figure 2.6*, come in different sizes and prices. Starting with a low-cost one will be suitable for our circuits. I have a small portable one. They have a dial so that you can select the function you need. A multimeter will have probes that we'll use to connect to the circuit to take measurements. You'll notice these are also black and red, following the same convention we've been using for our circuits, too. If your probes are removable, make sure the **black probe is in the COM port** and that the **red probe is in the mAVΩ** port. Additionally, note that the multimeter uses the convention of red wire for positive/power and black for negative/ground. You should read the instructions that come with the multimeter you buy, as they might have slightly different dials:

Figure 2.6 – Multimeters

In this section, we will be learning about the important ways multimeters can help in our circuits, covering the main ways you'll be using the multimeter. For additional learning, there are tutorials and videos online if you'd like to take it further.

Resistance

Let's measure a resistor. **Resistors** are often out of their packages or mixed up in their packaging, and this is a quick and easy way to find out whether we have the right one:

1. Turn the dial on your multimeter to the Ohm symbol, Ω, and place the probes on either side of the resistor that you want to measure.

2. *Figure 2.7* shows the probes on each side of the resistor, and the reading on the multimeter is 217 Ohms.

When you buy it, it's marked as a 220 Ohm resistor. Be aware that there is usually a difference in the readings. There is a tolerance value to resistors.

The common resistors we are using are usually plus or minus 10 percent, which won't make much difference to our circuits:

Figure 2.7 – Measuring resistance

If you can't hold the probes steady, you can make this easier by using use crocodile clips, attached to the probes and the component or part. You can check the resistance of the conductive thread or materials in your circuit. This is especially important if the thread has some distance to travel between components, which adds resistance (that is, less electricity) to the connection. An auto-ranging multimeter will find the correct range of your resistor. If your multimeter doesn't do this, you'll need to move your dial to the correct range:

Figure 2.8 – A close-up of a multimeter dial

Typically, when measuring a resistor value, you turn the dial to Ω, and then turn the dial to 2000. This will measure values under 2000; for example, LEDs will use 330 Ohms or 220 Ohms. If we are using a higher value, such as a 10K resistor, you would turn the dial higher, to the 20K setting.

You can also use a guide to calculate the resistance value yourself. One helpful resource can be found at `https://www.digikey.com/en/resources/conversion-calculators/conversion-calculator-resistor-color-code`.

Voltage

It's useful to be able to check the voltage of your battery, as this can often be why your circuit isn't working. You can check whether your components are receiving the amount of voltage they need. *Figure 2.9* shows a battery being measured at 3.8V:

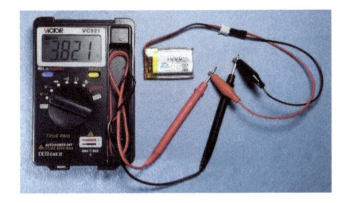

Figure 2.9 – Measuring voltage

Turn the dial on your multimeter to the **V with a straight line**. Place the probes on correctly according to polarity: ground to the black probe and power to the red probe.

If your multimeter has multiple settings on the dial for voltage, then turn the dial to the **DC Voltage** portion of the dial and choose a voltage higher than what you are expecting. Arduino circuits use **5 volts**, so your dial should be set to **20V**, not 2V. You'll know whether this is incorrect, as it will display the voltage incorrectly. If it's wrong, then move it to a higher voltage.

Current – continuity/conductivity tests

This is a quick and easy way to check whether your circuit is complete or whether the material you want to use is conductive. I have a portable multimeter that I can carry with me and use in shops if I'm curious about a piece of fabric, thread, or other material.

If you are unsure whether your wiring and connections form a closed circuit, perform the following steps:

1. Turn your multimeter dial to the **speaker**/audio icon. It's a little speaker because this test will make a sound. There will be a tone when there is a **closed circuit**.

2. Place the probes across the place you want to test. This could be across a wire you've soldered for example. It might be to see if a fabric is conductive. If you hear the tone, then it is a complete circuit.

3. If you want to check a broken circuit connection, place the probes onto the wires, pins, or part of your circuit are **not** supposed to be connected. If you hear a tone, that tells you it is connected, there is flow of electricity, when there shouldn't be. Note this is purely the physical circuitry, and it can't tell you whether your circuit will work according to your programming.

Figure 2.10 – Measuring no conductivity, shown with OL (left-hand side)
and conductivity registering a value (right-hand side)

Do you want to know whether it is a conductor or an insulator material? We can check conductivity. Again, turn the dial to the speaker symbol and place the probes in two separate places on the item you want to test. In *Figure 2.10*, you can see the reading is **OL**, which stands for Open Loop, so there is no conductivity between the two probes. This is a measurement of felt fabric. Often, I use felt to put my components on and map them out. However, in *Figure 2.10*, we can see that conductive fabric is being measured. Again, look at the reading; this material is conductive and shows a positive value reading. You will hear a tone, so we know we can use this conductive material because it will carry the current.

Some fabrics will have some conductivity in a different direction from what you are testing. Try testing the fabric in a few different directions according to the way it is woven because it might have conductivity. Then, you can use the fabric in that direction and sew on top of it.

> **Important to Remember**
>
> The probes must not touch each other when doing the reading. You'll notice that when the probes touch each other, you will hear a tone. That's because you are forming a closed circuit. So, if the probes touch, you are measuring your multimeter circuit and not the material.

The multimeter is a valuable tool to check our circuits, the flow of electricity, our battery charge, and whether a material is a conductor or an insulator. Now that we understand the basics of our multimeter, we will continue our journey into electronic circuits. We'll be using the multimeter again to help us work out the resistance when we have more than one resistor in the circuit.

Electronic circuits

Let's create some circuits. First, we will use crocodile clips, a battery holder, a battery, and LEDs to complete two circuits. We will look at circuit design with the following:

- Electricity in series
- Electricity in parallel

As we learned previously, as electricity travels through a circuit and its components, from a point of higher voltage to lower voltage, the electric potential is used up by the components it flows through until there is no more potential energy. So, how we arrange our components will influence how the electricity is consumed. Let's look at series and parallel circuits, using an LED to demonstrate.

Series

For components to be in a series, they are connected one after another. Electricity will pass through the first component, then through the next, and so on:

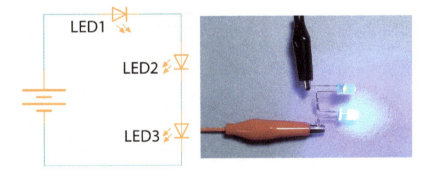

Figure 2.11 – A schematic LED in a series

The schematic shown in *Figure 2.11* shows three LEDs in a series. We can also see how this might look in a circuit using two LEDs. A quick way to see whether it is in series is to follow the current flow: start from the positive side of the power source and follow through to ground. The electricity gets *used* as it passes through each component before going to the next. If we don't have enough voltage, then only the first or second LED in a series will be lit. This is called a **voltage drop**. As electricity passes, it drops that voltage.

Typically, the LEDs we use have a forward voltage drop of 1.8V–2.2V. If we used a 3V power source, then the first LED would work and the second would get less voltage and work with less brightness. There wouldn't be enough voltage left to power any more LEDs on. You need to choose a battery with enough voltage – or you can wire up your components in parallel.

Parallel

Each component will receive the same amount of voltage, but the *current* is divided between them. If we wire our components side by side, they are in a parallel circuit. Electricity will pass through them all at the same time.

They are each connected to ground and power. This is shown in *Figure 2.12* where each component has a circuit that functions independently:

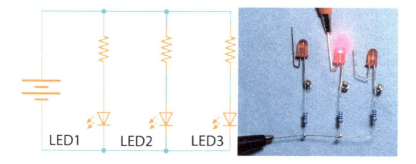

Figure 2.12 – A circuit in parallel

Figure 2.12 shows one LED is lit while the others are not. With a parallel circuit, we can see that there are distinct paths the current can take.

What else can be in series or parallel?

Using a resistor in series – where the electricity can only follow one path – means that if we add resistors, we add their values together. If we used three 10K resistors, the total resistance would be 30K. In a series circuit, the current is restricted to the same path, making it harder to flow. Using a multimeter, we can easily see the resistance when we add our resistors. Take a look at *Figure 2.13*, showing over 29K Ohms:

Figure 2.13 – A series circuit with almost 30K resistance (left-hand side) and
a parallel circuit with just over 3.3K resistance (right-hand side)

Resistors in parallel circuits work differently. There is more than one path for the circuit to take when we are parallel. Our supply voltage is the same, but there are more paths. If we have one 10K resistor, then it will have 10K resistance. However, if we have two 10K resistors, then each takes the electricity flow through it at once, making it half, resulting in 5K resistance. If we are using three 10K resistors, that results in 3.3K resistance.

Now that we understand the types of circuits we can make, let's put it all into practice! We'll use crocodile clips to test a circuit.

Activity 2.2 – using crocodile clips to create a circuit

Crocodile clips, also called alligator clips, are great for creating a temporary circuit. This is useful when we are connecting to fabrics or other soft components that won't easily fit into a breadboard. There are many different types. *Figure 2.14* shows the variety – some are very short and others a lot longer. My desk easily gets cluttered with these, so I like to use the shorter ones. Some also have what are called **DuPont** cable ends. This is a plastic connector on the wire ends, that have a plug (a metal pin) or socket version (a corresponding connector with metal inside to accept the metal pin):

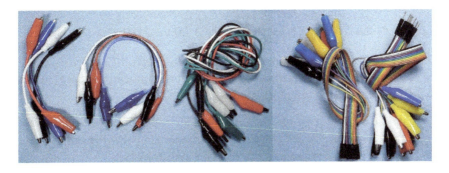

Figure 2.14 – Crocodile clips and DuPont ends

You'll find having a range of these clips is very handy for connecting components quickly and easily.

Our parts and the final circuit, as shown in *Figure 2.15*, include a battery holder, a battery, crocodile clips, and an LED:

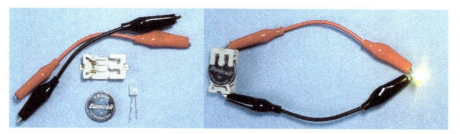

Figure 2.15 – Parts for the circuit (left-hand side) and the complete circuit (right-hand side)

Now that we have our parts and can see the finished circuit, let's put it together.

To connect the LED circuit, perform the following steps:

1. Connect the black crocodile clip to the - ground side of the battery holder.
2. Connect the red crocodile clip to the + power side of the battery holder.
3. Connect the short leg (ground) of your LED to the other end of the black crocodile clip.
4. Connect the longer leg of your LED (positive) to the other end of the red crocodile clip.
5. Put in your battery.

We have light! We don't have a switch yet though, so it stays on when the battery is in. We will improve this circuit later.

Now that we've created this circuit, let's use a breadboard to move our circuits once again. You will likely use a breadboard for most of your early prototyping because it's a quick way to check whether things are working as intended.

Activity 2.3 – creating a circuit using a breadboard

Using a breadboard is a great way to start prototyping your circuit. It can be more reliable and easier to move when you've used wires in a breadboard. If your circuit works and you have finished, we can solder or sew the components to create a permanent project.

A breadboard is a piece of plastic (*Figure 2.16*) with metal strips inside. These connect all the small holes on the top. The horizontal edges of the breadboard run horizontally. The smaller vertical strips run vertically. This means everything in that row will be connected:

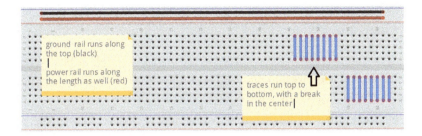

Figure 2.16 – A breadboard

If your breadboard has a red/black or red/blue strip on it, the long red horizontal strip is used as a power rail. Once you put power into it, it will power any components that are also connected to that rail. A breadboard is a much quicker way to prototype than having to sew all your circuits the first time. It can help solve a lot of errors:

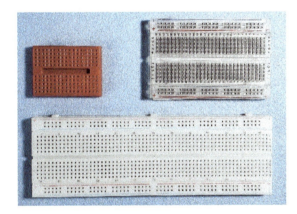

Figure 2.17 – Various breadboards

To make our circuit on a breadboard, we need (as shown in *Figure 2.18*) a breadboard, a battery holder, a battery, an LED, and jumper wires:

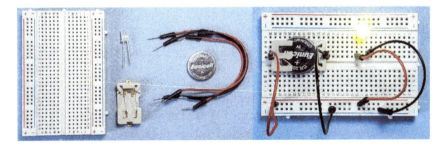

Figure 2.18 – Parts for the circuit (left-hand side) along with the completed circuit (right-hand side)

To understand how to connect (the completed circuit is shown in *Figure 2.18*, on the right-hand side), perform the following steps:

1. Using a red wire for power, connect the red wire to the + power side of the battery holder.

2. Plug the other end of the wire into the red power rail of the breadboard along the horizontal bottom (as shown in *Figure 2.18* of the completed circuit).

3. Using the black jumper wire, plug it into the - ground side of the battery holder.

4. Push the other end of the black wire into the horizontal ground rail on the breadboard. You now have power and ground in the breadboard for your circuit.

5. Push the LED legs into the breadboard. Make sure the legs are in two different vertical rails. For example, the ground leg is in row 20 and the power is in row 22. Use any rows:

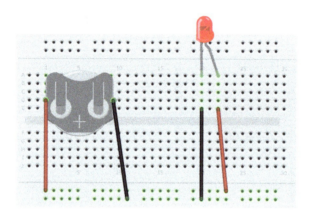

Figure 2.19 – A battery holder and an LED in a breadboard

6. Use a red jumper wire to power the LED. Push one end into the same row as the positive side of your LED (the longer leg); I've used row 22. Push the other end of the red wire into the horizontal power rail.

7. Plug the black jumper wire into the same row as the short leg of your LED (ground); I've used row 20. Finish the circuit by plugging the other side of the black wire into the horizontal ground rail of the breadboard.

8. Finally, put your battery into the battery holder.

You should now have an LED that is on and giving light. After completing this activity, you understand how a breadboard works and how to use it. Also, connecting ground and power in a circuit will be easier to figure out now that you've done it! If your LED isn't lighting up, check the legs are the correct way around. Maybe you have connected the ground side to the power side by mistake. Now, take some time to try different designs on the breadboard to better understand the layout of the breadboard and the circuit.

Now that we have created a circuit with crocodile clips, and one on the breadboard, it's time to get conductive! Let's work through a circuit using conductive thread to solidify our learning and continue our journey into wearables.

Soft circuits

We've been learning about the importance of testing our circuit on a breadboard and what happens when connecting components in series and parallel circuits. Now, let's look at LEDs, conductive threads, and conductive fabrics. Once we understand their foundations, we can create a soft circuit.

LEDs

LEDs come in many sizes and types (*Figure 2.20*). They can suit a huge range of purposes. It is a good idea to have a look online at some of the LEDs you can get so that you don't limit yourself to just using the most common ones. In this chapter, the LEDs are 5 mm, but they can be as small as less than a millimeter. They are low power, have a long lifetime, and are robust.

Some common places where you'll see LEDs are control panels, computers, traffic lights, car lights, electric toothbrushes, and streetlights. LEDs have a range of colors, opacities, and light intensities. The higher the voltage the higher the lumen, and the greater the intensity. Often, I see ultra-bright LEDs and some that are directional. Additionally, the light is very bright straight on, but not very visible sideways:

Figure 2.20 – LEDs

You can also buy flashing, bi/tri-color, and rectangular LEDs. For our projects, we will be using 3V LEDs – that's the one parameter you'll need to be careful to choose. This is because they can easily be controlled by **input/output (I/O)** pins. Later, we'll be using I/O pins with microcontroller boards.

Conductive threads

Conductive thread is great for circuits. It carries the current in the same way that wires do. This allows us to create flexible, soft circuits, without soldering. There are silver and steel-based threads, but there are also a lot of conductive materials that can be used (*Figure 2.21*). If you test the material with your multimeter, you'll know whether you can use it to carry electricity.

Because of the differences in the threads, it's best to try a few and decide which is best for your wearable project. Silver threads are often nylon-based, so they can't be soldered either. Lastly, silver thread can tarnish over time due to their silver content.

Steel-based ones are a little more rigid and can be soldered – with some practice. Also, if your components are very far away from each other, for reliability and longevity, you will want to eventually swap the sewing out with soldered soft (silicone) wires:

Figure 2.21 – Conductive threads for circuits

Because conductive thread conducts electricity, if your threads touch each other, it will create a short. Remember, a short will stop your circuit from working. The battery releases energy very quickly when there is a short, and that can cause heat, smoke, sparks, and more. When you plan out your project, make sure that you plan a circuit that won't have overlapping threads or that you know where to cover your thread to insulate it. You can insulate with thick fabrics, electrical tape, fabric paints, certain glues, a hot glue gun, 3D printing pens and plastics, and more.

Conductive fabrics

How do you know if a piece of fabric is conductive? We've seen how to use our multimeter to test the conductivity. This will help us decide what materials to use.

Try using the resistance measurement on your multimeter to see whether it registers there. A material is conductive if it can carry an electrical current.

The fabrics available can vary greatly. *Figure 2.22* shows a small section of what is available. These materials come in knits, jersey styles, rip-stop, and more. Some have a back sheet on them that allow them to iron onto another fabric easily. The conductive iron-on fabric can make it simpler to test out your design, as you only need to cut out the shape in the fabric and then iron it into place. If your fabric has folds in it, it's best (as it is with all fabrics you use) to iron it first to remove any folds or creases. Bear in mind that electronic fabrics will heat up. Iron carefully and only a small corner first to test your temperature. Some materials can scorch easily.

Here is a list of considerations to understand the type of fabric you can use:

- Will it fray?

- Will it wrinkle easily?

- Will it be too stretchy or not stretchy enough?

- Will it be too heavy?

Remember that conductivity varies greatly between the different fabrics, so always test that it will work well in your circuit before buying huge amounts:

Figure 2.22 – Various conductive fabrics

You can find a variety of conductive materials from the Adafruit website, which has great supporting documentation: `https://www.adafruit.com/category/845`. For UK-based readers, I've found silver, copper, nickel, and tin materials at `https://www.hitek-ltd.co.uk/technical-textiles` and a large supply of conductive textiles and materials at `https://www.tinkertailor.tech/conductive`. Note that nickel is used in most components, so be careful if you have a nickel allergy. Also, try not to have wearables with bare components that constantly touch the skin if not part of the interaction.

The **Shieldex** product range is one of the main supplier; you can view it at `https://www.shieldex.de/en/applications/`. As shown in *Figure 2.22*, information about the materials is helpful for gaining an understanding of their unique properties. You might have a local supplier that you can find and ask to purchase a sample pack. This is a great way to try small patches of fabrics before you buy larger quantities.

Many of these fabrics and materials are made for medical purposes. You'll notice there are materials with antiviral and antibacterial properties, and I've seen some that are sold, such as copper, to put on door handles to make viruses harmless in a short space of time. Additionally, you might have noticed that the tips in many gloves have a small pad of conductive material to allow touch screens to work.

After our look at LEDs, conductive threads, and fabrics, it's time to get sewing. Let's make a sewable circuit!

Activity 2.4 – sewing with conductive thread and LEDs

Now that we've learned about LEDs and conductive thread, we can make our soft circuit. For this example, we will be using the starter kit from **Adafruit** (or its equivalent components), which is available online at https://www.adafruit.com/product/1285#tutorialsstarter.

By the end of this activity, you will have sewn a circuit that is the same as the one we mapped out on the breadboard earlier. It's important to be able to take our circuits from a breadboard to fabric, and *Chapter 8, Learning How to Prototype and Make Electronics Wearable*, will cover this in more detail later. For now, let's get making!

> **Important Note**
> Always disconnect your power source before sewing the components or connecting them with wires!

The components needed to create this circuit are conductive thread, an LED, a battery holder, and a coin cell battery (*Figure 2.23*). You'll also need a sewing needle:

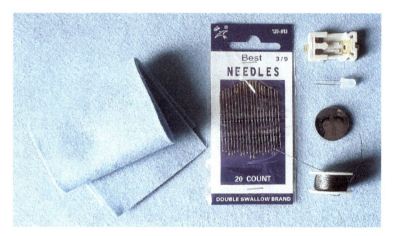

Figure 2.23 – The items needed for the circuit

Now we can prepare our components for a soft circuit. You'll need to get an LED, which we will shape so that we can sew it onto the circuit!

> **Through-Hole and Surface Mount**
>
> Through-hole, or thru-hole, mounting refers to the mounting technique of a component. If it is a component with *legs*, typically, these legs go through the holes drilled into a PCB. We call it a **surface mount (SMT)** component if the component stays on top of the PCB – no legs! Usually, they are very small and held by solder paste onto a board.

Let's use a through-hole LED as part of our circuit. We can shape it so that it will fit into a wearable design.

Preparing an LED

To sew a through-hole LED, it helps if we can use some pliers to bend the legs so that they are much easier to sew. *Figure 2.24* shows a quick way to alter your components. First, straighten out your LED legs so that they lay flat. Then, take one leg and hold it with the tips of the pliers.

Keep holding the leg and begin to turn the pliers to create a loop. Take a look at *Figure 2.25*, which shows that process. Do this on both LED legs and then flatten it so that you can sew through the holes. You can do this with resistors and other components that have legs:

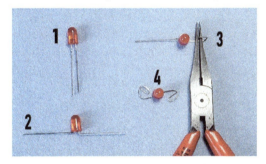

Figure 2.24 – Steps for the LED legs

I have a pair of small bull-nose pliers (with a square-shaped end), and that creates a square shape, not round. So, play around with what you want from your circuits and how you'd like them to look. You might want to bend them into different shapes to easily distinguish between + and -:

Figure 2.25 – Preparing an LED

Also, you might want to choose a needle with a slightly larger eye. The conductive thread can be thicker and fray more than a typical sewing thread. You might want to use a threader to make it easier and quicker to thread the needle:

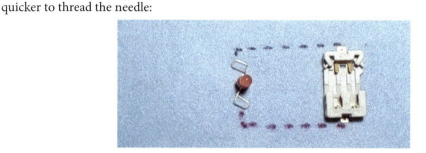

Figure 2.26 – Mapping out your circuit

First, I mark out my circuit on felt or fabric with a pen or piece of chalk. This is to ensure that there will be no shorts or overlapping wires. If some do overlap, I can plan to insulate them. *Figure 2.26* shows the mapped-out circuit. I've used red to indicate power and to remind me which way the LED should be.

Steps to create a soft circuit

This is optional: at the start, glue your components to the fabric you are using. This helps to hold your components in place as you sew. Sometimes, things move when we sew and can become unaligned. It can make a tidier circuit.

Step 1 – the ground side

Perform the following steps:

1. Measure out a quantity of thread. Cut your thread with very sharp scissors to make it easier to thread. Thread the needle. I fold the thread in half once it's threaded, so it's double thickness. Tie a knot at the end.

2. Begin your stitching. Push the needle through the ground side, -, sew tabs of your battery holder.

    Figure 2.27 shows the needle coming through the back side of the fabric through the battery holder. Be careful not to pull the thread all the way through to the other side:

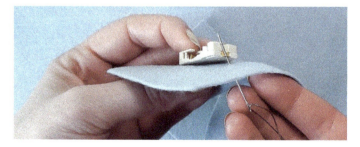

Figure 2.27 – Starting your sewing

Stitch back down alongside the sew tab to go back through the fabric (*Figure 2.28*):

Figure 2.28 – Sewing the battery holder tab

3. Make sure that you put a knot in the end, so your stitching stays in place (*Figure 2.29*):

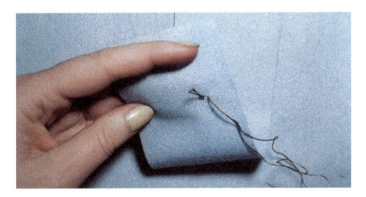

Figure 2.29 – Tying a knot on the underside

4. Sew a loop or two through the battery holder sew tabs to make sure they are secure.

5. Stitch all the way up the length of the ground side. We are using a straight or running stitch (*Figure 2.30*). This is a stitch where we pass the needle in and out of the fabric at the same distance.

6. When your stitching has reached the ground leg of the LED, sew around the bent leg loop you made earlier until it is secure (*Figure 2.30*):

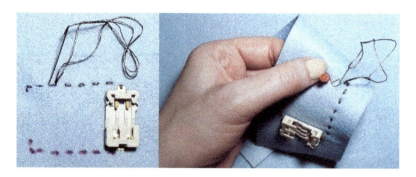

Figure 2.30 – The running stitch and the stitches securing the LED

When the LED leg has been securely sewn with a few stitches, knot the end of your thread on the underside of the fabric, as shown in the following photograph:

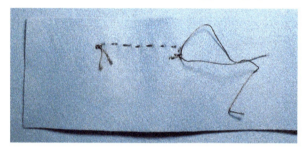

Figure 2.31 – Stitches securing the LED

Ensure that you don't have any long threads remaining, as this can cause a short in your circuit. Cut any ends short after knotting.

I put a dab of fabric glue or clear nail polish (*Figure 2.32*) on this knot to stop it from fraying or coming loose. Sometimes, the conductive thread can separate easily or have small fragments come off. This can cause a short, so covering it with a little nail polish will help prevent that, too:

Figure 2.32 – Securing the knot

Now that we've completed half the circuit, we can start to sew the positive side, where we follow the same instructions.

Step 2 – the positive side.

Perform the following steps:

1. Re-thread your needle with a new piece of conductive thread. Follow the same steps as earlier, but this time, push your needle through the back of the fabric to go up through the positive side, +, of the battery holder. Loop it to make it secure.

2. With a running stitch, sew along to the positive side toward the positive LED leg.

3. When at the LED, secure the leg with several stitches to loop it tightly.

4. When done, stitch through to the back of the fabric and tie a knot to secure it.

5. Trim the ends, and dab some glue or nail varnish onto the knot to secure it.

Notice that, on the back of your circuit, the two stitched areas are not crossing in any way. If they cross or touch, your circuit will short.

Hopefully, you can now put your battery in, and your circuit will work. See *Figure 2.33* for the finished front and the finished backstitching:

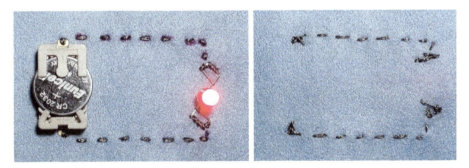

Figure 2.33 – The finished circuit from the front and the back

Congratulations! You've sewn a soft circuit and are well on the way to more complicated wearables!

Circuit not working?

If your circuit isn't working, you should check that your battery has full power. Swap out your battery. Also, check the polarity of your battery. The current flows in one direction, so you must have the LED legs in the correct position of your circuit. Check whether it is the following:

- Ground to ground: Is the ground (negative) sew tab from the battery holder and the ground (negative) leg on the LED connected through your sewing?

- Power to power: Is the correct side of the battery holder with the power (positive) sew tab sewn up to the power (positive) side of the LED (longer leg)?

Are there any shorts in your circuit? Does the thread touch a part of the circuit that it shouldn't?

If your circuit is flickering, or only working sometimes, then check for loose connections. The sewing on the connections needs to be tight. If there is movement, it can sometimes flicker as the current isn't constant. This is easily fixed: pull the thread tighter or sew on top to ensure you have a good connection.

Lastly, make sure there are no long ends of thread or any frayed thread pieces on the fabric. Any extra conductive material can create inconsistencies in your circuits, so it's good practice to ensure everything has been trimmed away.

Challenge yourself!

Get creative with soft circuits. *Figure 2.34* shows circuits created in a wearable workshop (and *Ahmed Zia* wearing his pocket bear design). First, he mapped it out and then used straight stitches to connect it. He covered the LEDs with felt to create the effect:

Figure 2.34 – Fun soft circuits created in a workshop

Now that you've learned about circuit types, how to use a breadboard, and taken a circuit from breadboard to creating its equal as a soft circuit, we can move on to sewing a creative circuit. This activity will consolidate your learning so that we can move on to more advanced topics with switches and buttons.

Activity 2.5 – sewing a creative circuit

Now that you've created your first soft circuit, let's add a few more components to it. We will use a few more LEDs and some sewable snaps to create a circuit that we can turn on and off.

We will use another battery holder, a battery, snaps, conductive thread, a sewing needle, and some sewable LEDs. These are a little different from what we used earlier. See *Figure 2.35*, which has a board of 10 sewable LEDs. These have sewable tabs, so we don't need to bend the LED legs:

Figure 2.35 – Materials for the circuit

The first part of your design will be to plan it out. What are you interested in making? A wrist wearable, a strap for your bag, or something else? I'm going to make the circuit on two pieces of gray felt, and then sew them to a vest I have at the waist. When I close the vest with the snaps, the LEDs will light up. Do you have something similar that you'd like to try?

Let's sew a parallel circuit so that all the LEDs get the same power at the same time. To make this circuit, follow these steps:

1. Measure out your fabric against the item you will be sewing. I've got a vest handy, and I've measured out where I'll be putting the circuit.

2. I measure it out and use a small cutting board to cut the felt straight and put it on top of the garment to check that it is the correct size. *Figure 2.36* shows the process of cutting and placing the fabric piece that you cut earlier and place it were you will sew it, to check it is the right size:

Figure 2.36 – Cutting the fabric and checking the measurement

3. Next, it's a good idea to lay out your circuit. *Figure 2.37* illustrates what I've done.

I've folded back one end on each piece of felt. When I sew the snaps, it's thicker to make sure the snap doesn't pull through.

4.   I put a little fabric glue under the flap, and I hold it into place while the glue dries with little sewing clamps:

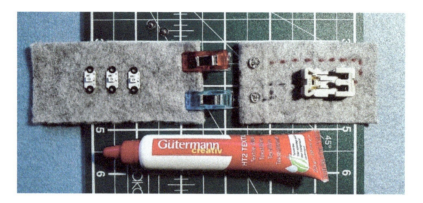

Figure 2.37 – Preparing your circuit

5.   Glue down your components with fabric glue so that they don't move when you sew or use a glue gun, which is quicker. You might want to glue the battery holder to the underside so that it isn't visible from the front of the fabric.

This is optional: I like to draw out the circuit stitches first to be sure none overlap. It's a good habit to get into and can save you a lot of mistakes in the future as your circuits become more complex. I've been caught out with an overly complex circuit that had too many crossing wires that I should have thought through before I started to sew.

6.   Put your snaps in place and make sure they line up.

Now that everything has all been laid out correctly, let's start sewing with conductive thread.

> **Tip**
>
> Close your snaps together and put them on the fabric so that you are sure which way round they go.

To sew the first part of your circuit, perform the following steps:

1.   Measure a piece of conductive thread and thread your needle. Starting at the positive end of our battery holder, sew up to the snap. Make sure that you go through the snap several times so that it becomes secure and that we have enough thread to conduct the current of electricity.

2.   Secure with a knot. Dab glue or nail varnish to stop the knot from fraying. Cut the thread ends short. *Figure 2.38* shows the knot and nail polish process.

3. Now, sew the other side of the battery. Start a new thread, and sew from the ground side of the battery all the way up to the other snap. Secure the snap with several loops of thread on all the snap holes:

Figure 2.38 – Dabbing the ends with nail polish to secure them

4. With both sides of the battery sewn, we can test our circuit to see whether this part has a good connection.

    Use one of your LEDs and place the positive side on top of the positive side snap. Then, fold over the fabric with the negative snap to cover the negative side of your LED. *Figure 2.39* shows how to do this. If it lights up, well done! Your circuit is halfway there and is already working:

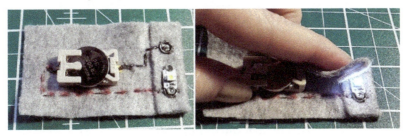

Figure 2.39 – Testing our circuit

So, we've finished part of this circuit and tested it. Now we need to sew the other side of the circuit.

To sew the other side of the circuit, the LEDs, and the back of the snaps, follow these steps:

1. Let's sew the other half of our circuit. The LEDs need power and ground to light up. Starting at the positive side of your LEDs, sew the bottom LED positive sew tab several times to secure it (*Figure 2.40*).

2. Continue to sew all the way up to the next LED positive sew tab and, again, secure it with several stitches. Sew up to your third LED, and sew that one in place, too:

Figure 2.40 – Starting to stitch

3. Once all three LEDs have been sewn, continue to sew stitches up to the snap (*Figure 2.41*). Sew the snap securely to ensure it won't break. Then, sew back one stitch to tie a knot:

Figure 2.41 – Sewing up to the snap

To keep our stitches hidden, we can do a different stitch. If you sew the longer stitches on the back of the fabric and very small stitches on the top, you won't see much stitching on the front of your fabric. This is called a **hidden stitch**. This is a good stitch to learn because we can use it for many of our wearable designs and sewing projects. The underside of a hidden stitch is shown in the following photograph:

Figure 2.42 – The underside of a hidden stitch

You can do any stitch you want, and often, using a nice color thread can add to the design. If you don't want the stitch to show, then use a hidden stitch.

4.   Protect the knots at the ends by dabbing a little nail polish onto them. Trim the ends so that we don't cause any shorts in our circuit.

5.   Let's do the same again, but this time, on the negative or ground side.

Start at the lower LED sew tab, and sew all the way up to the next LED and then the next. Continue to the snap and sew it in place with several stitches.

6.   When you have finished sewing, test whether your circuit works by snapping it together, as shown in the following photograph:

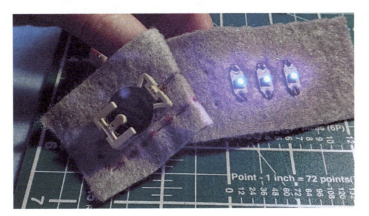

Figure 2.43 – Circuit testing

We tested the circuit earlier, so it should work at this point, too. Now with the LEDs on, you can finish sewing it into the wearable that you want to make.

Finishing your soft circuit

As I mentioned earlier, I have a vest that I'm adding this circuit to. Now that the circuit is finished, I'll put it in place, and using regular thread, I'll sew it to my garment. I'll use the hidden stitch again so that the stitching will show on the back but not on the front.

The finished modification to the vest is shown in the following photographs. You can see the hidden stitch that is on the underside of the vest, and the front of the vest is pictured up close so that you can see the 3-LED detail in the circuit. Lastly, the completed vest is shown from further away so that you can see how it has been placed onto the vest:

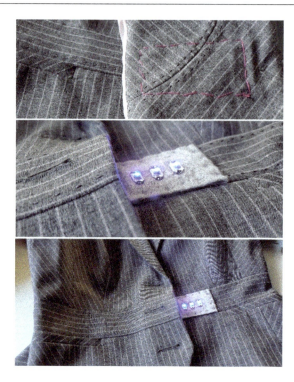

Figure 2.44 – The finished LED circuit on the garment

So, you have created a circuit and sewn it into an item you already have, or made it into a bracelet or even a light for your bag. Now that the circuit has been completed, you'll notice that we used snaps as a switch so that we can turn it on and off easily. We don't need to remove the battery to turn it on or off. So, what is a switch and how is it used?

Using switches and buttons will add a lot more interaction to your wearables – it's essential! So, let's head to the next section, which is all about switches and buttons, where you will be creating your own switches to integrate into your wearables. Let's jump right in to learn all about switches and buttons and also make some of our own!

Switches and buttons

Switches are breaks in your circuit that stop the current from flowing. In this section, we will learn about the various types of switches and buttons and how they work. Then, we will get creative and make our own switches.

In this section, I've included buttons. Although not strictly a switch, they also create a break in the circuit. We can use buttons and switches in similar ways. *Figure 2.45* is a photograph of some of the types of switches and buttons that are available. However, bear in mind that there are hundreds of varieties, colors, sizes, and more.

Note that only a small selection has been pictured, so always go hunting for new and unusual items for your own wearable projects:

Figure 2.45 – Switches and buttons

First, let's look at some of the types of switches we can use. The switches fall into two distinct categories, **momentary** and **maintained**. A momentary switch holds the connection for as long as the switch is held down. The maintained switch will hold the selection until it is deselected or switched in the opposite way. Let's take a closer look at the following:

- **Momentary switches**
- **Maintained switches**

To understand momentary and maintained switches, let's learn how a button or switch works. A break in a circuit is needed for a switch or button to provide the bridge or connection across the break. In *Figure 2.46*, you can see a button creating a break in the circuit to stop the LED from working. The schematic is also shown with a switch. This schematic is similar to our sewable snap and LED circuit:

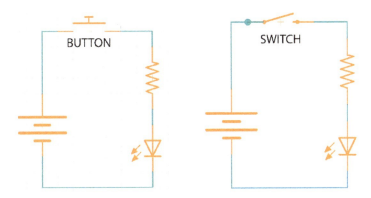

Figure 2.46 – Schematic of a button and a switch closing the circuit

When the switch is closed, it completes the circuit. This allows the current to flow through the entire circuit. The LED will light up. The switch and button have two possible states: on and off or high and low.

Momentary switches

This is a switch that will change state while you hold it. When you are actively engaging the switch, it will be *on* or *off*. Then, when you release it, it will go back to its original state. Momentary switches can be **normally open (NO)** or **normally closed (NC)**. This describes the default state for the switch. If the momentary switch is NC, then pressing it will open it, stopping the current in your circuit. If you've ever set the time on a cooker or watch, often, there are buttons that will count the time while you hold it. It will stop the time when you let go of the button. This is what a momentary switch will do. Another good example of this is a keyboard.

Maintained switches

This is a switch that holds its state until it changes into a new state. So, clicking on a button will activate it, and only when you click on it again, will it change state. One example is turning a desk lamp on, as the lamp will stay on until you turn it off.

Now that we understand the differences between a momentary (held for a moment) and a maintained (maintains the hold) type of switch and button, let's look at how these switches and buttons are often categorized.

Don't forget – the basis of all these buttons and switches is that there is an incomplete or opened circuit that will become complete or closed.

Example switches and buttons

Now, let's take a look at a few switches and buttons that can be either one of the two overarching types we just discussed.

Latching buttons

A latching button is an on-off switch that stays on or off with a press. When you press it, it will stay on. This can be a good choice for a wearable to make it easy for the wearer to turn the circuit on or off. This is a type of maintained switch because the latch is physically clicked on and locked into place or out of place. These can be very satisfying to click and, typically, have a great "click" sound.

Toggle switches

Typically, this is a switch that has a lever, so it might not be very comfortable if you haven't planned it into your circuit well. The toggle can stick out, so be sure to check the size when ordering. However, you can get really cute smaller ones. Making a forearm glove piece can suit it well. This is also a maintained switch.

Poles and throws

Some switches are called **single-pole, single-throw (SPST)** or **single-pole, double-throw (SPDT)**. They refer to poles and throws. In *Figure 2.47*, we can see the schematic of an SPDT switch:

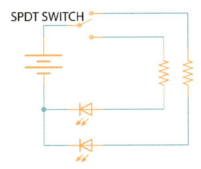

Figure 2.47 – Schematic of an SPDT switch

The pole is the number of circuits controlled by the switch, and the throw is how many positions the pole can connect to. Looking at the schematic, the SPDT switch has two possible ways to close the circuit. For example, if the switch is switched to the first throw, the LED in the bottom circuit will light up, and the other LED will be off. If the switch is thrown to the other circuit, this will be reversed. You don't have to use both throws; you can use it as an on-off switch – just don't connect anything to the other throw. That would mean you are using it as an SPST switch.

Slide switch

These can be very small and good in wearable designs. You slide them to create or break the connection. For example, underneath my mouse, there is an on-off slide switch.

Tilt switch

A tilt switch is an interesting switch. A tilt is opened or closed depending on how it is tilted. Mostly, it senses through a small metal ball that is located inside the switch. They can be very small.

Touch

Some buttons and sensors work on capacitive sensing and the signal that happens when you make contact. Often, these are standalone, momentary switches.

Other ways to use switches and buttons

We will explore touch capacity with certain circuit boards, or you can purchase a special touch sensor input board. When we look ahead to *Chapter 7, Moving forward with Circuit Design Using ESP32*, we will be using the input capacities of that board to work with touch.

There is a huge variety of switches and buttons available. I would suggest having a good hunt online, or finding a local electronics store, to see what fun components you can find. Some have LEDs in them or are very small and discreet – great for wearables – and some are very durable for more heavy-duty needs such as on a bag or backpack.

Now that we've gained an understanding of switches and buttons, the fun can begin. Let's look at alternative materials that we can use and jump into making our own.

Activity 2.6 – making your own switches

There is an endless list of materials and objects we can use to make our own buttons and switches. Now that we understand how a switch creates a break in the circuit (and then completes it again), we can get creative:

Figure 2.48 – Materials to make buttons

Most of the materials in *Figure 2.48* are from Adafruit, Tinker Tailor, or Proto-Pic, but there are also unusual items or household items. The small metal bee is used to decorate things; for example, I put them on purses. The silver studs go on the bottom of handbags as small feet, but they are metal, so you could use them creatively. This is the same for the stag head, which is used as a bag clasp. This is to illustrate that you should keep your eyes open to all the possibilities around you. You can even bring your multimeter to a haberdashery store!

Using the example of an LED, let's look at how we can create different switches and buttons. We've already learned how to use sewing snaps to create a break in our circuit, so let's see what we can do with the following:

- Conductive fabrics
- Hook and loop fasteners
- Zippers

- Copper tape/nylon tape

Using your multimeter, test the conductivity of materials around the home and see what you can find that could also be used for circuits. Do you have paper clips or pipe cleaners?

Conductive fabrics

Using conductive fabrics is a great way to make a switch. When the fabrics touch each other, a connection is formed. When they aren't touching, the circuit will be off. *Figure 2.49* shows the materials you need; three pieces of fabric work best. Here, I've used felt:

1. Using two pieces of conductive fabric, place them on another two pieces of fabric.

2. Cut out a shape on the third piece of fabric. Put that piece of fabric, with a pattern cut out (I've cut a heart), on top (*Figure 2.49*) of the conductive material:

Figure 2.49 – The fabrics needed, including layering fabric

3. The conductive material will be sandwiched between the two pieces of regular material (felt). This will allow you to actively *press* the button to get it to work.

    Putting the pieces together, you should have the following:

    - A piece of felt on the bottom

    - A layer of conductive fabric

    - A layer of felt with the cut-out shape in its center

    - A layer of conductive fabric

    - A piece of felt on the top

4. Sew your conductive thread to the top and bottom of your button to add them to your circuit. Be sure the conductive thread is sewn into the conductive fabric on one side, then sew into the conductive fabric on the other side (top and bottom of your button).

    Remember, it is about making a break in the circuit, so it will be sewn into where the break will happen (*Figure 2.50*); for example, just like the snaps we sewed earlier:

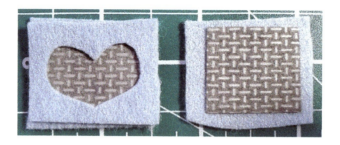

Figure 2.50 – Felt, conductive fabric, felt with the heart shape cut out (left),
then felt on the bottom and conductive fabric on top (right)

When you press this button together, the conductive fabric, which is only separated by that felt layer, will touch, completing the circuit. You can now make your own buttons and use them in your circuits to suit the body parts you are working on.

Another way to use conductive fabric as a switch is to sew it onto your wearable and then touch them together to close the circuit.

I made a glove out of felt and jersey fabric, and then sewed in some LEDs that were pre-mounted on long wires. I used conductive fabric on the thumb and pinky finger. This forms a connection, so when the thumb and pinky touch, it illuminates the lights.

These LED are also multicolor, so they switch between different colors the longer the connection is held in place. *Figure 2.51* shows the conductive fabric and how it works:

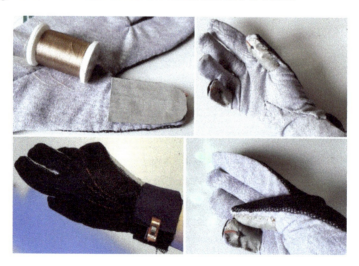

Figure 2.51 – Tri-color LED glove with conductive fabric sewn onto
the pinky and thumb pieces to create a switch

The preceding glove is just one example of using conductive fabric as a switch for your wearable. Think about where else you might incorporate a switch you can make. Spend some time sketching ideas, as you might use them for future projects!

Sometimes, when making simple sewable circuits, we use a battery holder, as we did in our first circuits. But what if you don't have one? We can use conductive fabrics to make our own.

Need a battery holder? You can make one!

This is another perk of having conductive fabric in your wearables project box. Conductive fabric can save you from running out of a battery holder. This can be used in the circuit easily and more discreetly.

For the following circuit, you'll need fabric, conductive thread, and conductive fabric (*Figure 2.52*):

Figure 2.52 – Battery holder items

With the conductive thread, sew a knot where you want the battery (negative side down) to go.

Make sure you have a big strong knot and sew over it a few times. *Figure 2.53* shows the knot on the reverse side of the fabric, after you have sewn through the conductive fabric (bottom layer).

The top piece of the battery holder has a square of conductive fabric under the blue felt square (shown on the right), which will be the positive side of the battery holder:

Figure 2.53 – Making a battery holder

Then, you can slide your battery into the pocket you made. This is a quick circuit that you can sew into your wearable design.

Hook and loop fasteners

Conductive hook and loop fasteners are a good way to get a switch working. Sew your power to the hook side from your battery power side. Then, sew the loop side to the power side of your LEDs. When the hook and loop touch, it will complete the circuit, and they will light up. In *Figure 2.54*, the circuit connects with a hook and loop fastener:

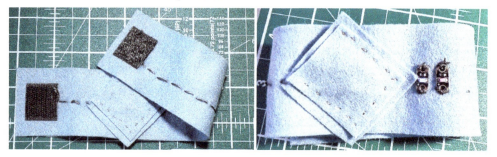

Figure 2.54 – The hook on one side and the loop underneath

Zippers

We could use metal or plastic zippers, but they will make a difference to the type of switch we use. If it's plastic, it will only connect exactly where the zipper bridges the connection. This creates a momentary switch. If you hold the zipper there, then it will maintain this bridge and keep the circuit on. I have made an example cuff piece. It has conductive thread high up where the zipper finishes. When you zip to that part of the zipper, it will keep a light on.

I used a cool light, which is a mock Edison filament. Normally, this is used as filament in a light bulb. They are made up of small LEDs in a row, so they look great! You can buy different lengths and colors. Be sure to get the 3V version for our wearable projects so that we can power it.

These can be purchased from: `https://www.tinkertailor.tech/product-page/led-filament-strips`

This example is running off a coin cell. The filament has a positive side and a negative side just like the LEDs we've been using. To make this fun project, thread your needle with conductive thread and sew your battery holder.

Create a conductive thread stitch from the positive side of your battery holder to one side of your zipper (*Figure 2.55*):

Figure 2.55 – Stitching from the battery holder

Sew very close to the zipper, and check that you can still pull the zipper over the conductive thread. Once you have a tight connection, sew back a stitch or two and knot (*Figure 2.56*):

Figure 2.56 – Sewing up to the zipper

To add the filament, we need to push the end through the fabric. Poke a hole into the fabric to push the end of the filament through to the underside. When it has been pushed through (*Figure 2.57*), sew conductive thread over it several times to make a knot:

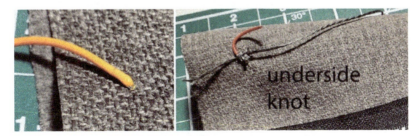

Figure 2.57 – Filament through the fabric

Make sure to test that your zipper can still go over the zipper teeth. *Figure 2.58* shows the zipper opened and closed, including the final working wearable glow cuff:

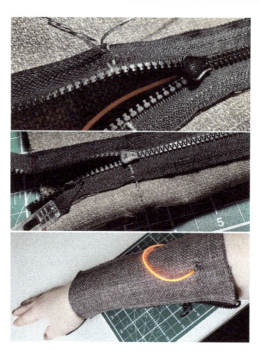

Figure 2.58 – Zipper working over the thread, and final glow cuff

When you pull your zipper up to that conductive thread connection, it will light. You can use this technique anywhere you'd like a zipper in a circuit. It's an alternative switch!

Copper tape/conductive nylon tape

When mapping out a circuit, you can use copper tape or conductive nylon tape. *Figure 2.59* shows conductive nylon tape:

Figure 2.59 – Conductive nylon tape

Conductive nylon tape can be purchased in different widths. This one from Adafruit is great at working the first time and with no overlap. This simple circuit works perfectly the first time, and the tape is a lot more flexible than copper tape. If you fold the tape back on itself, you can also create a switch that works to turn the LED on or off.

Copper tape can be a quick way to work out your traces and see which might overlap. It will help with planning. It isn't as flexible as the nylon tape. In *Figure 2.60*, the track uses copper tape. Sometimes, you will need to layer it up when you change direction, and it can take some pressing to be sure you have a conductive track. Most copper tape has a non-conductive glue on the underside:

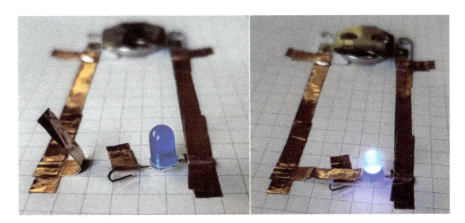

Figure 2.60 – Copper tape with a switch

Another good thing about using copper tape is that you can also solder wires to it.

Other random items

Always be on the lookout for random items that you can use to complete your wearable. Unique items can make a very creative circuit and an eye-catching design. Keep on the lookout for safety pins, foil, magnetic snaps, hooks and clasps, jewelry, pipe cleaners (with some of the "fuzz" scraped off), and other unique items made of metal.

Also, going to your local charity shop can be a great way to grab some bargains and be sustainable. There might be items with zippers, clasps, and similar that you can upcycle or practice your wearable journey on. I found these amazing snaps and hooks and eyes (*Figure 2.61*), which must be decades old but will work fine:

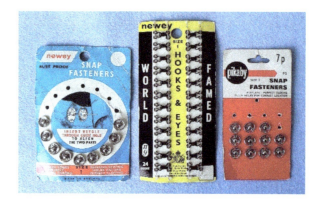

Figure 2.61 – Bargains from a charity shop

Being aware of other interesting items you can use for your wearables will keep it interesting, exciting, and unusual!

Summary

What an amazing journey you've just completed in this chapter. We went from learning about the basics of electricity to making simple circuits, to understanding how we can make our own buttons and switches. You used crocodile clips, breadboards, and conductive fabrics. I hope you tried the activities and made notes of circuits that you'd like to make in the future. Practicing these skills is a creative and rewarding experience.

The components used in this chapter can be found at `http://www.adafruit.com`, `http://tinkertailor.tech`, and `http://www.proto-pic.co.uk`.

Now we look forward to learning about e-textile toolkits. These are microcontroller boards and components made for creating wearable projects. They are different from a standard rectangular Arduino board, but we can still use Arduino to program them. All the knowledge from the upcoming chapter will help you to build upon the skillset you've just acquired and help us to create more complex and interactive wearable solutions.

Review questions and exercises

To help with your learning, try to answer the following review questions:

1. Try swapping the resistors in your LED circuit. How do 220-Ohm, 330-Ohm, and 550-Ohm resistors affect the circuit? What have you observed?

2. What are the two types of circuits that we looked at?

3. What is the difference between a closed circuit and an open circuit?

4. How would you wire a parallel circuit?

5. What are some advantages of making a soft circuit?

6. What are conductive materials and how do you know they are conductive?

7. Create a parallel circuit and a circuit in series using crocodile clips or a breadboard.

8. Create some sketches and notes for creative buttons and switches you can make. Take inspiration around you and draw some ideas out. This will be very useful later or if you're struggling to think of ways to create your circuits.

3

Exploring e-textile Toolkits: LilyPad, Flora, Circuit Playground, and More

In this chapter, you'll learn about e-textile toolkits. You will start by learning about the toolkits available, as well as some sewable components you can use.

We will begin by exploring **LilyPad** components and how we can connect them. Then, we will learn about **Flora, Gemma, Circuit Playground**, and other e-textile toolkits. We will also examine the differences and why you may choose one board over another.

Once you have a grasp of these toolkits and boards, as well as their capabilities, we can make electronic circuits. This will lead to using the **Arduino IDE** to program interactive elements into your designs. We will finish by setting up the software that will be needed throughout this book.

By the end of this chapter, you'll understand what e-textile toolkits are, and how we can use them to start creating and learning about wearables. You'll be able to choose an e-textile board confidently that suit your projects. Lastly, you'll have the Arduino IDE installed on your computer so that you can make more intricate electronic wearable circuits later in this book.

In this chapter, we're going to cover the following main topics:

- LilyPad e-textiles
- Understanding Flora, Gemma, and Circuit Playground
- Comparisons and observations
- Software setup and resources
- Troubleshooting

Technical requirements

This chapter has a practical element where you will experiment with circuits. You will need the LilyTwinkle ProtoSnap Kit for the circuits. It contains the following items, which you may choose to swap out or purchase separately:

- The LilyTwinkle board
- A sewable coin cell battery holder (switched or not)
- A coin cell battery
- Sewable LEDs
- Stainless steel conductive thread
- Sewing needles

For the last activity, we will use a Circuit Playground board, the Gemma M0 board, and the Arduino IDE, which is available for free at `https://www.arduino.cc/en/software`.

LilyPad e-textiles

The LilyPad boards were the most widely known and were developed for creating wearable circuits. However, as we'll learn, there are a variety of microcontroller boards to suit our projects. Many are based on the Arduino board with ATMEL chips. Therefore, we can use the Arduino **integrated development environment** (IDE) to program them. Learning about the different types of e-textile kits will help you with planning and making future wearable circuits.

A **microcontroller** is a small single-purpose computer with an **integrated circuit** (IC) that's made up of a processor, memory, and connections for inputs and outputs. It will store and run a program that we upload to it. Most of the boards have a reset button and a way to connect power to it.

A key feature of e-textile toolkits is that they all can be integrated into our wearable designs easier than traditional microcontroller boards.

The LilyPad Arduino was one of the first commercially available wearable Arduino-based microcontrollers. It was created at the MIT Media Lab by Leah Buechley. The board was released by SparkFun in 2007. This board spawned a movement of makers and creatives and over time, it helped launch a variety of boards and components. The unique feature of this board is that it has *petals*, or sewable tabs, so that we can connect our soft circuits to it. It has inputs and outputs, and we can integrate them into our electronics projects with conductive thread.

There are three varieties of LilyPad e-textiles:

- **Simple sewable**: Items we can connect with conductive thread, as we did with our battery board and sewable LEDs previously.

- **Pre-programmed**: A series of small boards that are already programmed for specific functions.
- **Programmable Arduino**: Fully programmable boards. There are a few varieties of these.

First, let's look at the non-programming options: the simple sewable circuits.

Simple sewable

The simple sewable range contains several items. There is a simple coin cell battery holder, similar to the ones we've been using, that has no switch. There is also a switched version.

Part of the LilyPad range includes colored LEDs, an RGB tricolor LED, and a Lily Pixel. Lastly, there are also buttons, reed switches, and slide switches that we can put in our circuit. *Figure 3.1* shows some of the available LEDs, battery holders, and switches:

Figure 3.1 – LEDs, buttons, switches, and battery holders

You can configure these components into circuits for some basic but fun prototypes. Using conductive thread, you can get started with very little extra knowledge required.

Pre-programmed

The pre-programmed boards from LilyPad are LilyTiny, LilyTwinkle, LilyTwinkle ProtoSnap, and LilyMini ProtoSnap. The ProtoSnap range provides kits on a board; *Figure 3.2* shows the ProtoSnap kit. The ProtoSnap version is already connected so that you can test the circuit before you sew it:

Figure 3.2 – ProtoSnap kit with power

LilyTiny is pre-programmed with different patterns for LEDs. Each of the four sew tabs, numbered 0 to 3, has a different effect. It's a fun way to get effects quickly and easily into a circuit. There's also LilyTwinkle. As its name suggests, it adds sparkle to your projects. This mini board is pre-programmed with random effects to mimic a twinkling star effect.

This board also has four sew tabs for sewing your LEDs to it. You can get this board on its own, or in the ProtoSnap version. We will be using this board to create a twinkling wearable in *Activity 3.1 – twinkling circuits.*

Programmable

Lastly, there are programmable LilyPad Arduino boards, as shown in *Figure 3.3*. These are the boards that will bring your projects to life with interactivity. They all have a few differences. These can be purchased from `http://proto-pic.co.uk` or `http://sparkfun.com`, and other electronics retailers:

Figure 3.3 – LilyPad programmable boards – Main, Snap, and USB Plus

The LilyPad Arduino 328 Main board has the most sew tabs for your projects. *Figure 3.4* shows a bag I modified where I used the LilyPad Main board to add interactivity. The board has 14 **digital I/O** pins and 6 **analog input** pins. It has the most I/O pins of all the e-textile toolkit boards. This means that it's a great board for those projects that have a lot of interaction and components connected. It operates at 2-5V. It has a special connector called an **FTDI** for its programming interface, so you need to have an FTDI cable to use this board with your computer:

Figure 3.4 – Message Bag with a LilyPad Arduino 328 Main board

Some research on the Message Bag is available in the paper, *Did you Pack your Keys? Smart Objects and Forgetfulness*, by Farion, Christine & Purver, Matthew (2014). Conference on Human Factors in Computing Systems - Proceedings. 539-542. 10.1145/2559206.2574809: `https://www. researchgate.net/publication/265652238_Did_you_Pack_your_Keys_Smart_ Objects_And_Forgetfulness`.

> **Input and Output Pins**
>
> To fully appreciate these boards, we need to understand what an **input/output (I/O)** pin is. An I/O pin is how we connect our components between the microcontroller and our circuit. We control these pins through programming.
>
> In the Arduino IDE, we configure how the pin is used – is it for output or input? The digital pins use digital signals. This has two values, HIGH and LOW, which is the equivalent of ON or OFF, or 1 and 0. An analog pin has a numerical range of values, and most Arduino boards have pins A0 to A5 as usable analog pins.

The LilyPad Arduino USB is my preferred board from the LilyPad suite. It's very easy to connect as it uses USB for the programming interface, and it has enough I/O pins that you can create a complex project. It has 10 digital pins and 4 analog pins or sew tabs. This board operates at 3.3V. *Figure 3.5* shows the LilyPad Arduino USB board in a near-body wearable prototype:

Figure 3.5 – A 1950s upcycled handbag prototype with a LilyPad Arduino USB

Another Lilypad board is the Simple Snap board. This has fewer sew tabs, with 5 digital I/O pins and 4 analog pins. It has an on/off switch and an onboard chargeable battery. The charge circuit is also on board, so it's very convenient and ready to be put into your projects. Also, because of the snap tabs, you can sew the snaps on many different prototypes and then just snap them off the board and use them in another project.

There is a modified version of the USB board, the LilyPad USB Plus, which has 10 digital I/O pins and 7 analog pins. It connects with a micro USB. The USB Plus has an RGB LED in the middle, and a row of six white LEDs that can be used as indicator lights.

Lastly, there is a specialist board known as the LilyPad MP3 player. It has an onboard LiPo charger, headphone jack, SD card socket, and stereo audio amplifier.

To complete our tour of the LilyPad e-textile range, let's look at the sewable components that are available for enhancing the circuits we make. *Figure 3.6* shows the components in the range. There are temperature, light, and accelerometer sensors, as well as buzzers and vibration boards for output:

Figure 3.6 – Components in the LilyPad range

The LilyPad range of boards and components allows us to be flexible in planning wearable designs. It's a good place to start our prototyping. However, before we jump in, let's create a circuit to try things out. Then, we will learn all about the Flora, Gemma, and Circuit Express boards. Once we have learned about them, you can decide which board is right for your projects.

Let's take a closer look at one of the pre-programmed boards, the LilyTwinkle. *Activity 3.1* is where we will make the circuit!

Activity 3.1 – twinkling circuits

As we learned in the previous section, there are pre-programmed boards in the LilyPad e-textile range. One of those boards, the LilyTwinkle, will add some *shimmer* to our circuit. The components in this activity are from `http://proto-pic.co.uk`, who provides an extensive range of components for making wearables.

The items needed to make this circuit are shown in *Figure 3.7*. These are the LilyTwinkle board, four sewable LEDs, a battery holder (with an on/off switch), conductive thread, a sewing needle, and some fabric:

Figure 3.7 – Items for Activity 3.1

I usually map my circuit out on the fabric before I begin to ensure I won't make any errors. Don't forget that you can also use your crocodile clips to test it if you are using the standalone pieces and not the ProtoBoard version.

Sometimes, the pieces have rough edges. I like to take a moment and just softly sand down the edges so that they are nice and round. You can do this with sandpaper or a nail file, as shown here:

Figure 3.8 – Smoothing rough edges

Follow these steps to make the sewable circuit:

1. Place your components on the fabric. Be sure to correctly *orient all the sew tabs in the correct position*. The ground should be facing toward the outside of the fabric and the positive (+) sew tab should be toward the LilyTwinkle board.

2. Glue the components into place to make them easier to sew. Fabric glue or a hot glue gun works well.

3. Thread your needle. Begin sewing from the ground sew tab on your LilyTwinkle board. Sew from the LilyTwinkle to the ground sew tab on the battery holder.

4. Loop several times over both sew tabs to create a secure connection. I usually sew three times through each sew tab.

5. Once secure, continue sewing the ground trace through all the ground sew tabs on the LEDs. When you have sewn through the last LED ground sew tab, loop the thread several times to make a secure connection.

6. Tie a knot in the underside of your fabric. Secure the knot so that it doesn't fray and cause a short in the circuit. You can do this by putting a little fabric glue or nail polish on the knot. Cut the ends short. *Figure 3.9* shows the first part of our circuit with our ground trace sewn completely through our circuit:

Figure 3.9 – The completed ground circuit

Now, it's time to sew the positive (+) sew tabs of your LEDs to the LilyTwinkle :

1. Re-thread your sewing needle. Choose one of the LEDs and sew the positive sew tab securely. Then, sew to one of the numbered (the closest to that LED) sew tabs of the LilyTwinkle. There will only be a few stitches to sew. Secure the LilyTwinkle with several loops on the numbered sew tab and then secure with a knot on the underside of the fabric. Again, dab with nail varnish and trim.

2. Do the same for the remaining three LEDs, securing the positive sew tab to one of the next free numbered sew tabs on the LilyTwinkle board.

3. Once all the LEDs have been sewn to their counterpart numbered sew tabs on the LilyTwinkle board, sew the final sew tab on the battery holder. Sew from the positive sew tab on the battery to the positive power sew tab of the LilyTwinkle board.

4. Once you have tied your knots and sealed them, pop the battery in. Turn on your circuit and see the twinkle effect (*Figure 3.10*). Well done – we've got a fun circuit working!

Figure 3.10 – The final LilyTwinkle circuit

Now that we've got our LilyTwinkle board working, we can jump straight into learning about other sewable circuit boards.

Understanding Flora, Gemma, and Circuit Playground

In this section, we will look at the exciting choices we have for creating wearable designs with circuit boards designed specifically for this purpose. Here, we will look at Adafruit Industries in New York, founded by Limor Fried in 2005 (Ladyada) and certified as *A Minority and Woman-owned Business Enterprise (M/WBE)*. We will look at their sewable circuit boards, including Flora, Gemma, and Circuit Playground.

We'll learn about the differences between these microcontroller boards. Then, we'll explore a range of components that connect to our circuits to add interactivity. Finally, we will investigate other systems that you may want to learn about through your research.

We will cover the following topics:

- Adafruit Flora, Flora sensors, and snaps
- Gemma M0
- Circuit Playground Classic, Express, and Bluefruit
- Other toolkits

Let's get started.

Flora, Flora sensors, and snaps

Let's start with the Adafruit Flora board (currently V3 – `https://www.adafruit.com/product/659`). Flora is a round, small, 1.75" diameter, sewable Arduino-compatible board. It has sew tabs so that you can easily connect it to a circuit. It uses a USB (micro USB) to plug in and program it. The board has a reset button, battery connector, and power switch. *Figure 3.11* shows some of the Flora range:

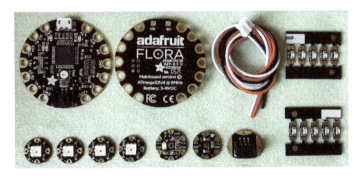

Figure 3.11 – Flora system

The Flora has four indicator LEDs and an RGB **NeoPixel**. One is for indicating power, the LED allocated to a digital signal shows bootloader feedback, and an LED for data received and transfer rx/tx. It has 14 sew tabs for connecting components, inputs, and outputs. It is a flat board so that it doesn't snag on fabric and offers very good value for money.

The Flora board is black, which looks great in most projects! Some of the Flora components that can add interactivity to your wearables include a color sensor, a wearable GPS module, RGB NeoPixels, a **Bluetooth Low Energy** (**BLE**) module, a UV index sensor, a lux light sensor, a sewable 3-pin JST wiring adaptor, and an accelerometer/gyroscope/magnetometer. A JST is a type of connector for connecting electronics, with the standards originally developed by J.S.T. Mfg. Co. (Japan Solderless Terminal).

A NeoPixel is like a super LED. It is bright and chainable, and you can individually control each one that you add. We will look at these amazing LEDs in detail in *Chapter 6*, *Exploring Reactions Through Outputs*. The GPS module is for outdoor location-aware projects that you may want to explore making. Flora Lux Sensor senses infrared, full-spectrum, and human-visible light. I've played around with the color sensor as a fun way to add color-matching interaction to a project.

The color sensor is shown with a NeoPixel strip in *Figure 3.12* in an electronic jewelry piece I made:

Figure 3.12 – Color sensor and NeoPixels

Lastly, the 3-pin wiring adaptor is a very handy component and such a great idea. With it, you can attach modules a lot quicker and more securely in your circuits.

Gemma

The Adafruit Gemma M0 board (`https://www.adafruit.com/product/3501`) is small, 1.1" round and has sew tabs for easily connecting components with conductive thread. Often, it's exactly the right size for a wearable project that may only need a few inputs/outputs.

We can use this board with the Arduino IDE. It also has USB support and there is a built-in RGB DotStar LED and sew tabs. Three of the sew tabs can be used as hardware-capacitive touch sensors. You can use NeoPixels on any pins with enough memory to drive thousands:

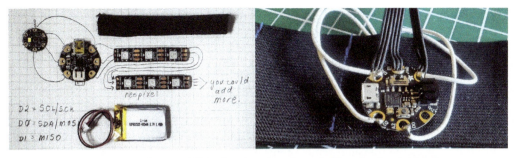

Figure 3.13 – Gemma M0 in the planning phase (left) and a circuit (right)

In *Figure 3.13*, the Gemma M0 board has been placed on paper to help map out the wearable circuit. I've mapped the connections that I'll be using and how they will work together.

When I remove the parts to put them in my circuit, I'll still have my drawn *map* to follow. There is also an image of the Gemma M0 in the completed circuit, with a lot of soldered wiring to it. Soldering your circuits is a good way to preserve them when you want to make them durable.

The Gemma M0 is a fun board that allows you to create discreet circuits due to its small shape. The size is not an indication of its power as I was able to run many NeoPixels and a color sensor off this little board. You can do a lot more.

Now, let's look at the Circuit Playground boards, which allow you to take prototyping to a whole new level!

Circuit Playground boards

These boards were launched in 2015 and have been improved over time. There are currently three boards available and they have different features:

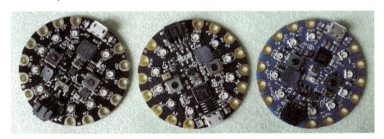

Figure 3.14 – Adafruit Circuit Playground e-textile boards

The Classic board provides all the base components, as do the other two boards, the Circuit Playground Express, and Circuit Playground Bluefruit. The Classic board consists of the following:

- 10 mini NeoPixels

- Sensors for motion, temperature, light, and sound
- Mini speaker
- Two buttons and a slide switch
- 8 pads with capacitive touch inputs that react to touch

It operates at 3.3V and uses a micro USB to connect. The **Circuit Playground Express** (**CPX**) has all the same components (listed previously) as the Classic, but it also includes an **infrared receiver and transmitter**. It receives and transmits remote control codes while sending messages between Circuit Playground Express boards. It also acts as a proximity sensor. The Express board has 7 (not 8) touch capacity inputs; the other pin is a true analog output for sound.

There are 10 NeoPixels around the board perimeter. They turn green when the bootloader is running, and they will turn red if it has failed to initialize. These boards also have a large library of code, tutorials, and resources.

This makes them a great starter board due to the amount of support available. Getting crocodile clips to connect other sensors and outputs is a quick way to start prototyping. *Figure 3.15* shows the components on the Circuit Playground board (image courtesy of `www.adafruit.com`):

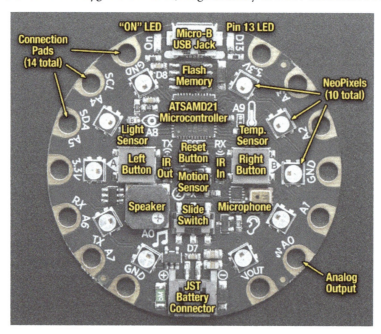

Figure 3.15 – Mapping the Circuit Playground functions

The following table states the pins that the sensors are using. It also lists their components and **General-Purpose Input/Output** (**GPIO**) numbers:

Item	GPIO Pins Analog/Digital
Speaker (can be turned off).	D11
You can use pin A0 as the true analog out, which has a connected amplifier.	A0
A light sensor that reads between 0 and 1023. A higher reading means higher light levels.	A8
Temperature.	A9
Button on the left.	D4
Button on the right.	D5
Slide switch.	D7
Infrared transmitter.	D29
Infrared receiver.	D39
Can be used for basic IR proximity sensing using the raw analog value from the LED.	A10

Table 3.2 – Pin use for Circuit Playground Express

The pins listed (except for A0) in the preceding table are all configured internally. This means that these pins are not connected with the sew tabs that we use to attach our components. There are no conflicting pins. The pins that are physically visible on the board are all freely available for us to use in our circuits.

As we can see, Circuit Playground is a powerful board and addition to any wearable project. We will explore using this board in *Chapter 4, Implementing Arduino Code Using Gemma M0 and Circuit Playground*.

Other systems

There are other e-textile components and items available. Some of them have been discontinued or aren't as widely used, so I haven't featured them here. You may want to continue exploring some of these other platforms as it's always a good idea to know what is available. A good place to start is Kitronik: `https://kitronik.co.uk/`.

They have many educational resources and make many wearable components, some of which are shown in *Figure 3.16*, that cost a lot less than others. It can be a great way to begin on a budget:

Figure 3.16 – Kitronik components

Now that we've looked at the different e-textile boards, let's compare them and understand which boards might be the most appropriate for our wearable designs.

Comparisons and observations

These comparisons and observations are largely from my experiences with using different systems across a variety of projects. It also comes from reading a lot of research projects and developmental workshop information, to learn about other people's perspectives and uses for these boards.

The LilyPad boards are usually purple and have a petal-style design. The Flora has larger sew tabs so that you can easily use your crocodile clips on them. In addition, the board is black, which I like for my circuits. The Gemma M0 is also black, and the size makes it a great fit for hiding in clothing easily.

You may want to consider choosing a board that has a lot of support and resource materials. Some boards have extensive libraries, for example, and great documentation. Also, I have found some boards difficult to source. From researching these boards, it looks like the LilyPad Arduino USB Plus will be the LilyPad board to support. Some of their other boards are being discontinued, so that may influence your decisions about projects and adaptability.

For functionality and features, you can't get better than the Circuit Playground boards. With the huge number of embedded sensors and features, these are a great way to start creating wearables – you can start getting creative right away!

When choosing a board, there will be trade-offs. You may want more pins, but it might be a larger board and might cost more too. Most of the boards have an LED on pin 13 and a reset button.

The e-textile board I have been using the most due to its size and being able to prototype smaller fun projects is the Gemma M0. It's a great board for the cost and you can have a lot of fun with it. It can be such a quick way to add NeoPixels to your designs! Now, let's choose a board for our projects.

Activity 3.2 – choosing your board

Now that we've had an introduction to some of the many different offerings from the boards made for wearables, it's time to choose one! But how can you decide when you're just starting? Here are some questions to help guide you through the process.

Think about what you want your wearable to do – what is the minimum feature set or interactivity that you want from this circuit? Plan your inputs and outputs – we will look at a huge variety of I/O components in *Chapter 5, Working with Sensors: All About Inputs!*, and *Chapter 6, Exploring Reactions Through Outputs*. So, don't worry just yet if you aren't sure. You can come back to the following table later to clarify the objectives for your wearable design:

Input – what would the wearable sense from the environment?
Output – how would your wearable react to what it senses?
Placement of the wearable – where would it be located? Is it an on-body or off-body system? Could it be used in more than one place? How close is it to the body?
Is the size of the wearable appropriate for its placement?
Cost of your project? Do you have a budget?
Connectivity with batteries/for programming?
Visibility? Do you want your circuit on show or to be hidden?

Table 3.3 – Guide for selecting an e-textile board

Often, when we prototype, we don't need to prototype the entire project at once. Try to get one aspect of your design working. Then, progress by adding to it and making it more complex if needed. We will look at the prototyping process in more detail in *Chapter 8, Learning How to Prototype and Make Electronics Wearable*.

Now that we understand these e-textile systems, let's get the Arduino IDE set up on our computer so that we can advance our wearables knowledge further. We will be able to program interactivity through the Arduino program, which will bring our wearables to an entirely new level!

Software setup and resources

Looking back at the simple LED circuits we've been discussing, they are good for understanding how an electronic circuit works. If we only ever wanted a simple LED to turn on or off, then we'd be done. But we're here to do something a lot more fun. Using a microcontroller will add interactivity – and life – to our wearables!

Let's set up the software that we'll use for all our circuits in this book and beyond. We'll be using the Gemma M0 and Circuit Playground boards for many of the wearable designs. As mentioned previously, the Gemma M0 is a small-sized board that is great for wearables because of its size. It has enough sew tabs for input and output. The Circuit Playground board has a larger number of possible connections, so we can use it for more complex circuits. It also has a lot of sensors on the board so that we can use it without connecting anything as we get started. So, with these boards in mind, let's walk through installing Arduino and setting it up.

Installing the Arduino IDE

This is a free application that you can download from `https://www.arduino.cc/en/Main/Software`. Be sure to download it from the official website. There are usually updates to the software, so choose whatever the most recent version is when you visit the site. The following screenshot shows version 2.0, which I'll be using throughout this book:

Figure 3.17 – Arduino version download

Choose the correct version for your operating system. Download and install it with the correct installer for your computer. This will open the **Save** dialog box for you, where you can save the file:

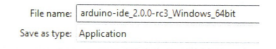

Figure 3.18 – Saving Arduino to your computer

When the download is complete, open the file. A dialog box will appear, asking you to agree to the terms of service. Choose your install location:

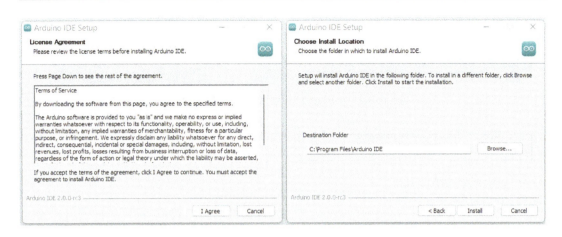

Figure 3.19 – License Agreement and Choose Install Location

Once you click **Install**, the program will install to your chosen location. At this point, you will be presented with the complete setup window:

Figure 3.20 – Installing Arduino and the setup complete

Click to **Finish** the install. Now, let's look at the program and connect our Circuit Playground board.

Arduino essential steps

The Arduino IDE can be used with all the Arduino devices and many other versions of Arduino-compatible boards. It has a built-in code editor where you can test your code and see problems with the code in a message window. As shown in the following screenshot, from left to right, the main program buttons allow you to check your code (verify it), upload your code, create a new sketch, debug, open, and save. The furthest icon on the right-hand side, which looks like a magnifying glass, allows you to open the serial monitor. We will look at the serial monitor in more detail later:

Figure 3.21 – Arduino buttons in the interface

There are other ways you can program an Arduino, but I'll be using the Arduino IDE throughout this book.

Opening the Arduino IDE

To configure the IDE to work with your circuit, you need to check three important settings. This allows your computer to communicate with your microcontroller board. You need to check the following:

- If your board is plugged in with the correct cable, it must be a data cable.
- Which board you are using.
- Which port you'll use for communication.

To select the board and port, we need to plug our board in. The port on the board communicates with a port on your computer when you plug it in. It's how the devices speak to each other. Plug your board in now.

> **Check Your Cable**
>
> Many people, myself included, have problems because they are using a charge-only USB cable. These will not work! We need a *data/sync* cable. You must have a good-quality syncing cable.

There is a board and port drop-down area in the center of the main program bar where we can choose the board we are using. Hopefully, Arduino will have found it for us. The following screenshot shows that Arduino has found **Adafruit Circuit Playground on COM33**:

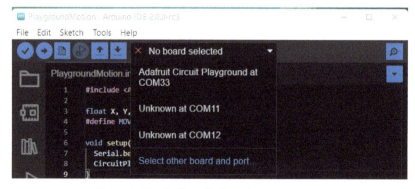

Figure 3.22 – Finding the board you are using

However, the Arduino IDE doesn't always find the board and port. You can specify it yourself by going to **Tools | Board** and then choosing the board you are using; for example, **Adafruit AVR Boards**:

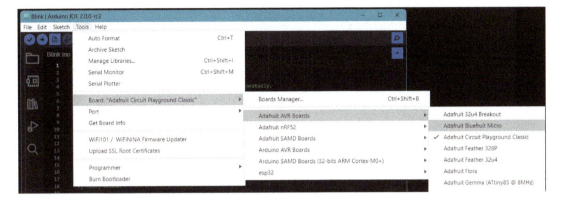

Figure 3.23 – Selecting your board

Next, choose the correct port by opening **Tools | Port** and looking for the COM port for Windows users. On a Mac, it is a **/dev/tty.usbmodem or /dev/tty.usbserial** port with numbers:

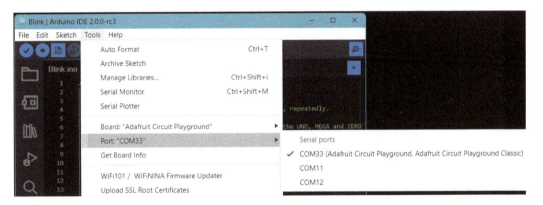

Figure 3.24 – Choosing the correct port

Don't forget that if your board isn't plugged in, it won't show up. I know it sounds obvious, but I can't tell you how many times someone changes something in their circuit, unplugs it, and forgets to plug it back in!

Now, let's have some fun and get a little piece of code running on our Circuit Playground board.

Activity 3.3 – Hello Circuit Playground

Learning a new programming language comes with the tradition of *Hello World*. It's a way to make the simplest program possible to demonstrate that the system is working. The Arduino equivalent is a blinking LED, usually on pin 13. It's the Arduino communicating to the world. It lets you know that your hardware and software are configured and working.

We will start by blinking an LED so that we can work through any issues if it doesn't work. We don't need to hook anything up for this; the Circuit Playground board has an LED on pin 13. We can use an example sketch that will blink the LED for us.

Go to **File** | **Examples** | **01.Basics** | **Blink**. This will open a sketch called **Blink**, as shown in the following screenshot. When we write a program in Arduino, it's called a sketch:

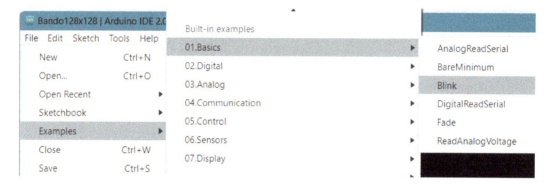

Figure 3.25 – Opening the Blink sketch

Looking at the code that is in the sketch, we can see it is minimal with only nine lines. We will look at it in detail after we upload it to our circuit board. This is the sketch almost all learners start with:

```
void setup() {
  pinMode(LED_BUILTIN, OUTPUT);
}

void loop() {
  digitalWrite(LED_BUILTIN, HIGH);
  delay(1000);
  digitalWrite(LED_BUILTIN, LOW);
  delay(1000);
}
```

Let's upload it to our board and see it working, then look at it in more detail. To upload the code to the board, click on the second icon or the arrow facing right, as shown in the following screenshot. Your board must be plugged into your computer and the correct board and port must be selected. If you've done this correctly, you should see the board's name in the drop-down menu:

Figure 3.26 – The Upload button and the board selected

This will take a few seconds. We can see the progress in the **Output** window. It will inform you of the percentage of bytes your program used, and the maximum available.

You should see an **upload complete** message in the **Output** window, as shown in the following screenshot. If you see this message, you should also see a red LED blinking on your board. We've done it!

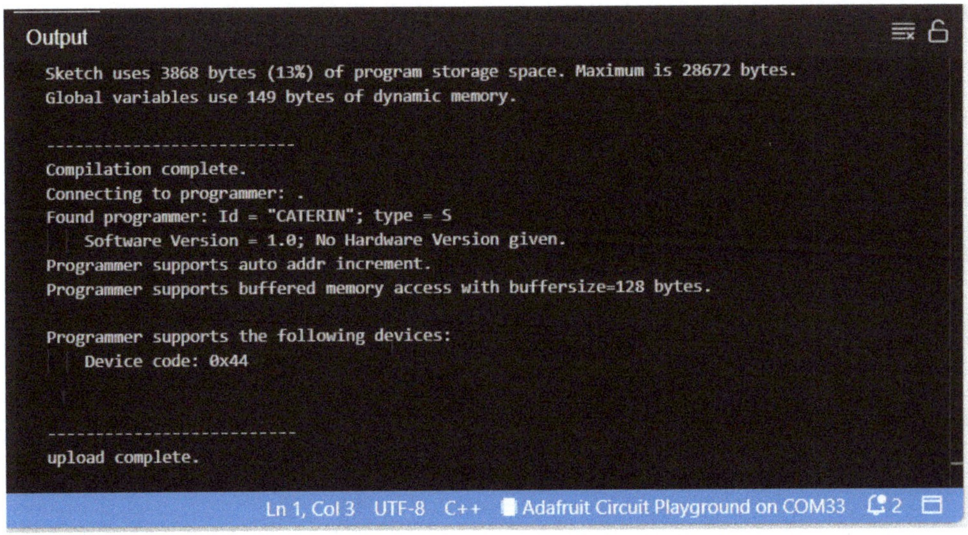

Figure 3.27 – Output window

Let's take a closer look at the **Blink** sketch and its parts before we look at troubleshooting any issues that may have happened. There are two main areas in an Arduino sketch: the setup() function and the loop() function. The setup() and loop() functions are the skeletons of every Arduino program. Let's look at them closer:

```
void setup() {
  pinMode(LED_BUILTIN, OUTPUT);
}
```

The setup() function runs once when you power up the board or press the reset button. The function is called when the sketch starts. This is where we initialize the components that we will be using in the code.

The setup() function sets initial values for **variables**, **pin modes**, and **libraries**. In this setup() function, we are defining that we are going to use the pin that the LED is connected to as an output. In this case, it is pin 13.

What is pinMode(pin, mode) for?

This sets a digital pin as either an input or an output. We need two parameters: the number of the pin and its mode, INPUT or OUTPUT. We put this command in setup() so that the pin's behavior is determined at the start of the program.

Following that, the loop() function runs. It repeats over and over, allowing your program to respond to inputs and outputs. It will control what the microcontroller does.

Let's take a closer look at the loop() code block in the Blink sketch:

```
void loop() {
  digitalWrite(LED_BUILTIN, HIGH);
  delay(1000);
  digitalWrite(LED_BUILTIN, LOW);
  delay(1000);
}
```

What is digitalWrite(pin, value) for?

In the Blink code, we use digital pins. We are setting it HIGH, to turn the LED on. This command is used to control a digital output pin. The first parameter is which pin you would like to control. The second is the value you want to set, which can be HIGH or LOW. HIGH will turn the pin on, sending out V+ at 40mA, while LOW will turn the pin off.

What is delay() for?

This is the amount of time to delay your program. Currently, it is 1 second, noted as 1,000 milliseconds. The delay() function will bring most of the other activities to a halt. For example, it won't read other sensors.

Try changing the microsecond amount, then upload the code again. Watch how the blink pattern changes. After the delay(1000) statement, there is another digitalWrite() function. This time, it sets the pin to LOW, meaning it won't send the LED on pin 13 any power, turning the LED off.

That's the basics of this first **Blink** sketch described. Looking through the code, I've mentioned **functions**. It's important to understand what their purpose is. So, let's look at functions in a little more detail.

What's a function?

A function is a way of organizing the code/instructions for the program that will go on your microcontroller. We can group statements and code blocks in a function. There are many pre-written functions in Arduino that can help us quickly program our boards.

> **Note**
>
> Also, notice that each statement finishes with a semicolon, ; . They are called a terminator, and it tells Arduino that we have finished with that statement. Your code will display an error if you forget to include it.

Another important aspect that you'll see in most code that you download or load from Arduino is that it will have comments in it. These are important to a sketch and worth discussing.

What are comments?

You'll notice there are other lines of text in the Arduino Blink sketch. These are comments. There is an initial multiline comment at the top and then there are several inline comments. A **single-line** comment uses // before the text you want in the comment. If you write // at the start or end of the code line, they are also referred to as an **inline comment**. A **multiline** comment is written between /* and */. These are not read by the program but are there to help us know more about the program.

I use comments a lot to remember code I have tried or code that needs to be changed. If I want the code to remain there but not be used, I can comment it out by using a multiline comment. The multiline comment at the top of your sketch is useful for providing notes, dates, attribution, and sometimes pinout information. Comments can also be used to remove lines of code, which is a useful way to remember what you tried.

Lastly, there is a Sketchbook in Arduino where your code is saved. This is saved inside the Arduino folder in your computer's `Documents` folder. You can access these in the Sketchbook dropdown in the **File** menu. You can change this location in the Arduino IDE settings.

Troubleshooting

Sometimes, we get error messages. The one you might see after trying to upload code is `Cannot run program "{runtime.tools.arm-none-eabi-gcc.path}\bin\arm-non-eabi-g++"`. This likely means that you are missing an important installation, in which case you must ensure that the **Arduino SAMD** boards package has been installed on your system. It is important to have *both* the Arduino and Adafruit SAMD board packages installed.

To fix this, you can navigate to the **Tools | Board | Boards Manager** menu, as shown in the following screenshot, but you can also click on the second icon down on the left-hand side of the program.

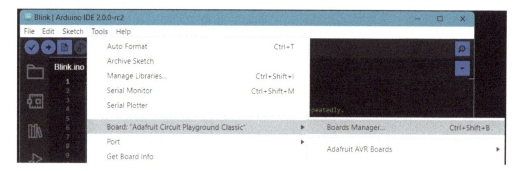

Figure 3.28 – Accessing Boards Manager

The second, quicker way to access the **Boards Manager** window is using the left-hand side menu. The icon that looks like a circuit board (highlighted in the following screenshot) opens **Boards Manager** too. This icon will open a side panel, as shown in the following screenshot, and a search bar. Type `Adafruit SAMD` in the search bar and when the entry appears, click on **Install**:

Figure 3.29 – The opened Boards Manager

You'll see confirmation of when the boards have been installed:

```
Tool arduino:bossac@1.8.0-48-gb176eee uninstalled
Configuring platform.
Platform adafruit:samd@1.7.8 installed
```

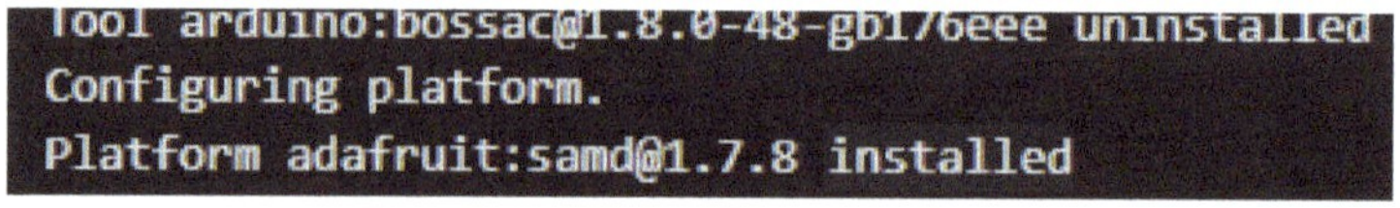

Figure 3.30 – Confirmation that the boards have been installed

Once you have both the Arduino SAMD and Adafruit SAMD board packages installed, the error message should stop. This will also install the Gemma M0 board for us to use in later activities. Your project should now be working – and that brings this chapter to a close!

Summary

This chapter explored the e-textile boards and kits that we can use to get up and running with our wearable circuits. We explored their differences and uses and how you can make decisions about which board will be a perfect fit for your projects. The Gemma M0 board is a great little board to start a project with due to its size and affordability, and the Flora gives us a few more options to add more interactivity to our wearables.

The Circuit Playground range of boards offers huge interaction possibilities in our projects due to their huge feature sets. At the time of writing, there isn't a more comprehensive board on the market. We also learned about the LilyPad range of components, which allows us to add sewable sensors easily. The pre-programmed boards allow us to create fun circuits that only require sewing. Then, we learned about the LilyPad boards with I/O pins, which can be useful for expanding the projects we create.

We finished by installing the Arduino IDE, which we will need throughout this book, and uploading our first program. With that, we saw how easily we can get functions working on a Circuit Playground board. In the next few chapters, we will continue our development with this board and others.

Spend a little time thinking about the sensors we looked at in this chapter. What types of projects could you plan out that would use them? Sketch some thoughts and ideas in a notebook – don't hold back. Make them as imaginative as possible because your skillset will develop, and you will be creating inspiration for yourself in later circuits!

In the next chapter, we will get busy with the Gemma M0 and Circuit Playground boards. These are likely to be the ones you choose most in your projects, so it's important we expand our knowledge about them. We will be creating a stretch/flex sensor and reading the data we get from it. It's going to be a busy and fun chapter!

Review questions

Answer the following questions to test your knowledge of this chapter:

1. What types of sensors are available with the e-textile toolkits?
2. How do these kits help us design our wearables?
3. Why do we need input and output pins?
4. What is the difference between digital and analog pins?
5. What are the first three things we need to check when using the Arduino IDE?
6. What is the purpose of the `void setup()` function?

4

Implementing Arduino Code Using Gemma M0 and Circuit Playground

Gemma M0, Circuit Playground, and other sewable boards are a great way to add more interaction to your wearables. As you learned in the previous chapter, their different sizes, functions, and I/O ports make them appropriate for different uses.

In this chapter, we will focus on learning through building a practical application with a Gemma M0 or Circuit Playground board so that you can expand the capabilities of your circuit. We will also explore flex sensors and the many ways to alter, use, and make them. Once you've considered their uses, you will connect a circuit. We will also read about how flex sensors have been used in research. Reading how components are used is a great way to inspire your projects. After that, we'll spend some time learning about the Arduino IDE, which you'll use to program your wearable. This will be followed by testing your circuits.

By the end of this chapter, you'll have a better understanding of designing, prototyping, and using the Gemma and Flora boards. You'll add flexibility to your wearable with an off-the-shelf flex sensor or one you've made. This will prepare us for the chapters that follow in which we will learn about the inputs and outputs that can be added to wearable projects. We will finish this chapter by hooking up and programming a Gemma M0 with a flex sensor and a servo motor!

In this chapter, we're going to cover the following main topics:

- Prototyping accelerometer and flex circuits
- Understanding flex sensors
- Research and innovation
- Troubleshooting
- The Arduino IDE

Technical requirements

In the practical part of this chapter, you'll use the Circuit Playground and Gemma M0 boards and create flex sensors. You'll also connect a flex sensor and servo motor to the same circuit. To follow along, you'll need the following items for the circuits. You can choose or swap items out from the following list:

- A Circuit Playground/Gemma M0 board and a micro USB cable
- Various flex sensors and a stretch sensor
- Conductive fabrics/textiles
- Velostat resistive plastic
- A 10KΩ resistor
- A servo motor
- The Arduino IDE: `https://www.arduino.cc/en/software`

Prototyping accelerometer and flex circuits

Previously, we connected our Circuit Playground board and programmed its LED to blink through the Arduino IDE. Now, we'll add to our skills by using an example from Circuit Playground and modifying it. We'll use the built-in accelerometer for this. We have a lot of exciting ground to cover, so let's jump straight in with our first activity.

Activity 4.1 – Hello_Accelerometer

Let's have some fun checking out one of the sensors on our Circuit Playground board to get to know it better. The accelerometer measures motion in your wearable. We will use the included example code from Adafruit. Plug in your Circuit Playground board and choose the correct board and port, as we've done previously.

As a reminder, go to the **Tools | Board** menu and select your board. Then, go to **Tools | Port** and select your port. The Arduino IDE may have found your board and port when you plugged it in, so you may not have to do this. Once your board has been found on the correct port, open the sketch.

The sketch can be found by going to **File | Examples | Adafruit Circuit Playground | Hello_Accelerometer**, as shown in the following screenshot:

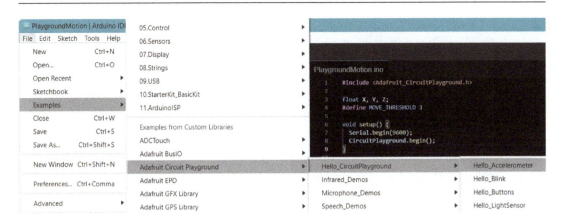

Figure 4.1 – Opening the sample sketch

Once the sketch is open, upload it to the board. Remember that the upload button is the second button from the left and looks like an arrow pointing to the right. Check for the confirmation message stating that the upload was a success – that is, **upload complete** – as shown in the following screenshot:

Figure 4.2 – Upload complete

Let's check if it's working. For this, we're going to open Serial Monitor. This is the last icon on the top right-hand side of the Arduino IDE and looks like a magnifying glass. Click the magnifier icon, as shown in the following screenshot. The serial monitor is integrated with Arduino 2.0, and it can be used as a debugging tool, to test out concepts, or to communicate with a microcontroller board:

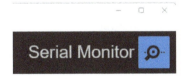

Figure 4.3 – The Serial Monitor icon

Once Serial Monitor is open, as shown in the following screenshot, make sure the baud rate is the same as declared in the sketch; that is, **9600 baud**. Then, move your Circuit Express board. You will see that the values change based on the movement and orientation of the board. What's going on?

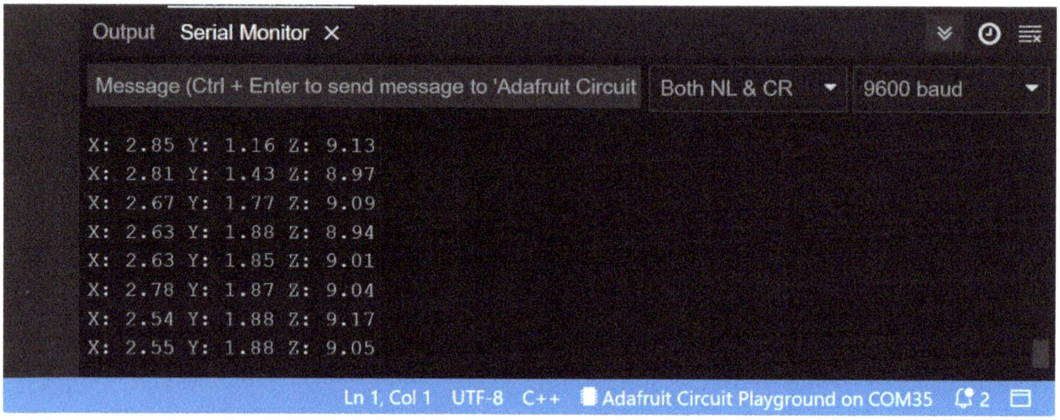

Figure 4.4 – Serial Monitor

Let's break down the code to understand it more. The first line is an #include statement. This adds libraries to the sketch and links them. These are premade files that contain code that adds a lot of functionality to our sketch. Then, there is a declaration of values that will be used in the sketch. In this case, we will need to use a float. float allows us to use decimal places in numbers.

Here, we create three instances of a float type – namely X, Y, and Z – that correspond with the directions of the accelerometer. We can also declare it in three separate lines.

The X, Y, and Z variables are used as directions:

- X is clockwise and counterclockwise.
- Y is for twisting the board left to right.
- Z controls back and forth motion.

You'll recognize the next part of the code: the setup() function. This contains our initial settings and a new function called Serial.begin(). We will use it in almost all of the code we write. This allows us to use Serial Monitor and send messages to it. It is very useful for finding errors in our circuit and reading messages to see what is working.

In this sketch, it will be used to display the values of the sensor. We only need to set the speed of the connection. As shown in the following screenshot, I chose **9600 baud**. This must match the speed "baud" in the Serial Monitor window:

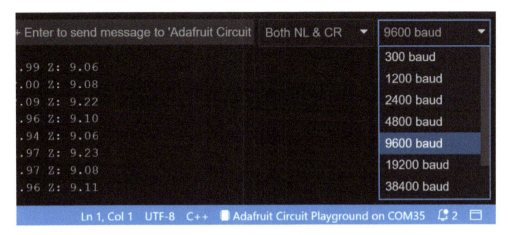

Figure 4.5 – Choosing the matching baud rate

Lastly, we must create an instance of CircuitPlayground by appending the .begin() function. This will allow us to access the code in the library so that we can use CircuitPlayground in the sketch to add features and functions:

```
#include <Adafruit_CircuitPlayground.h>
float X, Y, Z;
void setup() {
  Serial.begin(9600);
  CircuitPlayground.begin();
}
```

Next, let's look at what the code is doing in the loop() function. Here, we allocate a value to the three float variables we defined. We allocate position X to the value of the CircuitPlayground X coordinate.

This can be done by using a prewritten function called .motionX(). The same follows for the other two float values, where we will use two other functions, .motionY() and .motionZ(), for the Y position and Z position coordinates, respectively:

```
void loop() {
  X = CircuitPlayground.motionX();
  Y = CircuitPlayground.motionY();
  Z = CircuitPlayground.motionZ();
```

In the loop() function, we are printing to Serial Monitor. We can do this with the Serial. print() function. We program what to print, which can be the value of our variable data or a String, for example.

Try it now – add the `Serial.print(" Hello World");` line to your code, upload the code change, and see what happens:

```
Serial.print("X: ");
Serial.print(X);
Serial.print("  Y: ");
Serial.print(Y);
Serial.print("  Z: ");
Serial.println(Z);
delay(1000);
}
```

The output from the `Serial.print()` function will provide the output shown in the following screenshot. As we can see, using quotation marks around text prints the text (String) we want, `X:`. To print the value held in the x `float` variable, we just use `(X)`. The following output shows `X: value` for X, and so on:

Figure 4.6 – Output

The last `Serial.println(z);` function adds a carriage return or new line to the output. This is what happens when we use `.println` instead of `.print`.

The block of code in our `loop()` function ends with a `delay()` of 1 second written in milliseconds, as 1000, as we've seen previously in this book.

It's great that we've got our board to work with the serial monitor, but it's still not very exciting! Let's change the code so that it uses some of the onboard NeoPixels to respond to our movements.

Activity 4.2 – Hello NeoPixels

Now that we've successfully connected our Circuit Playground board to our computer and uploaded code with the Arduino program, let's add a bit more visual fun!

It would be great if, when we moved the board, the NeoPixels responded. By doing this, we can put our circuit on a band for our wrist, and if we wave hello – or goodbye – the NeoPixels will light up!

We'll need a Circuit Playground board, a pack of screw mounts, and a LiPoly battery for a completed circuit. I'm using hook and loop (Velcro) to close the wristband. I'm also using sturdy fabric to support the board and battery.

Let's upload the code. It's available at `https://github.com/cmoz/Ultimate/blob/main/C4/Activity_4_2.ino`. You can watch the video to follow along: `https://youtu.be/0CC6KjrWmQY`.

So, what's the code doing?

As with the previous code we used, we are including the Circuit Playground library and the three float variables, but this time, we are including a #define:

```
#define MOVE_THRESHOLD 3
```

The preceding line is adding a new variable and allocating it a value at the same time – a value of 3. A maximum value of 10 is allowed; the lower the number, the more sensitive it will be to motion. Our setup() function is also the same as in the preceding code we used. There are a few changes in the loop() function. Here, we use the .clearPixels() method to turn off all the NeoPixels:

```
CircuitPlayground.clearPixels();
```

Then, we allocate the values to our three floats, as we did previously. This time, however, we are using calculations for the movements, which we are still printing to Serial Monitor so that we can see that our program is working correctly:

```
double storedVector = X*X;
storedVector += Y*Y;
storedVector += Z*Z;
storedVector = sqrt(storedVector);
Serial.print("Len: "); Serial.println(storedVector);
```

The following code will check if there is motion by using an if statement. An if statement tells our code to do something if it is true. In this example, if there is movement larger than our MOVE_THRESHOLD, then our code will be executed:

```
if (abs(10*newVector - 10*storedVector) > MOVE_THRESHOLD) {
    for (int x=0; x<10; x++){
    int randomValR = random(255);
    int randomValG = random(255);
    int randomValB = random(255);
    int randomNeoPos = random(10);
    CircuitPlayground.setPixelColor(randomPos,
                            randomValR, randomValG, randomValB);
    delay(100);
    x = randomNeoPos;
    }
    }
```

We are going to light up to 10 NeoPixels in this `for()` loop. It will run the code very fast to light up the NeoPixels, so we added a short 100 ms delay. We want the colors and the location of the pixels to be random, so we used the `random()` function.

We also created three random function calls, one for each of the three color (R, G, B) possibilities. `setPixelColour()` takes four variables. First, it takes the position of the NeoPixels. 0 is top left all the way around to the top right position, which is 9. Then, it takes three values of 0-255 for the colors red, green, and blue. Each color has light levels in a number range of 0 to 255. 0 means no light while 255 means maximum light. If we have a pure blue color, the values will be 0, 0, 255, while if we have a more jade-color blue, the values will be 0, 100, 255. This means no red, a medium green, and a full blue color that all mix.

Lastly, I've included `x = randomNeoPos;` to allocate x a random value. This is so that the number of NeoPixels that light up will also change with the movement.

You can change the code if you only want blue, for example, and not random selections. How would you do this? You would have to alter the following line:

```
CircuitPlayground.setPixelColor(randomPos, 0,  0,   255);
```

You could also choose which NeoPixels you would like to light up by changing the first value. *Figure 4.7* shows our lit Circuit Playground board:

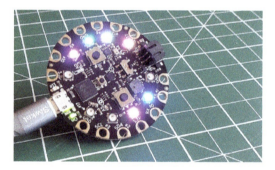

Figure 4.7 – Light-up NeoPixels

Your turn!

Modify the code to change the colors and positions of the NeoPixels. What effects can you make? How does moving the board change your color choices?

Making it wearable

Lastly, I'm going to use the bolt mounting kit to quickly add this to a thick piece of material. I've got this fake leather fabric that is thick and can take holes being punched into it. You can use felt that's 3 mm thick as an alternative. I'm going to put a few holes through where the holes match up with the board. Then, I'm going to push through the screws to mount the board. This is a super quick and easy way to put a circuit onto a wearable when testing it and making a prototype (*Figure 4.8*). The board will be reusable too!

Figure 4.8 – Mounting the board with screws

It looks pretty funky! Now, I only need to sew a pocket for the battery and sew hook and loop (Velcro) so that I can attach it to wear. Now, when I wave, the board will be flashing! Woop! The completed project is a super quick hack when you need to prototype and test something you've been working on. We don't always have to commit it to a permanent form. *Figure 4.9* shows the version for testing:

Figure 4.9 – Completed project

Now that we've completed this quick prototype, let's explore the world of flex sensors and make some of our own.

Understanding flex sensors

Because we move in all sorts of ways, a flex sensor can be a great way to track some of that movement. Where do we bend? Elbows, wrists, fingers, toes, ankles, knees, and the waist are a few examples. We can buy flex sensors, that are of various lengths. To get an accurate reading, you need to consider the position and how you can protect the sensor. Be sure it isn't too delicate a sensor if it is placed somewhere with vigorous bends.

In terms of sensors, you can get a carbon-impregnated conductive rubber cord or a flex sensor/bend sensor, which is like a variable resistor. As it bends, the resistance values change. There are also a variety of linear soft pot ribbon sensors, square force-sensitive resistors, circular soft potentiometers, and round force-sensitive resistors available. We will look at these in more detail in *Chapter 5, Working with Sensors: All about inputs!*.

By measuring the resistance, we can tell how much bend there is. We can read the sensor by connecting it to a fixed-value resistor, 10kΩ (Ohms), which creates a voltage divider. A voltage divider is a linear circuit that produces the output voltage, which is a fraction of the input voltage. Essentially, it changes a large voltage to a smaller one.

We connect one end of the sensor to power and the other to a pull-down resistor. The fixed-value resistor and the flex sensor are connected to the **analog-digital converter** (**ADC**) input of Arduino. This creates a variable voltage output that Arduino reads.

We can use our multimeter to see these changes. Let's try that now.

Activity 4.3 – using a multimeter to read our flex sensor

Using your multimeter, you can take a resistance reading. I put this flex sensor in a small breadboard because it was easier to read the values that way. The two metal probes at the bottom are too close together to get an accurate reading otherwise. *Figure 4.10* shows the sensor flexed with the reading at almost 400 Ohms. A straightened-out sensor has carbon particles very close together, so a value of 0 should be noted when flexed as these particles space out a lot more:

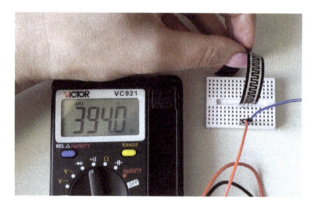

Figure 4.10 – Multimeter readings of the sensor flexed

Now that we've looked at traditional flex sensors to understand them, we can build our own! We know we are looking for changing resistance values. Let's look at how flex/pressure sensors are used in real-world applications. This next section is all about research and innovation.

Research and innovation

Flex sensors are used in some of the wearables that we looked at in *Chapter 1, Introduction to the World of Wearables*. Their use in sports clothing and medical monitoring devices are some of the most common. Flex sensors, such as the stretchable graphene thermistors researched by Khan, Y., Ostfeld, A. E., Lochner, et al. (2015), which also detail respiration knits and patches that are used for **monitoring vital signs.**

Human finger tracking was explored in Ponraj, G., & Ren, H. (2018). In their paper, they observed how much human hands are used every day, including in *"gesture recognition, robotics, medicine and health care, design and manufacturing, art and entertainment across multiple domains."* Other interesting research is regarding **sitting postures** and the health issues that may come with them. The system described by Hu, Q., Tang, X., & Tang, W. (2020) uses six flex sensors to create a *"novel posture recognition system on an office chair."*

Monitoring **neck posture** also involves using flex sensors (Guo, Y. R., Zhang, X. C., & An, N., 2019). Two are attached to the neck to warn users about neck posture for better neck health. The research by Hiader, S. A. A., Nasir, A., et al. (2021) focuses on the design and development of low-cost **3D prosthetic hands** using flex sensors. Additional work in the field includes developing gloves for **communicating sign language**, **gloves for motorbike drivers** to measure hand forces during motorbike riding, and wearable bands for stress detection. Smart garments for monitoring body posture also make use of flex sensors, such as **controlled robotic hands** for people with disabilities. Smart gloves are also a popular wearable and if you search, you will find inspiring examples and good starting points for your wearable projects!

There is more information on these types of sensors in the paper by Kamara, V. (2019), *A Comparative Characterization of Smart Textile Pressure Sensors*. 2019 41st Annual International Conference of the IEEE **Engineering in Medicine and Biology Society (EMBC).**

Please check out the *Further reading* section for the full references to these papers so that you can explore flex/force sensors in greater depth.

Now that we understand the potential for flex/pressure sensors in real-world applications, let's make one!

Activity 4.4 – making a flex sensor

Let's start making a flex sensor. Being able to make components is a good skill to have because, for wearable technology, we can mold and create sensors to fit the curves of the body. We can make them fit smaller or more unique places. Also, when you make a sensor, you know what materials are in it and exactly how it will work:

Figure 4.11 – Materials for the flex sensor

The materials (*Figure 4.11*) that we use for this sensor are as follows:

- Conductive fabric. I'm going to use steel ribbon as it's already a good size and easy to use. You can also use sticky nylon sheets or other conductive fabric that you have.
- **Velostat**, which is a resistive plastic. It will change resistance when there is force on it, so we can use it as a force-sensing resistor, or in this case, flex.
- I'm using felt as my fabric base for this flex sensor.
- A sewing needle, clips, thread, and conductive thread.

Once you have collected these materials, measure out the size of the sensor that you want. The main thing you need to remember is the Velostat must cover all of the conductive fabric or conductive steel ribbon.

You'll need two pieces of felt (or other fabric), one piece of the Velostat that will go in the middle of this sandwich, and two pieces of conductive fabric, or as I'm doing, the steel ribbon. I've laid these out as shown in *Figure 4.12*, with the pieces in place of where they will be once sewn:

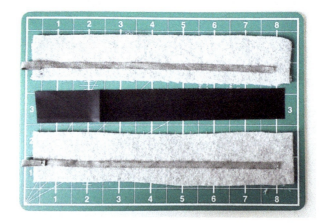

Figure 4.12 – Placed materials

I flipped over the end of the steel ribbon (*Figure 4.13*) to make it easy to sew into the circuit without it unraveling. I sewed it in place with conductive thread. If you're using a conductive material, you may not need to fold it over, though it does give it additional strength. Balance conserving material with your sensor reliability. Also, be sure to not cause a short within your circuit:

Figure 4.13 – Sewing the edge over

Once your materials are secured in place, layer them like a sandwich. You'll have a layer of felt, then conductive material (steel ribbon), then Velostat. Then, you'll have the other conductive material and lastly the other piece of felt or fabric. *Figure 4.14* shows how the layers should be created:

Figure 4.14 – Layering the materials

Once they have been layered, we will sew them together. Just use a simple running stitch all the way around. First, I'll clip it into place (*Figure 4.15*), and then start sewing from the top corner.

Important Note

Be sure you don't pierce the Velostat, and make sure that the two conductive material pieces are not touching each other – this will create a short circuit!

The finished stitching and sensor are shown in *Figure 4.15*. Notice that the tabs are not touching:

Figure 4.15 – Clips holding the fabric (top) and the completed sewing (bottom)

Once you've finished sewing, use your multimeter to measure the circuit when it is pressed, flexed, and bent (*Figure 4.16*). You are looking for a change in values to indicate there is movement in the sensor:

Figure 4.16 – Checking for changes with a multimeter

Now that we've measured our flex sensor and know that it works, let's connect it to our Circuit Playground board!

Activity 4.5 – connecting your circuit – an LED reaction to flexing

Now that we've made a flex sensor, we need to connect it to our Circuit Playground board. There are only two pin-outs on the flex sensor. One will go to power on our board, while the other will connect to an analog pin on the Circuit Playground board – first to the ground and then to a **10K resistor** to the ground tab on the board. We made sew pads for the sensor so that we can use croc clips to connect it up and see it all working. Let's take a closer look – *Figure 4.17* is a mapped-out plan for our flex sensor circuit:

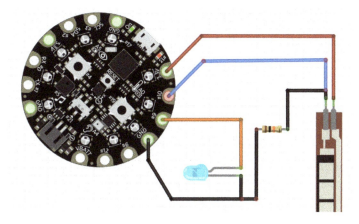

Figure 4.17 – Mapping the circuit

Mapping the circuit is a great way to find errors and be sure of our connections before we commit to sewing or soldering!

Don't Forget

Always choose the board and port you are using from the **Tools** menu in the Arduino IDE before trying to upload your code!

The circuit mapped on paper will look like the connected version shown in *Figure 4.18*. One of the tabs on the flex sensor connects to power. The other tab connects to pin 10 and connects a ground wire that has a 10K resistor, completing the ground circuit. In my example, the resistor has been connected to the board using the screws we had earlier:

Figure 4.18 – Connected board and flex sensor

Now that the circuit is connected, let's look at the code. You can watch the video at `https://youtu.be/MzdQFUCvan0` to follow along. The code for this can be found at `https://github.com/cmoz/Ultimate/blob/main/C4/Activity_4_5.ino`.

First, let's define the pin for the LED. We need to choose a pin that can do a PWM output. This is because we don't only want an on or off value – we want to see a variation in brightness. On the Circuit Playground Classic board, I've chosen pin 9.

Also, define `flexPin` as an analog input pin. Here, I've chosen pin 10. If you are using a different board, be sure to choose a PWM pin for the LED and an analog pin for the sensor. This is because we want a range of values and not limited to 1 or 0.

The Circuit Playground Classic board has the following pins:

- D6, D9, D10, and D11 digital/can be analog inputs
- D3, D6, D9, and D10 digital/can be PWM outputs

Lastly, we have a variable of `int` type called `flexValue`. These are used to hold the value of the flex sensor reading:

```
int ledPin = 9;
int flexPin = 10;
int flexValue;
```

In the `setup()` function, we set the LED pin as an output and start `Serial` communication:

```
void setup(){
  pinMode(ledPin, OUTPUT);
  Serial.begin(9600);
}
```

In the `loop()` function, we start by reading and saving the analog value that we are getting from the flex sensor. We print that value to Serial Monitor to check if it is working correctly. We can open Serial Monitor and read the values as we flex the sensor:

```
void loop(){
    flexValue = analogRead(flexPin);
    Serial.println(flexValue);
    flexValue = map(flexValue, 700, 900, 0, 255);
    analogWrite(ledPin, flexValue);
    delay(100);
}
```

There is a new function in the `loop()` code block. We use `map()` to map values 0-1023 and 0-255 of **pulse width modulation (PWM)**. This re-maps a number from one range (in this example, the values 0-1023 of the analog input) into a different range (0 to the maximum 255 color value). Here, we are mapping to the max value that we can use with the LED (255) as we want light from the values.

Test your flex sensor and find out what your values are. Test it by using your multimeter, as we've done earlier in the chapter. Flex, press, and bend your sensor and write down the lowest and highest values you are getting a reading for. I've remapped mine to hold the values `848` to `1015`, so I've modified that line of code to read as follows:

```
    flexValue = map(flexValue, 848, 1015, 0, 255);
```

You will need to change these values since your flex sensor is different from mine.

After the `map()` function, we must write the value from the flex sensor to our `ledPin`. This will change the LED's brightness. The code sends the PWM amount to the LED. Finally, we can complete the code with a short delay to see the changes in the LED's brightness.

Let's take a closer look at the Arduino IDE. We'll be using it for more wearables throughout this book, and of course for your wearable technology projects afterward too!

So, let's go ahead and hook up the Gemma M0 board with a flex sensor and servo motor.

Activity 4.6 – hooking up the Gemma M0 board with a flex sensor and servo motor

This super little board is a great way to start many wearable technology projects. It's a great choice for circuits that need a discreet board with enough inputs and outputs to make a wearable design interactive.

While we're here, let's talk about servo motors. Servo motors are used where there is a need for small, accurate movement or position. They are good for applying low-speed and accurate positions. These motors are used in robotic arms, flight controls, and control systems.

Servo motors are available in different shapes and sizes. For this circuit, we will use a 180-degree servo that is common to many kits. It's often called a Tower Pro servo motor and weighs 9 g and is 23 x 12 x 29 mm in size. A servo motor has three wires – one for voltage, another for ground, and another for the position setting. The **red** wire is for power, the **black** (or **brown**) wire is for ground, and the **yellow** wire is the signal wire.

Let's hook this up with crocodile clips to check our circuit planning. As you already know, the flex sensor has two pins. It's a resistor, so the pins are interchangeable.

> **Important Note**
> Always unplug the circuit board from its power source whenever you are making any changes!

The following diagram shows how to hook everything up. Here, the servo has three wires. Don't forget that there are two wires going to one pin on the flex sensor – the analog pin, A0 (blue), and GND (black):

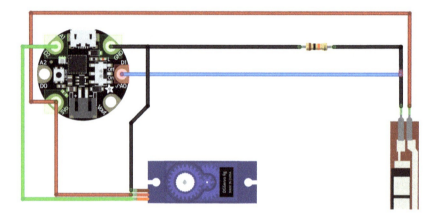

Figure 4.19 – The circuit with the Gemma M0 board, the flex sensor, and the servo motor

Let's take a closer look. You can use the preceding diagram to follow along. First, let's hook up the flex sensor:

1. Connect one of the pins to ANALOG IN pin A0 on the Gemma M0 board. Connect the **same** pin, through a 10K ohm resistor (brown, black, orange), to GND.

2. Connect the other pin to 3.3V

The servo has a cable with three wires; hook them up as follows:

1. Connect the RED wire (power) to 3.3V.

2. Connect the YELLOW wire (signal) to pin A1.

3. Connect the BLACK wire to ground (GND).

The hook-ups and pins are shown in *Figure 4.20* with crocodile clips. These are connecting the flex sensor and servo motor:

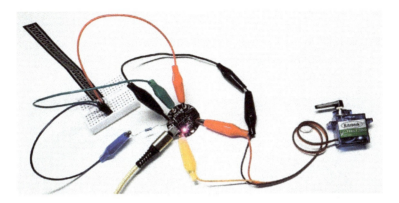

Figure 4.20 – The Gemma M0 board with crocodile clips

The complete code isn't too complicated for this circuit. It is shown here and available online at https://github.com/cmoz/Ultimate/blob/main/C4/Activity4_6.ino:

```
#include <Servo.h>
Servo servo1;
int flexpin = A0;
void setup()
{
 Serial.begin(9600);
 servo1.attach(A1);
}
void loop()
{
  int flexposition;
  int servoposition;
  flexposition = analogRead(flexpin);
  servoposition = map(flexposition, 600, 1000, 0, 180);
  servoposition = constrain(servoposition, 0, 180);
  servo1.write(servoposition);
  Serial.print("sensor: ");
  Serial.print(flexposition);
  Serial.print("  servo: ");
```

```
    Serial.println(servoposition);
  delay(20);
}
```

Before we investigate the code in more detail, plug in your Gemma M0 board and upload the code to it. Don't forget to select your **board** and **port**; otherwise, the code won't upload:

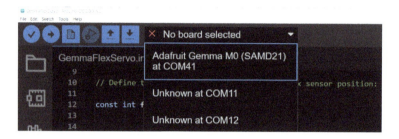

Figure 4.21 – Board and port selection

Let's look at the code in more detail to understand what's happening and what variables you may need to change. If you want to follow along, there is a video of this circuit working at https://youtu.be/oO9nMhIsxog.

We start the code by adding our servo library so that we can access servo functions to control it.

Then, we create a servo *object* called servo1. Each servo object controls one servo. You can have a maximum of 12, but not on this little Gemma M0 board – you'd need to use a board with more I/Os.

We define the analog input pin to measure flex sensor position, which is **A0**. Remember that if you are using a different board, you may need to change this so that it matches your board. Then, we write our void setup() function, where we set up this sketch. All we are doing is starting the serial monitor and defining that servo1 will read analog data from pin **A1**.

Moving through to the void loop() function, we create two integer variables to hold the values of the flexposition and servoposition. We set up the value for flexposition to be the analog reading from the flex pin. We servoposition define based on our flex, which we then map to the servo range of 0 to 180 degrees. I've mapped my flex sensor so that it has a range of 600 to 1000; yours may differ. Start with a range of 600 to 900 and see how it maps.

Important – bend the flex sensor and make a note of the minimum and maximum values. If you replace the 600 and 900 values in the map() function, you'll match the flex sensor's range with the servo's range:

```
servoposition = map(flexposition, 600, 900, 0, 180);
map(value, fromLow, fromHigh, toLow, toHigh)
```

Because every flex sensor, including the ones we've made, has different resistance, the range in the map() function may not cover the flex sensor's output. To tune our program based on the flex, we can use the serial port. This will print out the flex values to the Serial Monitor window.

Because the map() function may return values outside the range, we can use a function called constrain(). This function clips the numbers into a range. So, if the number is outside the range, it makes it the largest or smallest number. However, if it's within the range, it remains as it was.

Then, we can enable control of the servo and move it into the mapped position.

Note that almost all of the lines for print() are the same, except the last line, which is println(). Without the ln appendix to print, it will put everything on one line. println() will send a carriage return to move to the next line.

After you upload the sketch, turn on Serial Monitor (the magnifying-glass icon to the right of the icon bar). You'll be able to see the sensor's values.

Activity 4.7 – using Serial Monitor

Serial Monitor is a great way to look inside our program and find out if it's working as expected. We had a brief look at this earlier in *Activity 4.1 – Hello_Accelerometer*, when we looked at what the output was when moving the Circuit Playground board. There are other uses for Serial Monitor and if we add Serial.println("some text"); to our code, we can start to understand which function/method/statement of the code is being executed.

You can use USB-serial communication and Serial Monitor in the Arduino software to view what sort of values you're getting in. To use the serial monitor, we need to initialize it in our code using Serial.begin(speed). Include this code in your setup() function. Set the speed of communication by writing the value in parenthesis. A standard rate that's used in examples is 9600 baud. Serial.println(val) sends the value followed by a new line. Using Serial.print() will keep the responses on the same line.

When you open Serial Monitor, you should see the values and responses from Arduino. There is a drop-down menu for the rates of communication, or baud rate, that you can select. The baud rate is the rate of communication that the computer and Arduino use to talk to each other. Check if the baud rate of your serial monitor matches the value you set in the Serial.begin() function. You'll quickly find out if they don't match because the output will not be readable!

Let's look at Serial Monitor as we flex and bend our sensor:

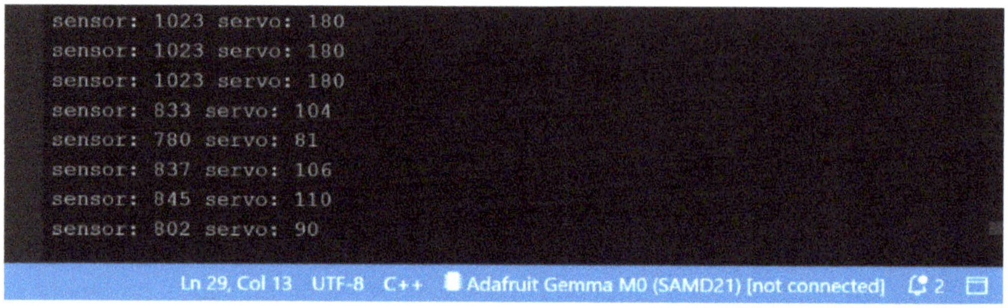

```
sensor: 1023 servo: 180
sensor: 1023 servo: 180
sensor: 1023 servo: 180
sensor: 833 servo: 104
sensor: 780 servo: 81
sensor: 837 servo: 106
sensor: 845 servo: 110
sensor: 802 servo: 90
```
Ln 29, Col 13   UTF-8   C++   Adafruit Gemma M0 (SAMD21) [not connected]   2

Figure 4.22 – Serial Monitor output

If everything is fine, you should see a change in resistance as you bend the flex sensor, as shown in the preceding screenshot.

The following is an example of how we could display information:

```
Serial.print("sensor = ");
Serial.print(sensorValue);
Serial.print("\t output  = ");
Serial.print(outputValue);
```

The preceding code will result in the following output:

```
Sensor = 250        output = 33
```

\t places a tab space between the output.

Serial Monitor is a good way to check that your sensors are working how you expect. In the wearables you make, you'll be using this feature of the Arduino IDE often. We can test our circuit by flexing it and reading the values on the screen. This will help us make sure it works as we expect.

Now that we've seen the output on Serial Monitor and that the code is working, we can decide how and where we might like to incorporate this circuit.

Troubleshooting

Is your circuit working fine? Does your servo move when the sensor you made is pressed and flexed? If not, you may want to investigate these things first. Don't forget that there are many great places online for resources to help you on your journey. For more information about the servo library that we used in our code, you can visit https://www.arduino.cc/reference/en/libraries/servo/. For a clear hookup guide, you can visit https://docs.arduino.cc/learn/electronics/servo-motors.

If your servo is not twisting, I would first look at the connections. Even with the colored wires, you may have put it in backward. Check your connections to see that power is going to the power pin on the Gemma M0 board. If the servo is not moving as you are expecting it to, remember that this sensor works best in one direction, or sometimes with pressure. Try flexing it in different directions to see if your flex sensor responds. If you find that your servo doesn't move very far, remember that we looked at modifying the map() function in the code. You need to modify the range of values according to what your sensor is outputting. Lastly, make sure the pin you are using (you may have connected it to a different board, for example) has analog in and PWM out for the LED. Be sure to change these pin numbers in the code too!

I hope that helps – if not, search online; there are usually many people who will have had the same issue as you.

The Arduino IDE

We've used the Arduino IDE for a couple of projects, so the interface should be familiar to you. In this section, I want to cover a few basics of programming and the interface.

This section is for beginners so that they feel more comfortable with using Arduino. If you are a seasoned programmer, you may want to jump ahead to hooking up the Gemma M0 board.

Let's take a brief tour of a few of the terms and what they are:

- Functions
- Variables
- Other tips/syntax

We'll start by looking at functions, which we covered briefly earlier in this book.

Functions

Functions are important for segmenting code into modular pieces. These perform a defined task and then return to where that code was called from. It's useful if there are a series of steps that we want to repeat. An example is the digitalWrite() function, which we can use to write a HIGH or LOW value to a digital pin. We can write our own functions, but digitalWrite() is one that is prewritten in Arduino for us.

Variables

A variable is used to store a value. Think of it as the container we use. It can hold different types of values, depending on what we need to use in our program. We have already used integers, whole numbers, and float values for decimal places. We can also use strings for strings of text. To use a variable, we must declare it. We can also use characters and Booleans as variables.

To declare a variable, we must give it a *type*, a *name*, and a *value*. We can declare variables without giving them a value, but we can't give a value to something we have not declared yet. This will always give us an error message. Earlier, we declared three variables of the `float` type with three names – X, Y, and Z:

```
float X, Y, Z;
```

We could have declared it this way for clarity:

```
float X;
float Y;
float Z;
```

Because they are all the same type, we can declare them together. When we were using the variable, we assigned it a value:

```
X = CircuitPlayground.motionX();
```

In this example, we are assigning the X float variable a value of the x movement of the board. The variable name must be the same every time you use it in your sketch; otherwise, it won't be recognized.

> **Variable Naming Conventions**
>
> There are a few conventions to follow when naming a variable: it can't start with a number, it can't have any spaces in it, and it can't be a word that the Arduino language already uses for another purpose (for example, we can't use *delay* because it's reserved by the Arduino language). If your code does not compile or throws an error, often, variables are the place to look to troubleshoot the issue.

Also, it's good practice to name your variables something that indicates their purpose, as shown here:

```
int randomValR = random(255);
```

We named this integer variable `randomValR` because it holds the randomly generated value for the red portion of the code.

Other

We've already looked at the structure of the Arduino sketch, which has a `setup()` and a `loop()` function. There are also control structures we will learn along the way. We saw a `for` loop and an `if` statement too.

A `for()` loop repeats a block of statements enclosed in curly braces. We used a variable to increment and terminate the loop. A `for()` loop is useful for repeating code.

The `if` statement checks a condition and if the condition is `true`, it will run the code. Also, curly braces signify when we start and end a block of code.

Lastly, there is always more than one way to write code. Don't worry if you do it differently than someone else. All you have to do is look online at examples and you will see that there is always a selection of people doing the same thing, but they program it differently. It's more important to try your circuits and your code. You can always go back to it later to tidy it up or edit it.

Summary

This has been a very busy chapter where you have been making circuits, programming them, and learning about new sensors and servos. We started by using the Circuit Playground board to explore one of the many sensors: an accelerometer. We used this onboard sensor with NeoPixels to track movement. This was a great way to see firsthand the fun we can have with NeoPixels! Using the sensors on the Circuit Playground board is a great way to add interactivity to future projects. It demonstrates that we can use the sensors onboard to test code and circuits quickly.

Then, we jumped straight into understanding flex sensors. We looked at using an off-the-shelf component, but also how we can build our own. Being able to build sensors opens a whole new world for your wearables. You can start to plan your circuits and make the sensor fit easily with the body part you desire. We also used a multimeter to help us take readings from the sensor to make sure it was working.

Lastly, we learned how to hook up and incorporate our handmade flex sensor with a servo motor for output. This involved you also learning about Serial Monitor, which can be a useful tool for finding errors. We looked at using Serial Monitor to read the values from the flex sensor and servo motor to ensure it was working as we expected. We managed to connect our components using the Gemma M0 board because it's small and great for wearables. It has enough power to use both components to add interactivity to our wearable technology.

Hopefully, you've found this a useful chapter to keep your wearable journey full of curiosity and explorations. Making a component is great fun and I hope you've started to plan how you would integrate these two components into a wearable item.

Will you bend your finger so that it moves like a flower or butterfly? Does the bending control a little flag or message? Does it connect to your knee and when you bend, the servo hits a small drum for noise?

In the next chapter, we take our explorations further by learning about the sensors that can collect data from our environment. We'll look at how we can use these sensors, what sensors there are, whether we can make them ourselves, and how to do some basic hook-ups into our wearable designs. It's all about input!

Further reading

To learn more about the topics that were covered in this chapter, take a look at the following resources:

Khan, Y., Ostfeld, A. E., Lochner, C. M., Pierre, A., & Arias, A. C. (2015). Monitoring of Vital Signs with Flexible and Wearable Medical Devices. *Advanced Materials, 28(22), n/a--n/a*. Available at `https://doi.org/10.1002/ADMA.201504366`.

Ponraj, G., & Ren, H. (2018). Sensor fusion of leap motion controller and flex sensors using Kalman filter for human finger tracking. *IEEE Sensors Journal, 18(5), 2042-2049.*

Hu, Q., Tang, X., & Tang, W. (2020). A smart chair sitting posture recognition system using flex sensors and FPGA implemented artificial neural network. *IEEE Sensors Journal, 20(14), 8007-8016.*

Guo, Y. R., Zhang, X. C., & An, N. (2019, August). Monitoring neck posture with flex sensors. In *2019 9th International Conference on Information Science and Technology (ICIST) (pp. 459-463). IEEE.*

Hiader, S. A. A., Nasir, A., Ameen, M., Raza, A., Waleed, A., & Ali, Z. (2021, November). Design and Development of Low Cost, Wireless Controlled, 3D Prosthetic Hand using Flex Sensors. In *2021 International Conference on Innovative Computing (ICIC) (pp. 1-6). IEEE.*

Zubair, M., Yoon, C., Kim, H., Kim, J., & Kim, J. (2015). Smart Wearable Band for Stress Detection. *2015 5th International Conference on IT Convergence and Security (ICITCS).* Available at `https://doi.org/10.1109/ICITCS.2015.7293017`.

Abro, Z. A., Yi-Fan, Z., Nan-Liang, C., Cheng-Yu, H., Lakho, R. A., & Halepoto, H. (2019). A novel flex sensor-based flexible smart garment for monitoring body postures. *Journal of Industrial Textiles, 49(2), 262-274.*

Latif, S., Javed, J., Ghafoor, M., Moazzam, M., & Khan, A. A. (2019, August). Design and development of muscle and flex sensor controlled robotic hand for disabled persons. In *2019 International Conference on Applied and Engineering Mathematics (ICAEM) (pp. 1-6). IEEE.*

Review questions and exercises

Answer the following questions and complete the following exercises to test your knowledge of this chapter:

1. How do we know our flex sensor is working?

2. What happens if you name my variable something that is not allowed?

3. Why do we use Serial Monitor?

4. Why did we need to choose a PWM pin for the LED?

5. Can you complete the circuits created in this chapter? Add them to a part of the body, sew them into a design, or plan where you may want to incorporate them.

6. Spend some time planning a flex sensor for a different part of the body. What do you need to consider if you are planning for a finger? For the knee? How will these sensors differ? Be aware of the size differences and the pressure or flex on different parts of the body. The knee will need to track a wider movement, but the finger will involve smaller, more precise movements.

Part 2:
Creating Sewable Circuits
That Sense and React Using
Arduino and ESP32

In this part, you will learn to add inputs and outputs to your circuits to create dynamic, fun, and exciting wearables. You will expand the capabilities of your wearable projects.

This part of the book comprises the following chapters:

5

Working with Sensors: All About Inputs!

This is going to be a fun chapter! Adding interactive elements to our wearables can be done with sensors. Sensors are used to listen to the world around us. In this chapter, we discover what sensors can be added to our projects, what protocols we use to add them to our circuits, and how we can use the data they provide. Most of the wearables we create will sense something – our touch, the sound, the light, and so on.

In this chapter, you will learn about the types of sensors we can include in our wearable designs to input information into our system. This input is then used to create a reaction or response. For example, we might use a temperature sensor to collect temperature data, and when the temperature reaches a programmed level, to provide heat or cooling to the body. We will also look at some alternative ways to use a sensor.

By the end of this chapter, you will understand and be able to use sensors in your wearables. Also, you will have the knowledge needed to use the protocols to connect sensors to your Arduino -based boards. Lastly, you'll also be able to use and install a library in the Arduino IDE to add a lot more functionality to our code.

In this chapter, we're going to cover the following main topics:

- Sensors for listening
- Using libraries
- Understanding the I^{2}C and **Serial Peripheral Interface (SPI)** protocols
- Using conductive materials as sensors

Technical requirements

This chapter is all about learning how to use different sensors and inputs. A selection is featured in the chapter so there isn't a required list. However, you may want to give a few of the electronic circuits a try so you can choose items from this list:

- Arduino software as the IDE

- Circuit Playground/Gemma M0/Flora board

- A kit available at `https://www.tinkertailor.tech/product-page/sense-a-tional-fun-pack` with a variety of sensors and outputs, or various sensors of your choice, such as the following:

    - Ultrasonic distance sensor

    - Tilt sensor

    - Stretch sensor

    - Sound sensor

    - UV sensor

    - Conductive textiles and materials

Sensors for listening

This chapter is where we learn an overview of some of the sensors we will use in our wearables. I've organized them into four categories. We will explore each category and then work through activities to create a sample circuit to see them in action! In this section, we will learn about the following:

- Distance and movement

- Force, flex, and stretch

- Environmental sensors

- Communication and other inputs to try

This will give us a knowledge base to help with planning our wearable designs. It will support our decision-making process for choosing the correct board. This is because we will have a better understanding of the number of I/O pins we need to connect for these types of inputs.

Sensors are all about input; they are listening for us. We can use data collected from these sensors to produce an output of some type. It could be an output or reaction/response with sound, light, movement, or something else.

Let's look at the first category: distance and movement.

Distance and movement

There are several sensors that can measure distance and movement. Many are low-cost, off-the-shelf sensors so you have a choice of different sizes and capabilities for your projects.

Often, when prototyping, it's a good idea to go for the lowest specification and lowest cost until your idea is tested. It's important to remember though that sometimes these components can be less reliable too. They may be inconsistent or give errors, especially the cheaper versions. Also, if you are testing the sensor out with croc clips or DuPont cables, they can come loose or not have a solid connection, which can affect your output:

Figure 5.1 – Distance and movement sensors

If you are aware of these potential issues and keep them in mind, then they are great sensors to use. Some of these sensors are shown in *Figure 5.1*. From left to right, you can see an accelerometer, two **time-of-flight** (ToF) sensors, a Sharp distance sensor below them, an ultrasonic distance sensor in the middle, a **passive infrared** (PIR) sensor, and lastly, a Maxbotix high-performance sonar module.

A **ToF** sensor measures the time it takes for light to bounce back to the sensor. This is done with a small invisible laser. The area of sensing is very narrow, meaning it is for objects directly in front of the path of the sensor. Two are shown in *Figure 5.1*: a black one on the top left, and a purple one next to it. Not all ToF sensors look like this.

The **ultrasonic distance sensor (HC-SR04)**, shown in the center of *Figure 5.1* with a blue circuit board, is designed to work on the voltage range that the Arduino range of products uses, so 3.3V to 5V. The HC-SR04 module has an ultrasonic transmitter, a receiver, and a control circuit. This works with sound; the transmitter emits a high-frequency sound. This travels and if it finds an object, it bounces back to the module. The receiver receives that reflected sound. There are also ultrasonic rangefinders that often cost more but have different ranges, from 1 mm to 5 meters of sensitivity, depending on your project needs. They are also about half the size of the HC-SR04.

Another distance sensor is the **Sharp distance sensor**, shown on the bottom left of *Figure 5.1* (black with two mounting holes). It comes in a variety of ranges and capabilities. It is an **infrared** (IR) analog sensor used for a variety of distances, so choose one that would suit your project. The sensor outputs the voltage corresponding to the distance detection so it can also be used as a proximity sensor.

For detecting motion, you could choose a passive infrared, **PIR sensor**, the large white and green sensor in *Figure 5.1*. It senses the change in IR radiation to detect motion up to about 7 meters. These sensors are typically used in rooms to trigger a light or a wildlife camera.

The **Maxbotix high-performance sonar** is shown on the furthermost right of *Figure 5.1*. These sensors are high-quality sensors that you may want to upgrade to when making a high-fidelity prototype. There is a large selection of sensors, and you can read more about the differences on their site, which also has a distributor list so you can purchase in your own country: `https://www.maxbotix.com/Ultrasonic_Sensors.html`.

In addition to these sensors, we've also already tried an **accelerometer** that was on the **Circuit Playground** board. We can buy an accelerometer component (shown in *Figure 5.1*, furthermost left) and use it with any of the circuit boards. Some of these boards also have a gyroscope function included. If you remember, we can collect information from three axes over time along *x*, *y*, and *z* for gravitational acceleration. We can then also collect *x*, *y*, and *z* for the rotational velocity.

Lastly, we can use a **tilt switch** as a sensor (not shown). This is a switch, as we can use it to close a circuit the same as when we used switches. However, using a tilt can be a way to detect, or sense, that there is movement in a wearable.

Force, flex, and stretch

These sensors come in a wide range; *Figure 5.2* has some of the range of sensors you can find. **Force sensing resistors (FSRs)** will allow you to collect any physical pressure or squeezing, or weight. These sensors measure changes in resistance. They might not be the most accurate or consistent, but they will work for prototyping and send us the data we need.

We looked at the flex sensor in detail in the previous chapter, so we won't add too much here, but they can be great to use placed on fingers for gloves to add interactivity to a wearable project:

Figure 5.2 – Force and flex varieties (left) and stretch (right)

If the sensor has a wide or large area, it will be good to a large general press or hold. If it's a smaller sensor, then it will be a more precise press or hold, with better accuracy.

Environmental sensors

There are many sensors that are great for collecting data, so let's look at some of them. We can collect temperature and humidity data from a **DHT11** sensor. These can detect temperature ranges around 10°C–40°C and humidity around 60% or below. There is also a temperature-only sensor that you can add to projects at a very low cost.

Other sensors range from gas, smoke, rain, water, light, sound, **ultraviolet** (**UV**), and GPS. We can also connect thermal cameras. *Figure 5.3* shows a range of sensors that can be added to our wearable designs.

Environmental sensors can bring the environment into our wearables for amazing interactions. Bringing the world around us into the wearables we make can be a great way to highlight social awareness issues:

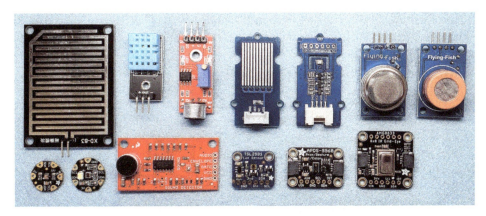

Figure 5.3 – Various environmental sensors

Environmental sensors can also help build our connection with the community, or care for ourselves and those around us. The UV sensor, for example, tells us or our families when we need to protect our skin, or sound sensors indicate there is an alarm for a hearing-impaired person. *Figure 5.4* (photo credit to Neosensory) shows Buzz haptic feedback for the hearing impaired. Buzz uses sensory substitution to feed sound information directly to the brain through the skin. It benefits those who were born deaf as well as those who were born with hearing but currently use hearing aids or other assistive listening devices. The website `https://neosensory.com/feelthesound/` provides more information about this wearable technology.

Figure 5.4 – Buzz haptic technology to feel the sound

We can use these sensors to bring a socially responsible design to our society. How will you use these sensors? What planning can you do for wearable projects? How will they fit into your wearable designs?

Communication and other inputs to try

There are other input devices we can use to add interactivity to our wearables. We can use **radio frequency identification** (**RFID**) boards (a reader) with corresponding tags, for example, to trigger events. We will look at this in more detail in *Chapter 13, Implementing the Best Solutions for Creating Your Own Wearable*, where we will use an RFID board in an off-body system. The most common of these boards is the RC522, which comes with corresponding tags:

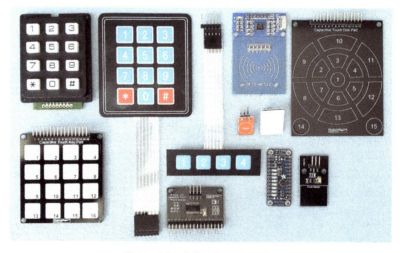

Figure 5.5 – Other inputs to try

RFID (shown in *Figure 5.5*, right side and blue) works by radio frequency and an antenna that generates an electromagnetic field. The tags we use are passive, they don't have a battery, but each one has a microchip that stores information as well as an antenna to receive and transmit a signal. When these tags are close enough to our reader, it gets enough power through the antenna to send the stored information to the reader.

Other ways we can have data input to our circuit boards are through **keypads** and **touchpads**. You can buy different types of touchpads (*Figure 5.5*); some are singular, with just one touch area, but others are like a number pad with many pads as inputs.

The variety of inputs that receive data that we interpret is huge. It's also fun to look through component websites and see what possibilities there are. Also, there are often new and exciting types of inputs to try. Once you understand the basics of hooking these components up, you can be more adventurous and try others.

Before that, there are a few other things to consider and know about, including datasheets, which we cover in the next section.

Other things to consider

When creating your wearables, there will be a variety of points to consider. Now that we have an overview of some input sensors, we can plan a little better:

- What information does your sensor provide?
- Consider the sensitivity. What range of values will you need?
- The output will be used in your program to respond in some way, so what information do you need?

Lastly, when using these sensors, or if you come across any interesting sensor you'd like to use, it's always a good idea to look at the sensor's datasheet.

What's a datasheet?

The **datasheet** will tell us all the information about a component. Any component, even the LEDs we used at the start of this wearable journey. One of the most important things we are looking for is the **operating voltage**. If we use too high a voltage, we risk burning out that component. If we use too low, it probably won't work. Also, it usually will show us the pin-out information. Importantly, we need to know where the power and ground connections are. *Figure 5.6* is part of a datasheet for an LED:

Absolute Maximum Ratings at Ta=25℃

Parameter	MAX.	Unit
Power Dissipation	100	mW
Peak Forward Current (≦1/10 Duty Cycle, 0.1ms Pulse Wide)	100	mA
Continuous Forward Current	20	mA
Derating Linear From 50°C	0.4	mA/°C
Reverse Voltage	5	V
Operating Temperature Range	-40°C to +80°C	
Storage Temperature Range	-40°C to +80°C	
Lead Soldering Temperature [4mm(.157") From Body]	260°C for 3 Seconds	

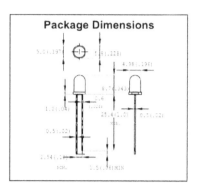

Figure 5.6 – Part of an LED Datasheet

Datasheets should be your first stop when using a new component. Often, when I order a new component, I'll download the datasheet at the same time. That way, when it arrives, I'll already have a lot of the information I need.

> **Remember**
>
> It's always good practice to look up a component's datasheet. The most important information to check is what the power requirements are, and how to hook up ground and power correctly!

Now that we've learned about some of the sensors available and the importance of checking a datasheet, let's have some fun and jump into some activities to practice using them!

Activity 5.1 – Distance and movement

Adding sensors for distance and movement to trigger an event is possible with a variety of sensors. The most common one is the ultrasonic distance sensor, HC-SR04. These are also low-cost. Adding one to a project is simple. *Figure 5.7* shows using this sensor with lighting and other outputs to create a physically distanced hat. The hat was from a charity shop.

Charity shops have lots of items we can use to upcycle, repurpose, and reuse to create prototypes for our wearables.

Hooking this sensor up to our board is easy to do, and it's a good sensor to start with because you get data through the serial monitor with only four pins to connect:

Figure 5.7 – Physically distanced hat using an ultrasonic distance sensor

You can start to consider the many ways we can integrate it into a wearable garment, and we will add one now to a circuit to see how to hook it up.

Using an ultrasonic distance sensor

There are only four pins that we need to connect. I'm using DuPont plug connectors on croc clips to easily connect the sensor in the mini breadboard and then clip it to a Gemma M0 board:

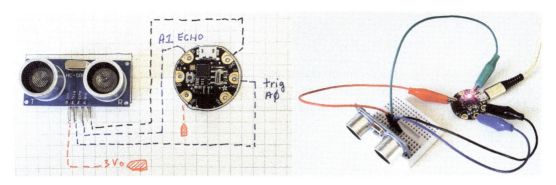

Figure 5.8 – Hooking up a distance sensor and Gemma M0

Figure 5.8 shows the pinout illustrated in my notebook (it is a good idea to keep a notebook with your connections, so you don't forget what you tried) and the hooked-up circuit.

I've also mapped it out in Fritzing, which is a software you can buy to map out your circuits. *Figure 5.9* shows this diagram:

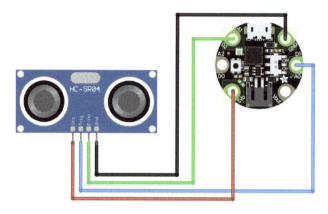

Figure 5.9 – Connecting your Gemma M0 and distance sensor

If you want to check your circuit is working, you can run sample code to see whether your sensor is receiving values. Let's look at the code now. First, we'll initialize our variables:

```
int trigPin = A0;
int echoPin = A1;
long duration, cm, inches;
```

The variables are our **trigger pin** for input, the **echo pin** for output, and then variables to hold the measurements: duration, centimeters (cm), and inches. The setup () function for this sketch is to initialize our serial monitor and define the input and output we are using:

```
void setup() {
Serial.begin (9600);
pinMode(trigPin, OUTPUT);
pinMode(echoPin, INPUT);
}
```

Let's look at the loop section of our code. Here, the sensor is triggered by a HIGH pulse for 10 or more microseconds. A short LOW pulse is given to make sure the HIGH pulse is clean:

```
void loop() {
digitalWrite(trigPin, LOW);
delayMicroseconds(5);
digitalWrite(trigPin, HIGH);
delayMicroseconds(10);
digitalWrite(trigPin, LOW);
```

The signal is read from the sensor. This is the duration of the time of **sending the ping** to **receiving the ping** from an echo off of an object in the path:

```
pinMode(echoPin, INPUT);
duration = pulseIn(echoPin, HIGH);
```

This time measurement is then converted into a distance. The value will be displayed on the serial monitor. For centimeters, we divide by 29.1 or multiply by 0.0343, and for inches, we divide by 74 or multiply by 0.0135:

```
cm = (duration/2) / 29.1;
inches = (duration/2) / 74;
```

Here is the code snippet for displaying the information to our Serial Monitor:

```
Serial.print(inches);
Serial.print("in, ");
Serial.print(cm);
Serial.print("cm");
Serial.println();
delay(250);
}
```

The completed code is accessible online: `https://github.com/cmoz/Ultimate/blob/main/C5/Activity5_1.ino`.

Test your circuit and code. If it's working, you can push this circuit further by thinking about what reaction you'll want your wearable to have when there is a certain distance (or distances) sensed.

Circuit not working?

If it isn't working, be sure you have correctly hooked up your ground and power pins. Also, check you've plugged your board into your computer – I've sometimes gotten excited and didn't have my board connected! If you're using crocodile clips, check whether they've slid or moved from where you placed them. They can often slide or move away or touch other pins, which will make it not work or be inaccurate. Did you check the ping and echo pins are correctly placed on the right pins?

It could be a code-related issue – make sure the pin numbers in the code match the pins that you have used for the echo and trigger pins.

Lastly, another example of using the ultrasonic distance sensor (shown in *Figure 5.10*) is a project my students made during a rapid prototyping session (photo credit: Yunwei Liu and Lexi Chen, pictured). The sensor is on the front of the mask so that as you approach someone, it will be triggered:

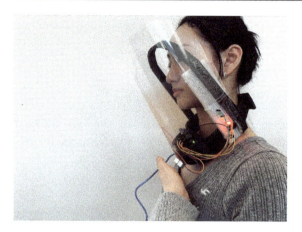

Figure 5.10 – Face shield with an ultrasonic distance sensor

This group chose the ultrasonic distance sensor and created a shield for protection from potentially dangerous situations. It's a rapid prototype that was made up in one afternoon using foam board and electronic components. A great way to test a wearable concept.

Another way we can detect motion in a wearable technology piece is by using a tilt switch as a sensor. Though not strictly a sensor, let's have a closer look at how to do it.

Activity 5.2 – Using a tilt, shock, or knock sensor

Shock and knock sensors give out a high signal when resting, and a low signal when they are moved or bumped. These sensors only have three pins to hook up: a power, ground, and sensor pin, which reads the values that the sensor is receiving.

Because these sensors only read a high or low value, what pin type do we need on our circuit board? We can use a digital pin. Analog or **pulse-width modulation (PWM)** isn't needed. *Figure 5.11* shows the hook-up for the sensor with a Gemma M0. I'll connect a sewable LED so we see the result of moving or knocking the circuit. If you look at the sensor, there are three pins. One pin has an *S* beside it, the pin on the left. This is a **signal pin**, and this will send the signal to our circuit board. The middle pin is **power**, so connect it to the 3Vo sew tab on the Gemma M0.

Lastly, the third pin, the pin on the right, has a "-" near it, and this is for **ground**. This will connect to the GND sew tab on the Gemma M0:

Figure 5.11 – Hooking up a KY-020 tilt sensor

The code can be used for either sensor (and for the tilt sensor). When the sensor is moved, the value reading for the sensor changes. This will turn on the light for half a second. Don't forget to modify the pin numbers to suit the board you're working with. In this example, I'm using the Gemma M0, and my LED is on pin 2, and the sensor pin is Gemma M0 pin 1:

```
int sensorPin = 1;
int ledPin = 2;

void setup() {
  pinMode(sensorPin, INPUT);
  pinMode(ledPin, OUTPUT);
}

void loop() {
  int read = digitalRead(sensorPin);
  if (read == LOW) {
    digitalWrite(ledPin, HIGH);
    delay(500);
  }
  else {
    digitalWrite(ledPin, LOW);
  }
}
```

We start the sketch by declaring our pin variables. In `setup()`, we define `pinMode` for these two pins; the sensor is an input because we want the values from our environment to be read, and the LED will output our light, so it is an output. In the `loop()` section, we declare an `int` variable called `read`, `int read = digitalRead(sensorPin);`, which will hold the value of the sensor pin.

The `if/else` statement tells the Gemma that if there is a low reading, turn on the light for half a second (*Figure 5.12*). But, if the reading is high, then we want the LED off:

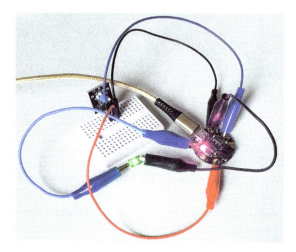

Figure 5.12 – The sewable LED is on when the sensor is moved

These sensors have different sensitivities, and as with all these sensors, it's best to try them and work through how they work best in your own projects. Try different orientations and placements to get the most effective results. The completed code is available here: `https://github.com/cmoz/Ultimate/blob/main/C5/Activity5_2.ino`.

Now, let's move on to using force, flex, and stretch sensors. These are used often in sports wearables, but we can use them for many fun, wearable garments. The next activity will help us to understand them a little more and tell us how to hook them up.

Activity 5.3 – Force, flex, and stretch

We made our own flex sensor previously in *Chapter 4, Implementing Arduino Code Using Gemma M0 and Circuit Playground*, so we won't explore that in detail here. However, we didn't explore the stretch sensor. The **stretch sensor** works the same way as the other flex sensors and is usually made from a conductive rubber cord. It has a relaxed state, and when you pull on it, the resistance increases. It measures the stretch, displacement, and force. These sensors come in different lengths with different resistance values so you will need to measure the sensor you have with your multimeter.

Let's measure your stretch sensor.

Holding the sensor ends, place the ground probe on one end and the voltage or power probe of your multimeter on the other. I'm using croc clips to hold the sensor. Use the resistance setting on the multimeter and gently stretch the sensor.

What happens to the value? Do you notice any changes? The value should be changing (see *Figure 5.13*). As you can see in the photos, I have an initial reading of 20.08 Ohms that moves to 27.91 when stretched. You might want to register your lowest reading (at rest) and a new reading when it is stretched. Don't overstretch your sensor!

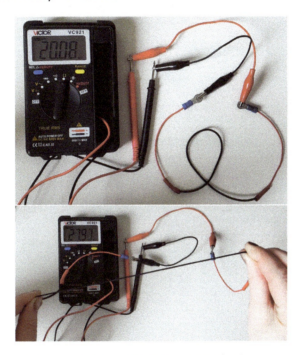

Figure 5.13 – Taking multimeter readings for the sensor

The stretch sensor will connect to the circuit the same way we connected our flex sensor in *Chapter 4, Implementing Arduino code Using Gemma M0 and Circuit Playground*. The stretch sensor has two ends, so one end will be connected to power, and the other end will be connected to a 10K resistor to ground, and that same side will also be connected to an analog pin. On the Gemma M0, I'll be using pin A0.

The circuit prototype with croc clips is shown in *Figure 5.14*. If it is connected correctly, we will see the readings from the sensor in the serial monitor when we run the Arduino code:

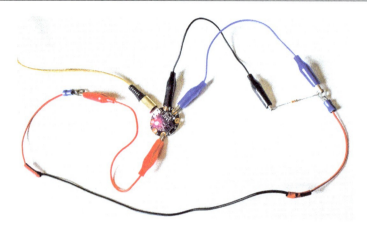

Figure 5.14 – The connected circuit with croc clips

The following code can be used to check whether the circuit is working and we are receiving values. We start the code by defining our resistor value (we know this is 10K), and then we define the pin number.

The pin is what we take the analog readings from, which is A0. Your pin may be different if you are using a different board, so don't forget to change this value. Then, we define setup(), which will only require initializing the serial monitor:

```
#define MYRESISTOR 10000
#define STRETCHPIN A0

void setup(void) {
  Serial.begin(9600);
}
```

The loop() function is where our code takes place to display the reading we get from the sensor in the serial monitor. First, we define a float variable called float reading;, which will hold the value. Then, a reading is taken from the analog pin we defined for our sensor:

```
void loop(void) {
  float reading;
  reading = analogRead(STRETCHPIN);
```

The rest of our code will convert the reading and display it in the serial monitor:

```
  reading = (1023 / reading)  - 1;
  reading = MYRESISTOR / reading;
  Serial.print("Resistance ");
```

```
    Serial.println(reading);

    delay(200);
}
```

Upload your code to the board. Don't forget to always choose your board and port from the `Tools` menu or your code won't upload. Open the serial monitor once the code has finished uploading and check that the values change when you stretch the sensor.

My circuit has a base level of around 5000 for the reading. When I pull the stretch sensor, it reduces to various values from 2800 onward. Take the readings from your sensor (they will be different from mine), based on the length and so on, and we can add the following code to provide the interactive or reactive element to the circuit.

Add this next block of code after `Serial.println(reading);` and before `delay(200);`:

```
if (reading > 4700) {
    Serial.println(" No stretch");
    } else if (reading < 4000) {
        Serial.println(" stretch");
    } else {
        Serial.println(" relaxed");
}
```

Then, you should still have the `delay(200);` code after that block:

```
delay(200);
}
```

This block of code uses the reading value in an `if` statement, `if (reading > 4700)`, which means that if the reading is greater than 4700 (near the value of our relaxed sensor), then do something. In this example, it prints to the screen, but you can connect LEDs or other outputs for different effects. The completed code can be found here: `https://github.com/cmoz/Ultimate/blob/main/C5/Activity5_3.ino`

Now that you have a working prototype of the circuit, take some time to think about how you might use it. Should we add it to a small bag, for example, on the handle? As the weight of the bag increases, maybe a light shows red to indicate that it is heavy.

Or, maybe we use this sensor on our wrist and if there is little movement, we get a warning light or sound to remind us to move every 15 minutes or so if we are at our desk.

What ideas can you think of for the uses of this sensor? What part of the body do you think it would be most suitable for? Once you've had a chance to think about this sensor and maybe plan out a circuit, let's look at some of the environmental sensors.

Activity 5.4 – Environmental sensors

The most common and obvious environmental sensor is probably the DHT11 temperature and humidity sensor. There are numerous tutorials for this sensor online, so I'd like us to use a different environmental sensor for this activity.

Using a sound sensor

Sound is an interesting sensor to use. The two most common sensors are KY-038 and LM393. We can use them to directly trigger an event by making the noise ourselves, or we can use the noise in the environment around us to trigger an event.

There are only three pins we need to connect, a ground pin, a power pin, and one pin for data (this is marked *D0* if you're using the four-pin sound sensor). We will connect it to a Gemma M0 on pin 0:

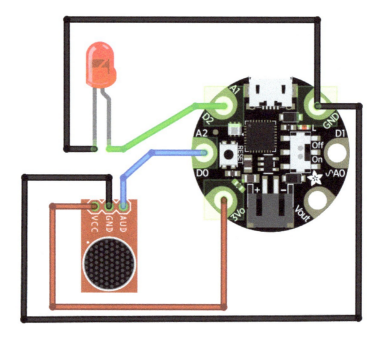

Figure 5.15 – The circuit

Let's hook up the sound sensor. See *Figure 5.15* and *Figure 5.16* for the circuit connection. Using your croc clips, attach the sensor to the Gemma M0. I've also connected an LED (filament style) to pin 2:

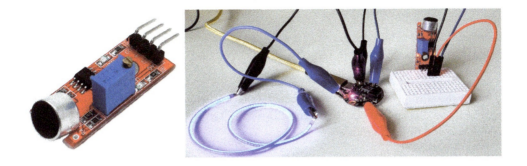

Figure 5.16 – Sound sensor hookup

Now that you've connected your sensor, let's write and upload the code. We start by defining the pin that our sound sensor is connected to. Then, create a variable to store the time when the last event happened:

```
#define sensorPin 0
unsigned long lastEvent = 0;
int ledPin = 2;
```

The setup() function is where we set the sensor pin as an input, and we initialize our serial monitor as we have done previously:

```
void setup() {
        pinMode(sensorPin, INPUT);
        Serial.begin(9600);
}
```

In the loop() function, we read the sound sensor pin. We then have an if statement that is testing whether the pin is pulled low. If it is, it executes the code in the parentheses:

```
void loop() {
  int sensorData = digitalRead(sensorPin);
  if (sensorData == LOW) {
    if (millis() - lastEvent > 25) {
      Serial.println("Clap detected!");
    }
    lastEvent = millis();
  }
}
```

If enough time has passed (in this case, 25 ms), it means a clap is detected. The code then remembers when the last event happened. In this example, it will write to our serial monitor when a clap is detected. If we wanted it to do something else in response to the clap sound, where would we write the code?

Did you say after the `Serial.println("Clap detected!");` line? That's right. After this line, and before the closing curly bracket, we would write any behavior we wanted this circuit to do. We've used LEDs before, and I'd like to use an LED filament to light up when there is a clap sound. What do we do to add this to our code?

1.   Define the LED pin number at the start of the code:

     ```
     int ledPin = 2;
     ```

2.   In `setup()`, we set the LED pin as an output:

     ```
     pinMode (ledPin, OUTPUT);
     ```

3.   Lastly, we want the LEDs to light up, so we will set the LED pin to `HIGH`. We only want it to flash with the clap, so we'll delay it for less than a second, and then turn it off again:

     ```
     digitalWrite(ledPin,HIGH);
     delay(200);
     digitalWrite(ledPin, LOW);
     ```

If your sensor isn't registering the claps very well, turn the small dial on the sensor. This alters a potentiometer in the sensor to increase or decrease the sensitivity.

Don't forget that the sensor does have a limited range too, so don't be too far away from the sensor when you clap or make noise. The completed code is available here: `https://github.com/cmoz/Ultimate/blob/main/C5/Activity5_4.ino`.

Test that your circuit works. Then, you can plan where you want to put it or how you want to develop it. I'm going to sew mine onto some stiff needlework fabric (16-count Aida) so it can pop into a shirt pocket.

Figure 5.17 shows the sensor, which is visible and facing up so it can sense the sound correctly. When you clap, it lights up the LEDs. The LEDs are diffused slightly from the shirt fabric as it is quite thick. This should be a consideration in your own designs:

Figure 5.17 – Shirt pocket clap-o-meter

Using environmental and other sensors not only adds interest to your wearable design but there can be real benefits of applications for people who use them. Let's look at some of the research and development where sensors are used. This can help provide context for the real-world application of wearables that will solidify our understanding of their usage.

Examples of sensors used in the field of wearables.

Applications for using sensors span many fields, from healthcare, positive mental health, visual or hearing impairment, security, sport, and fashion.

There are many documented use cases for the varied application of sensors. Perspiration analysis (*Gao W., Emaminejad S. et. al., 2014*), wearable sensor arrays for recording muscle activity (*Supuk, T., Skelin, A., Cic, M., 2014*), wireless systems for neonatal care that have "skin-like" modules (*Chung H., Hoon Kim B., et al., 2019*), and self-powering sensing systems for wearables (*Lou Z., Wang L., Shen G., 2017*).

One very innovative wearable I came across was an in-body system, TONG. It is a device that uses tongue movement to control a computer (*Figure 5.18*):

Figure 5.18 – photo credit: Dorothee Clasen, TONG, a masterthesis project

Described as an intra-oral wearable, it's placed inside the mouth. You move a small magnetic element back and forward with your tongue. This generates an input, then a Wi-Fi module behind the user's ear transfers the information to other connected devices, such as a computer.

Emotional clothing (*Figure 5.19*) is a focus of *Iga Węglińska*, who says, "*By interacting with the pieces, the wearer can not only be informed about their own body changes, but they can help us to focus more about the intimate relation with clothing, control the body reactions, or even set goals to achieve by playing with smart materials reactions like color changes or movement*":

Figure 5.19 – Iga Węglińska's emotional clothing

These sensors and the artifacts created merge technology, fashion, and physical design. This offers intelligent clothing and a unique experience. *Figure 5.19* shows the garments with the sensors in.

Figure 5.20 – Sensors for measuring heart rate and temperature

Węglińska explores the relationship of these sensors to human skin to emphasize the intimate relationship that these sensors have (*Figure 5.20*), through being placed directly on the body. Wearables that are on the skin offer another unique way of interacting with us.

Northwestern University has created many sensors that are both functional for health purposes, and beautiful (*Figure 5.21*). They describe this integration in their temporary tattoo sensor as "*bio-integrated engineering and interconnected technology will provide continuous measurement of electrolyte loss, non-intrusive screening for disease, and in the future could go inside our bodies to correct an irregular heartbeat, improve the function of our brain, and achieve better control of our health.*"

This is an example of a next-generation wearable.

Created by the Rogers Lab in Northwestern's McCormick School of Engineering, it is soft and flexible wearable technology. This device is placed on the skin to capture and analyze the chemistry of sweat:

Figure 5.21 – Photo credit, John A. Rogers/Northwestern University

It is similar to a temporary tattoo. This provides a snapshot of the wearer's health. For more information, go to their website (`https://news.northwestern.edu/stories/2017/october/biointegrated-technology/`), which has details about other sensors they are creating.

We can experiment a little with these types of sensors, too. Integrating kinesiology tape (muscle aid tape) is a potential way to make an on-skin wearable (*Figure 5.22*). Layering up this tape with conductive fabric is a cheap way to make a thin conductive trace that you can attach to the body. It will stay on the body for up to five days and is water-resistant:

Figure 5.22 – Kinesiology tape (black), and conductive material (silver)

You can make cuts into the conductive fabric to give it more flex. This is something that you'll want to play around with to make it work well for your circuit. *Figure 5.23* shows this placement on the finger, with a bend:

Figure 5.23 – Flexing the circuit

This method is a temporary solution, but it's an interesting way to create an on-body system for rapid prototyping. You might want to have the conductive fabric exposed so you can easily connect other components to it. *Figure 5.24* is an example of using Shieldex© Köln, a copper-plated fabric:

Figure 5.24 – Copper-plated fabric for conductivity

Using muscle tape in this way allows great flexibility. We can see the natural twist of a forearm works easily with this form. The copper fabric is also available as tape; you can purchase the tape and other conductive fabrics from `https://www.hitek-ltd.co.uk/product-page/copper-tape`. These copper traces are just an example, but you can solder to the copper beforehand and attach your wires or LEDs and then secure it with this tape. **Always check for allergies** when using a metal next to the skin!

Other research I've seen includes smart knee braces for knee joint issues and a wearable sensor to help with independent living for older adults. This includes fall detection wearable sensors and sensors for recognizing teeth brushing for "elder care." Research indicates that failing to regularly brush teeth has serious health consequences, and this problem could potentially be addressed with a wrist-mounted wearable.

Considering the shaping and maneuvers we do every day with our bodies, we need to be aware of considerations when choosing sensors to use. The next section will discuss exactly that and will help guide you to making your own decisions for your wearable circuits.

Activity 5.5 – Choosing sensors

There are several factors to consider when choosing what sensor to use in your wearable.

Over time, learning to put a sensor in the right context is important because location and orientation will alter its performance. **Context** includes location, range, and the orientation of the placement. For example, facing our UV sensor upward toward the sky makes a big difference. Also, limiting other external factors that may affect its performance will make a difference.

What are you sensing? Is it a movement? Is it sensing something the wearer does or interacts with? Is it an external factor away from the wearer but the circuit reacts in a way to it? This will make a difference in the placement of the device. Does it need to be on the body, or can it be an off-body item?

Time is important. How long will they be wearing the device? If it is worn for an extended time, do you need to find a smaller, more discreet sensor or can you embed it into an item of jewelry or an accessory that they would want to wear for a long time? Is it something they wear when they go shopping or will they use it over an entire weekend? Can they get it wet, or does it need to be removed?

Which part of the body are you designing it for? The **location** is important. Be aware of the curves, or the areas where it will be comfortable. If it's possible, position sensors where the body doesn't twist or bend (unless it's a flex sensor). Finding a flatter area of the body can make it a lot easier to place a sensor.

Be aware of the **weight** that a sensor or straps and similar will have. Are the people using your wearable happy to have the extra weight? If so, for how long? It's a good idea to make a weighted item that you can then ask some people to wear over time to give you feedback.

Make sure the **placement** won't restrict the wearer's natural movement. If they can't go about their typical day, then they just won't use it. Also, be sure it isn't too loose. It can be very annoying for someone to have to keep fixing a strap or placement. If it's too loose or needs to be in a position where size can vary, be sure to have a strap that can be easily adjusted.

Will your sensor control something? What is the **purpose**? If it does control something, how will that affect the placement? Does the sensor need to be near the other circuit elements?

Lastly, **cost** is always a consideration. Can you start with a generic cheap sensor? Then, if your prototype is working and you're after more accuracy or durability, upgrade the sensor.

To summarize, when using the many sensors available, it's always worth creating and testing a prototype. Once you have your concept working, then look around for a possible sensor to swap out if you have a particular need for a smaller area or more accuracy.

Consider the following:

- What are you sensing?
- How long will you be wearing it?
- Where on the body is it for? Can you find a flat area?

- What is the weight of the circuit?

- Does it restrict movement? Is it too loose?

- Will it control something?

- How much does it cost?

Don't forget, if you just can't find that perfect sensor, you can think about making it. We'll look at that in more detail using conductive textiles as sensors, but first, we need to learn more about protocols we can use to connect sensors and about installing and using libraries.

Using libraries

We can connect sensors to our Arduino-based microcontroller boards using the I²C and SPI protocols. We can also make use of the sensors and components quicker and easier using a library. Let's take a closer look at these areas now. We'll start with libraries.

How do we use a library?

You will use the **Library Manager** a lot when you're making your wearables. Libraries provide your sketches with extra functionality. What are libraries? The Arduino website says, "*Libraries are a collection of code that makes it easy for you to connect to a sensor, display, module, etc. There are hundreds of additional libraries available on the Internet for download.*"

They can be written by anyone, and you can create your own and share it. When I last checked, there were over 4,000 libraries! Libraries are used in many of the sketches we write in the Arduino IDE. We can easily install them and, typically, they include sample code to help us get our sensors working quickly. This is a great way to test your circuit. Let's install a library now.

Activity 5.6 – installing a library – UV sensor

Which library should we install? Because this chapter is all about inputs, let's use the UV sensor from the environmental sensors. Earlier, we saw the smallest wearable, which consisted of a UV nail sensor. Let's use the Flora sewable UV sensor in a wearable to see how it works.

The library for this sensor is `Adafruit_SI1145`, and this is declared at the start of our code. When you find sketches online or in books, look at the first one or two lines of the code. It will show you what libraries are needed for the code to work (or execute). If you don't have the library installed, you'll get error messages, as shown in *Figure 5.25,* showing the output window:

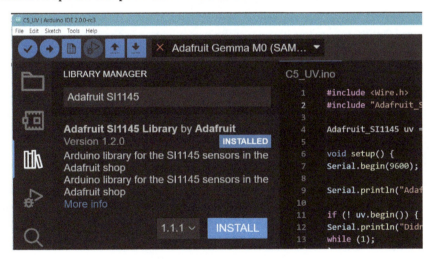

Figure 5.25 – Error message if the library isn't installed

Looking at the code for the UV sensor, we see the first two lines' reference libraries, one called Wire, and one called Adafruit_SI1145:

```
#include <Wire.h>
#include "Adafruit_SI1145.h"
```

The Library Manager in the new version of Arduino is very easy to access. It is the third icon down on the left side menu, and it looks like books. This is where you can access the libraries (*Figure 5.26*). Clicking that icon opens a side panel and a search bar:

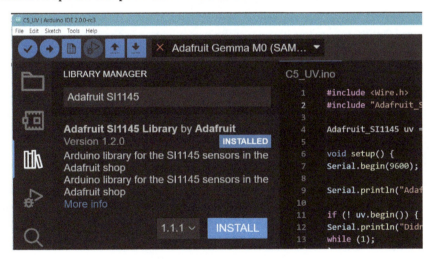

Figure 5.26 – Searching for the library

Let's type Adafruit_SI1145 in the search bar because this is the library we want to install. Once you've searched and it's there, click the **INSTALL** button. There will be a notification (*Figure 5.27*) saying that it's successfully installed:

Figure 5.27 – Success notification

Now that the library has been installed, if you navigate to **File menu** | **Examples** | **Adafruit SI1145 Library**, you'll see the example code file (*Figure 5.28*). Open this code and this is what we'll use to test our circuit!

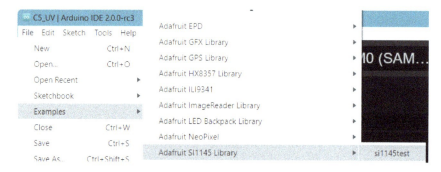

Figure 5.28 – Accessing the sample code

You'll have noticed that there were two libraries at the start of our code, the UV library and one called `Wire`. The `Wire` library is one of several standard libraries that are part of the core distribution with the Arduino IDE. This means we don't have to install it, as it's already there!

Test your code by connecting your board with the UV sensor. The sewable UV sensor (as part of the Flora range) is a sensor from SiLabs that uses a calibrated light-sensing algorithm to calculate the UV index. This is done through calculations based on visible and IR light from the sun. It doesn't sense the actual UV as such. The digital sensor works over I²C, which we will look at closer in the next section, but for now, let's connect it to the Gemma M0 board.

Although we'll connect it to a Gemma M0 board to see the connections (*Figure 5.29*), you may want to move it to a Circuit Playground or other board to expand its capabilities. For example, modify code so that the NeoPixels on the Circuit Playground will change colors based on the UV reading. You can then incorporate the board and sensor into a hat, jacket, purse, or another item.

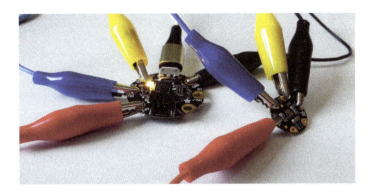

Figure 5.29 – UV sensor and Gemma M0

Making the connections to the Gemma M0 board with croc clips is quick. Start with your board unplugged from the computer.

To connect the sewable UV sensor, make the following connections:

- Connect the UV sensor **3V** pin to the Gemma M0 **3Vo** pin.
- Connect the UV sensor **gnd** pin to the Gemma M0 **GND** pin.
- Connect the UV sensor **SCL** pin to the Gemma M0 **A1/D2** pin.
- Connect the UV sensor **SDA** pin to the Gemma M0 **A2/D0** pin.

It is important to note that the sensor needs to face the sky, so plan to sew it in a place where it can be exposed to the sun. If you're using a handbag, then it might be good to sew it to the top strap area that will go over your shoulder. Remember though, you'll need to have long enough wires to connect the circuit up to the board you are using, too.

The data from the sensor will be like mine (shown in *Figure 5.30*), which is the output on the serial monitor:

Figure 5.30 – Serial monitor output

The UV levels are measured in ratings. From https://www.epa.gov/sunsafety, we learn that a UV index reading of 0-2 means low danger from the sun's UV rays for the average person. A reading of 3-5 means a moderate risk of harm from unprotected sun exposure. A reading of 6-7 means a high risk of harm from unprotected sun exposure. Protection against skin and eye damage is needed. The readings indoors will likely be under 1, so you'll need to take your sensor outside to get other readings.

Now that we know how to install libraries, we can install them for other components we will add to our wearables. Just refer to this section if you forget. This UV circuit used pins that we called I²C, which is a communication protocol.

Let's move on to understanding more about protocols.

Understanding the I²C and SPI protocols

Connecting our sensors and devices is mostly done using two different **protocols**. Some devices can use both, offering you the choice. First, let's learn about **I²C**.

What is I²C?

I²C (also written as **I2C** and **IIC**) is an acronym for **Inter-Integrated Circuit**. It is a two-wire serial communication protocol (*Figure 5.31*), using **serial data** (**SDA**), and **serial clock** (**SCL**) lines. It is for communicating with sensors and devices. You can tell whether the sensor or device uses the I²C protocol because it has two pins specifically for **data** and **clock**. It uses these two connections for transmitting and receiving data. The data communicated is transferred bit by bit through the SDA line.

The I²C protocol is synchronous, meaning that the output of bits is synchronized by a shared clock signal. This is shared with a **microcontroller** and **sensor** (previously called master and slave). You will still come across these terms, which are being phased out. We can use the terms *microcontroller* and *sensor* in their place, for example. The clock signal is handled by a controller. This serial communication bus was invented in 1982 by Philips Semiconductors:

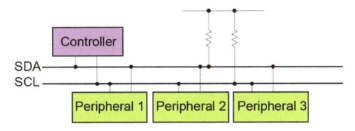

Figure 5.31 – The I²C protocol

The main advantage of using I²C is that it only needs two wires – even if you have many devices – so it is easy and quick to hook up. All the data is passed across the two wires, to and from the controller and peripherals. Each peripheral device has an address, which identifies it so the controller device can send data.

The two wires have specific purposes:

- The **SDA** wire is used for sending the actual data back and forth between the controller and peripheral devices.

- The **SCL** wire carries the clock signal for communication timing.

We saw earlier that the UV sketch used a `Wire` library. This library has I²C functions to make it easier for us to program. To use the functions in the `Wire` library, we add it to our sketch, which is done with `#include <Wire.h>`.

Once we have the library added, we need to add the devices to the I²C bus. If you have more than one device, it's helpful to check the addresses of your devices.

You can search online for a sample code. I've used the following code in the past, which displays the address of your devices in the serial monitor (`https://create.arduino.cc/projecthub/abdularbi17/how-to-scan-i2c-address-in-arduino-eaadda`):

Figure 5.32 – Scanning for I²C devices

This code will give you the output as shown in *Figure 5.32*, so you can note the address of your device. Usually, you'll only need to do this if you are connecting to more than one I²C device.

To connect an I²C device, follow these steps:

1. When connecting any device using the I²C protocol, look for the SDA/SCL pins on the device you want to connect.

2. Find out what the SDA/SCL pins on the circuit board you are using are; some boards have SDA/SCL marked near the pins.

3. Connect the SDA on the device to the SDA on the board.

4. Connect the SCL on the device to the SCL on the board.

An overview of this protocol is that we are using an I²C bus that has connected SCL and SDA lines. The SCL is the clock line that synchronizes the data, and the SDA is the data line. We can connect many devices on the SDA and SCL lines; we just need to check their addresses so the data goes to/from the right device.

Now, let's look at the SPI protocol and then compare the two.

What do we use SPI for?

Serial Peripheral Interface (**SPI**) is a four-wire protocol, and the SPI bus allows for duplex communication to and from the primary device simultaneously (*Figure 5.33*). However, we need a larger number of pins to use an SPI device. It uses a clock and data line, and a select line that we choose so we can identify the device we are trying to control. The SPI interface was designed by Motorola in 1979:

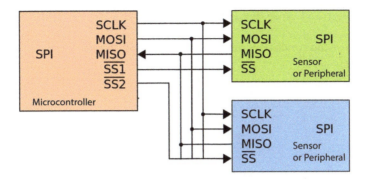

Figure 5.33 – The SPI protocol

Pin names for devices using SPI will vary. You will see different terms being phased out by many manufacturers. The protocol naming convention and depreciated names include MOSI, MISO, and SS (`https://www.oshwa.org/a-resolution-to-redefine-spi-signal-names`). You can read more about this change online. Currently used conventions are MISO and MOSI, which is for microcontroller in and sensor out, and microcontroller out and sensor in.

The simplest way to use the SPI protocol is with the SPI library. To use the library, we define the pins in our code, but we will be looking at using a **Radio Frequency Identification** (**RFID**) reader example later in the book.

The advantages of using the I²C protocol are that you can have a longer distance communication than with SPI, each device is independently addressable, and I²C only requires two lines. The disadvantages are that it draws more power, there is typically a limit of around 12 devices, and it can get overly complicated and hang. The SPI protocol is better for high-speed communication. It is also low-power but has a shorter range so components can't be too far away.

Now that we understand a little more about these communication protocols, let's use some conductive material to make our own sensor and use it with the Circuit Playground board. The code we'll use has both protocol libraries and a new library we'll have to install. Let's get started!

Using conductive materials as sensors

By using conductive materials, fabrics, tapes, and other various items, we can create our own sensors. In the previous chapter, we used a zipper as a switch, but we can adapt it to alert us if a zipper is opened or closed, for example. We might have it on a backpack, and if the wearer hasn't closed the zipper, we can alert them.

Activity 5.7 – Sound and touch

Another way we can use the conductive materials is to sense our touch. We're going to use touch to create a musical circuit:

Figure 5.34 – Conductive tape as a touch sensor

The Circuit Playground Classic board has eight hardware touch inputs. We can use these to sense our touch as a sensor input. Using conductive fabric, we can cut to shape the sensor we want and then attach it to the board.

To make this, you'll need conductive material, a Circuit Playground Classic board, and conductive thread to sew it together. You can use the bolt-on kit if you don't want to sew the fabric, or you can use conductive tape. I used conductive nylon tape (*Figure 5.34*) for an LED circuit before and it works great for this circuit too.

The code begins with defining a library; the `Adafruit_CircuitPlayground` library gives us access to a lot of functions to make our wearables interactive. To initialize the library with the board, we use `CircuitPlayground.begin();` in our `setup()` function. We also initialized a pixel number and allocated 10 `capsense` positions. This is the hardware on the board that will react to our touch:

```
#include <Adafruit_CircuitPlayground.h>

uint8_t pixeln = 0;
int capsense[10];

void setup() {
   CircuitPlayground.begin();
}
```

The void() loop looks for any touches on the capacitive pins, and if there is a touch, we will play a frequency on the piezo. I've added code to display a lit NeoPixel when we tap one of the sensors. This will light up just enough to see it and then turn off again:

```
void loop() {
    capsense[0] = CircuitPlayground.readCap(3);
    capsense[1] = CircuitPlayground.readCap(2);
    capsense[2] = CircuitPlayground.readCap(0);
    capsense[3] = CircuitPlayground.readCap(1);
    capsense[4] = CircuitPlayground.readCap(12);
    capsense[5] = CircuitPlayground.readCap(6);
    capsense[6] = CircuitPlayground.readCap(9);
    capsense[7] = CircuitPlayground.readCap(10);
```

After taking readings for touch, we make sure the frequency is at 0; this is the sound that will be emitted, which is nothing.

There are if statements to determine which cap has been touched. Each one then has its own frequency attributed to it. This will give it its own distinct sound:

```
int frequency = 0;
if (capsense[0] > 100) {
  frequency = 523;
  CircuitPlayground.setPixelColor(0,75,0,130);
} else if (capsense[1] > 100) {
  frequency = 587;
  CircuitPlayground.setPixelColor(1, 0,0,255);
} else if (capsense[2] > 100) {
```

The code continues for all the capsense conditions. Lastly, we set a color for the corresponding NeoPixel. This is done with CircuitPlayground.setPixelColor(0,75,0,130);. The first number refers to the pin that will be affected, and the three following numbers are corresponding **red, green, and blue (RGB)** values. You can look up RGB values online to change the colors that are displayed.

We complete the code with a short delay() and to play the tone briefly:

```
delay(10);
CircuitPlayground.clearPixels();
CircuitPlayground.playTone(frequency, 200);
}
```

The completed code is available here: `https://github.com/cmoz/Ultimate/blob/main/C5/Activity5_6.ino`.

I've chosen a variety of RGB colors to display, but you might want the same color to display every time, or to have no color. Adapt your code so it suits your purpose. This circuit can now be integrated into your wearable design.

Activity 5.8 – Using alternative sensors

If we want to use other circuit boards to register a touch, and if we want to use almost any material to register our touch, there is a great library that we can install. The `ADCTouch` library (*Figure 5.35*) will allow any analog pin on your board to register your touch:

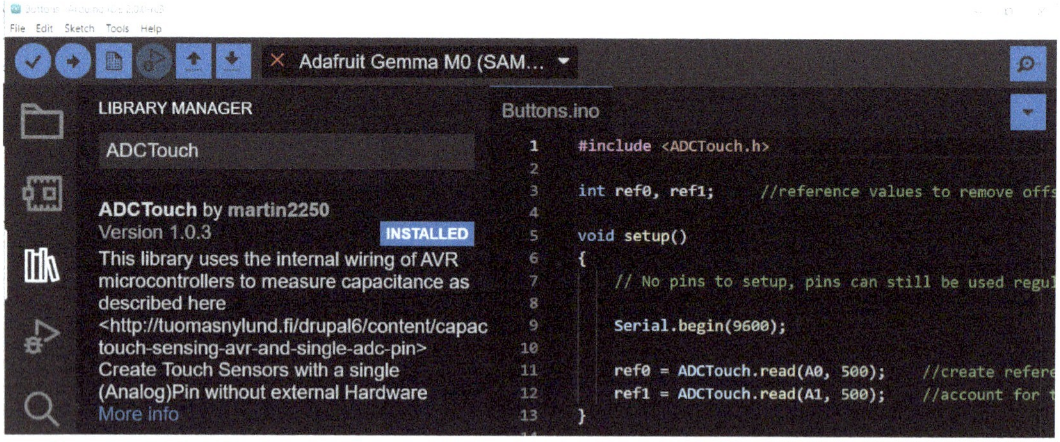

Figure 5.35 – The ADCTouch library

Using this library, you can add touch capabilities to a lot of interesting and unusual items! During a workshop, Dr. Andrew Quitmeyer (of `https://www.dinalab.net/`) demonstrated using nature as a sensing device. Students first collected items from nature. They then used rapid prototyping techniques, 3D printer pens, glue, threads, and similar to create designs. The exercise is for exploring and experimenting, learning about using tools, and gaining confidence in prototyping. After they collected these items, they started making garments, as shown in *Figure 5.36*.

Using alternative materials is an exercise you should try yourself. It really pushes you to learn how you can create a wearable using alternative items, and no one else will have the same design. It can really help if you are struggling for solutions or want to try something different:

Figure 5.36 – Nature on garments

Putting it all together, once the designs were made, they installed the ADCTouch library, chose some analog pins on a circuit board, and connected a croc clip to the items from nature.

The twigs, flowers, and other forestry items all became sensors. To see the sensor activity, they opened the serial plotter in the Arduino IDE. You can see that when the sensor is touched, there is a spike in the values. This works on capacitance, so you might want to use your multimeter first to check the items you are using. In general, any plants or materials with **water content** work well. A dead dry twig will not work.

The basic hookup is shown in *Figure 5.37*, and consists of the sensing pin having a croc clip attached to it and then attaching the other end of the croc clip to the item of nature you want to have touch capability.

This is the simplest circuit you will make! Yes, it really is just one wire to pin A7 (on the Flora board)!

Figure 5.37 – Hookup for touch sense

Now that you've seen the hookup, which is a simple one-croc setup, open the example file. Navigate to **File | Examples | ADCTouch | Buttons**. Load this sketch.

This code uses default pins A0 and A1 as touch sensing pins. Hook up a board you want to use: for example, on the Flora, we can choose digital pins D9/A9, D10/A10, and D6/A7:

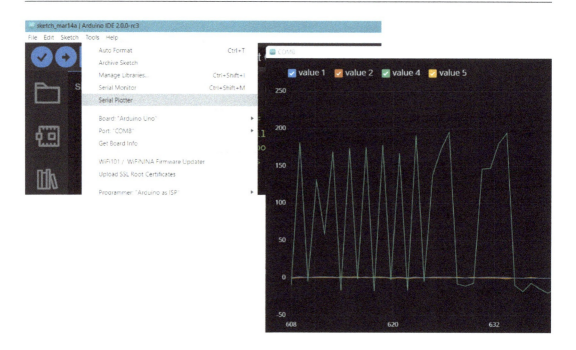

Figure 5.38 – Serial Plotter in Arduino IDE

Plug your board in and after uploading the code and connecting the croc clip to the item collected in nature you want as a sensor, open the serial plotter. This is in the **Tools** menu. It should look like mine in *Figure 5.38* with spikes and jumps when the item is touched. *Don't forget to select your board and port menu, especially if you are changing boards like I am.*

> **Important – Default Sensor Reading**
>
> When you load the code, it takes an initial reading of the sensor at rest. This should register at 0, then when you touch the sensor, it registers high above the 0 line. Be sure to reset your board and wait a second or two for the initial reading value to register.

To add interactivity to this wearable, you could hook up a servo motor, for example. In the next chapter, we will look more closely at outputs such as servo motors, but for now, my completed circuit is shown in *Figure 5.39* and there is a diagram of it in *Figure 5.40* if you do want to try it now:

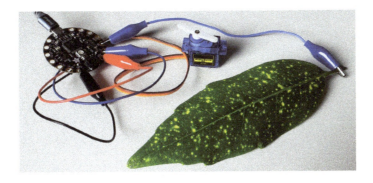

Figure 5.39 – Servo hooked up with a leaf as a sensor

When you touch the leaf, the servo motor moves. You can attach anything you like to the servo to create movement. Maybe you put a flower on it, or another leaf is hiding the servo beneath – when someone touches the leaf, another leaf moves. Have fun with this!

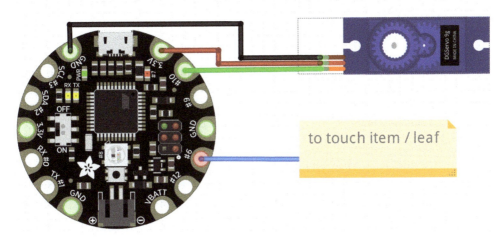

Figure 5.40 – A servo and touch connection with Flora

Here is the last example of a garment being "hacked" by nature. The items are collected from nature and are attached to clothing with a 3D pen (using TPU, a pliable printing plastic filament). Then, an Arduino-based board is attached and can be hidden. You'll want to have some battery packs nearby to power these while you're testing and playing with them.

These are rapid prototypes that took an afternoon to make. The photo in *Figure 5.41* shows the items in use with moving parts and lights that flash:

Figure 5.41 – Prototypes in progress, and with wearable electronics

To program the added servo, we can use code that is a modification from the ADCTouch library, and sample button code provided by *Martin2250* (https://github.com/martin2250/ADCTouch). You'll notice we're using that library (ADCTouch) and a library (Servo) to control our servo. This is also a built-in library so you shouldn't need to install it.

There are two values you might need to change in this code and the sample button code. First, val0high = 350; should be changed to the highest value that your sensor puts out on the serial monitor when it is touched. So, run the code, open the monitor, wait for it to register the sensor (a few seconds), and then touch the sensor. Note the highest number and use that value. For the leaf I used, it was 350:

```
#include "ADCTouch.h"
#include <Servo.h>

Servo myservo;

int ref0;
int touchPin1 = A7;
int val0constrained = 0;
int val0high = 350;
```

```
int val0low = 0;
int threshold = 10;
int pos = 0;

void setup()
{
    Serial.begin(9600);
    myservo.attach(12);
    ref0 = ADCTouch.read(touchPin1, 500);
}

void loop()
{
    int value0 = ADCTouch.read(touchPin1);
    value0 -= ref0;
    Serial.println(value0);

    myservo.write(0);
    if (value0 > threshold) {
        myservo.write(180);
    }
delay(100);
}
```

Secondly, `threshold = 10;` can be modified. This is the number that your sensor must sense above for it to trigger a reaction. If your sensor is jumping a little around the lower numbers, you might want to make this a little higher value. However, if your sensor is consistently at 0 when it is waiting for touch, then you can safely lower this if you want to. Think of this value as the sensitivity. The completed code is available here: `https://github.com/cmoz/Ultimate/blob/main/C5/Activity5_7.ino`.

Using nature as a sensor in our wearable is so much fun! I hope you'll be inspired to try it because it's a great way to free up your thinking. We started with using conductive material to create touch with the Circuit Playground, and now we're using nature to create elaborate garments. The wearable journey can take you through so many interesting routes of exploring. Having excitement and curiosity can keep your wearables interesting and help your learning journey.

Summary

This chapter explored so many concepts and fun components that it was a lot to take in. It's a great idea to get yourself some of the sensors you find interesting and try them out, as it's the best way to learn. Often, making mistakes helps us to improve our skills. Hopefully, you've learned enough about sensors to have a look online for the sensors that interest you the most. You could also find a local electronics store so you can have a look at some components, too. Try creating some wearables with pre-made sensors or try creating sensors of your own. Don't forget when choosing a new sensor to look up the datasheet for it. This is important for finding out how to connect it and also its power requirements. You'll be looking for 3V or 5V sensors, as these work with the Arduino system.

The challenges of choosing the right sensor were discussed. You have been guided through some main points to consider before building your prototypes. For example, thinking about the placement, size, and weight of sensors becomes very important when designing an on-body system, especially if it will be worn for an extended amount of time.

We also learned about the protocols that we can use to communicate with a circuit board. These protocols are used to connect our sensors and components and use either a two-wire or a four-wire connection. Some sensors will use specific libraries too, and we learned how to install them using the Library Manager. Lastly, we finished on some wacky nature sensors that used a simple library to add touch capabilities to our designs.

All these concepts will come in handy for our next chapter, where we explore the huge variety of available outputs. This is where our designs will become a lot more exciting. We will add reactions when our sensors send data. This could be like some of the wearable devices we've been learning about, to alert, guide, support, and monitor people.

Let's head to the next chapter now. Get ready for more connections and projects to try!

Review questions

1. What are the two protocols we learned about for communicating between the sensors and our circuit boards?

2. Can sensors only be bought?

3. Why is it a good idea to make our own sensors?

4. Why should we use a library?

5. Because these sensors only read a high or low value, what pin type do we need on our circuit board?

6. Were there sensors you found more interesting than others? Do some research into these sensors and look up their datasheets to find out more. Do you remember what information we should always check for on a datasheet?

6

Exploring Reactions Through Outputs

Getting a response through and with our wearable is exciting. The world of outputs and actuators can help us do that. If a wearer must create the input themselves, it can become a burden. **Implicit interaction** (Schmidt, A., 2000) is possible by using sensors to capture the data. Then, we can process this with Arduino for the wearer; that can be stored or is interpreted for an output.

> **Important note**
> Implicit interaction is about putting humans first and having technology as a background system. It is an approach that engages a wearer and creates systems that don't require *extra steps* or actions to allow them to work as intended. Making systems fun and engaging for a wearer is a great way to enhance a system's use.

This chapter describes the outputs that bring your projects to life. We will experiment with light, from LEDs to NeoPixels, and more. We will also learn about sound, movement, and heat. Learning these skills will enhance the capabilities and interactions we can make with our wearables. Let's make things happen!

In this chapter, you will learn about the outputs that can add huge value to a wearable. After defining the types of outputs and why they are useful, we will put what we've learned into practice and create circuits that react to the inputs they receive.

By the end of this chapter, you will know about a range of outputs that you can add to your wearable designs and be able to code your circuit board to react and display visual effects, auditory properties, and haptic feedback, **based on the sense of touch**.

In this chapter, we're going to cover the following main topics:

- About action – outputs and responses
- Visual – light, color, and vision

- Auditory – sound, tone, and audio

- Haptic – actuators, motion, motors, and vibration

Technical requirements

This chapter is all about learning how to use different outputs to show reactions, or actions when we receive sensor data. Many outputs are featured in the chapter, so there isn't a required list. However, you may want to give a few of the electronic circuits a try so that you can choose or swap items out from the following list:

- Arduino as the IDE

- Flora V3/Circuit Playground Classic/Gemma M0 boards

- Various sensors and outputs – NeoPixels, OLED, piezo, and a vibration motor

- Components for hooking up the motor – 10 KΩ resistor, PN2222 transistor, 270 Ω resistor, diode, and a small 3-5V miniature cooling axial fan or motor

About action – outputs and responses

Output responses provide a wearer with essential **feedback**. It can also enhance the wearer's experience. Besides that, delight and fun are an important part of people's experience of technology. Offering *long-term value* makes the difference between a wearable being worn or being left in a cupboard somewhere!

In this section, we will learn about outputs. Then, we will try some sample circuits to solidify our knowledge. These circuits will be more complicated than previous examples we've tried because we will create a circuit with an input that sends data to the board, which will perform an action, cause a reaction, or provide an output of some description based on that data.

Let's start by learning about some of the outputs we can use, starting with visual output.

Visual – light, color, and vision

Materials that glow and light up always add an element of excitement or wonderment to a wearable. The good news is that we can add light to our wearables in many ways!

There are a few ways we can enhance our projects with both light and vision. In this section, we will look at the following:

- LEDs

- NeoPixels

- EL wire

- Display screens

Throughout this book, we have played with LEDs, so we already know about these in a basic way. Let's start with an overview of LEDs, then explore other ways we can add light to our wearables!

LEDs

An LED is a diode, as we've seen previously. Since it's a diode, electricity travels through it in one direction. The color of the light is determined by the energy gap distance inside the LED. They come in a huge variety of sizes, shapes, and colors. LEDs can also be ultraviolet and infrared, so we can't see the light, but we can use them to control other devices by sending a signal. An LED has *low power needs* – you've already tried using LEDs with coin cell batteries – but they also have a *long lifespan*. Many new cars use LEDs in their lights because of their efficiency.

When buying LEDs, you may also want to check their lumen value, which is a light intensity rating. More intensity can require more power, so also check the power requirements. Generally, for our wearable projects, try to find LEDs that are around 3V so that they work with your circuits easily. Remember, we can look at a components data sheet to find out more about it.

Filament-style LEDs offer a variety of effects. One end of the filament has a very small hole in the metal connector. This end is for power. The end with no hole in it is the ground connection.

LEDs can have their brightness controlled through a higher resistor value; try a 330 or a 550 Ohm resistor in your circuit if the LED is too bright. Our eyes always perceive a green LED as brighter than others, so I typically use a higher resistor when I use green. We can also alter how the LED is viewed by diffusing it. This can be done by using layers of fabric, adding sequins or a covering, or using plastic pieces such as Perspex or acrylics of different colors and thicknesses. These can be molded and shaped too:

Figure 6.1 – LEDs – matrix and segment styles

There are also LEDs in a matrix shape, 7-segment displays, and bar graphs with tombstone-style LEDs, as shown in *Figure 6.1,* the filament style is also shown here.

Lastly, there are interesting wireless LEDs, as shown in *Figure 6.2*. They have a conductive main coil around them, which is their power source. The LEDs have coils at their base that conduct power from this main powered coil. The closer the LEDs are to the power coil, the brighter they will be. You can get the LEDs in a variety of colors and sizes:

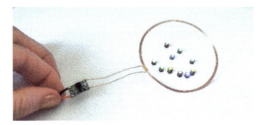

Figure 6.2 – Wireless LEDs – magic!

These coil-style wireless LEDs can be a lot of fun and if you embed the power coil into a thin garment area, it adds a little magic to a wearable!

NeoPixels

A NeoPixel, as shown in *Figure 6.3*, is an individually addressable RGB color pixel strip that is made with an LED driver with a single wire protocol. The NeoPixel was the first widely accessible, programmable, maker form of digital RGB LEDs. There is one data wire to transmit the data between devices. It is an Adafruit brand and its lights need a microcontroller to be used. They are very quick to hook up because of the single wire protocol – we just need to define a data pin! There are also many libraries and code examples to help you get started and, of course, the mega guide on the Adafruit website (`https://learn.adafruit.com/adafruit-neopixel-uberguide`):

Figure 6.3 – Styles of NeoPixels

They can be used individually or in much larger chains with many lights. As you may recall, when we connect a single LED, we also hook up the power, a resistor, and ground. A NeoPixel is a full-color LED (red, green, and blue), with a driver chip embedded. There is also an RGBW version that has a white LED. You can connect many through one data pin, so it is really exciting to get them working. I love NeoPixels so much and they always add so much interest and visual interactivity to a project.

From my experience and observations, once someone learns about NeoPixels, they usually stick with them! They come in many shapes and forms, including grids, lines, and circles. You can buy them in different quantities along a long strip, a strand, or in matrices and shapes. See what types you can find because they are always fun to experiment with. The strips also come in a variety of weather-proofing thicknesses. Some can completely keep water out while others are good at repelling it. You can also usually get black or white strips so that they match your project better.

If you want individual NeoPixels, you can buy ones that are sewable with sew tabs. Typically, strips come in quantities of 30/60/144. These can be cut to the amount you need for your project. You'll need to solder the connective ends onto it if you cut it. We'll look at this in more detail in *Chapter 10, Soldering and Sewing to Complete Your Project*. The strand versions are more flexible and work best for sewing organic shapes or if you want to wrap them around something. There is also a version of the strip with croc clips on the end so that you can get started right away!

When buying NeoPixels, be sure to note the type that you are buying as it will have implications for when you code it later. Typically, you need to know if you have an *RGB* or *RGBW* version. The W version also has true white. You'll recognize that it's RGBW if you look at the NeoPixel and it's divided in half with a yellow semi-circle. There is also a version of the strip NeoPixels that is an angled sidelight. They face downwards and not facing the top of the strip. They can be good for putting a strip between a seam or on the bottom of something.

Electroluminescent (**EL**) wire is great for adding interesting effects to a wearable (*Figure 6.4* shows a variety).

You might have come across something that looks like a *Tron*-style item, with a hue of color outlining an item of clothing, for example. It's often used to add light to cosplay or costumes. The copper wire core is coated with phosphor and when we add electricity, it glows. It's covered in clear plastic or colored plastic for different effects. It's quite bendable and you can find a style with a sewable edge. That's usually the style I buy. It makes it a lot easier to add to your wearable projects.

EL wire comes in different colors, styles, and lengths. You must buy it with a driver/inverter (this converts DC voltage into a higher AC voltage) battery pack to power it. The inverters give off a little noise, so be aware of that. It's like a slightly high-pitched hum; some are louder than others. You can always wrap the inverter in padding or bubble wrap to quieten it:

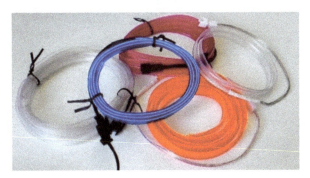

Figure 6.4 – EL wire samples

Note that EL wire seems to have a life span of a few years, so you may want to consider how you include it in your projects as it may need to be replaced. Lastly, you can cut EL wire if it is too long for your project, and it will glow up to the end of where it was cut.

Lastly, there is also EL panel and tape. These are thin sheets that glow and tend to be brighter than the wire. It's a larger area too, so think through where it would best suit your wearable. You can see these panels and more at `https://elpanelandtape.co.uk/el-panel/`.

I hope you enjoyed the fun factor that an EL wire can add to your wearable. Now, let's look at display screens.

Display screens

We can add a display screen to our wearable as an output that relays information or messages to the wearer. There are a few different types, and they offer different features. In this section, we'll look at OLED, LCD TFT, and eInk/ePaper screens because they can be integrated into our wearable with minimal wires, and they offer a crisp display. Then, we'll finish by looking at 16x2 LCD screens.

OLED

An **Organic Light-Emitting Diode (OLED)** is a display that comes in several sizes (*Figure 6.5*). There are small OLEDs with crisp text output because of their high contrast.

One of the more popular ones is the 0.96-inch display, which has 128×64 pixels. There is also a 0.91-inch display that measures 128x32 pixels, and a 1.12-inch display comprising 128x128 pixels. Each pixel is turned on or off by the controller, so they are very bright, and it reduces the power consumption. They have different display colors to choose from, including white, blue, and yellow.

Most of these displays have two pins for I²C for communication, and a ground and power pin. Some versions have a RESET pin. Other OLED displays communicate using the SPI protocol:

Figure 6.5 – A selection of OLED displays – SPI (left) and I²C (right)

The OLED display is a self-light-emitting technology. It's made from a thin, multi-layered organic film that is placed between an anode (negative) and a cathode (positive).

> **Important Note**
> The order of the pins on the OLED screen can be different for different brands. Always check the pins before you hook it up and turn it on. I've lost an OLED this way by "cooking" the component with a short circuit! This means it was shorted because the pins were hooked up incorrectly.

Lastly, there are **transparent** OLED displays. A new-to-the-market OLED from DFRobot has blue illumination color, is 1.51 inches, and has a resolution of 128x64, as shown in *Figure 6.6*:

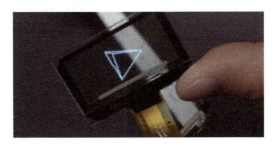

Figure 6.6 – A transparent OLED

You can read more about this OLED at https://www.dfrobot.com/product-2521.html.

LCD TFT (thin-film transistor)

These are colorful and bright displays that can add great feedback to a wearable (*Figure 6.7*). An LCD TFT is a thin-film-transistor, liquid-crystal display. This is a variant of a liquid-crystal display, which improves the image through thin-film-transistor technology. The screens come in many different sizes and most follow the SPI protocol (see *Chapter 5, Working with Sensors: All about Inputs!*).

Larger than the OLEDs we learned about, there is a 2.4-inch LCD TFT module with a display with 240x320 resolution and 65K RGB colors. Usually, the displays have small mounting holes to make them simple to incorporate into your design. Adafruit has a 1.44-inch display with a 128x128 color pixel TFT LCD that includes a Micro SD card reader on it. It uses a TFT driver so that it can refresh the images at a fast rate, though this will also depend on the circuit board you use with it.

Because of the card reader, you can load full-color bitmaps from a FAT16/FAT32-formatted Micro SD card. Lastly, there are also circular TFT screens that you can add to a project. They are the size of a standard watch face:

Figure 6.7 – Various LCD TFT displays

Creating a touch screen for your project is possible with an **in-plane switching** (**IPS**) Super TFT. Some have a capacitive touch option and IPS is considered an advanced screen because the technology that it uses improves viewing through a wider angle. All these displays can be used with extensive libraries, which we will look at in more detail later in this chapter. The libraries will help us get the most out of these amazing displays!

The main difference is that an OLED is generally a single color and super bright definition, while the LCD TFT is great for displaying color images.

eInk/ePaper

These displays vary in size and color (*Figure 6.8*). There are monochrome versions, such as the 2.9-inch Grayscale eInk display that's 296x128 pixels from Adafruit. There is also a 2.9-inch version with red, black, and white as the display colors. Also, they come in sizes of 1.54 inches, 200x200 or 152x152 pixel displays, and 2.7 inches. eInk is a type of static display. When used, the image is written to the screen, and it will stay there when the power is off.

Their surfaces make them easy to read because they don't have a shine to them. These displays need a lot of pins to connect, so be aware that you'll have to choose a circuit board with three SPI pins and possibly up to four control pins for an SD and SRAM.

An eInk without color will refresh a lot quicker than the tri-color (red, black, and white) versions:

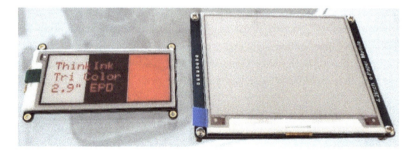

Figure 6.8 – eInk/ePaper displays

If you are using a Circuit Playground Express board (the Classic does not have enough RAM) and if you want to easily add one of these screens, there is a bolt-on *gizmo* that has a screen with M3 standoffs that complete the connections between the screen and circuit board.

16x2 LCDs

Lastly, these are very common and at one point, they would have been used in many projects. Typically, they are included in basic Arduino kits and are very low cost. Many have a 16-pin design, so you need to use a circuit board that can handle that many pins, though increasingly many come with an adaptor board so that you can use the I²C protocol. This does add to the bulky size of the screens though! *Figure 6.9* shows an example of this screen. They come in different single colors, such as white, blue, and red, and some have different backlight options, so you can have white text on a blue background, for example:

Figure 6.9 – LCD with an I²C adapter board – front (left) and back (right)

Because of the crisp, bright, and low cost of the OLEDs and TFTs, they seem to be used less in wearable designs. They can be chunky and heavy, so, as we have discussed previously, this should be a consideration when creating a wearable.

Take some time reflecting on the light sources we've identified in this section. Write notes in a journal about how you could incorporate light and vision into a wearable. Often, making notes, doodles, or drawings as reflections spawn ideas to build on later. Think about how the visual element would work – does the wearer actively engage with it, or is it triggered by a sensor? Is the visual component communicating to the wearer or others around them? How noticeable will it be, is it for fashion purposes, or does it enhance someone's daily life?

Light and vision are a very important part of feedback on a wearable technology design. There are so many options when choosing how to communicate the information the wearer needs to be aware of. Consider when the light should be on and what its role is – communication with the wearer or those around the wearer. Let's jump into some activities for using light and vision.

Activity 6.1 – learning about NeoPixels – a Hand HEX system

This is going to be the biggest project so far in this book. In this activity, we are going to get complex and build a system that will be useful to visual designers in many different fields. As we've seen, HEX codes and RBG values are important when we are programming NeoPixels. Using a HEX code is how we choose the colors to display. We use three values – red, green, and blue – which make up the output color.

In this circuit, we want to use a color sensor to detect any color around us, even if it's a color on a drink can nearby! Then, we want to use that color to light our NeoPixels. We aren't going to stop there, though! We will also hook up an OLED screen so that we can see the HEX values as their numerical values on a screen for additional output. This is so we can use that exact color in any other sketches we are writing, or for any designers so that they can use it in their work. Pretty cool, hey?

This activity will take us through mapping, hooking up, and programming our circuit board to get it to function. If you want to sew it together, you can do that here or you can wait until a little further into this book. In *Chapter 10, Soldering and Sewing to Complete Your Project*, we will learn more about techniques to complete wearables.

> **A Note for Future Circuits You Design**
>
> It's always good practice to *connect the power pin last*. Sometimes, especially if we didn't disconnect our board from the computer, we can get a surge on the power connection. This can damage our components!

You can use a glove that you already have if you think it is suitable or get creative and make your own. It's great practice and then you'll have an additional skill for creating your wearables. Remember: it only needs to be a prototype.

The parts list for a Hand HEX system is shown in *Figure 6.10*. They are as follows:

- Sewable or another color sensor

- NeoPixels, in your chosen form – strip, strand, or shapes

- A glove (buy one, make your own, or upcycle an existing glove)

- An OLED screen. Choose your preferred color and size – I'm using 128x128 yellow/blue

- An Adafruit Flora board

- A rechargeable LiPoly battery

Now that we have the materials, my first step is to map out the circuit in my notebook. I will assemble all my parts and then work through the pinouts:

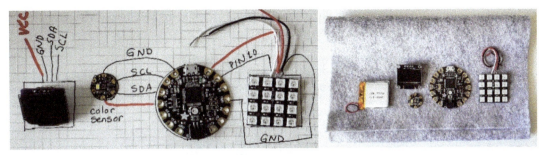

Figure 6.10 – Mapping the complete circuit and the parts for the Hand HEX system

Figure 6.10 also shows my map of the circuit connections that I'll follow. We'll build this project in stages. This is a great way to work because then, as we proceed through the circuit in complexity, we can fix errors as they happen. We'll know that our circuit works as we build it. There will be *three parts*: the *color sensor*, then the *OLED*, and then the *NeoPixels*.

First, let's add the color sensor.

Part 1 – color sensor

I'll start by hooking up the Flora sewable color sensor to the Flora board. It uses the I²C protocol that we learned about in the previous chapter. To connect the sensor and Flora, you must set the following:

- Sensor 3V to Flora 3.3V
- Sensor GND to Flora GND
- Sensor SCL to I²C Clock on Flora (SCL pin 3)
- Sensor SDA to I²C Data on Flora (SDA pin 2)

Once you've connected them (*Figure 6.11*), plug the board into your computer so that we can try out the sensor:

Figure 6.11 – Color sensor connected to Flora

Let's open the Arduino IDE and install a library to use this sensor. Open the **Library Manager** area (*Figure 6.12*) and search for Adafruit TCS34725:

Figure 6.12 – Installing the library for the color sensor

The color sensing library didn't come up when I searched the exact name, so if you don't see it in the list, try searching for color sensor – that worked for me. When you do click **Install**, it will ask about dependencies. As shown in the following screenshot you'll want to choose **Install all**:

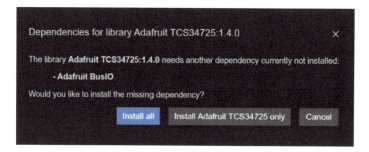

Figure 6.13 – Installing the dependencies

Be sure to wait for the notification stating that you have successfully installed the library. Sometimes, there is a glitch with the Arduino IDE 2.0 where you need to repeat this process and try the install process more than once as it may not install the library the first time. If you have the installed messages in the output window, then you're good to go!

Because this library is used for a slightly different color sensor, we'll use my modified code at https://github.com/cmoz/Ultimate/tree/main/C6/C6_ColorSensor for this example:

```
#include <Wire.h>
#include "Adafruit_TCS34725.h"
Adafruit_TCS34725 tcs = Adafruit_TCS34725(TCS34725_
INTEGRATIONTIME_50MS, TCS34725_GAIN_4X);

void setup() {
  Serial.begin(9600);
```

```
    Serial.println("Color View Test!");
    if (tcs.begin()) {
    Serial.println("Found sensor");
    } else {
    Serial.println("No TCS34725 found");
    while (1);
    }
}

void loop() {
    uint16_t clear, red, green, blue;
    tcs.setInterrupt(false);
    delay(60);
    tcs.getRawData(&red, &green, &blue, &clear);
    tcs.setInterrupt(true);
    uint32_t sum = clear;
    float r, g, b;
    r = red;
    r /= sum;
    g = green;
    g /= sum;
    b = blue;
    b /= sum;
    r *= 256; g *= 256; b *= 256;

    Serial.print("HEX: \t");
    Serial.print((int)r, HEX); Serial.print((int)g, HEX);
    Serial.print((int)b, HEX); Serial.print("\t \t RGB: \t");
    Serial.print((int)r ); Serial.print(" ");
    Serial.print((int)g); Serial.print(" ");
    Serial.println((int)b); Serial.println();
}
```

Upload the sketch to the Flora board and open Serial Monitor. You should see a display of the color values in the output, as shown in the following screenshot:

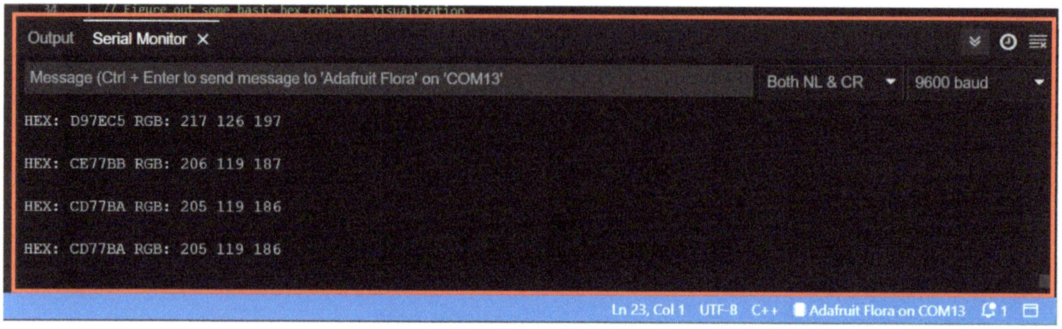

Figure 6.14 – Serial Monitor output from the color sensor

Your color sensor blinks as it's sensing. The output to the monitor depends on the color of the item you hold over the sensor. I held a pink item, which is why I was given that readout.

Now that we have one part of our circuit working, we can connect the NeoPixels, which we'll use to display the color of the item we are sensing. Remember, though, that this will only be as accurate as the LEDs can create, so it won't be an exact match.

Part 2 – OLED

Unplug your Flora board from your computer and hook up the OLED display. Connecting the OLED should be familiar to you now because it follows the same I²C protocol that we covered in *Chapter 5, Working with Sensors: All about Inputs!*. The OLED also has four pins, two of which are for the I²C protocol. As mentioned previously, connect SDA on the screen to SDA on the Flora, and connect the SPI on the screen to the SPI on the Flora. Then hook up the ground pin and finish with the power pin.

We are using the same SDA and SCL pins because each of the components we are putting on these pins has a unique address. If you are curious about the address for your components, then you can run the sketch that outputs the address of your I²C devices.

To easily program the OLED, let's install a library. Open the Library Manager area and search for `Adafruit_SSD1306`. This library will also ask you to install **Adafruit_GFX** at the same time, so install both (see *Chapter 4, Implementing Arduino Code Using Gemma M0 and Circuit Playground*, if you need more guidance on installing libraries):

```
#include <Wire.h>
#include "Adafruit_GFX.h"
#include "Adafruit_SSD1306.h"

#define SCREEN_WIDTH 128
#define SCREEN_HEIGHT 64
```

```
Adafruit_SSD1306 oled(SCREEN_WIDTH, SCREEN_HEIGHT, &Wire, -1);

void setup() {
  Serial.begin(9600);
  if (!oled.begin(SSD1306_SWITCHCAPVCC, 0x3C)) {
  Serial.println(F("SSD1306 allocation failed"));
  while (true);
}
  delay(2000);
  oled.clearDisplay();
  oled.setTextSize(3);
  oled.setTextColor(WHITE);
  oled.setCursor(0, 10);
  oled.println("Hello World!");
  oled.display();
}
```

This time, there isn't anything in our `loop()` because this code is just checking everything is working. The OLED should now be displaying text that says *Hello World*. Play around with this code to have it display something else, such as *Ultimate Wearables*! This is a good way to get to know the code. When you've finished trying different effects and code, we can put the color sensor and OLED code together.

Open your code for the color sensor and save it as a new file. Then, add the libraries we are using, add the initialization, and then the rest of the code.

Your turn: try to combine the code. It's good practice to combine the code yourself first. You can build it up with each new function you want your wearable to perform. Try it now with the two components:

Figure 6.15 – The OLED display showing the HEX reading taken from the color scanner

The code from `https://github.com/cmoz/Ultimate/tree/main/C6/C6_ColorSensor_ andOLED` will contain both elements – that is, the color sensor and the OLED. Upload it to your Flora board and then run it. Test it by holding something of color against your color sensor. *Figure 6.15* shows the OLED displaying a HEX value for a blue pencil I scanned by holding the end against the sensor. We now have an input that is receiving data and creating an output based on that data!

Part 3 – NeoPixels

Let's create a second output that will visually echo the color that we are scanning with the color sensor.

Make sure you unplug the Flora board from the computer before you hook up the NeoPixels. Once *unplugged*, connect the NeoPixels to the Flora board. Your configuration of NeoPixels might be different than mine. I'm going to use the strand version. Whatever version you choose, there will be *one data pin* and a *power* and *ground* pin:

1. Connect your NeoPixel *Data In* pin to a pin that is available of your choice. This pin will be added to the code. I'm choosing pin 10 on the Flora board.

2. Then, connect the power and ground of the NeoPixel to the power and ground of the Flora.

3. In the Arduino IDE, add the **Adafruit NeoPixel** library. This will install sample files for us that we will use to test whether our lights are working. Open the `strandtest` file by going to **File** | **Examples** | **Adafruit NeoPixel** | **strandtest**.

Change the `#define LED_PIN 6` line of code so that it contains the same value as your pin; I chose pin 10. The new line of code will look like this: `#define LED_PIN 10`. The line after that one is a count of the number of NeoPixel LEDs being used. Count the lights you are using in your strip, strand, or shape, and put this number in. Mine looks like this: `#define LED_COUNT 8`. Note that if you are using *RGBW* pixels, then you need to change NEO_GRB in the following code line:

```
Adafruit_NeoPixel strip(LED_COUNT, LED_PIN, NEO_GRB + NEO_
KHZ800);
```

You must change it to NEO_RGBW:

```
Adafruit_NeoPixel strip(LED_COUNT, LED_PIN, NEO_RGBW + NEO_
KHZ800);
```

The NeoPixels will still work if this isn't correct, but you will see some *unlit* NeoPixels when they are supposed to be white, for example. Some strange lighting effects will happen, so you will know that you should change the code. **Upload** the sample `strandtest` code to the Flora board.

Once uploaded, you should see a wonderful display of colors and effects.

Do they light up? If not, make sure you're using the **Data In** (**DI**) line and not the **Data Out** (**DO**) line. Have you got power and ground to your NeoPixels? Check those connections. Are you using the right pin? Did you change the pin's number in the code to reflect the pin that the NeoPixels are connected to on the circuit board?

I always find this an exciting part of the process; seeing a NeoPixel in action is always fun!

Understanding how to control a single NeoPixel is good knowledge to have. It will help with your programming and controlling NeoPixels for your future wearables. Let's look at the sample code for seeing the NeoPixels light up one at a time with one color.

You can use the following code to do this. Looking through the code to understand it can be a good way to learn how to control NeoPixels:

```
#include "Adafruit_NeoPixel.h"
#define LED_PIN 10
#define LED_COUNT 8

Adafruit_NeoPixel strip(LED_COUNT, LED_PIN, NEO_GRB + NEO_
KHZ800);

void setup() {
  strip.begin();
  strip.show();
  strip.setBrightness(50);
}

void loop() {
  for(int i=0; i<strip.numPixels(); i++) {
  strip.setPixelColor(i, (0, 0, 220));
  strip.show();
  delay(1000);
  }
}
```

Note that the color values for each of the three colors can be set to a maximum value of 255. Full brightness is also a value of 255. `strip.numPixels()` will take our predefined number of pixels in our strand, and use that number to count up to light each one. In the `strip.setPixelColor(i, (0, 0, 220));` line we are setting the i value to the LED number, so it will increment, lighting the first, then the second, and so on. Then, it sets the values of the color we want. Here, it is 0 = no red, 0 = no green, and 220 = almost full blue. If you wanted to only light up the fourth pixel in a string of eight, for example, how do you think we would write the code? If you wrote `strip.setPixelColor(4, (0, 0, 220));`, you'd be correct.

Setting these values to all 0s will turn off the lights.

Putting it all together

Now, we can combine the code further. At `https://github.com/cmoz/Ultimate/tree/main/C6/C6_ColorSensor_andOLED_Neo`, I've created a file of the completed code that has all three parts put together. When the code is working, you'll see flashing on the color sensor. This means it is taking a reading:

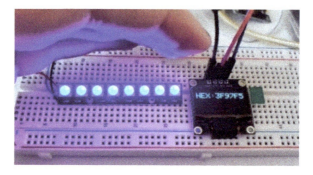

Figure 6.16 – The color sensor and two outputs – an OLED screen and NeoPixels

Then, the HEX code is written to the OLED screen, and the color is sent as RGB values to the NeoPixels (*Figure 6.16*). I've also checked the HEX code that was displayed on the screen and typed the value into a color HEX website, `https://www.color-hex.com/`, to check whether the value is close to what I'm expecting.

To make it into a wearable glove, you can sew the components to a glove that you already have. However, if you have some felt, you can use that to create a quick prototype fingerless glove. We just need a piece of felt big enough for our hand, front and back:

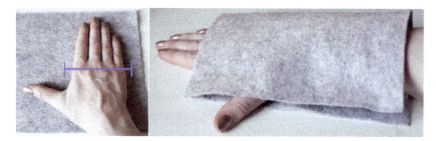

Figure 6.17 – Checking the size of the fabric

Place your hand on top of the felt, and measure across where your knuckles are. This will be the widest part of the glove. The material will need to cover that part of your hand and account for the thickness of your hand too. *Figure 6.17* shows the area we need to measure, and the felt draped over the hand to be sure there is enough of the fabric.

Then, once you've cut the felt, fold it over your hand to be sure there is overlap to it so that it will fit once it is sewn (or glued) together. To start putting it together, it's a good idea to use safety pins to hold the shape in place. Then, put the glove on to feel where the components will fit. Keep in mind that the purpose of this glove is for it to be used by someone typing on a computer because we want to help them with finding HEX code. So, make sure you can hold a mouse easily (*Figure 6.18*) when the components are on it.

Once you are satisfied with the placement, place the components on the felt and glue them into place:

Figure 6.18 – Trying it before sewing the final version

The sensor is just out of view on mine because I want it near my pinky. Once the glue is dry, you can sew the components into place. I map out my connections before I sew to be sure I know where the threads might overlap. This rapid prototype in felt is a good way to test your wearable and find if there are usability issues.

I'm going to transfer my circuit to a glove design made from scuba style fabric *neoprene* for a stretchable fit. This would become a prototype iteration to test a more permanent solution because I like the functionality of this wearable!

Once you build upon your skill set, you may want to look at soldering NeoPixels yourself, which can be a great way to have the freedom to put these lights anywhere into a wearable technology garment (see *Chapter 10, Soldering and Sewing to Complete Your Project*).

Now that we've had a look at a complex circuit, let's see how we can attach EL wire to a wearable.

Activity 6.2 – sewing EL wire

Adding EL wire to a wearable is a fun way to create an impact. It's great to put on a backpack, for example, so that it can be seen at night. This could be a good idea for cyclists. You can add EL wire to an existing item or make a garment/bag and plan for the EL wire to go in the seam of it. Either way, it's easy to do and only requires a few steps. To add EL wire to an existing bag, you'll need the EL wire in the length that will work for you. You can cut it down to size, though. You'll also need the inverter battery pack to power it.

Figure 6.19 shows an example of EL wire being sewn into a bag that I made by hand. The EL wire is sewn between all the seams as the bag was made. If you choose a simple shaped bag with light fabric, you can modify it by adding EL wire. You'll need to choose a bag where you can open the seams easily and sew them back together again!

Turn the bag inside out. Using a seam ripper or small sharp scissors, gently pull up one or two stitches. Once you've cut through one or two, you'll be able to tease the seam apart slightly. After you have a few inches of open seam, place your EL wire with seam into the gap. The EL wire should be on the outside of the seam, and the sewing tab on the wire should be between the pieces of the bag fabric, layering them together. Note that you'll want to place the battery pack inside the bag to keep it safer and quieter:

Figure 6.19 – EL wire sewn into a handmade backpack

Once your EL wire is in place, sew the seam together. This can be a great way to give an old bag a new life! What other garments or accessories can you modify? Think of the different colors and sizes of EL wire you can buy; this might help you create your own EL wire wearables.

A technology that focuses on connectedness, while not a wearable, is an application where this can be adapted, is BodyPods (Roseway, A., Dimitris Papanikolaou, D., 1999). It is "*...a remotely paired set of communicating chairs that facilitate a sense of presence by leveraging implicit actions such as sitting to communicate that someone you care about is home.*" This uses light for communication across distances and is a meaningful example of using light in alternative ways.

Now that we've looked at the different ways we can use light and vision, let's learn about using sound as an output. Let's make some noise!

Auditory – sound, tone, and audio

Sound can be an important indicator for the wearer, calling attention to potential errors, or for confirmation that something has happened. If we use sound effectively, we may not need to have a display for messages – if the tones are clear in their use. Understanding a person's comprehension and interpretation of distinct sounds, pitches, and even the length of time a sound is emitted will enable effective communication. We can make interactions meaningful.

We can use buzzers and speakers (*Figure 6.20* shows examples), though for more complex sound, there are MP3 boards that we can hook up to our circuits. We won't be exploring MP3 boards as it's a little outside the scope of this chapter, but it's important to know that they exist. They can be great for providing better sound or communication through an audio file. It may provide a soundtrack to tasks or sensor input, for example. You may want to do some research about the types of boards that are available for sound, and what speakers and memory cards you need to use them:

Figure 6.20 – A variety of piezo buzzers, speakers, and audio boards

If your wearable needs pre-recorded sound, you can use a sound FX audio processor board with bone conduction headphones so that only the wearer will hear it.

A passive or active piezo buzzer or speaker works similarly. Active usually has more height to it than passive and it's sealed. The passive buzzer has electronics visible on the underside of it. It's called active because it has electronics inside it. The passive buzzer will need other electronics to be used. The taller leg is the power side, while the shorter leg is for ground, just like an LED.

There is usually an indicator to show which side is positive as well, marked with a + symbol. If we connect the active buzzer, it will start buzzing right away because of the components inside. If we use the passive buzzer, we need to send a signal to it.

Buzzers produce simple sounds but many libraries exist that have tones. The example from Arduino (`https://www.arduino.cc/en/Tutorial/BuiltInExamples/toneMelody`) includes a file called `pitches.h` that contains pitch values, as shown here:

```
#define NOTE_AS2 117
#define NOTE_B2 123
#define NOTE_C3 131
```

When using sound in a wearable, it's important to think it through and try it with other people. Their interpretation of the sound may not be the same as yours. Consider the following:

- What is the input that triggers the sound?
- What is the environment that it's being used in? If it's in a quiet place, people may not want a sound – vibration may work better.

- Is the sound for the wearer, or a warning for others around them?

- What sound will work best for your wearable?

- What location on or near the body will the speaker or buzzer be placed?

Let's try a couple of exercises to get a buzzer working in a circuit so that you can hear the sound it makes.

Activity 6.3 – connecting and using sound

Connect a buzzer to the Gemma M0 board. *Figure 6.21* shows the piezo connected with croc clips to Gemma M0 pin 0:

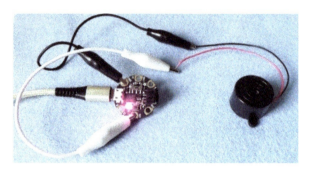

Figure 6.21 – Piezo and Gemma M0 connected

Choose the longer leg of the piezo, which is the power side (it might be marked with a + symbol), and connect it to pin 0. Then, connect the shorter leg, which is ground to GND on the Gemma M0 board.

The simplest way to check your buzzer is working is by using code to create a tone:

- No code is needed in `setup()`

- Type the code in the `loop()` function of the sketch: `tone(1, 2000, 500);`

The pin number is the first argument in the `tone()` function. The second number is the frequency, which is 2 kHz. The final argument specifies the amount of time we want the sound on. In this example, it's half a second. Play around with these values to listen to other tones and durations. It's a quick way to check your speaker and sound.

You can also use the following code for your buzzer, similar to the **LED Blink** code:

```
int buzzerPin = 0;

void setup() {
pinMode(buzzerPin, OUTPUT);
```

```
}

void loop() {
digitalWrite(buzzerPin, HIGH);
delay(500);
digitalWrite(buzzerPin, LOW);
delay(3000);
}
```

You'll recognize we are initializing an int variable and have called it buzzerPin. We will use this to hold the value of the pinout that the buzzer is on. We define the pin as an output in setup(). Then, in loop(), we make the pin *HIGH* or *LOW* if we want a sound or no sound.

Now that we've used a buzzer that we've hooked up to a circuit board, let's try the onboard speaker on the Circuit Playground Classic board.

Activity 6.4 – using the Circuit Playground's onboard sound

The Circuit Playground board has a surface mount speaker. We used it for our touch sensor input in the previous chapter. Let's look at a quick demo of using it with the two buttons on the board. The library for Circuit Playground allows us to get this working quickly. The speaker is connected to pin 5, and we're using the two buttons on the board to control the sound. The left button is on pin 4, while the right button is on pin 19:

```
#include <Adafruit_CircuitPlayground.h>

void setup() {
 CircuitPlayground.begin();
}

void loop() {
 if(CircuitPlayground.leftButton()) {
 CircuitPlayground.playTone(440,100);
 CircuitPlayground.setPixelColor(3, 138,43,226);
 CircuitPlayground.setPixelColor(4, 138,43,226);
 }
 else if(CircuitPlayground.rightButton()) {
 CircuitPlayground.playTone(1760,100);
 CircuitPlayground.setPixelColor(6, 138,43,226);
```

```
CircuitPlayground.setPixelColor(8, 138,43,226);
  }
```

Let's take advantage of the many sensors the board has and use the light sensor to play music. This is a version of a light theremin that reads values from the light sensor – between 0 and 1023. We'll use map again to map the input values so that they are within a playable and pleasant range:

```
#include <Adafruit_CircuitPlayground.h>

void setup() {
  CircuitPlayground.begin();
}

void loop() {
  uint16_t value, sound;
  if(CircuitPlayground.slideSwitch()) {
  value = CircuitPlayground.lightSensor();
  sound = map(value, 5, 1000, 131, 1760);
  CircuitPlayground.playTone(sound, 100);
  }
}
```

Now that we understand sound basics, let's do another activity. Here, we'll build a circuit that uses a sensor input and has a sound output, depending on the data received from the sensor.

Activity 6.5 – Touch Together – a socially playable instrument

Touch together, a game for social connections – it takes two to play this instrument! The way this wearable is designed is that you can't touch the battery and the circuit together by yourself. I'm creating it out of neoprene fabric so that it is fitted but can stretch to a variety of sizes. I'll use a zipper to close the forearm piece. The pieces that are needed for the circuit (*Figure 6.22*) include two pieces of large neoprene (or other fabric with some stretch to it) to fit around a forearm, a smaller piece of that fabric to hold the battery in place, zippers (or Velcro) to close the wearable around the arm, a Circuit Playground board, a battery, conductive fabric, glue, conductive thread, clips, pins, and an optional vibration motor:

Figure 6.22 – Pieces needed to create this wearable

We'll start by creating our two forearm pieces – one will have the battery and conductive fabric for the ground and power connections across to the circuit playground. Then, there are linked pads for the sound that you can play. This means we need the following:

- *One forearm piece* for the battery and conductive fabric pads for GND, PWR, and the pads for touch input.

- *One forearm piece* for the Circuit Playground board, GND, PWR, and pads for receiving the touch input from the other wearable piece, as well as an optional vibration motor.

Follow these steps to create this circuit:

1. Measure out the neoprene for the forearm. Place your or a friend's arm on a piece of paper or tissue paper. Wrap that paper around the forearm. Measure and *allow extra fabric* for placing the zipper/hook and loop edge and seams to sew. Also, make sure it's not so tight that it stops circulation!

2. Cut two forearm pieces from your neoprene.

3. Once cut, check the neoprene's shape. Wrap it around the forearm to make sure it's sized correctly. This is a wearable that will be tried on and worn by many different people. With it being an alternative social musical instrument, it needs to fit a variety of arm sizes or cover various clothing thicknesses that someone might be wearing.

4. I mapped out where the circuits would be placed on a spare piece of neoprene. This is so I can choose the flattest part of the arm and possible connections. *Figure 6.23* shows this part of the process. You could do this on the paper from earlier:

Figure 6.23 – Mapping on neoprene in situ

5. Place the zipper/hook and loop on the fabric where it should be sewn according to your plans for zipper placement. Use clips/pins to hold it in place.

6. Sew the zipper/hook and loop in place.

7. Then, create the conductive pieces of fabric that will be needed. *Plan for the touch inputs.* If you are going to use all the touch pads on the Circuit Playground board, you'll need 2x7 pieces of conductive fabric – one piece for each connection and then a corresponding piece to connect across the other piece of neoprene. I'm going to use a circle design, with two different sizes of circle pieces. This way, they will connect across the conductivity. You will also need two power, two ground, and various pieces for connections back to the circuit board.

    You can cut out the shapes you want. First, I ironed double-sided Bondaweb® to the back of my conductive fabric (*Figure 6.24*). I used a Brother Scan and Cut machine (`https://sewingcraft.brother.eu/en/products/machines/scanncut/scanncut-machines`) to cut my shapes out (you can do the same with a Cricut machine: `https://cricut.com/`). The resulting cuts from the Scan and Cut machine give me consistent parts and takes less time than cutting:

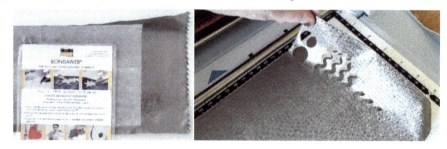

Figure 6.24 – Bondaweb® and the Brother Scan and Cut machine

Figure 6.25 shows the conductive fabric pieces after cutting. Cut them into any shapes that you want for your piece:

Figure 6.25 – Conductive fabric shapes for the circuit

Place the conductive fabric on the neoprene forearm pieces so that they will touch when two different people's forearms come into contact.

Figure 6.26 shows how the connections will touch:

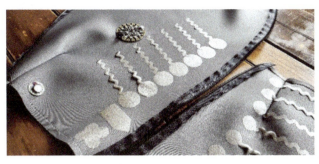

Figure 6.26 – Connections spanning across both forearm pieces

Measure the placement of your connections across both forearm pieces and hold them into place to ensure they touch before fixing them in place.

8. When you have the conductive fabric pieces cut and ready, *glue them into place*. Don't use too much glue because sometimes, it prevents us from sewing smoothly through the material.

9. Take chalk and map out the circuit connections. This is where you will be sewing the connections, so *make sure that none of the connections overlap.*

    Start sewing the connections! When the connections have been sewn, you'll want to add a holder for the battery so that it's secured. Make a snug pocket for it so that you can pop the battery in and it will stay in place:

Figure 6.27 – The sewn connections

10. Double-check that all your connections are snug. Secure all the ends with nail varnish (or fabric glue) and make sure none of the conductive threads are overlapping.

Once you have finished with all the sewing and making sure your connections are secure, we can upload the code.

This code will be the same that we used previously for our touch circuit, but we will add a tone and color sequence at the start so that we know we've made a successful connection when we touch forearms. Also, you should change the colors that light up; I'm altering this to have blue lights.

The code from *Chapter 5*, *Working with Sensors: All About Inputs!*, is available online at https://github.com/cmoz/Ultimate/tree/main/C5/C5_ConductiveTouch. You'll need to add the following code to setup() if you'd like to have all the NeoPixels light up blue and with a tone playing when the social music maker starts. Why will the music only play on startup? Look at the following code:

```
void setup() {
  CircuitPlayground.begin();
    for(int i=0; i< CircuitPlayground.strip.numPixels(); i++) {
    CircuitPlayground.setPixelColor(I, ( 0, 0, 255));
    CircuitPlayground.strip.show();
    CircuitPlayground.playTone(984, 30);
    delay(40);
  }
  delay(1000);
  CircuitPlayground.clearPixels();
}
```

The code to play the music is in our setup(), so it will only play when the code initially loads. Once the code has been uploaded, pop in the battery and find a friend! Test this socially connected instrument out (*Figure 6.28* shows the completed piece, worn by Xiang Li and Qiwen Sun):

Figure 6.28 – The friends-connected wearable in use

I hope you've enjoyed creating a fun wearable with a socially focused goal.

One final note: as with most wearable projects, using them will give you valuable feedback. This wearable activity is no different, and after use and observations, I noticed that it can be difficult to line up the conductive circles for the wearers. I decided to add magnetic buttons that repel if it is the wrong connection or attracts and "locks" into the correct positions. *Figure 6.29* shows the magnetic metal snaps in place. They should be directly on the conductive fabric for where you want them to connect. You can see the opened and closed positions when two people wearing the sleeves are near each other:

Figure 6.29 – Adding magnetic snaps – opened (left) and closed (right)

The outputs we've looked at so far have allowed communication through vision and sound. Lastly, we're going to focus on haptic feedback while learning about motors and vibration for additional communication and interactivity.

Haptic – actuators, motion, motors, and vibration

I will admit, I used to avoid motors! I thought they were complicated to use. However, I've come to realize that using motion can create amazingly interesting pieces and is a lot of fun. Movement has a magical element when we see it, and it's in our nature to try to figure it out. Why did a motor respond to our data? How did it physically create a reaction in response to data received? It's exciting!

Haptic devices can deliver feedback to our skin and bodies. We can use our sense of touch as a form of communication. Does a motor vary in its intensity to give us information about a system? How about the pressure that we feel? Do we alter the duration and pattern of a motor based on our incoming sensor data?

These questions form considerations for our wearable projects. Haptic feedback can be a powerful way to communicate with visually impaired people, or for situations where a screen would be a distraction or hindrance.

Zhan, M. and Khan, A.A., (2022) created an obstacle avoidance system for visually impaired people:

Figure 6.30 – Photo credit – Manuel Zahn, Inside the haptic sleeve

Part of their system uses a haptic feedback sleeve, as shown in *Figure 6.30*. They state that "*The system is independent of lighting conditions and can be used indoors and outdoors. Therefore, the obstacle avoidance system demonstrates a promising approach to using technology to enable more independence for the visually impaired*."

Another multi-object recognition system for the visually impaired can be made using off-the-shelf components like we are using. Park, H., Ou, S., and Lee. J. (2021) prototyped an object recognition system to allow people with a visual impairment to walk safely when alone.

Not only can movement help with communication, but some projects explore other ways to use motors and motion. One beautiful example (*Figure 6.31*) I came across was Finger Orthosis – a prototype for energy harvesting through movement as an alternative power source, by Franziska Kinder. This uses a stepper motor with gears. For more information, visit `https://www.whoisfrancis.de/` Kinder says, "*...about sustainability, I prefer to work transparent and open source. Projects should be easy to reproduce, and the technology should be understandable as well*," which is a great ethos for wearable projects:

Figure 6.31 – An elegant motor prototype. Photo credit – Franziska Kinder

So, how can we add haptic, touch, or feeling to our wearables? There are several ways to add touch elements.

We'll investigate the following:

- DC motors, vibration, and fan (axial motor):

  - Heating pad

- Servos – 180, 360, and continual rotation

- Linear actuators

Motors, servos, and fans all have similarities as they all have movements. Looking at *Figure 6.32*, we can see the different forms they take. A heating pad has also been included because we feel the temperature heat up with this component:

Figure 6.32 – Varieties of feeling output, servo motors, axial fans, and vibration motors

We'll begin looking at each of these areas in a general way so that we understand how we can integrate them into our wearables. We'll follow that with activities so that we can integrate them into our circuits.

DC motors, vibration, and fan (axial)

A **direct current** (**DC**) motor is fairly common and will be included in most standard Arduino kits you buy. They have two wires – a ground and a positive. When connected, it will rotate. Typically, a driver circuit will need to be used to power the spikes of power a motor uses.

In wearable designs, small vibration motors are often used. This is a DC motor with a weighted part that moves when the motor spins. There are different types of vibration motors, so always check the size and if the weighted part is internal. If you think about your mobile phone, you may have it set to vibrate for notifications. We can buy similar small vibration motors to have the same vibrations in wearables to alert the wearer in some way.

Some projects and research that have used vibration for communication include the following:

- Alerting visually impaired people of their surroundings

- Communication between people over distances

- A belt for children with hearing impairments to feel feedback

- A glove for haptic sensations during movies

- Notifications and positive feedback

- Heartbeat communication for wearers or family

- Posture monitoring systems

Vibration is also good for confirming input, for example, on a keypad or number pad. I've used vibration motors as positive feedback for when a wearer performs an action. You may have vibrations turned on when you type on your mobile phone for example. It can save a person time if they sense the feedback immediately, rather than looking to a screen to see confirmation of this. Also, it can be discreet enough that only the wearer is aware of it. A vibration motor can be a good solution for designs where you don't want a sound as an alert. However, if they are placed near or against other things, they can be noisy, so plan and map out your circuit and test it. Harder items amplify sound, while softer materials absorb it.

Webster (2000) prototyped a fingertip search device for visually impaired people. It used an 8x8 array of motors and its primary aim was to allow for research into the *importance of fingertip exploration*. This early work helped the field gain important knowledge about feedback systems. Another vibration system is a project that Stanford researchers are collaborating on. It's a vibrating glove they are testing, to help improve hand function after a stroke. *Figure 6.33* shows such a prototype:

Figure 6.33 – Haptic prototype for hand function after a stroke

Georgia Tech graduate Caitlyn Seim started the project. She hoped that the glove's stimulation may have a similar impact as more traditional exercise programs. She developed an early prototype as a proof of concept. More information is available online at https://neuroscience.stanford. edu/research/funded-research/pts-glove-passive-tactile-stimulation- stroke-rehab-renewal. These projects and research are only a few examples of the ways we can use motors in real-world situations.

Let's start our journey and connect a motor.

To hook up a motor, you'll need the following components:

- 1x PN2222 transistor
- 1x small DC motor
- 1x 1N4001 diode
- 1x 270 Ω resistor

Figure 6.34 shows these components. I'll connect them to a breadboard to show the connection when using these types of motors. I'm trying this circuit with two different DC motors, so there are two in the following figure. The one in the square housing is called an axial fan. We will use the axial fan in a later activity; it connects in the same way, so the motors are interchangeable:

Figure 6.34 – DC motors for a circuit, a diode, a 270 Ω resistor, and a transistor

Considerations for an axial fan include the supply voltage, fan speed, and noise levels. Again, check your datasheet for details about the component you are using. You may also consider the shape, which is typically square, as shown in *Figure 6.34*, or circular. Usually, axial fans are used for cooling. They are the types of fans we have in our computers for example. The connection for a working DC motor is shown in the following diagram (left) as well as the photo (right) in *Figure 6.35*. An important part of the circuit to be aware of is that the transistor, which has three legs, should have the *flat side* facing into the circuit:

Figure 6.35 – Motor components connected

This flat edge is visible in *Figure 6.35*, where you can see the connected components. The transistor has three pins, with the *flat* edge facing you:

1. The *left* leg is for the ground connection to the circuit board.

2. The *middle* leg is where the resistor is connected. The other end of the resistor connects to the pin on your board, so in my example, I'm using A2 (D9).

3. The pin on the *right* is where the diode starts, which is also connected to the ground connection on the motor.

4. Lastly, the other side of the diode connects to the power or both the circuit board and the motor.

Check your circuit before connecting your board to your computer. I've connected mine to a Circuit Playground board in this example.

> **Important Note**
>
> The 1N400 diode has **polarity**, meaning it must be inserted in the correct direction. This allows the current to flow in only one direction – that is, toward the silver marking. So, check and double-check that yours is the correct way around.

Using a motor with an Arduino based board is easy to implement. The following code allows a motor to be turned on:

```
int motorPin = A2;
void setup() {
  pinMode(motorPin, OUTPUT);}
void loop() {
  digitalWrite(motorPin, HIGH);
}
```

The preceding code uses the same code that we used for our LED, in that we turn on the pin that the component is connected to. We are sending the voltage to that pin, and this will turn on the motor.

To add *feeling* as an output, you can use a *heating pad* (*Figure 6.36*). It uses the same code and circuit setup as the one we've just used. Swap the motor out for the heating pad to add warmth to your wearable. Electric heating pads are thin and slightly flexible.

You can add them to wearables for a mild heat sensation. The heating pad uses the same circuit we created for the motor, with a transistor, diode, and resistor. We can sew a pocket for this pad and then use it in a belt circuit to help if we suffer from back ache:

Figure 6.36 – Heating pad

A *stepper motor* is usually described by the number of steps that happens per revolution. The ones usually included in Arduino kits are 32 steps, with the gears inside of the motor housing. It is capable of 513 steps (32x16). It will do a full rotation in equal steps. You may have seen larger versions of these motors on 3D printers, for example, as they are great at making precision movements. Also, note the voltage that this motor will use because you will likely need a driver board. It uses the `Stepper.h` library. You can change the number of steps per revolution, choose the pins your motor is attached to, and then set the speed in the `setup()` function of the sketch. In the `loop()` function, you can control the revolutions – clockwise or counterclockwise. There are sample sketches in the library; it's a good idea to open them and have a look through the code.

Other types of motion can be made with servos. Let's take a look.

Servos – 180, 360, and continual rotation

Servo motors can be programmed for very specific positioning. These are accurate positional types of movements. There is a set of gears that rotates to the number of degrees that we define in our sketch. Some servos will move 0 to 180 degrees, and you can also get 360-degree servos or continual rotation servos. In *Chapter 5*, *Working with Sensors: All About Inputs!*, we connected a Flora board with a servo motor that was controlled by touching a leaf; it was shown in *Figure 5.39*:

Figure 6.37 – Servo with croc clip connections

One of my favorite servos for prototyping is the servo that has croc clips (*Figure 6.37*) for connections.

For this, you can use the `Servo.h` library. There is a sketch in the Arduino `examples` folder called `Sweep` that shows the 180-degree movements. You can add more than one servo to your wearable and be on the lookout for some of the smaller versions, which can be great additions to projects.

These servos usually perform sharp, quick movements, and they can be noisy too, so you will need to figure out how they should be placed in your wearable. It's a good idea to play around with them, get to know how they move, and discover what is most appropriate for your circuit. You could use them to move parts of your garment or move things that are placed on it. They can be used to create stunning and dynamic pieces that shift and move in deliberate ways.

Linear actuators

A linear actuator pushes or pulls something in a straight line. You can find some very small linear actuators that can be embedded in your wearable projects. It may move something in a straight direction for effect or connect other parts of your circuit. They have two wires – ground (negative), which is usually black, and power (positive), which is usually red. These motors keep their positions when the motion is stopped while extending or retracting. Look for the lower voltage linear actuators so that your circuit board can power them.

Overview

With all these motors and movements, you can use the input as data to control your motor. We can use sensors to control the output. This is why we looked at sensors first. It's worth spending time exploring the varieties of motors, specifically for the following purposes:

- Weight
- Size
- Shape
- Features
- Voltage requirements

Understanding these properties will help you when you plan your wearable. You'll understand what components are available and how they can be controlled to add those important interactive elements to your projects.

Now that we have read about these motors, let's make a wearable circuit!

Continuing our journey into haptic feedback, we'll make a circuit that uses a sensor for input and with the data received, a reaction will be made by the appropriate output. In this instance, sound and vibration will be used as alerts.

Activity 6.6 – haptic feedback with a UV sensor

Putting a sewable UV sensor on a hat is sensible. We wear a hat to protect ourselves from the sun and skin cancer is often caused by overexposure to the sun. This can help reduce our chances of getting sunburnt and of exposure to harmful UV levels since it alerts us with a sound to remind us to put on sunscreen. We'll also use a color reference, similar to what's used in UV charts. The one shown in *Figure 6.38* shows the lowest level at 1, which is green, to the extreme level of 11+, which is a harsh red:

Figure 6.38 – UV light level indicators

We will connect a UV sensor and when the UV sensor detects a high reading and it reaches dangerous levels, a buzzer will make a noise and the NeoPixels will change color to alert the wearer to apply more sunscreen lotion.

For this circuit, we'll use the components shown in *Figure 6.39*:

- A Circuit Playground Classic (with vibration or a standalone vibration motor)
- A sewable UV sensor, though you can use other UV sensors and sew them
- Conductive thread
- A battery
- A cap/hat

Note that you could use a Gemma M0 but I'd like to add additional outputs and functions to this activity, so I'm going to use a board (Circuit Playground) with more outputs:

Figure 6.39 – Items used for this wearable

First, let's map out the circuit. As we've seen previously, we will connect the UV sensor using the I²C protocol. To make this circuit, we will connect the UV board to the Circuit Playground board. Connect the following:

- UV board SDA pin to Circuit Playground SDA
- UV board SCL pin to Circuit Playground SCL
- UV board GND pin to Circuit Playground GND
- UV board PWR pin to Circuit Playground PWR
- Vibration motor GND to Circuit Playground GND
- Vibration motor PWR to Circuit Playground pin 1

I'm using croc clips again for the prototype to be sure it works. I'll upload code at this point to check my connections are correct and working before I sew it all in place:

Figure 6.40 – Using the fold for the battery

Position the components on the hat with the *UV sensor facing upwards toward the sky*. Place the Circuit Playground and battery where they will be comfortable for the wearer (*Figure 6.40* shows the battery hidden in the hat's underside). Glue them down to make it easier to connect them (*Figure 6.41*). I used a glue gun to make a strong bond:

Figure 6.41 – Gluing the components into place to make them easier to connect

Let's add the code. Open the Arduino IDE and connect your Circuit Playground. We already have the UV library installed from *Chapter 5, Working with Sensors: All about Inputs!* , but if you didn't grab it, then you'll need to open the **Library Manager** and search for Adafruit_SI1145 library. Once installed, open the sample si1145test file and upload it. Check that you have your **Board** and **Port** chosen. Open Serial Monitor to see if your program output is correct. The test code checks the UV sensor and if it is working. We want to add sound, vibration, and light to it. The complete modified code can be found at https://github.com/cmoz/Ultimate/tree/main/C6/C6__UV_ColorVibration.

Let's look at a snippet of the code.

In the code, look for the if statements and conditions that have been set. The first one defines that the reading should be larger than the threshold we set. This is the threshold for an indoor reading. If the reading is higher than the indoor reading and it's smaller than a value of 689, then the UV levels are low. It will color the NeoPixels a blueish color.

Looking at the next if statement, we can see that the values are higher, so we defined it as moderate UV levels. We created a yellow-colored NeoPixel, set a vibration as an alert, and set a tone to play to warn the wearer:

```
if(uv.readUV()>= UVthresholdIndoors && uv.readUV()<689 )
{
 Serial.println("LOW");
 neoColor(0,255,100);
} else

if(uv.readUV()>=690 && uv.readUV()<1379)
{
 Serial.println("Moderate");
 CircuitPlayground.playTone(345, 200);
 neoColor(255,191,0);
digitalWrite(vibePin, HIGH);
} else
```

Once the code has been uploaded, test your circuit outside. Note that values won't register if you use the UV sensor indoors. The completed cap is shown in *Figure 6.42* with an indoor and an outdoor reading:

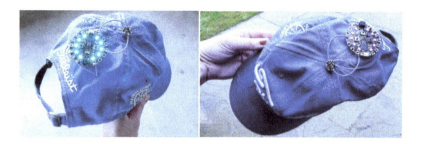

Figure 6.42 – The completed cap – sensing UV

This has been a fun and important wearable for our skin's health. We incorporated a sewable UV sensor to help parents, caretakers, or ourselves know when we need to put on sunscreen. However, we can take this an extra step forward. In the next activity, we'll look at how the temperature can also affect our wearer.

We are going to use the onboard slide switch to add more functionality to our cap. If we slide the switch one way, it will run the UV code, but if we slide it the other way, it will run a temperature check. Let's complete the next activity to see how this works!

Activity 6.7 – using temperature and motion

We will continue with the last circuit, but this time, we will use the *slide switch* (see *Chapter 2, Understanding and Building Electronic Sewable Circuits*, for more information about switches) to control which program we want to run:

- Sliding the switch to one position, we can use our cap outside for UV sensing, which we just completed: the outdoors cap.

- Sliding it to the other position, it will use the temperature sensor for when the cap is worn indoors. When a certain temperature is reached, it will turn on a fan that will blow air to cool us down: the indoors cap.

The Circuit Playground board has a temperature sensor built-in, so we need to access it.

First, we need to add the circuit for the axial fan. The circuit has a fan, diode, transistor, and resistor. These can be sewn on a piece of felt. Refer to the circuit shown in *Figure 6.35* on the breadboard to check that you are putting the components in the correct place, then curl the ends of the components, as we did in *Chapter 2, Understanding and Building Electronic Sewable Circuits*, to make these components sewable.

The axial fan is connected to pin A1 in the code, which is marked as TX1 on the Circuit Playground Classic board. The servo is connected to pin 12. The servo is used to move the fan into position. It's an optional part of this circuit, but it makes it look very cool!

Then, I glued them into place (*Figure 6.43*) to make them easier to sew. Remember, when using conductive thread, don't overlap any of these connections!

Figure 6.43 – Sewing the diode, transistor, and resistor

For adding the servo, a little clip-on hinge (*Figure 6.44*) was made for this circuit by *Fergus Fullarton Pegg*. It was designed in Fusion 360 and printed using TPU on a 3D printer. This is to connect the fan to the brim of the cap:

Figure 6.44 – Servo/fan mount with a hinge for the cap

You could glue the 3D hinge in place/sew it or mount it in another way. I wanted a hinge so that the servo could move the fan if the temperature changed. The final one was printed in a darker blue to match the cap. You can place your fan onto the cap by gluing the servo to it, and then glue the fan to the moving part of the servo.

Append the code so that it includes the functionality we've added:

- The switch feature of the Circuit Playground (to select our program)
- Temperature
- Servo

You can access the code with this functionality at `https://github.com/cmoz/Ultimate/tree/main/C6/C6_UVBuzzTempMotion`.

The completed cap is shown in *Figure 6.45*, with the fan added to our original circuit:

Figure 6.45 – The completed cap

Working iteratively is how you might start creating wearable projects. We start with one feature, then build on it. Working iteratively allows us to increase the complexity of our circuit in a way that we can still find errors as they happen. If we had just put everything together at once and then tried the code, chances are that there would be a few errors – at the least! We will investigate building up projects in more detail in *Chapter 9, Designing and Prototyping Your Own Hyper-Body System*, and *Chapter 10, Soldering and Sewing to Complete Your Project*.

Summary

This chapter worked you through some difficult circuits that implemented both the inputs and outputs that we've been learning about. Through the exercises, we increased complexity in our circuits, to help us to understand how to build complexity in wearables that can serve a purpose. As we progress through this book, the way to make and consider social conscience wearables will become clearer, and I hope that thinking about wearables in this way motivates you to also consider the purposes behind the wearables you make.

Some of the pitfalls when using different outputs is that we need to be aware of the I/O pins we need and select an e-textile board that will suit our needs. This sometimes means that we must compromise on the size or shape of the wearables we make. Also, sometimes, these added complexities add to the code complexities. This will take time and practice to get right but there are a lot of forums and resources available for you. Arduino is a good place to start (`https://support.arduino.cc/hc/en-us`) and, as mentioned previously, there are great resources on Adafruit (`https://learn.adafruit.com/`), Proto-Pic (`https://proto-pic.co.uk/`), and Kitronik (`https://kitronik.co.uk/`), to name a few.

When using NeoPixels, be aware that you can have voltage drop issues. Along some of the longer NeoPixel strips, you may have seen multiple power in points (solder tabs). You can connect power and ground at multiple places along the strip to be sure it has full power all the way along it. This can sometimes fix low brightness and flickers. Additionally, when creating circuits that are a bit more spread out in distance with components, the conductive thread may start to lose its effectiveness. You will have to start thinking about soldering some circuits to create more permanent connections. Luckily, we have *Chapter 10, Soldering and Sewing to Complete Your Project*, coming up!

Having a variety of outputs to communicate to the wearer gives us many options to suit many people. We can design accessibility and inclusivity into the designs by using different modalities such as vibration or bright light.

Now that you have completed this chapter, spend some time reflecting on the types of wearables you have seen or read about and how they can be inclusive.

- Are there designs that you could implement different outputs in so that they would suit a wider audience?

- Have you seen products that are too exclusive because they don't communicate effectively with a wearer?

- What designs would you like to implement, and for what types of people? It would be great to make some notes, drawings, and collections of things you have seen so you can refer to them later when your confidence grows and your ambitions to create larger projects can be fulfilled.

Now that we have our inputs from the previous chapter, and our outputs from the one we've just finished, it's time to build on that knowledge and get busy making! We'll explore an exciting integrated circuit called the ESP32 and some of its varieties in the next chapter.

References

The following references were provided in this chapter:

Schmidt, A. (2000). *Implicit human computer interaction through context. Personal technologies, 4(2), 191-199*. [Available online] `https://www.researchgate.net/publication/2532959_Implicit_Human_Computer_Interaction_Through_Context`.

Ju, W., & Leifer, L. (2008). *The design of implicit interactions: Making interactive systems less obnoxious. Design Issues, 24(3), 72-84*. [Available online] `https://www.researchgate.net/publication/249563448_The_Design_of_Implicit_Interactions_Making_Interactive_Systems_Less_Obnoxious`.

Papanikolaou, D., Brush, A. B., & Roseway, A. (2015, January). *Bodypods: designing posture sensing chairs for capturing and sharing implicit interactions*. In Proceedings of the *Ninth International Conference on Tangible, Embedded, and Embodied Interaction (pp. 375-382)*. [Available as a PDF online] `https://d1wqtxts1xzle7.cloudfront.net/38570953/tei275-papanikolaou-brush-roseway_light-with-cover-page-v2.pdf`.

S. F. Frisken-Gibson, P. Bach-y-Rita, W. J. Tompkins and J. G. Webster, *A 64-Solenoid, Four-Level Fingertip Search Display for the Blind*, in *IEEE Transactions on Biomedical Engineering, vol. BME-34, no. 12, pp. 963-965, Dec. 1987*, doi: 10.1109/TBME.1987.325937.

Zahn, M., & Khan, A. A. (2022). *Obstacle avoidance for blind people using a 3D camera and a haptic feedback sleeve. arXiv preprint arXiv:2201.04453.* [Available online] `https://arxiv.org/pdf/2201.04453.pdf`.

Park, H.; Ou, S.; Lee, J. *Implementation of Multi-Object Recognition System for the Blind. Intell. Autom. Soft Comput. 2021, 29,247–258* [Available online] `https://www.researchgate.net/publication/351719067_Implementation_of_Multi-Object_Recognition_System_for_the_Blind`.

Review questions

Answer the following questions to test your knowledge of this chapter:

1. How many wires does the I²C protocol use and what are they?

2. What is the golden rule when making circuits so that you don't accidentally burn out your board?

3. What does the `strip.setPixelColor(4, (0, 0, 220));` line of code do?

4. What are some of the ways we can use light and vision in our wearable?

5. What useful purpose does the switch on the Circuit Playground board have?

6. What additional components do we need to add to our motor circuits to make sure the motors work?

7. Reflection: Which outputs did you enjoy the most? What planning can you do to use these different visual, audio, and haptic communication methods with the wearer? Take some time to think about some of the communication methods you've seen in existing products or items. What did you find effective, annoying, or unusual? Could you swap one output for another? How would that affect its use?

7

Moving Forward with Circuit Design Using ESP32

In this chapter, we will delve deeper into designing circuits using alternative microcontrollers. These are circuit boards that aren't specifically "sewable," but we can use them for wearables. Using **ESP32** will add more interactivity to our sewable circuits. It's a powerful and adaptive microcontroller board. Although the ESP32 development board form factor is not typically made for a wearable project, we'll look at how we can add them and why this is beneficial. Using these techniques, you can adapt other microcontroller boards and components to your future wearable projects too. We will learn to program these boards using Arduino software.

In this chapter, we will learn about the ESP32 board. We will prepare the Arduino IDE so we can use it to program the ESP32, and we will write a first sketch. Then, we will advance our knowledge so that we can use it to connect to **Wi-Fi**. We will then work through several activities, including making a touch-activated wearable as a device for good mental health and wellbeing. This will collect current data from a website through an **application programming interface (API)**.

By the end of this chapter, you will understand why using alternative boards can be beneficial. You will get to know some of the features of an ESP32 board and be able to use it to connect to Wi-Fi. Lastly, through the activities, you'll understand what an API is, how we connect to one, and how we can update information with it. You will have completed another wearable item too!

In this chapter, we're going to cover the following main topics:

- Understanding microcontroller boards
- Taking a closer look at the ESP32 board
- Connecting to Wi-Fi
- Creating a map for far away friends and family: for mental health and wellbeing
- Using an **application programming interface** (**API**) for live data

Technical requirements

This chapter involves creating a wearable that will connect to the internet and you'll need the following to complete the circuit:

- Arduino Software as the IDE

- Access to Weather API – create an account at `https://openweathermap.org/`

- An ESP32 board: Adafruit Feather HUZZAH ESP32

- An OLED display

- Conductive fabrics and conductive thread

Now that we know what this chapter involves, we can start learning about microcontroller boards.

Understanding microcontroller boards

A microcontroller is generally regarded as a simple processor that does a specific task. Sometimes they are referred to as **microcontroller units** (**MCUs**). The microcontroller is the brain of our project. They are small, very versatile as we've already seen, and usually inexpensive. Microcontrollers also allow a wide range of people with varying skillsets to program and control them, from complete novices to experts. Often, they are used for doing one job repeatedly. The name consists of "micro" because they are small and "controller" because they offer control functions. They are controllers for the physical world, sensing our actions and then using that information to have a reaction.

As we've seen before, they have inputs and outputs that are pins or metal sew tabs. We attach our components to those pins and the microcontroller will allow us to control them. So far we've mostly been using *ATMEL* microcontrollers. The **ATMEGA328** is the processor on the Arduino Uno board. Also, the Circuit Playground Classic we've used contains the ATmega32u4 as its device core.

Development boards have a chip, which is the processor, a power circuit, a hardware connector for programming, and indicator LEDs. Most have a reset button too. The microcontroller **Integrated Circuit** (**IC**) has the following:

- A processor

- Memory (volatile, which is temporarily lost when the board is reset, and nonvolatile, where the memory stays even when the power is off)

- I/O peripherals

A development board integrated with a microchip is shown in *Figure 7.1* (an Arduino Uno). A microcontroller generally has a low clock speed – it's not complex in the tasks it can perform, has no operating system, low power consumption, small internal memory, several I/O pins, and is low cost.

Figure 7.1 – An Arduino Uno microcontroller, the anniversary edition (left), and the R3

To understand the difference between microcontroller and microprocessor boards, we can look at the Raspberry Pi. The Pi can have an operating system, Linux, running on it and you can use a keyboard and display with it as if it were a computer. It is a microprocessor but also a device known as a single-board computer.

The **Gemma M0** board that we have used was initially made using an ATMEL ATtiny85 but that was changed to an ATSAMD21E18 32-bit Cortex M0+ chip. This has a 48 MHz 32-bit processor, which is six times as fast as the previous ATtiny85 version.

The Arduino IDE supports more than 1,000 official and non-official boards, so that will give you some context as to how many boards are available for our use. To have a look at some of this huge selection, you can browse online to see the boards that are Arduino compatible. Look to the end of the chapter for links to online shops where these are available.

We will be focusing on the ESP32 chip for this chapter. As we'll see, it is embedded into many different packages and board styles. Let's take a closer look.

Taking a closer look at the ESP32

The ESP32 is a single 2.4 GHz Wi-Fi and Bluetooth **system on a chip** (**SoC**) and a general-purpose microcontroller, designed by **Espressif Systems**. You can find more information online about their processors at `https://www.espressif.com/`.

Figure 7.2 – Varieties of ESP32 dev boards

This chip has been added to different boards (*Figure 7.2*) and it is these development boards that we'll be using. The prices for these boards vary. Consider what the features are for the different boards and the cost trade-offs. ESP32 offers capacitive touch, I2C, SPI, PWM, and much more.

A guide accessed online at `https://lastminuteengineers.com/esp32-pinout-reference/` contains the common pinouts (GPIOs) for the ESP32-based boards.

> **Important to Note**
>
> Although these are the common standard pin layouts, I would highly advise you to always check your specific board for the GPIOs. Some boards have 30 pins, others 36. You don't want to connect something incorrectly and waste a lot of time trying to fix what is a simple error.

The ESP32 chip is designed for many types of circuits, including mobile, wearable, and **Internet of Things (IoT)** applications. It has capabilities that make these projects possible, including Wi-Fi and Bluetooth capabilities. You can buy it in chip form or as a development module (dev), which is what we'll be using.

For the most up-to-date information, there are documents on the Espressif website `https://docs.espressif.com/projects/arduino-esp32/en/latest/getting_started.html` for reading about developments and different guides to get started. Currently, the ESP32 family is divided into these main categories:

- ESP32 – Wi-Fi and BLE
- ESP32-S – Wi-Fi only
- ESP32-C – Wi-Fi and BLE 5

The ESP32 is an upgrade from an earlier chip, the ESP8266, which was very popular when it was released. It allowed makers, developers, and hobbyists to integrate Wi-Fi into their designs at a far lower cost than what was possible before that point in time. Typically, people would purchase a large shield (*Figure 7.3*) that was placed on top of an Arduino Uno, so the ESP8266 also allowed much smaller prototyping.

Figure 7.3 – Wi-Fi shields and the ESP8266 (the small one in the center)

The ESP32 has more pins, analog in and out, and two cores with a higher-speed processor. As a result, many makers and developers have switched to the ESP32. **DFRobot** makes a series of ESP32 boards, `https://www.dfrobot.com/` called **FireBeetle**, which come with no headers soldered so that you can use them for a variety of projects. They are reasonably priced, allowing low-cost prototyping with an ESP32-based board. They also have a Beetle that is sewable and is only 35 x 34 mm in size, as shown in *Figure 7.4*.

Figure 7.4 – A DFRobot Beetle ESP32, front and back

For this chapter, we will be using the **Adafruit Feather HUZZAH ESP32** (Feather), which came out in May 2017. Note that there is also an updated version of this board, which is the Adafruit ESP32 Feather V2 - 8MB Flash + 2 MB PSRAM. There are several reasons why I've chosen the Feather board. For a start, it has a reset button, not the typical reset and boot button. For many (indeed, most) of the ESP32 development boards, you need to press the boot button to upload your code. On the Feather board, you don't have to do this. It also has a connector for a battery, which is great for our wearable projects. The final reason is that it is breadboard friendly – most of the other dev boards do not fit onto a breadboard conventionally and you need to arrange it across two boards. You can get it in a soldered version, with pins or stackable headers, or one that isn't pre-soldered.

The Feather board has a dual-core ESP32 chip (Arduino sketches run on one core by default, but we can create tasks to use both cores), with 4 MB of SPI Flash memory, as well as Wi-Fi and Bluetooth, so there are plenty of options for our wearable projects.

Also, there are over 50 *wings* that can be used with this board. A wing is like a shield or a hat that goes on the Feather board that you are using. This gives it extra capabilities, such as adding an OLED screen easily, for example. They should all be compatible so you can swap out the main board or extra boards without any problems.

Lastly, it's worth mentioning a tiny board, the **QT Py ESP32-S2**, introduced in December 2021, with the ESP32-S2 chip on it. In *Figure 7.2*, this is the first board on the left, so you can see the size comparison. It has fewer available pins and only uses one of the two available cores for processing.

Let's get started with how we can use and program an ESP32 board. You'll need to follow this next section to use your ESP32 board, regardless of which board you are using.

Activity 7.1 – Programming the ESP32, libraries, and tweaks for Arduino

Now that we know more about the ESP32 boards, we need to do a few things to be able to use them with the Arduino IDE. The ESP32 Arduino board support package is currently part of the *2.0.0 or later* release, so you may want to check whether your version of Arduino already has this package installed. If not, then you'll need to follow along in this section. The board information is also online at `https://github.com/espressif/arduino-esp32#using-through-arduino-ide`.

To use versions of an ESP32 dev board with the Arduino IDE, we need to add the ESP32 boards. There are two things we need to do to add them. You won't need to do this again unless you delete Arduino or install it on another computer, for example.

Modifying preferences

With the Arduino IDE opened, go to the **Preferences** window, which is **File | Preferences**, or use *Ctrl + Comma (PC)* or *CMD + Comma (mac)* on your keyboard. If you look near the bottom of this window, there is an **Additional boards manager URLs:** field, with a field that is empty. If you already have a URL there, (it's likely you already have the Adafruit boards package), then add a comma and paste the URL, which adds a stable release of ESP32 boards to the Arduino IDE. There is also a development release link online (`https://raw.githubusercontent.com/espressif/arduino-esp32/gh-pages/package_esp32_index.json`).

Figure 7.5 – Additional Boards Manager URLs

See *Figure 7.5*, which shows the preferences view with the URL field for where the URL should be added. Click **OK** when you have added the board.

Using the Boards Manager

Now, you need to go to the Boards Manager. You can get to it by clicking the second icon down on the left, which looks like an Arduino board. You can also go to the Boards Manager by going to **Tools | Board | Boards Manager**. Search for ESP32 (it will be by Espressif Systems) and click **Install**. The boards should now be installed. *Figure 7.6* shows a new menu item, **esp32**.

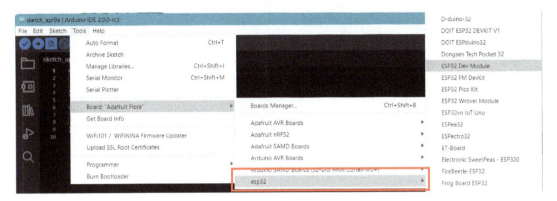

Figure 7.6 – ESP32 boards are now available in the Board menu

We will be using the Feather ESP32 version, so look for **Adafruit ESP32 Feather** in the list of boards under the **esp32** section. There will now also be example code that we can access to try new things on this board.

We will be going through Wi-Fi technologies with the ESP32, so there will be a few activities to follow. These include the following:

- Establish a connection with the Feather Huzzah ESP32, uploading an example sketch
- Make tweaks to code if using different ESP32 boards
- Connect to Wi-Fi, scan networks near us, connect to our own network
- Apply this new knowledge to a project

Now that we know what's coming up, let's get started with the first activity, connecting and communicating between our ESP32 board and computer. Let's get an LED to blink and upload our first sketch on the Feather!

Activity 7.2 – Hello World, does it blink?

This will be a quick activity but it's very important! We need to establish a connection between our ESP32 board and computer. When your board is plugged in, first check that the **board** and **port** are both correctly selected (in the **Tools** menu).

Once you have the correct board and port selected, open the **Blink** example that we used earlier when we installed Arduino. It's in the **File** | **Examples** | **Basics** folder. Upload the code to your Feather (*Figure 7.7*).

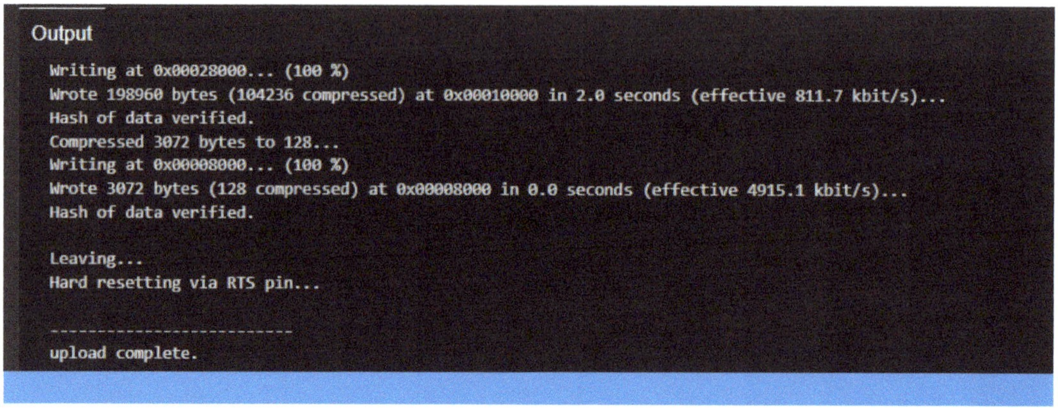

```
Output
  Writing at 0x00028000... (100 %)
  Wrote 198960 bytes (104236 compressed) at 0x00010000 in 2.0 seconds (effective 811.7 kbit/s)...
  Hash of data verified.
  Compressed 3072 bytes to 128...
  Writing at 0x00008000... (100 %)
  Wrote 3072 bytes (128 compressed) at 0x00008000 in 0.0 seconds (effective 4915.1 kbit/s)...
  Hash of data verified.

  Leaving...
  Hard resetting via RTS pin...


  -----------------------------
  upload complete.
```

Figure 7.7 – Code successfully uploaded

It's important to note that this exercise is for the **Adafruit Feather Huzzah ESP32** board. When we upload the code, we will see the upload process and associated messages in the output window. Some boards will behave differently and have other messages.

Using a different ESP32 board

If you are using a generic ESP32 or just another ESP32-based board, you might have to also follow this advice. If you cannot find your board in the menu, I default to choosing **ESP32 Dev Module**, as that seems to work most of the time when uploading.

> **Important to Note for ESP32 Boards**
>
> If you are using other ESP32 boards, then you might have to hold down the **BOOT** button on your board (*Figure 7.8*). In the output window, it will display **Connecting........_____.....___** when you see that message – press (then release) the **BOOT** button. The display window should then show a message similar to **Writing at 0x0000e000... (100 %)**.

If you don't hold down the **BOOT** button, you will see a message similar to the following in the output window:

```
A fatal error occurred: Failed to connect to ESP32: Timed out
waiting for packet header
Upload error: Failed uploading: uploading error: exit status 2
```

We won't get this message with the Feather Huzzah boards as they are made so that they will enter this boot mode for programming. This is actually a great feature.

Figure 7.8 – The boot button on other ESP32 boards

The default code in the **Blink** sketch will also need a little tweaking. It is likely that it won't recognize the BUILTIN_LED variable that is used. So, we'll edit the code to select pin 2 to get our LED to flash. Modify the blink code. Create a const int ledPin = 2 variable and use that variable to replicate the blink action. The code is the following:

```
const int ledPin = 2;
void setup() {
  pinMode(ledPin, OUTPUT);
}
void loop() {
  digitalWrite(ledPin, HIGH);
  delay(1000);
  digitalWrite(ledPin, LOW);
  delay(1000);
}
```

That should work for versions of the ESP32-based board. You should now have a blinking LED (likely blue) on your board. Well done, this is the first step to getting to know a very exciting and versatile board. Now, let's look at one of the exciting features that make the ESP32 board stand out from the others – Wi-Fi. Let's get connected!

Connecting to Wi-Fi

One of the main features of using an ESP32-based board is the Wi-Fi functionality. Let's jump straight in and learn how to connect to Wi-Fi so that we can get more out of our board. We can also use **over-the-air** (**OTA**) updates for this board. If our ESP32 board is installed somewhere that's not easily accessible, we can program it through Wi-Fi. This does require installer code (this code must be in all your uploaded sketches to that board for it to continue working) to be on the board first before it can be used this way; it's a good feature.

Activity 7.3 – Let's get connected

There are a few examples we can use for connecting to Wi-Fi. We will look at these examples so that you can start to see the potential of using an ESP32 board for your wearable projects. We will look at the following:

- Scanning to see the networks near us
- Connecting to your Wi-Fi network

Let's start by scanning for networks around us so that we know our board is working and able to see internet connections.

Scanning to see the networks near us

One of the main reasons we are looking at ESP32-based boards is because we can use them for Wi-Fi. Let's open some code to use our Feather board to display the list of available Wi-Fi networks where we are. There is an example file that we will use. Go to **File** | **Examples** | **Wifi** | **WiFiScan** and upload it to your board. The Wi-Fi library is one that should be installed when you installed Arduino, but if you can't see this example sketch, check whether you have the Wi-Fi library.

One thing to point out is that we typically use faster communication methods with an ESP32 board. You'll notice a line of code in the sketch defines the serial speed of **115200**. Don't forget to change the speed in the Serial Monitor through the drop-down menu. If you don't, you will see foreign characters in the window that look like errors.

When you open the Serial Monitor, you'll see a scan (*Figure 7.9*). It will list the number of networks found and their names. Hopefully, your local network will be there as well.

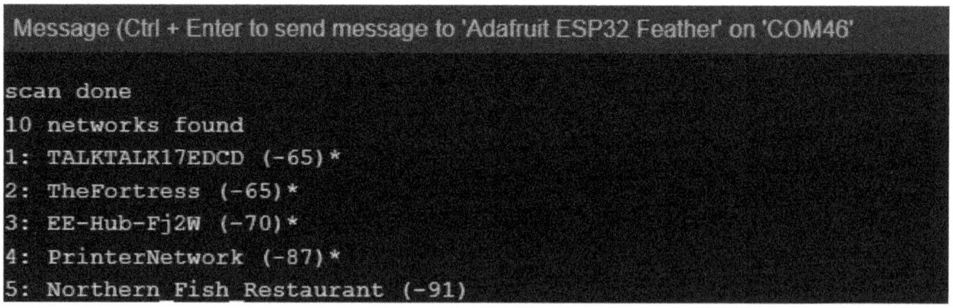

Figure 7.9 – Scanning for Wi-Fi networks

Now that we can see that our ESP32 board has found the networks, let's connect to one of them.

Connecting to your Wi-Fi network

There are several sample files in Arduino that will help us make a connection to our Wi-Fi network. Let's do the following:

1. Open **File | Examples | WiFi | SimpleWiFiServer** (see *Figure 7.10*).

2. Change two values in the file to start a connection between our Wi-Fi and the ESP32 board: the **ssid** name and the **password** input for the network you want to join.

Figure 7.10 – The SimpleWiFiServer file location

Once the file is open, change the values in the following fields to start with:

```
const char* ssid     = "yourssid";
const char* password = "yourpasswd";
```

3. Change these values to your personal network ID and password. After the ssid and password fields have been changed, create your variable for the LED.

4. Edit the LED pin number to 13 for Feather ESP32, or 2 for generic ESP32 boards. The LED pin number is located in three places within this code, so we should follow good practice and create a variable for our LED pin.

5. Create a variable. Remember variable creation requires a type, a name, and a value. The type is **int**, the name I've chosen is **ledPin**, and the value is the pin that the LED is on, **13**. This would be int ledPin = 13;.

6. Find the code with the LED's current pin number (5). Amend those three locations, remove the number 5, and in its place, put our variable, ledPin, into three lines, the first in setup() and the other two in loop():

```
if (currentLine.endsWith("GET /H")) {
digitalWrite(ledPin, HIGH);
```

```
    }
if (currentLine.endsWith("GET /L")) {
digitalWrite(ledPin, LOW);
}
```

Using a variable can save you a lot of time and potential errors.

A Note about Using a Variable

If we use a variable to define a pin number, instead of changing the pin number in every place throughout the code, it will make it a lot quicker for us to change the pin number or a value in the future. Also, using a variable helps to eliminate errors that can happen if we forget to change one of the pin numbers or values in the code.

---

7. Then, upload your code to your board. Reminder: if you're using a standard ESP32, you may need to hold down the **BOOT** button on your ESP32 upload.

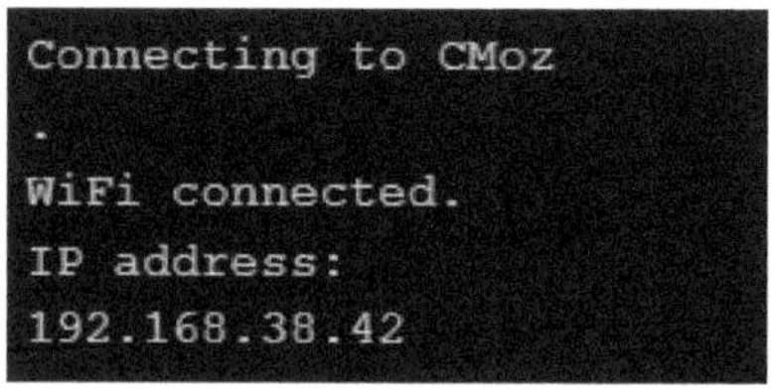

Figure 7.11 – Output to Serial Monitor

8. After the code is uploaded, open the Serial Monitor, and you'll see your board connecting to your network (*Figure 7.11*). The output monitor will display an IP address. Copy this number so that we can visit it. If it doesn't appear, press the **BOOT** button or the **RESET** button on your board to reset it to load the code.

Important Note

You need your computer and your device to be on the same network to visit the web page that will be generated when we go to the IP address.

---

9. Paste the IP address from the Serial Monitor into a browser. When the page loads, you should have the following (*Figure 7.12*) page view. This allows us to control the LED on our ESP32 board. Click the links to check whether yours is working correctly. If it isn't working, check you've changed the pin number to the correct pin for your board's LED. Make sure to also check that you have changed this pin number in three places throughout the code. Lastly, check that the network is working.

Figure 7.12 – A browser window with the web page connected to the ESP32 open

You'll notice that this web page says, **Click here to turn the LED on pin 5 on**. This is because the HTML in our file has this exact text written, so we should also amend that. In the sketch, you'll see the following line:

```
client.print("Click <a href=\"/H\">here</a> to turn the LED on
pin 5 on.<br>");
```

Amend this line to reflect the correct pin (13) that you used for your board.

Extra challenge!

Spend some time looking through this code and playing around with it. We can see from the code written that appending the URL with /H will turn on an LED as we've done previously in the code using `digitalWrite(ledPin, HIGH)`. You should spend some time playing with the code in small ways, adding an LED, for example, and amending the code to turn that extra LED on or off.

Have a look through the code and the way that it is displayed in the browser and change its appearance too. I have uploaded modified code that will have buttons to click. It has a .h file, which we can store our credentials in so that they are not stored in the main code body. The code is here: https://github.com/cmoz/Ultimate/tree/main/C7/C7_ESP32_LED_On. In *Figure 7.13*, there is an example of using buttons and controlling two LEDs. You can modify the colors and look of the website too.

Figure 7.13 – The web interface for the program

Now that we've successfully found networks we can connect to and connected to our network, let's look at a project that addresses how we can add interactivity to a wearable design using the advantages of the Feather.

Creating a map for far away friends and family: for mental health and wellbeing

We will be creating a map reminding us of our faraway friends and family! Sometimes, it can be difficult for families to stay connected. I know I have family far away and I think of them a lot. It's not always easy to call or speak with them because of the time differences too. *Heshmat, Y., & Neustaedter, C. (2021)* studied family and friend communication over distance during the pandemic. Their paper (`https://dl.acm.org/doi/pdf/10.1145/3461778.3462022`) shows the results of design lessons for these times of extreme disconnection.

I realized that I have my family's time zones that correspond to where they are and what the weather is like on my mobile phone. In a way, it makes me feel closer to them to imagine what the weather or conditions are like for them. Do you have a similar way to form some of these small connections with friends or family that are far away? We will be creating a wearable to remind us of where our loved ones are. The final project is shown in *Figure 7.14*, a vest with map locations to interact with that display live location data, styled as a pocket watch concept.

Figure 7.14 – "Touch me" live mapping of friends and family (modeled by Sushmita Joshi)

This project focuses on creating a wearable that could allow us to feel close to missing loved ones. I'm going to make a vest with touchable areas that will display the current weather conditions for where my family members are located.

For this activity, you'll use the following:

- Adafruit Feather HUZZAH ESP32 (or your own ESP32 board)
- An OLED

- An optional vibration motor
- Conductive material and conductive thread or wires
- An article of clothing that you can upcycle

Once you've gathered the required items, think about what connections would make you feel closer to your friends and family, and then let's start the next activity.

Activity 7.4 – Making your maps using symbols that work for you

To start this activity, I thought that having a map shape to represent where my family members are located would be the first step in order for me to feel closer to or think about them. I went online to find usable shapes to represent where they live and I will cut these shapes out of conductive material. The map is from `https://www.worldatlas.com/maps/canada/ontario`, where you can get your map too. *Figure 7.15* shows where family or friends live.

Figure 7.15 – Map shapes

I'll use these shapes and will cut them out of conductive fabric. I'll use the ScanNCut machine again but it's fine to cut shapes and symbols out with scissors. When you've decided on your symbols and cut them out, put them aside for now. We'll look at the **touch capacity** of the ESP32 next to get this part of our circuit working.

Activity 7.5 – Touch me! Building your touch pads

Let's create our touch circuit on the Feather. The touch pins on an ESP32 sense variations in electrical charges. These can be generated from our touch, or from items that are conductive, such as conductive fabric. Often people use these touch pins to wake the ESP32 from sleep. The ESP32 has several sleep modes that reduce power consumption. There are five different sleep modes: active, modem, light, deep, and hibernation. We won't be using these here for this sketch but it is something to consider for your future wearables.

Figure 7.16 – A pinout diagram for Adafruit Huzzah32 ESP32 Feather

To use touch capabilities with the Feather, we read the values of the pins that we define in our code as being touch-sensitive using the touchRead(GPIO) function. There is a possibility of 10 **capacitive pins** and these allow us to replace a traditional button or other standard inputs. This can reduce the wear on components.

The touch pins defined in the Huzzah32 ESP32 Feather pinout diagram are from Adafruit (*Figure 7.16*, courtesy of Adafruit https://learn.adafruit.com/assets/111179) and Attribution-ShareAlike Creative Commons (http://creativecommons.org/licenses/by-sa/3.0/).

These touch pins are the same for most ESP32 boards but other boards may have additional touch inputs. Always check the development board that you are using to see which pins have been broken out or made accessible. Have a look at the Feather to see where these pins are located.

All we need for this activity is the board and the USB cable. Plug in the board, select the Feather from the **Board** menu, and find your **port**. Open the file, copy the code, and paste it into a new sketch. See the following link: https://github.com/cmoz/Ultimate/tree/main/C7/C7_TouchInterruptESP32.

Let's look at the code in detail. We start with declaring our variables; this includes the threshold and three bool values. The **threshold** is how sensitive the touch will be. A lower number is more sensitive. Then, the three bool values define whether a touch is true or false. We initialized these to all be **false**. This means **no touch input**:

```
int threshold = 40;
bool touch1detected = false;
bool touch2detected = false;
bool touch3detected = false;
```

In our setup() function, we open the Serial Monitor so that we can see the touches registering. We also define what pins we are using for touch input through the touchAttachInterrupt

`(T5, gotTouch1, threshold)` function. This allows us to define the pin and threshold; it will also run a function when a touch is detected:

```
void setup() {
Serial.begin(115200);
delay(1000);
Serial.println("ESP32 Touch Interrupt Test");
touchAttachInterrupt(T5, gotTouch1, threshold);
touchAttachInterrupt(T3, gotTouch2, threshold);
touchAttachInterrupt(T0, gotTouch3, threshold);
}
```

In the `loop()` function, the code is checking for any touches on the pins. It then executes code if a touch has been detected. It will set the `bool` value back to `false` and print to the Serial Monitor. You could add some LEDs to turn on here, for example, to test your code and work through the example in further detail:

```
void loop(){
if(touch1detected){
touch1detected = false;
Serial.println("Touch 1 detected: GPIO 12");
}
if(touch2detected){
touch2detected = false;
Serial.println("Touch 2 detected : GPIO 15");
}
if(touch3detected){
touch3detected = false;
Serial.println("Touch 3 detected: GPIO 4");
}
}
```

After the `loop()` function, we have the three functions that will change the `bool` value to true when there is a touch. This will then trigger the touch detected in `loop()`:

```
void gotTouch1(){
touch1detected = true;
}

void gotTouch2(){
```

```
touch2detected = true;
}


void gotTouch3(){
touch3detected = true;
}
```

Open the Serial Monitor and you should have a functional readout of the touches when you touch the pins on your Feather or other ESP32 board.

Experiment a little with the code: display other messages or use other pins for touch. Maybe add an extra pin or two and get that working.

Once you've had a chance to expand the code a little, we will add an OLED to our circuit. This will be used to display information.

Activity 7.6 – Adding an OLED for displaying information

We will add an OLED to our circuit to initially display the touches registered. Then, we will move on to a more complicated and interesting feature of our wearable, displaying the weather data from our conductive map pieces. Here are the necessary steps for this activity:

1. First, let's hook up the OLED. As previously, we only need to use the I²C wires, SDA and SCL, as well as the ground and power. The I²C pins on the Feather are marked with SDA and SCL, and they are located near the top end of the board where the antenna is. Other ESP32 boards have SCK/SCL on pin 22 and SDA on pin 21.

    Once connected, we should run sample code to test whether the OLED is working and connected correctly. You'll notice now that we've done several activities that we often follow a similar procedure. We connect one type of input or output and then we run a small sample sketch to check whether things are working. This is usually the best way to work, as it is a lot easier to solve problems when the components are isolated.

2. With the OLED connected to the Feather, open the example code in **File | Examples | Adafruit SSD1306 | ssd1306_128x64_i2c** (*Figure 7.17*):

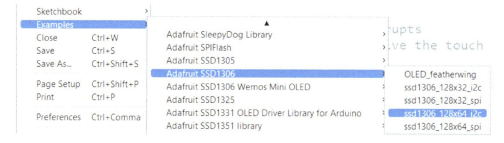

Figure 7.17 – Open the example sketch

3. Upload the code to your board. You should see the OLED displaying all the sample graphics that are included in this sketch. If yours isn't displaying any graphics, then check that you have supplied ground and power to your OLED from the Feather. Ensure to also check that your SDA and SCL pins are the correct way around. Lastly, check that all your wires/connections are secure and not loose.

4. Now that we know the connection works, let's merge our code with the sketch that registered touch inputs in the previous activity. Open that sketch again and we'll combine both working sketches together. *Try this yourself first*. If you do it step by step, it is a good way to understand what the code is doing:

    I.   Begin by adding the libraries that the OLED uses at the top of the sketch.

    II.   Then, work towards the `setup()` function where there is an initialization of what we are using.

    III. Follow with the behavior that you want the code to execute. We want the OLED to *display which touch is registered*, so where do we add that code and what should it say?

To check your code, visit GitHub online to view and download my completed version if you'd like to check it against mine, at the following link: `https://github.com/cmoz/Ultimate/tree/main/C7/C7_TouchInterruptESP32_OLED`.

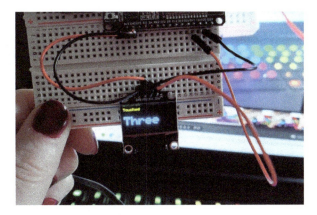

Figure 7.18 – OLED and ESP32 connected with the touch code

Now that we have our OLED displaying the touch information (*Figure 7.18*), we can get it to display something far more interesting – the weather data for our chosen locations. To achieve this, we will learn how to use an API to connect to services.

Using an Application Programming Interface (API) for live data

An API allows two computers to talk to each other. When you check the weather or access services, you're using an API. In a sense, it's a messenger; it sends a message to a service, such as the weather service, saying that you are requesting data and what the data that you're requesting is, and then it is returned to you. The API key is the code that gets sent to identify who you are (whether a user or a developer) and it sends the requested information to you if the key is correct. This often is based on the type of account you hold with the API provider.

We'll be setting up a free account to access an API for weather data. This next activity will take us through the process step by step.

Activity 7.7 – Connecting to an API

In this activity, we'll use the ESP32 to request the weather data relevant to our specific predetermined locations, using an API for live data. We will use a service provided by https://openweathermap. org/ to access the information that they have about the weather. To start, we need to make an account with them (*Figure 7.19*). Once we make our account, we can generate an API key that is needed to connect the requested data.

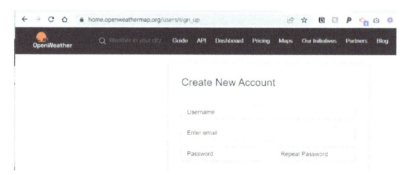

Figure 7.19 – Create an account

To create an account, you'll need to enter a *username*, *email*, and *password*. We only need to access the free service at this point, but in the future, if you use them for more API calls or other services, you may need or want to upgrade your account.

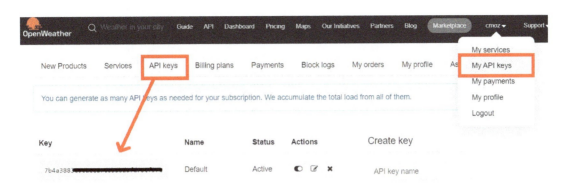

Figure 7.20 – Your API keys

After your account is created, do the following:

1. Navigate to the **My API keys** section (*Figure 7.20*) in your account. It should look similar to mine.

2. I've generated a new key called `current weather`, but the **default API** key works fine.

3. Copy your API key. Note that if you have just created a new key, it can take 10 minutes or so to be ready for use.

Check that it's ready to use by sending a call to your browser using `http://api.openweathermap.org/data/2.5/weather?q=Toronto&APPID=yourAPIkey`. Change `yourAPIkey` to the key in your account. If it's working, you'll have output similar to *Figure 7.21* with weather information from the city selected.

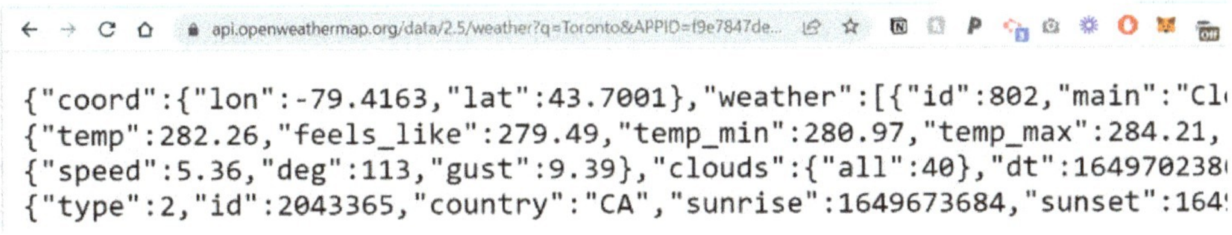

```
{"coord":{"lon":-79.4163,"lat":43.7001},"weather":[{"id":802,"main":"Cl
{"temp":282.26,"feels_like":279.49,"temp_min":280.97,"temp_max":284.21,
{"speed":5.36,"deg":113,"gust":9.39},"clouds":{"all":40},"dt":164970238
{"type":2,"id":2043365,"country":"CA","sunrise":1649673684,"sunset":164
```

Figure 7.21 – The API call comes back if it has worked

Now that we are connected, we will access a current weather call. Details on this part of the API can be read at `https://openweathermap.org/current`, which details what we will be doing.

If you skim through to the **API call** section, you'll see (*Figure 7.22*) how to form the call to request the information.

Figure 7.22 – OpenWeather API forming the API call

One of the calls is for the URL appended with the city we are requesting and our API key. For this, we use the following:

```
https://api.openweathermap.org/data/2.5/weather?q={city
name}&appid={API key}
```

We'll start by checking whether the simplest form of this code works with our Feather and that we can retrieve a basic weather call:

1. The code at `https://github.com/cmoz/Ultimate/tree/main/C7/C7_API_testCall` demos access to the full API. You'll need to fill in your API key, your SSID, and password.

2. Upload the code to your ESP32.

3. Open the Serial Monitor. There should be a request for the information through the API call that we wrote.

Now that we have a working API call, a working OLED, and the ESP32 with several bits of implemented code functions, we will bring it together. This is exactly what's covered in the next activity.

Activity 7.8 – Connecting all the parts

Well done for making it this far already. We've covered a lot of ground! You've gotten the ESP32 board working with code to connect to Wi-Fi, you've gotten input touches to register touch, and you have also hooked up an OLED to display when touches have been detected. You have also connected to an API to access live data. Now, we will add all of these working parts together to continue creating our map for faraway friends and family.

This is our biggest task to date but don't let that worry you. We will go through it step by step and there is no rush to finish in a hurry. Take the time you need to process and work through the information, as it's a fun and rewarding project when you get to the finish. It also teaches you a lot of new and exciting concepts that you will take forward in your wearable technology journey.

To complete this activity, we will need access to the completed code and all of our components to make the physical circuit.

The items are as follows:

- Completed code: `https://github.com/cmoz/Ultimate/tree/main/C7/C7_WeatherAPI`
- An ESP32 board
- Conductive fabric pieces
- Conductive thread/wires
- An OLED (I'm using a yellow/blue style OLED)

There are a few steps to follow for completing this activity, but first, let's look at the ways we can make a typical development board wearable.

Some of the development boards come with pins, called header pins. We can use needle-nose pliers to gently bend these pins back so that they are flatter, rather than pointing straight down (*Figure 7.23*).

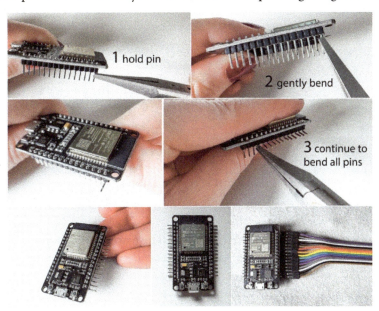

Figure 7.23 – Making a microcontroller board wearable

Once the pins are flat, we can place the board on a piece of fabric, such as felt. We can then sew these connections using multiple stitches over each pin. Alternatively, you can attach a DuPont cable with a socket end to these pins and sew it into place with thread. Both methods are appropriate, depending on your wearable placement and the durability needed.

We can use these techniques for other types of circuit boards. This way, it opens up the range and diversity of types of boards with varying features that we can use in our wearables. We can also solder wire directly to the pins or the board. This is a great way to improve the durability and longevity of our wearables. We will cover this in more detail in *Chapter 10*, *Soldering and Sewing to Complete Your Project*, where we discuss soldering.

Now that we have made our board compatible with a wearable sewable circuit, we can begin to put it together.

Here are the steps to make our wearable:

1. Let's start with creating the touch connection on an upcycled piece of clothing. Choose and source your clothing item. I've got a vest that I'll modify. We need to extend the touch inputs that are working on our Feather. We don't want to have to touch the pins directly; they are too small and it's not wearable. So, we will use conductive thread, DuPont connectors, or wires to extend the conductivity to where we want to have touch capability (*Figure 7.23* illustrates the DuPont connectors.)

2. I've used wires that I'll connect to the touch pins on the Feather. I have three map locations, so I'll continue with the three touch inputs that we tested earlier. Decide where to place your conductive pieces on the item of clothing, as in *Figure 7.24*:

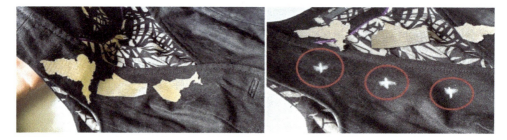

Figure 7.24 – Chalk marks for where the wires will push through

3. The underside of where the conductive fabric will be placed is where you will start. This is where I put my wires, which I *push through the back of the fabric*. You can carefully cut open a small part of the fabric inside and slide the wire into it for a neater finish.

4. The wires need to be poked through the fabric from behind so that they will touch the conductive fabric on the front. *Figure 7.25* shows the wires that I have run along the inside of the vest and then poked through where I left the chalk marks.

Figure 7.25 – Wires through the vest

5. In my wearable, I taped down the wire until I was ready to sew. The tape stops the wires from slipping back into the garment. I also mapped the ends of the wires to which pins on the ESP32 board they would connect. I wrap masking tape around the wire and write the pin number on it. Always *test and check the connections* before sewing them in place.

6. When you have your wires in place, sew them with conductive thread to the fabric. When the wire is sewn, the conductive fabric will register our touch.

Figure 7.26 – One of the map pieces sewn into place

7. After sewing the wires with conductive thread, *place your conductive material shape over the top* of these sewn wires.

    Stitch the conductive fabric in place with conductive thread. You can use quite large stitches for this. You also don't have to use conductive thread for it necessarily. I used conductive thread mostly for the aesthetic. Then, knot it to the sewn wire piece on the underside.

8. Test the connection again once it is sewn into place (*Figure 7.27*). Your screen should light up with the location's current weather data.

9. Follow this method for all the other shapes in your wearable:

    A. Sew the wire underneath with conductive thread

    B. Place your conductive material shape on top of that sewn piece of wire

    C. Sew the shape into place

Figure 7.27 – Testing the touch connection

10. Once you are happy with your circuit and how you've mapped and planned it out, decide whether you want to include a vibration motor. A vibration motor can be a great way to send immediate feedback to the wearer that they have successfully touched the map piece.

An additional design consideration for the wearable is that I've decided to mimic a pocket watch style design for this vest/waistcoat. With a 3D printer, you can make shaped casing that will hold your components. *Figure 7.28* shows a 3D printed pocket watch casing for the OLED, with a front and back piece:

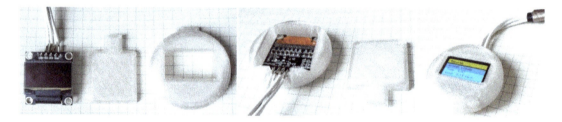

Figure 7.28 – 3D printed casing for an OLED

This was designed and made for me by Fergus Fullarton Pegg, and he's made it available on Thingiverse if you'd like to print your own in a color of your choice: `https://www.thingiverse.com/thing:5469722`. As part of the overall piece, it completed this wearable nicely!

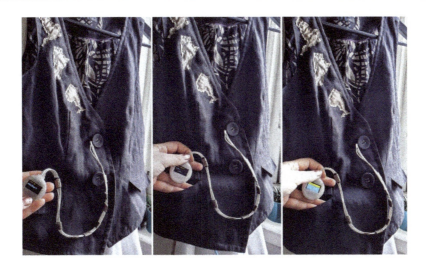

Figure 7.29 – The finished piece

The photos in *Figure 7.29* show the final piece with the touch maps made from conductive fabric, the OLED screen as a pocket watch, and the ESP32 board hidden behind the button area.

One thing to note is that if you want to use the circuit wherever you are, I often set the Wi-Fi network to one shared from my mobile phone. I create a mobile hotspot and connect to the hotspot in the code, adding my SSID and password.

When you have finished assembling your circuit and double-checking that your connections are secure, we can begin the process of coding the circuit.

Installing the library and uploading the software

Open the code (`https://github.com/cmoz/Ultimate/tree/main/C7/C7_WeatherAPI`) and copy it. Create a new sketch and paste the code into it. Then, plug the Feather board into the computer.

We need to install a library to get this code working. Open **Library Manager** and search for the **ArduinoJson** library. We need this library in order to parse JSON files. Parsing JSON files means extracting the information that we are getting back from the API request and being able to display it in a useful, readable way. When we tested our API connection earlier, we were presented with all the information returned from the weather website on the web page. This wasn't very easy to read, as shown in *Figure 7.21*.

This library will help us to display the exact information we want on the OLED. Using the library means we only need to add a few lines of code to our Arduino sketch and it will do all the hard work. There is a lot more information online at `https://arduinojson.org/` about this library.

Once we have the library installed, let's look at the code.

What's the code doing?

This is undoubtedly the most substantial code we've worked with so far. There's a lot in it, but if we look through it, you can start to read through and understand what each part is doing. Let's look through some parts of the code so we can understand it better.

Let's start here:

- The `long getRate = 15000` line declares that our variable called `getRate` will run for 15 seconds. This is our way of capping how often the calls to the API will happen. On our free account, we can make 60 calls a minute, but we want time to read the output and we don't want to max out the account.

- The next part of the code is about *defining a string variable* for each location. This is the information we are requesting through the API. You'll have different information here depending on the locations relevant to your own project.

- I've called these variables `base_t` for Toronto, `base_w` for Winnipeg, and so on, so that I don't forget which variable refers to what place.

You might want to rename your variables to match your project better. Here is the code:

```
String base_t = "http://api.openweathermap.org/data/2.5/
weather?q=Toronto,ca&units=metric&appid=yourAPIkey";
String base_w = "http://api.openweathermap.org/data/2.5/
weather?q=Winnipeg,ca&units=metric&appid=f yourAPIkey";
String base_y = "http://api.openweathermap.org/data/2.5/
weather?q=York,uk&units=metric&appid= yourAPIkey";
String units = "metric";
String weatherUrlT = base_t;
String weatherUrlW = base_w;
String weatherUrlY = base_y;
```

I followed this convention further along in the code, for the `weatherUrlT` string, for example. Be sure to change *all the locations* where this variable appears.

One feature of Arduino 2.0 is that we can select the variable name we want to change, right-click to see the sub-menu, select **Change All Occurrences** from the menu (as in *Figure 7.30*), and then start typing the new name for your variable. This will update them throughout the code for you.

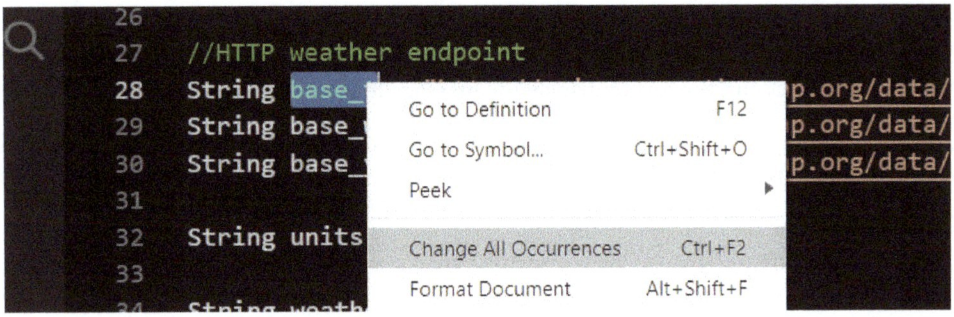

Figure 7.30 – Changing a variable name throughout the entire code

The next part of the code that you may need to adjust is the size of the OLED screen that you are using:

```
#define SCREEN_WIDTH 128
#define SCREEN_HEIGHT 64
```

In the setup() function, you'll notice a function being called, oledStart(). This is a function that we want to run when everything has been loaded in the setup() function. If you scroll down to near the bottom of the code (around line 200 or so) to find this function, you'll see the following:

```
void oledStart(){
  oled.invertDisplay(false);
  oled.clearDisplay();
  delay(500);
  oled.setTextSize(1);
  oled.setTextColor(SSD1306_WHITE);
  oled.setCursor(0, 0);
    oled.write(0x03);
  oled.println(" How's the");
  oled.setTextSize(2);
  oled.setCursor(0, 20);
  oled.println("weather?");
  oled.display();
  delay(2000);
}
```

This code will display a message that reads, *How's the weather?*, with a heart character too, as defined in oled.write(0x03). The oled.setCursor() code comprises the .setCursor() function, which is the prewritten code that will set the cursor location, and oled is the object that we want the .setCursor() function to affect. The function defines where we want the text to start: the first number corresponds to the horizontal placement and the second to the vertical placement. Play around with these values and the text to display the message that you want.

Our loop() function has one main part of code, an if statement that will react when the touch has been determined. The if(touch1detected) statement is repeated three times, once for each possible touch.

This code clears the display, sets the touch1detected bool to false, and calls the displayMessage(String) function; this has a String parameter. The function takes the String sent to it – in this example, the displayMessage() function, passes a String value containing "How's Toronto" – and uses it in the code.

We could write all the OLED instruction code directly into this block and not put it in its own function. However, we would end up writing a lot of *repeated* code. Putting code in its own function is a good idea to save repetition:

```
if(touch1detected){
    oled.clearDisplay();
    touch1detected = false;
    Serial.println("Touch 1 detected: GPIO 12 TO");
    displayMessage("How's Toronto?");
        if((millis() - prevWeatherCall) > getRate){
                updateWeather(weatherUrlT);
                prevWeatherCall = millis();
                delay(100);
                oledDisplay(parsedWeather);
                delay(getRate);
                oledStart();
        }
}
```

The code will check the rate of our call to the API, and if it is bigger than the getRate variable we set earlier in the code, we can make another call.

If this if statement is true, it will do the following:

1. Get the updated weather.
2. Set the new timer.
3. Display the parsed weather information on the OLED screen.
4. Then, it will wait to give the wearer a chance to read the weather information.

We end this `if` statement by launching the `oledStart()` function again to reset what's visible on the OLED screen. This lets the wearer know that they can press a different conduct map shape for another location.

Let's have a look at the `updateWeather()` function that is called. This first allocates the `payload` String, with the function `httpGet(location)`. The value of the `location` String is the URL to the API service. This was provided by calling the `updateWeather(weatherUrlT)` function in the code. This has our location information and API key, in this example, it's appended with T so we know it's for Toronto. When we called this function, we called it with the String location argument, which was this line of code, with the `weatherUrlT` String sent to the `updateWeather(weatherUrlT)` function:

```
void updateWeather(String location) {
 payload = httpGet(location);
 if(payload != "HTTP Error") {
 DeserializationError error = deserializeJson(jsonWeather,
payload);
    if(error) {
      Serial.print(F("deserializeJson() failed: "));
      Serial.println(error.c_str());
      return;
    }
    parsedWeather[0] = jsonWeather["name"].as<String>();
    parsedWeather[1] = jsonWeather["weather"][0]
["description"].as
<String>();
    parsedWeather[2] = "Temp: " + jsonWeather["main"]["temp"].
as
<String>() + " " + tempUnit;
    parsedWeather[3] = "Wind: " + jsonWeather["wind"]["speed"].
as
<String>() + " " + windUnit;
   }
  else parsedWeather[0] = payload;
  oledDisplay(parsedWeather);
 }
```

The `parsedWeather[x]` String array contains the information about the four fields that we want to display. Then, we call `oledDisplay()` to display that information as processed by the JSON library we are using.

If you look through the code, you'll see many functions that we have written and that we are using. If you look through them line by line, you will see code that you can edit to alter the way information is presented, for example.

Extra challenge

That is a lot of information, making, and coding. One of the best ways to consolidate your learning is to challenge yourself and play around with the code.

Look through the following functions:

- `void oledDisplay(String parsedJson[4])`
- `void oledStart()`
- `void displayMessage(String message)`

Edit some of the OLED code for the visual representation of the information. Try to look through some of the other code snippets to see where the information is passed through to a function and how altering some code can change the way that things function.

You can also add code to *include vibration*. When should this happen? This is great feedback for the wearer, so look at your code, revisit how to add the vibration motor, and what code to add.

When you're done, run a check through your code first to be sure it compiles. When it has compiled, upload it to your board. Be sure to check that the board and port are correctly selected after you've plugged your board into your computer. If there are errors, check it against the original code that was in the link provided.

Now that we've built a project with a focus on wellbeing, let's look at some of the real-world examples of projects to connect people.

Examples of design and innovation for wellness purposes

Sensory tools, wearables, and fabrics are used in various ways with the goal and effect of improving wellbeing. Research by *Tan, J., Chen, A., Shao, L., Kim, H., & Ge, L. (2022)* details an e-textile sensory tool for people with dementia. Touch triggers different effects, from flashing illumination to sounds, such as bird calls and the sea. They have used embedded conductive cushions, knitted conductive tassels, and hand-stitched conductive feathers. This is a co-design process and they are hoping to encourage the use of e-textiles in dementia care.

Another example of keeping close and connected in this way is within the work of *Warraich, M U; Rauf, I; and Sell, A., (2018)*. This research also uses a co-design process to design wearables with the purpose of monitoring and improving the emotional wellness of the elderly. They highlight the importance of including the elderly in the design process. They point out that wearables that track the state of the wearers exist but only with a "one-size-fits-all" approach. Designing and making a more personal item with the involvement of future wearers themselves could produce a more suitable item for them to wear.

Figure 7.31 – A Spire health tag

Another designed product used for emotional sensing includes the Spire health tag (2018), as seen in *Figure 7.31*, a *discrete clothing-adhered health monitor* that is attached to a waistband or bra. It tracks breathing patterns to determine the level of stress a wearer might be feeling. It is marketed for health and wellness. This started as a Spire Stone but that was discontinued in 2019. The tag stays on the clothing you choose to attach it to and its battery lasts 1.5 to 2 years. The tags are washable, so it's anticipated that you leave them where you stick them, and they continue to track you consistently throughout the year.

This is an interesting wearable because it's one that the wearer doesn't have to think about using. It stays charged and is washable, so the idea is that you have several, all placed on items such as underwear, and then you leave them in place.

Another wellness wearable that I've come across is Cove (shown in *Figure 7.32*). This is a headset to be worn twice a day for 20 minutes and vibrations activate areas to keep you calm and emotionally balanced. The potential benefits are better sleep, less stress, and improved mental performance.

Figure 7.32 – A Cove headset

There is also a tested prototype, Dormio, which is a hand-worn sleep tracker (*Figure 7.33*, credit: Oscar Rosello `https://creativecommons.org/licenses/by/4.0/`) and an associated app. This records dream reports (using Bluetooth to a mobile or computer). Interaction with Dormio happens through different stages of consciousness. This includes waking, during the onset of sleep, during sleep, and so on. You can find out more about the project at `https://www.media.mit.edu/projects/sleep-creativity/publications/` and `http://www.adamjhh.com/dormio`.

Figure 7.33 – Dormio (credit: Oscar Rosello)

The wearer decides what they want to dream about, whether solving creative problems, reflecting on an emotional issue, or finding a new perspective on something specific. It's explained that *the potential utility for a device like Dormio is to specifically enhance performance on a task pre-determined by the user*, with the researchers citing that correlations between *dream content and sleep-dependent memory processing have been reported in several studies*. This paper, *Dormio: A targeted Dream Incubation Device*, is cited at the end of the chapter.

One last tip – a dynamic SSID and password

From our examples, we've been coding in our SSID and password information. This is okay, but if we do want our device to change locations or to use another network, what do we do? We must reprogram our ESP32. There is another solution. We can create a **Wi-Fi manager**.

This is beyond the scope of the book, as our focus is on the wearables themselves. However, a Wi-Fi manager will help you move forward with making your own wearables. You can come back to this little section later when you have completed more ESP32 projects and you want to implement one; it's an advanced skill.

The ESP32 has two main modes for Wi-Fi. They are **Station Mode**, where the device connects to another Wi-Fi router, and **Access Point Mode**, where the device acts as the Wi-Fi router. We want the Wi-Fi credentials to come from us or a user. This means that the ESP32 will need to be in Access Point Mode first, then it waits for credentials, then it shifts to Station Mode.

The library (`https://github.com/kurimawxx00/wifi-manager`) consists of three main files. There is an HTML file loaded (*Figure 7.34*), which presents the form for users to enter their credentials. There is the `.ino` sketch, which checks for saved connection information. If none is found, it will load the credentials form. It saves the information in memory called **EEPROM**. We will use EEPROM in *Chapter 13, Implementing the Best Solutions for Creating Your Own Wearable.*

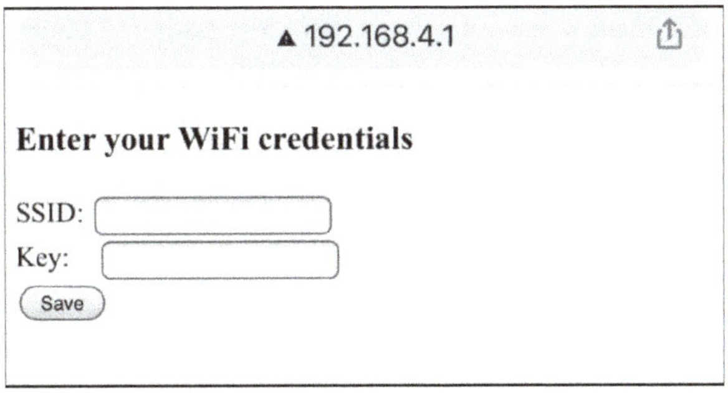

▲ 192.168.4.1

Enter your WiFi credentials

SSID: [   ]
Key: [   ]
(Save)

Figure 7.34 – Wi-Fi credentials

Lastly, there is also the `WiFiManager.h` file, which does the communication. Rather than me explaining more in detail, if you want to implement this, then you should visit GitHub, where there is a tutorial link for how to implement the code. You'll need to *add a button* on pin 13, to trigger it to search for the Wi-Fi credentials, see whether there are any, and launch the HTML page.

Another tip to make sure the files work is to put them in the same folder together. Then, they will open in tabs (*Figure 7.35*). You will get an error message if the `HTML.h` file doesn't load with the `WiFiManager-example.ino` file.

Figure 7.35 – The files opened in tabs in the Arduino IDE

Once you have advanced your skills with the ESP32, you might want to try this out. You should edit the HTML page so that it suits your wearable.

This brings us to the end of the chapter, and it's been a full one!

Summary

This chapter has explored the world of microcontrollers and how we can use them to bring more life to our wearables. We looked at what a microcontroller is and what its main features are. We then focused on the powerful ESP32 after learning about its predecessor, the 8266, which started a huge shift in wearables because of its inclusion of Wi-Fi capabilities at a much lower cost. Our board of choice was the Adafruit Feather HUZZAH ESP32 for several reasons, and it fit our project well. We looked at creating a wearable that would allow us to keep family and friends in our thoughts. This was a positive mental health and wellbeing project so we felt connected to loved ones who were at a distance.

To enable this technology and interaction, we looked at creating symbols that represented them and then accessing live data online. This was achieved through accessing an API service: in this example, it related to weather data. We then looked at making a non-traditional e-textile board usable in our wearable projects. We then put it all together, which included displaying data on an OLED screen when the conductive map symbols were touched.

Overall, this was a very involved chapter with a lot of new concepts introduced. I hope you have realized how much progress we are making. Now, we are ready to learn about prototyping. This will contain a mix of theory and practical activities. So, let's get our thinking caps on and jump straight into the next chapter!

References and further reading

Tan, J., Chen, A., Shao, L., Kim, H., & Ge, L. (2022). Customization of e-textile sensory tools for people with dementia. The Design Journal, 25(1), 104-125. `https://www.mendeley.com/catalogue/8a2d539d-9f27-31fa-8d1b-58357ad3232a/`.

Hua, D., Wei, H., & Blevis, E. (2018). MemoryPin: Turning digitally co-present moments into tangible memory keepsakes. In DIS 2018 - Companion Publication of the 2018 Designing Interactive Systems Conference (pp. 253–258). Association for Computing Machinery, Inc. `https://doi.org/10.1145/3197391.3205445`.

Warraich, Muhammad Usman; Rauf, Irum; and Sell, Anna, Co-creation Model to Design Wearables for Emotional Wellness of Elderly (2018). BLED 2018 Proceedings. 6. `https://aisel.aisnet.org/bled2018/6`.

Haar Horowitz, A., Cunningham, T. J., Maes, P., & Stickgold, R. (2020). Dormio: A targeted dream incubation device. Consciousness and cognition, 83, 102938. `https://doi.org/10.1016/j.concog.2020.102938`.

Carr, M., Haar, A., Amores, J., Lopes, P., Bernal, G., Vega, T., ... & Maes, P. (2020). Dream engineering: Simulating worlds through sensory stimulation. Consciousness and cognition, 83, 102955. `https://www.sciencedirect.com/science/article/pii/S1053810020300325?via%3Dihub`.

Heshmat, Y., & Neustaedter, C. (2021). Family and Friend Communication over Distance in Canada during the COVID-19 Pandemic. In *DIS 2021 - Proceedings of the 2021 ACM Designing Interactive Systems Conference: Nowhere and Everywhere (pp. 1–14). Association for Computing Machinery, Inc.* `https://doi.org/10.1145/3461778.3462022`.

Singhal, S., Neustaedter, C., Ooi, Y. L., Antle, A. N., & Matkin, B. (2017). Flex-N-Feel: The design and evaluation of emotive gloves for couples to support touch over distance. In the proceedings of the *ACM Conference on Computer Supported Cooperative Work, CSCW (pp. 98–110). Association for Computing Machinery.* `https://doi.org/10.1145/2998181.2998247`.

A selection of online shops for Arduino-compatible boards:

- `https://www.tinkertailor.tech/`
- `https://proto-pic.co.uk/`
- `https://www.adafruit.com/`
- `https://uk.rs-online.com/web/c/raspberry-pi-arduino-development-tools/arduino-shop/`
- `https://www.arduino.cc/en/hardware`
- `https://www.sparkfun.com/categories/300`

Review questions

1. Can we only use e-textile boards for our wearables? Explain why or why not.

2. What are the three main parts of the microcontroller?

3. What are the two main advantages or extra features that an ESP32 board offers us?

4. Describe the process for developing a wearable in stages and why it is a good idea to carry it out this way.

5. What is an API used for?

6. Why did we need an API key?

7. Can we edit all occurrences of a variable or other element in our code at once, or do we need to do this one by one throughout the code?

Part 3:
Learning to Prototype, Build, and Wear a Hyper-Body System

In this part, we will understand through making. We will look at hyper-body systems involving three or more senses. You will prototype, sew, and solder to make your own hyper-body system.

This part of the book comprises the following chapters:

- *Chapter 8, Learning How to Prototype and Make Electronics Wearable*
- *Chapter 9, Designing and Prototyping Your Own Hyper-Body System*
- *Chapter 10, Soldering and Sewing to Complete Your Project*

8

Learning How to Prototype and Make Electronics Wearable

Prototyping is essential for all your circuits. What do we mean by prototyping and what do prototypes prototype? Also, what do we need to understand to make a wearable wearable? This chapter provides guidance to help generate thoughts and knowledge about human behaviors. We will learn about prototyping from breadboard to body, making it work on uneven surfaces and the natural curves of our bodies, and learning how comfort, usability, and someone's style universe affects their relationship with a wearable. Lastly, we will examine materials and layout considerations that will get you on your way to developing your own hyper-body system to practice your new skillset.

In this chapter, you will learn the theory behind prototyping. We will understand the advantages of prototyping in different ways to get different outcomes. These methods will contribute to creating informed wearables that are functional and desirable for the people we are designing for. We will look at the **Houde and Hill model**, as well as **quick and dirty** methods of prototyping. You'll see examples created during prototyping sessions. Hopefully, this will inspire you to understand how these methods can benefit your own practice.

By the end of this chapter, you will understand how to progress rapid prototypes by choosing materials, fabrics, and items that are suitable and appropriate for the informed wearables you make.

In this chapter, we're going to cover the following main topics:

- What do prototypes prototype? – the Houde and Hill Model
- Breadboard to body – how to make wearables usable
- Comfort, usability, and style universe
- Materials and layout considerations

Technical requirements

These are optional items, as you can follow the activities that suit you, but the following will be useful:

- For rapid prototyping, a timer and foamboard or cardboard
- A glue gun with glue sticks, or a 3D printer pen and TPU flexible thermoplastic filament for experimenting
- Various fabrics, threads, conductive materials, and so on

What do prototypes prototype? – the Houde and Hill model

We will be looking at prototyping through a **Human Computer Interaction** (HCI) lens, as prototyping is understood differently in other disciplines. A prototype is a representation of part or all of a system. Prototyping methods and explorations have varied greatly over many decades. As digital media and ways to create and build artifacts have evolved, so has the need for prototyping. Some methods of the past, although still useful for idea generation, might be less appropriate for the types of challenges we might be facing in physical computing. Why do we prototype? There are several reasons. Prototypes are important to *understand how a thing might work*. They are important to help **communicate** our thoughts and ideas, facilitating ideas and **conversations**. They are useful for getting **feedback** to improve our designs and concepts. They can also be good for **generating ideas**.

A prototype can represent different states or features of a design. However, for all the many reasons we need for prototyping, the paper by *Houde, S., and Hill, C., (1997)*, defines three key questions that should be the focus of designing prototypes:

- What **role** will the artifact play in a user's life?
- How should it **look and feel**?
- How should it be **implemented**?

They suggest that a focus on the purpose of a prototype – namely, what it prototypes – is the way to build a much better prototype. The systems we are building for wearables often have complex features and components. Their model (see *Figure 8.1*) represents a space corresponding to those three key questions:

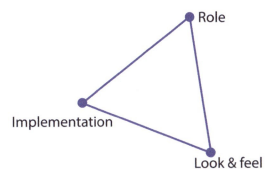

Figure 8.1 – The Houde and Hill model of what prototypes prototype

This allows a designer to separate the system components, typically into the way the artifact would work. The **role** prototype is important to work through what purpose it fills in someone's life. How would it help solve societal issues, improve society, or a situation for a person in some way? Also important when prototyping a wearable is considering that you may need to focus on a particular location on the body. You might spend time prototyping the placement aspect, through researching fabrics and flexibility of materials. This could result in a **look and feel** prototype to test your design (some describe it as a looks like prototype).

According to Houde and Hill, "*implementation usually requires a working system to be built; look and feel requires the concrete user experience to be simulated or actually created; role requires the context of the artifact's use to be established*."

Lastly, an **implementation** prototype will address its workings (some describe it as a works like prototype). In the wearables field, I see this as trying to get the components and electronics working together. In *Chapter 1, Introduction to the World of Wearables*, I also defined this as electronic prototyping. *Figure 8.2* shows an example of an electronic prototype for a wearable I was making:

 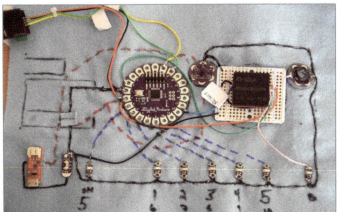

Figure 8.2 – Electronic prototyping – an implementation prototype

Using their model, as a designer you decide where you think your prototype will fit in this remit. Is it going to be predominantly a look and feel prototype, or is there an aspect of the role to be considered? You could mark this on their model, similar to what I've marked out in *Figure 8.3*, showing the placement of the relationship of the prototype:

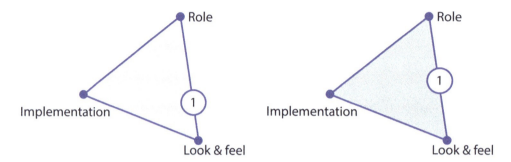

Figure 8.3 – A wearable prototyping a particular body location

As shown in *Figure 8.3*, you might give the role function an almost equal split of the prototype function, but that has no implementation in this case. In the case of a role prototype, the question you should ask should be, what will change in this wearer's life? The look and feel should reflect how it feels; this is the sensory aspect for the wearer.

There is also a central position that emerges when there have been prototypes created that satisfy all three questions; this is an **Integration** prototype, and the space is mapped as shown in *Figure 8.4*. These integration prototypes answer several of the design questions. It represents *the complete user experience of an artifact*. These are time-consuming to build because all parts should be working or good representatives of the final prototype.

However, this model from 1997, which I use in my own prototyping thinking, offers other areas for consideration:

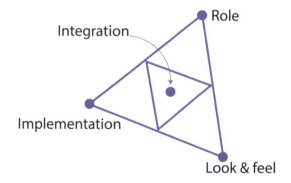

Figure 8.4 – The integration prototype – Houde and Hill

We briefly spoke in *Chapter 1, Introduction to the World of Wearables*, about other important issues when designing informed wearables. Do you remember what other issues should be considered?

We discussed the following:

- Ethics
- Environmental factors and sustainability

We should also consider, particularly for wearables, the intersections of the following:

- Society/social considerations
- Context
- Technological advances

The importance of these issues, and us reflecting on them, is a priority for informed wearables. The triangle areas intersect, as the social elements also play an important role in both the context and ethics in a design, for example. Equally, this applies to the sustainability aspect. We use the Houde and Hill model but include considerations for these other areas to encompass a wider remit when designing in this field. When trying to work through the implications, *Figure 8.5* shows a possibility of where these topics intersect. This could be a launch pad for a point of discussion when designing your wearables. Consider the ethics and environmental impact throughout the project:

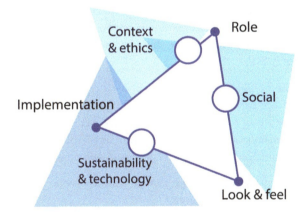

Figure 8.5 – Adding layers to prototyping

Lastly, it's important to also understand the concepts of **low-fidelity** and **high-fidelity** prototypes. When we speak about low fidelity, it could be as simple as making the prototype out of card or foamboard just to work out placement issues. We call this low fidelity because it won't resemble the final version of our prototype. *Figure 8.6* shows a diagram of starting with making a low-fidelity prototype, and as time and the number of iterations increase, so too does the fidelity and quality of the prototype:

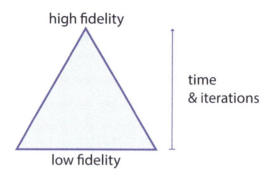

Figure 8.6 – Fidelity of prototypes

A low-fidelity prototype does not necessarily look like the final version. Typically, different materials are used. It might also have an altered configuration; however, it will encourage reflection. This is important because to resolve issues, reflection is needed. Having a prototype makes this easier to do. Sometimes, I start with an initial proof of concept as a role prototype (industry may call this a feasibility prototype), just to establish whether there is any scope for further development in an idea or concept.

After exploring the work by Houde and Hill, undertook during their years at Apple, we will also look at Lim, Y. K., Stolterman, E., & Tenenberg, J. (2008) and the anatomy of prototypes – prototypes as filters and manifestations of design ideas. They view prototypes, "... *not only in their role in evaluation but also in their generative role in enabling designers to reflect on their design activities in exploring a design space.*" I've included a link to their research, which you may want to read to develop your knowledge further. Also, at the end of the chapter, there are references that you can follow up on to learn more about prototypes.

Lastly, to add to iterative prototyping, in industry you will also come across **parallel** and **competitive** prototyping. Parallel is a concept based method where you create more than one prototype and test them at the same time. Competitive prototyping is similar, but the concepts are developed by different people or teams, and these prototypes are tested at the same time. You can then compare the results from the testing to make the emergent design as the proposed outcome.

Now that we've read some theory about prototypes, let's do an activity that will help us to understand the quick and dirty concept – **rapid** prototyping.

Activity 8.1 – quick and dirty

We are going to do an activity in which you can practice a quick and dirty prototype. Before we begin, let's look at the benefits of using this method. Being able to quickly and cheaply create a prototype allows you to get initial concepts mocked up so there is a conversation space around it. Rapid prototyping should be exactly that – rapid. It isn't about working everything out perfectly. It's about getting a concept or a thought together quickly enough so you aren't focused on those tiny details that don't matter initially.

The more you can work in a rapid way to test initial ideas, the more time and effort (and money) it will save down the road. Sometimes, we create a prototype that has taken a long time to make and has been costly, and we only want to hear positive feedback and praise about it. This isn't helpful. This won't improve the design, it won't make it wearable, and you'll be hesitant to make changes. Also, sometimes, we feel the idea is too big or difficult, so we just don't actually start making it. The thought of excessive work that might be needed to create a prototype can lead people to inaction. Practicing low-fidelity, quick and dirty prototyping should be seen as an opportunity to learn.

> **Making Mistakes**
> Failures should be embraced at this stage as a learning experience. It also allows you to make progress fast, moving forward in your design planning and creating. Also, sometimes making mistakes can inspire a new idea or a new way of working too.

Also, if your prototype looks like it was made in a hurry, people offering feedback won't feel like they are crushing your dreams. They can be honest and give you feedback on what might be improved. I've found that sometimes if we show a prototype that looks near perfect, people will think that is the final design. They might focus on one particular aspect. This might disappear in your final design, and they will be disappointed.

Here are the advantages of a quick and dirty approach:

- Quick to make.
- Low cost.
- Encourages conversations that can be open and honest.
- Designed to educate/inform.
- People can focus on your concept and not on minute details.
- Find and fix problems.

Here are the disadvantages of a quick and dirty approach:

- Can be hard to get targeted feedback.
- People might find it difficult to understand the full idea if very simplistic.
- You will need to make many prototypes.

You might want to take feedback from these early and often prototypes and put them on a wall with sticky notes. You can pin this raw data up and look through it easily and spot the common and different thoughts. Organizing the information in this way is done with an **affinity diagram**:

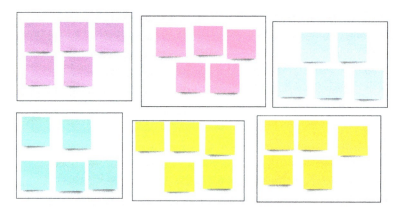

Figure 8.7 – Online Affinity mapping exercise

It might be organized by **themes** or patterns you see. It's about grouping similar ideas together. When they are organized, give them a heading for the topic or grouping. This was developed by *Kawakita Jiro*, an ethnographer in the 1960s, as "the KJ method for organizing notes." If you prefer working on a computer, then use an online service such as Miro (`https://miro.com/`), or Mural (`https://www.mural.co/`) and you can create your sticky notes online (*Figure 8.7*) from the feedback you get.

Lastly, I did a talk about a rapid prototyping session I ran, and it's an activity we can repeat. Visit the talk (done for *Arduino Week 2022*) at `https://youtu.be/EENeQGhTTAM?t=3997`. The main idea is we use foamboard as a material, which isn't normally bendable or used as something we wear, but it can make a great rapid prototype. Let's do the activity!

Activity 8.2 – rapid prototyping with foamboard

We can use this solid material to create the shapes we need to test our initial concepts out. I challenged participants to create a wearable item for a body part – with no electronics. This will be your activity now. For this activity (do it with friends?), you'll need the following:

- Foamboard/foamcore

- A sharp knife, a metal ruler, and a cutting mat

- Glue and a glue gun

To learn techniques for cutting foamboard, there is a great guide online with drawings: `http://www.fastefoundation.org/resources/foamcore_construction.pdf`. This will show you basic cuts to manipulate the material.

Your challenge is to create a prototype that has no electronics at this point:

1. Choose a part of the body (upper arm, forearm, leg, waist, neck, ear, head, hand, wrist, ankle, knee, back, torso, abdomen, or calf). Maybe choose a part you haven't designed for yet?

2. Set a timer for 15 minutes.

3. Create an item for that body part using foamboard.

Consider the following:

- **Weight**: It should be light enough to stay in place.

- **Position**: Make it for the body part that you've chosen and ensure that it fits it well.

- **Comfort**: It needs to stay securely where it is but not so securely that circulation stops.

- **Movement**: Does it impair movement at all? It shouldn't restrict someone.

- **Size**: It should be an appropriate size for the part of the body.

Having done this myself and with students, it is a useful activity to free your thinking because there are so few restrictions:

Figure 8.8 – A foamboard prototype on the wrist

Using a low-cost material in a general way can help with idea generation. *Figure 8.8* shows an example of foamboard that has been cut to fit around a wrist area.

Done the activity? Reflect

Think about your design. Consider the position, weight, movement, size, and comfort of it. Ask a friend to try it on. Can you take their picture in it? Would they wear it all day? If not, why? What would you alter for this design in the future? How would you make it better? Take photographs of your work and results.

Also, it's always important to consider the impact of our designs and prototyping. Could you reuse cardboard, for example, or other materials that you already have to hand? I often use secondhand, donated, old worn clothes when making first prototypes, for example.

After your reflection, let's move on to the next activity.

Activity 8.3 – rapid prototyping – adding components

Now that you've completed your basic prototype, think about the electronics. Keep it rapid, using a breadboard and croc clips:

1. **Planning**: What components will add an interactivity element to this prototype?
2. **Mapping**: Spend 15 minutes mapping out the circuit and how you would do it.
3. **Build phase**: See how much you can get finished in an hour.

Again, after this second exercise, test it with a friend. Take photos and talk about the design. What other designs could you have made from the initial foamboard prototype you made? Did you have other possible solutions?

Other rapid prototyping ideas

There are other ways we can rapid prototype, and using a **3D printer pen** is a good way to mount components fast. These pens are usually oversold as an amazing tool to 3D-print things, but the results never look like how it's advertised. However, we can use them for creating quick prototypes. In *Figure 8.9*, student Jiwon Lee uses a 3D pen to mount an electronic circuit on clothing:

Figure 8.9 – Using a 3D printer pen

We can use the 3D pen with **TPU**, which is a filament that is very pliable. Because it's softer than other plastics for 3D printers, we can push it into the fibers of material or board. It isn't going to be permanent, so you could even do it on clothes that you wear and peel it out eventually:

Figure 8.10 – Using a 3D printer pen for mounting electronics

Figure 8.10 shows a Makey Makey board that was used for a sound-based wearable prototype. It's in a cage made from TPU with a 3D printer pen. You can use the pen to stick items together, or if you put masking tape over the top of an item or structure, you can then create containers or pockets. These techniques were demonstrated in a workshop by *Dr Andrew Quitmeyer* during a week of Wild Wearables. You can read more about his work at `https://www.dinalab.net/`.

Now that we have looked at and tried a couple of techniques, you should have a prototype or two with some interesting results. Hopefully, you will be able to build on them later. For now, let's look at how we go from breadboard to the body in this next section.

Breadboard to body – how to make wearables usable

"*You need a goal and a reason for making a wearable. It shouldn't be a wearable just to be a wearable. It needs to be useful and serve a purpose.*"

*–From the creators of Bolu, a monitoring system for kids and parents for tracking
type 1 diabetes*

You will have created an electronic circuit on a breadboard to test how it functions. From this, you may have decided that it should be used in a wearable. So, why are we turning this into an electronic item we can wear? Is this an item that we need to carry with or near us, and if so, why? Is the item giving us information that we need to be current and up to date? Are there visual or auditory signals or cues that we need to pay attention to? Will this item improve something we are currently doing, or hope to do?

If you have decided that we need this to be a wearable for one of those reasons, or countless others, then you might be working through thoughts of how to take it from breadboard to the body.

Ehn and Löwgren (1997) use the term **quality-in-use** to refer to a range of aesthetic, ethical, and functional qualities that need to be considered in the design. Qualities such as enjoyment, fulfillment, and fun are not properties of technology. These properties, which add so much engagement and interaction between us and a wearable, could be considered as outcomes of certain kinds of experiences. These experiences could be enabled with – or through – technology. So, understanding what might make a particular product or design more pleasing or enjoyable to use could be achieved through trying to analyze or observe the experience of use.

Here are some examples of wearables that were created with breadboards in the first instance, as part of a rapid prototyping exercise. This was part of a wider project examining the relationship between people and nature. The examples shown in *Figure 8.11* and *Figure 8.12* are focused on wearables for the hand:

Figure 8.11 – Using crochet to hold components

Details of the projects and contributors are given at the end of the chapter. This was a student collaborative project during *Winter School at The Glasgow School of Art*'s Innovation School, at the Highlands Campus, which was collaboratively taught with colleagues, and other participating universities from Germany (Köln International School of Design, KISD) and Barcelona (University School of Design and Engineering of Barcelona, ELISAVA). In *Figure 8.11*, we see an elegant solution to obscure a breadboard and **radio frequency identification** (**RFID**) tag reader. It is hidden in the crochet wrist piece created by Lisa Nikelowski. She created the main wrist and hand area and, to improve wearability, added the two ring-attached portions, which made it a more elegant and thoughtful solution. The wearable hugs the hand, creating a more intimate solution. The hand approaches the RFID card that is on the table, causing the lights within this piece to become illuminated.

In *Figure 8.12*, another group workpiece, the ultrasonic distance sensor is pushed into a small breadboard. This triggers movement in the collar piece around the neck of the wearer. But the solution for rapid prototyping is a simple design partially obscuring the technology. A servo motor in the collar portion is completely concealed allowing a more immersive solution or experience. The handpiece is attached simply with pipe cleaners for a fast and effective solution. A close-up of the hand part of this wearable piece is shown in *Figure 8.13*. These are great quick prototyping solutions to allow someone to test their usability and feasibility, or even to test their concept and conceptual ideas:

Figure 8.12 – A hand and neck wearable worn by Elisabeth Seider

This allows these students time to reflect on what they are building. They are also able to get feedback in a much quicker way than if they spent many hours refining essentially the same design:

Figure 8.13 – The wearable top and a close-up of the handpiece

Lastly, when moving from the breadboard to the body, placement for wearables is easiest on the collar area, the upper arm, forearm, wrist, ribcage area, waist, hips, thigh, shin, and upper foot area. When we come to the *Materials and layout considerations* section, we will explore practical ways to connect components and our wearables to the fabrics that we wear.

Now, let's learn more about the comfort, usability, and style factors that affect wearable designs and adoption.

Comfort, usability, and style universe

A fascinating thought is an idea of making technology *invisible in use*. Wearables should be invisible to those around the user (Healey, M., 2007). This is not a new idea; it has been researched within the **Human Computer Interaction (HCI)** field (Card, S., Moran, T., Newell, A., 1980). The term HCI was first used in 1975 (Carlisle, J., 1976).

Are there technologies that you currently use that are seamless in their purpose? The notion of **Ubiquitous Computing** is appropriate for the field of wearables, as it is about computing appearing anytime and anywhere. Wearables should also not require continual attention (Amft, O., Lauffer, M., et al., 2004).

The approach for this book is to learn and become confident in making wearables from an informed perspective. However, learning these skills will also allow you to apply your own creative freedoms and explorations, which doesn't necessarily follow the more traditional routes I am describing. You could look up the work of Madeline Schwartzman, for example, at `http://www.madelineschwartzman.com/art-and-interaction` or even in the example of *Figure 8.13*. You can see Schwartzman's work in *Figure 8.14*.

When considering comfort, usability, and style universe in our wearables, we should design so there is **minimal effort required by the wearer**, little disturbance, or distractions, and keep notifications to a minimum. This can sometimes be termed **pervasive** computing (Nieuwdorp, E., 2007) or, a term I like to use, **everyware** (Greenfield, Adam, 2006), which is an easier-to-understand descriptive term.

If we go further back, we can reference the thoughts of J. C. R. Licklider: "*Man-computer symbiosis is an expected development in cooperative interaction between men and electronic computers." (Licklider, J. C. R., 1960)*. This is the idea of mechanically extending humans!

Figure 8.14 – Madeline Schwartzman – Face Nature

From my studies and research, I learned that acceptance, adoption, and comfort are important to people wearing the designs. Having a useful and usable design is great, but it should also be *aesthetically pleasing, age-appropriate, fashionable, and culturally and socially acceptable*. Devices that look as though they were designed specifically for accessibility are not adopted (King, 2001). Starner (2001) also states many challenges of wearable computing, which are still relevant – particularly that "*a user's taste is an important factor for acceptance.*" Echoing Starner's observations, Ariyatum, Holland, Harrison, and Kazi (2005) state in their research that the physical appearance of a wearable plays a significant role in its acceptance. They also note that a wearable should fit both the users' lifestyle and their personality.

When considering factors for a successful wearable, we can look to McCarthy and Wright (2004). Their perspective, to *"view technology as experience"*, captures the thinking behind the design of a wearable or technology device. They noted: *"Perhaps the most important aspect of experience that it makes visible is the potential for surprise, imagination, and creativity, which is immanent in the openness of each moment of experience."* Defining acceptance when considering our wearable designs means we consider how a wearable will become part of a person's everyday routine. For this to happen, it needs to fit in with the social aspects of the wearer. An important part of designing a wearable is that you identify social boundaries that could limit a wearable's use.

Currently, and for several years, one area of the body that has become acceptable for wearable technology is the wrist. Smartwatches, step trackers, and similar are socially accepted. These devices are mostly passive in that they are reporting devices, so interaction with them is minimal. One way to drive acceptance is to consider fashion. Can your wearable enhance someone's everyday style? Does it allow personalization?

Here are some thoughts for consideration on our wearable journey:

- Are there wearables that are not wearable?

- Do people wear electronics or do they wear jeans, jumpers, and so on? Should we focus on the style and not that there are electronic components in the item?

- Do wearable products need to be invisible and unobtrusive?

- What should a wearable's basic requirement be? Is it comfort, safety, and control of the wearable?

- What cultural differences impact a product's properties and its acceptability?

- What are the environmental impacts of what we make or how it's used?

A primary concern for wearers is the **style** of the wearable. Following that is **price**, then **technical** function, and whether it has a widespread use – or not – will also affect its adoption. Comfort, bulk, and the fit of a device are all considerations. The comfort of a wearable can be affected by its physical properties. This includes the size and weight of the system and the effect the wearable has on movement and pain. It could be limited by the psychological responses of the user – for example, the pride of the user when wearing it. To successfully "mount a computer on a body," comfort issues need to be taken into account. Excess stresses could cause discomfort, which could affect how a task is completed. A user expects both comfort and ease of use, as well as a product that is efficient.

Also, wearers today consider the ecological impacts of wear and use, including waste in the fashion industry – for example, what waste will there be if they purchase and use a wearable? If a product is seen as very wasteful or made from materials that are contributing to environmental impacts, then it is likely they will not want to wear it or be seen using it. Equally, we all have a responsibility to ensure our impacts are reduced as much as possible.

The questions raised in this section are to provoke thought and discussions, which you can return to after doing your own research. There aren't necessarily clear-cut answers. Another consideration is how a domain affects the wearable, which we will learn more about now.

Activity 8.4 – how does a domain affect the wearable?

One of the predominant goals of this book, besides understanding and building hardware and software wearables, is to understand what **long-term value** they can bring – the importance and, I feel, the necessity of making wearable technology meaningful. Considering how a domain affects the wearable will allow you to plan more clearly and accurately.

Embodiment theory (Hinton, 2014) states that "*our brains are not the only thing we use for thought and action; instead, our bodies are an important part of how cognition works.*" This considers that all the sensory information our bodies receive, the environment we are in, and the way we interact with it contribute to how we process information. If we have an overly complex device, we are increasing our mental workload, and that will make the wearable feel more of a burden or a challenge to use.

We've seen already that wearables are developed for so many vastly different domains, including healthcare, entertainment, performance, and sports monitoring. This activity will be more speculative in nature. This can serve as a future guide as part of the planning for your informed wearables.

Deciding the purpose or need for your wearable – *why do we need this?* – upfront can help you work through other essential considerations, such as the following:

- **Comfort**: This is freedom or a lack of discomfort or pain. If your wearable is comfortable enough, they may not sense it after extended wear, for example. Consider the temperature, not only the environment around them, but does your circuit emit any heat? Consider the texture and material – is it itchy, for example, or smooth on the skin? Is there any significant weight or unacceptable tightness when wearing or using it? Consider abrasion, impacts, humidity, dust, flexibility, and water resistance.

- Will your wearable allow **natural movements**? Will it burden the wearer in any way? Are there constraints that may be physical but that can also be **psychological**? There have been studies about memory devices, for example, where the device is so cumbersome or large that they are embarrassed to wear it – even if it improves their condition. Will they experience anxiety when using this item? Does it restrict movement?

- Will you have flexible or elastic materials particularly near or around joints or areas of flex in the body? **Measurements** for the human body also differ greatly from person to person. How will you consider a person's shape, size, and dimension?

- Will you account for someone's preferences or wishes, allowing customizations? Consider size, color, general appearance, and volume. Will the wearable fit in with their existing clothing, or is it added to it – perhaps worn with or instead of?

- **Ease of use**: Does it have or need a simple interface? Can you make it intuitive so that it does not require learning or training? Engage someone to use it by using both inputs and outputs (such as buttons or the screen) to help the wearer understand its functions.

- What **ergonomic factors** will you consider? The physical shape should allow easy use and not constraints. There is a correlation in studies that indicates how stylish a wearable is can alter the wearer's perception of it and its usefulness. Help a wearer to understand how interactions and communication work intuitively. Don't make the wearable obtrusive. Consider the anatomical characteristics of the part of the body you are designing for.

- Does the wearer's **privacy** get affected? Is there a subtle interaction? Is it discreet or will it draw attention to the wearer? How will they feel if there is attention drawn to them? Can you avoid confidentiality issues, and can the wearer choose their level of privacy? Make sure there is no harm to them by using a wearable. Safety implications should be considered, including the accuracy of data or information, to be precise and accurate. Reliability will encourage a wearer to trust the wearable. Create effective responses for the wearer, paying attention to the speed of reactions, so that the wearable isn't slow to react or becomes frustrating or confusing. Is **feedback** needed in real time? The responsiveness should benefit the wearer.

- **Satisfaction concerns**: Will it meet a wearer's expectations and requirements and be effective and fashionable? Keep in mind the fulfillment that you will be giving to the wearer, both emotionally and physically. Subtle communication can be effective. Notifying a wearer, for example, shouldn't add to any social burdens they may feel; they may want to ensure they are not disturbing others.

- **Sustainability** is important. This can be seen from several angles, including the impacts of the way the wearable is made, what materials are used, but also the disposal or recyclable capabilities too. For example, there are some tags that come with a battery deemed to have a 2-year life, after which the product has to be thrown away. This isn't the type of model that we should be following. Consider the recyclability and lifespan of the wearable – reduce, reuse, recycle, repair, and repurpose. Can the wearable be disposed of in an ecologically friendly way? Will it be obsolete after a short period of time?

Overall, these points are describing the wearability, the relationship between the item you've created and the person wearing (and hopefully benefiting from) it. A balance of comfort, aesthetics, and functionality will ensure the wearer has a sense of satisfaction when wearing it.

Your turn... consider the domain

Looking through the previous questions, they will have varying answers based on the activities and the domains that you are designing for. Imagine a wearable created for a firefighter compared to something that a dancer may need to wear. Take some time and in a journal, Miro board, or your preferred way of working, make notes while thinking through the domain considerations.

How will they access information? What information is urgent or essential? What are the safety considerations? How do their unique environments affect the physical nature of the device? I don't know, but we can find out. How?

What is the best way to be able to design for these different domains in an effective and meaningful way? Speaking with people who are in the field professionally, personally, or have experience of your chosen topic or domain, is the best way to gain an understanding of what their needs are. What are their stories?

Allowing them to have meaningful input allows for **meaningful impact**.

Looking at implicit human computer context

The term **implicit human computer context** was defined by Schmidt, A. (2000), describing this implicit shift from explicit in HCI. Implicit interaction is recommended as a way to allow successful input for wearers without excessive burden on them.

Traditional computing and HCI studies involve us actively requesting actions that are performed with computers. It is an explicit action. We are very much aware of and deliberately doing an action. However, with wearables, this can often become challenging. We don't necessarily want many buttons or screens, we don't want to take someone's focus away from a task, and we may not want someone to have a constant focus on a wearable device. Often, we are monitoring or assessing a situation, and only when a certain condition is met do we want to inform or interact with a wearer. Also, we are in motion a lot of the time, and input may require additional thinking, time, effort, or attention. It might take us away from an essential task or interrupt us. Imagine walking with a keyboard placed on your arm, and you are required to input information while walking to a meeting or while doing gardening. It would be difficult, awkward, and probably not possible without a lot of typos. Often, we are busy doing other tasks and only have one hand free, or we have changing environments.

Implicit HCI is a way to describe a computer or processor recognizing input from a wearer even if they aren't primarily interacting directly with that computer or processor. This might be an action or movement we do that triggers an event or process, but we haven't actively stopped what we are doing to focus on inputting some information or source directly ourselves into that processor. This could be a situational context. One example is illustrated in the Schmidt, A., Gellersen, H. W., & Merz, C. (2000) paper that detailed an RFID system linked to objects. When objects were interacted with, it triggered related URLs to open up. For example, picking up a wooden spoon triggered recipes to be loaded, or lifting a wallet triggered showing a person their stock portfolio.

What is the research telling us?

Usability is defined by "*the extent to which a product can be used by specified users to achieve specified goals with effectiveness, efficiency, and satisfaction in a specified context of use.*" (ISO 9241, 2010).

Sometimes, a wearable solution requires teaching someone how to use them and a wearer to use a foreign item. Some wearables are so bulky that it makes the person using them feel uncomfortable or socially awkward. Therefore, the social implication aspect needs to be considered.

Important factors to consider are easy setup, customization, and use. Developers should design a setup to be intuitive and possibly similar to tools or products or items that a wearer is already familiar with. It is also desirable that devices require minimal user input and minimal maintenance. Durability is another consideration; a wearable must be durable, but it should also be lightweight and, for example, able to sustain a fall to the ground without damage. Wearables need to be portable, inexpensive, and address the individual's end goals. The success of a device is a combination of its functional improvement, the technological improvements, and being personally meaningful in its impact on a user's quality of life.

Devices that are ubiquitous and monitor an environment have ethical considerations as well. Often, wearables are designed to promote independence for the individual, but a varying amount of privacy is compromised due to the nature of tracking and data collection to ensure systems are effective. From my own research, I conducted testing for prototypes to establish that design features for a wearable object must consider appropriate styling. Appropriate styling is essential. Styling issues featured throughout the research – so much so that it inhibits a wearer from using the device even if it is helping them. Additionally, a user who likes the styling or feels it reflects them will regularly use the wearable, particularly if the item was a fashionable one. However, negative styling indicated they would not use it.

Considerations for success that have been used for systems include looking at **usability**, **user ability**, and **learnability**. Also for consideration is the **memorability** and **environmental** factors. One aim for a wearable is for the system to function with accuracy. This will allow a wearer to achieve their goals. Also, it should be efficient, meaning that it won't require arduous tasks or unnecessary steps to get to that goal. The wearer needs to find the system comfortable for their lifestyle. Multiple sources (Rodden et al., 1998; Dix, 2009; Bevan, 1995; Bevan & Macleod, 1994) also detail usability and its definition according to the item's learnability, efficiency of use, user satisfaction, and retainability. A wearer's ability to learn and retain the knowledge of how to use or operate the wearable happens with their mental model. This can be learned and retained, which makes the system more usable. It makes a wearer more effective, efficient, and satisfied with their wearable.

A wearable, especially an informed wearable or one that provides something useful for the wearer, should let the wearer know when part or all of the system is activated or engaged, using easily understood cues. An example of this could be that the wearer hears an audible signal. They might feel a vibration as a response to input. There may be a visual output that signals to them that they were successful in achieving their task. In terms of *user ability*, if a task is to be actively performed, not just monitored through the wearable, can it be done easily? If someone is new to using the wearable, or they are a first-time user, will they understand how to use the system easily? Will they need training, or are the instructions clear enough to follow? Let's look at five considerations:

- **Learnability**: This can be measured to figure out how long it takes for a new wearer to do their tasks successfully: "*Simpler aids are most successful.*" (Collerton et al., 2014). A wearable should have good mappings (Norman, 1988). Mappings help a wearer to determine what actions the controls/sensors/input have and their responses or effects. Can the wearer determine the relationship between the actions and reactions? Levels of attention of a wearer or fatigue can depend on the time of day, or even when in the week they are using the wearable.

- **Memorability**: If the wearable isn't used over a period of time, can they remember how to use it? Also, how long will it take the wearer to remember how to do the tasks? The aim is to improve their lives in some way, so creating additional steps or unnecessary tasks will add to someone's burden.

- **Visibility**: Visibility is important; it is about the wearer being able to tell the state of the device by looking at it (Norman, 1988), or if they can't, then they should know the alternatives for action. Is the wearer able to, just from looking at the device, understand how it functions or the state of it – for example, that it is ready for input, or is processing something? Collerton et al. (2014) found that participants in their study did show an interest in technologies but *"found them too complicated and not adapted enough to their needs."* If the device or wearable is too complicated, the wearer will not be able to use it or understand how it works. This creates a barrier to its use. We can see the importance of this when looking at the sports wearables of today. Are we able to glance at a Fitbit or watch to see our steps, heart rate, or calories counted?

- **Physical environment**: It is also important to consider where a wearable will be used. Is it in a home environment, work, or entertainment, and how will that affect elements of the design? For example, an individual may be at home in the morning. Maybe they need to use the wearable and you've designed audible feedback. It might be noisy in the house due to typical morning routines. Maybe there are family members packing lunches, making coffee, and generally preparing for the day. Adding a visual or haptic cue could be important to include alongside the sound. Also, the way a device is carried or worn should be factored in too. The wearable might be shoved, squashed, or placed in small or squished places, particularly when traveling on public transport. The elements should also be considered, such as dust or rain. This could have a potential issue. The technology should be water-resistant, with the technology safe from rain if it is used outside or in wet environments. Also, the battery housing for a wearable should be located inside so that it is protected.

- **Social environment**: The social environment of the wearable should be considered; this is an understanding that it will be used in work or other settings. Will the device cause an awkward situation for the wearer, or draw too much attention (negative or positive) to the user? Does the device have positive effects, and does it fit in with their surroundings?

Now that we understand some of the research and theory, we will jump into the physicality again by looking at materials and layout considerations.

Materials and layout considerations

Both the materials and layout considerations will affect the wearable, its comfort, usability, and adoption. We need to consider how different fabric properties can make a difference in the structure and construction of the wearables too. Let's look closer at understanding fabrics.

Activity 8.5 – understanding fabrics

Understanding the different properties of the fabrics we use will make your wearable journey a little easier. There are fabrics that can easily shape and move with the body and that provide stable support. If you can find a local fabric shop, you should go for a visit and make notes of how they feel, drape, and can be shaped. This will provide you with a richer learning experience. When looking for fabrics, there are a few things to consider. Let's look at how we can better understand what to look for when searching for materials to use.

Fiber types affect how the fabric feels and is used. There are **plant-based** fibers, which include cotton, linen, and hemp. These can be more durable, and the care is usually easier with no special requirements. **Animal-derived** fibers include silk, wool, and other hairs such as cashmere. These are often lightweight, more expensive, and usually require more care. Lastly, **man-made** fibers can include plant cellulose (rayon, for example), which is made into threads. Petroleum-cased fibers are fabrics such as acrylic, nylon, polyester, and spandex. These can be durable and often less expensive than both the plant and animal-based types. Unfortunately, because of their cheaper nature, there could be an environmental impact.

How are fabrics made? Fibers and yarns form the structures by being **knitted**, **woven**, or **non-woven**. Fibers can be bonded together, using heat or a mechanical or chemical process.

Knit fabrics are made through a machine that forms rows and loops, and then it continues to create rows and loops through the previous row. These form interlocking loops, and it's what gives a knit fabric its stretch. Typically, this is good for swimwear, t-shirts, and clothing with places requiring stretch. Think of a knitted jumper as a good example of a very visible knit structure.

A **woven fabric** is made on a loom and has one set of yarns lengthwise and one set crossways. These yarns cross each other. This makes a fabric that holds when stretched and maintains its shape. Woven fabrics are typically denim, and even satin. They are used to make jeans, dresses, and similar. It is far less "loose" than a knit fabric.

Non-woven fabrics are made when fibers are molded, bonded, or felted. Faux leather is made through this technique. When thinking about non-woven materials, the most common is felt, which can be synthetic or 100% wool, for example.

One way to remember these differences is that knits are made from a single yarn and woven fabrics use multiple yarns (threads) that cross each other.

> **Skill Levels and Fabrics**
>
> Just a note to add about fabrics – some are easier to work with than others! If you are new to sewing, then cottons and durable fabrics (denim and so on) are a good place to start. Fabrics that are lighter, such as a rayon or satin, are very difficult to sew if you're a beginner and usually require additional skills in finishing edges, adding interfacing, and similar.

Now that we have some basics about fabrics, let's look at the stretch factor. Some terms you'll come across when sewing is selvage (or selvedge), cross-grain, straight of grain, and diagonal bias, as shown in *Figure 8.15*. The selvage edge is a tightly woven edge on the side of a woven fabric to stop it from unraveling. It's usually a narrow border, with a different weave:

Figure 8.15 – Selvage, cross-grain, straight of grain, and diagonal bias

The selvage, a self-finished edge, is usually cut off and thrown away, as it's not considered a part of the usable fabric. If you look at the photos of the stretchy denim fabric in *Figure 8.15*, the selvage edge is very different from the rest of the fabric. It's a cream color and is just loose ends of the material. We can see that where this selvage edge is, the fabric that runs in the same direction along the top of the fabric is straight of grain. Think of it as following the grain. Cross-grain is perpendicular to the selvage.

This is also important in the layout consideration for a wearable. If you had a straight of grain over a knee, for example, it would have very little bend in it. Using the diagonal bias will be a more comfortable solution for the wearer.

A fabric that has minimal movement in the straight of grain and cross-grain will still have a bias or diagonal movement. See *Figure 8.16*, which shows an upholstery fabric:

Figure 8.16 – Checking the grain orientations

This means that the fabric is a tight weave and will be sturdy. It's a good choice for your first few wearables and if you are new to sewing. It will provide a stable backing to your projects. Looking for upholstery fabrics can be a great find for near-body items such as handbags and similar. Tight-weave denim is also a really good choice, and I make things out of denim a lot. But do check for any elastic or stretch to these fabrics, which will make them a little more difficult to use.

Tip – Reuse and Upscale!

Recycling your old jeans is a great way to start building up your fabric collections. Repurposing or upcycling clothing from friends and family is a great way to stay conscious of materials and waste too. It also helps you to practice your sewing skills.

Finding a medium-weight fabric is a good choice because it will be easy to sew by hand; the needles should not have too much movement when you push it through. It's almost as if the cloth helps to hold it in place. This is a good fabric to choose. I also love to use neoprene as a fabric for wearables. Neoprene was made by Dupont as an alternative to natural rubber in the early 1930s:

Figure 8.17 – Neoprene fabric

Neoprene is shown in *Figure 8.17*, which also has a selvedge with small holes in it. However, this goes slightly against my own advice, as this fabric is very pliable, soft, and flexible, but it makes for a great wearable. The stretch and bend fit the body so well, and it is thick enough to be stable. Neoprene is essentially a man-made synthetic rubber center with soft jersey cloth on both external sides of it. It can be a polyester or nylon on the outside and have spandex mixed in to give it a little more stretch too. It has great stretch recovery. Cut it with a *rotary cutter* for a crisp edge, and the edges don't need finishing, which is another reason why I like it. It is suitable for skirts, arm pieces, and other body-fitted wearables. It also can be used either side up, as it has no right or wrong sides.

When you follow tutorial steps, they often talk about the **right side (RS)** of fabric, and the **wrong side (WS)**. The right side is the side facing outward, with the nice pattern or the side we want to see. *Figure 8.18* shows an example of the RS and the WS of the stretchy denim. The WS is the side of the fabric that will be toward the body or on the inside of what we are making:

Figure 8.18 – Shows the RS and the WS of the fabric

Regardless of which material you choose, sewing your components and circuits on the grain or cross-grain will make it a bit of an easier sew. There will be a lot less movement. Sewing on the diagonal will have a lot of movement.

Another material that I use a lot and has been used in examples throughout the book is felt. You can buy felt in varying thicknesses, from about 1 mm to 3 mm. Within these sizes, there is a range of felt types, from wool to acrylic (*Figure 8.19*). Acrylic is a lot more affordable, but be careful to choose soft, or foldable. It is often very firm and not great for wearables. Wool is very expensive and good-quality. When you are moving past the prototyping stage, you can upgrade the acrylic felt base material to a wool-based felt. This adds considerable cost to a project, so use it when you've made and tested your proof-of-concept wearable. Finding a 100% wool felt and with varying thickness – for example, the thicker 3 mm variety – is luxurious but very expensive per meter:

Figure 8.19 – Thick 3 mm felt (left) and soft acrylic felt (right)

A stretchy jersey-style fabric can be more difficult to sew with and has a lot less support, but it can be great for making gloves or other wearables that have a lot of movement. In *Figure 8.20*, we see the stretch that a jersey fabric can have, and it is also soft and feels nice against the skin:

Figure 8.20 – Jersey fabric and the stretch

Jersey is a soft, stretchy knit fabric; often, it's made from cotton but can be made from synthetic fibers too. Using a jersey fabric has a lot of layout options for the body because it is so stretchy. I sometimes combine it with a felt layer for the components and then sew that felt layer to the jersey. In *Figure 8.21*, I am tracing my *left hand* to make a glove. The outcome will be a *right-hand* glove because you'll sew the edges and then turn it inside out. Tracing round your hand to allow for seams can be a quick way to prototype:

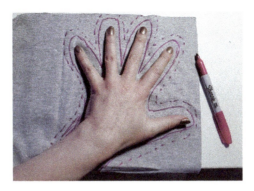

Figure 8.21 – Making a rapid glove prototype

You can even get a t-shirt and trace it to modify it for a wearable. This can help to keep costs down and make it specifically for the purpose you want. Other things to consider when thinking about the layout of your wearables include comfort, placement, and durability.

When discussing **comfort**, you should consider the following as essential considerations so that your wearable is wearable:

- Size

- Weight

- Shape

This includes thinking about how large, heavy, and bulky the components might be and how this affects the draping or the way your wearable is positioned. Also, how much surface area do these components need? They need to be placed somewhere – will your fabric need more structure or strength for it? How much do the electronics stick out from where you've put them? Are they against the body, or do they hang or protrude somewhere where they might catch on something? Are they placed so closely together that it restricts movement or becomes a big hard obstruction on your wearable?

Placement is important. Your comfort will be affected if components are placed in inconvenient places. I always temporarily attach components to feel if they are comfortable first. Then, I'll glue them and then sew or solder them in place. Do your components need to be in a protected location? Are they sensitive or delicate? Should they be hidden?

Some guidelines that are useful to consider are that if your components are heavy, try to directly attach it. If it's loose, it may deform the fabric or hit and knock things. This could mean attaching it to a wrist or ankle, for example. So, keep your heavier items closer to your core. Connections are easier to manage if you keep them near a seam. *Figure 8.22* shows a trim or bias tape that you can place your wires inside. Then, you can sew this to the edges of your wearable. You'll know where all your wires are! Sew inside bias tape to completely encase the threads, to protect them.

Figure 8.22 – Hiding wires in trim or bias tape

I've had to open wearables many times to fix or upgrade things, and if I've put things away from the seam, it can take a lot longer and be a lot more work.

Pockets can also be a great place to hide and support wearable technology. Using pockets that exist in a clothing item already will save you time, effort, and money, but if the pockets aren't suitable, it's very easy to make one that perfectly fits your wearable. An item of clothing with a lining is a great find. It's a good place to put components. Using a seam ripper and pulling apart seams to hide components inside works well. You can even incorporate a zipper and make your wearable removable! See *Chapter 10*, *Soldering and Sewing to Complete Your Project*, for specific tools and uses.

Lastly, **durability** is important to consider. When we wear things, we bend, move, walk, run, sit, and so on, and electronics can get hit, moved, sat on, and stretched. Consider what strain relief you'll have for your circuit. It can be a good idea to use stretchy conductive fabrics, or just make your wires longer than they need to be in case they need the slack. I sometimes use thin fabric, a mesh (*Figure 8.23*), to cover components. This can help diffuse bright LEDs and adds a layer of protection:

Figure 8.23 – Mesh to cover electronics

Selecting conductive fabric is a different consideration, as it might be used in small amounts. There are many types, but they can be difficult to find in varieties. For details on these types and styles, you can visit `https://www.shieldex.de/en-us/`. Also, you can find sample packs online, such as at `https://www.tinkertailor.tech/conductive`. Most common is the ripstop type of conductive fabric. This is a nylon and metal fabric that you'll recognize because of the little squares on it. Copper is very luxurious and thicker, but you'll also need to consider whether it might oxidize in your project. It can be sensitive to moisture. Conductive fabrics are often made as a blend of metals. *Figure 8.24* shows the various ways these fabrics drape. As you can see, there is a luxurious silver-based fabric:

Figure 8.24 – Conductive fabrics and how they drape

Keep in mind that silver-based fabrics may tarnish over time. Also shown in *Figure 8.24*, right, is a conductive fabric that has conductivity in strips. When working with conductive fabrics, you'll need to check the resistance and how this affects your circuit. If it has a high resistance, you won't want to use it over long distances. Try to use the same measurement when testing your fabrics, of ohms per foot or similar. You can keep a record of these measurements. Use these fabrics for LEDs and similar evenly distributed electronic components, but motors and other high-powered items will not work well:

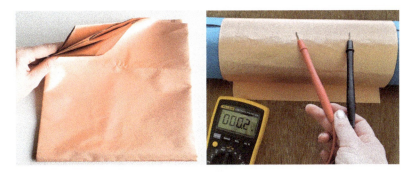

Figure 8.25 – Checking resistance

There are also steel-based conductive ribbons, which are very expensive, but they work really well so should be considered for a more permanent prototype. These conductive fabrics come as ripstop, knit, plated, woven, or non-woven. They are also composed of several layers, with a base non-conductive layer or a substrate of nylon or polyester. The non-woven ones tend to be thicker and don't fray at all. They are very conductive. You can cut them with scissors, but using scissors over time for these metal-based materials can dull them quickly. You can buy a rotary cutting tool that you glide through the material, and blades are easily replaced. A woven fabric will fray a bit, and some of them can fray a lot, which could cause a short in your circuit. Cutting the edges neatly with this rotary blade or laser-cutting the fabric will reduce this greatly. Also, sewing edges, hemming over, or using a surger/overlocker can stop the edges from fraying.

Don't forget to have fun with these fabrics. You can create unusual and beautiful shapes to add interest and intrigue to your wearable. Also, the materials themselves are often shiny and feel luxurious. Remember that your prototype might turn into a showpiece!

Activity 8.6 – adding strength with interfacing

Interfacing is a great material that we can add to fabrics that need a little more stability or structure. It comes in several different weights – lightweight, medium, and heavy – and usually the colors black, gray, or white. Sometimes, manufacturers refer to it as firm, medium firm, and so on. This can be a great way to add strength to places on the clothing that might have greater stress too. I always add interfacing to handbags, for example, to give them a little more rigidity and durability.

There are also interfacing stabilizers that you put onto your fabrics just to give them stability while you are working on them – for example, during embroidery. These then can tear away or wash away with water. There are also flexible varieties. For wearables, you might also consider the double-sided types of interfacing. *Vilene Bondaweb* is a good example of a product that can be applied carefully to the back of conductive fabric. It is an iron-on adhesive that is double-sided. This can then be easily cut, and you can then iron your conductive pieces onto your clothing item because it has glue on both sides. This can also help with some of the fraying edges:

Figure 8.26 – Bondaweb for adding conductive fabric

You can buy a sample pack of different interfaces to try and experiment with at `http://tinkertailor.tech`, which can be a good way to start without a commitment to the many types of large pieces of interfacing that you might not use. Usually, *Güttermann* and *Vlieseline* interfacing are the brands you want to look out for. Some use *spread* glue, and other types use *dot* glue. Spread and dot refers to the amount of glue on the interface. You will need to increase your heat times if you are using *dot glue* interfacing because the glue coverage is more sparse than other types of interfacing.

Figure 8.27 – Interfacing thickness, lightweight on the left, medium, and heavyweight

Lightweight (seen on the left of *Figure 8.27*) has a weight around 25–150 GSM, medium weight is 150–350 GSM, and heavyweight (seen on the right of *Figure 8.27*) is 350+ GSM. **Grams per Square Meter (GSM)** is a metric measurement. This is the measurement of how much 1 square meter of fabric weighs. The higher the GSM, the denser the fabric, giving it that weight or thickness. This can be useful to know, as often the packaging refers to these weights, so you'll know how heavy or thick it is. Generally, the advice is to use an interfacing weight under the weight of the fabric you're using; otherwise, it gives it an unnatural look.

Now that we understand fabrics, let's have a look at ways to connect components.

Activity 8.7 – exploring ways to connect components

When we connect components, we need to be aware of insulation for the conductive thread and materials. Because we are using beautiful fabrics, we might not want to cover them up, so always be aware of your traces, and map them out first. Always make sure none of the traces will touch each other. This is also important to consider when you are using the wearable. Will it come into contact with other parts of the circuit? What about if it was worn and then tossed somewhere? Are the important electronic connections safe?

One thing we can do is add protection to our conductive thread. Using fabric paints is a quick and easy way to add insulation. *Figure 8.28* shows a conductive thread stitch that has been covered by fabric paint. It will take time to dry, so do this as the last step. You can also insulate by adding a piece of felt on top of your stitching when you are finished:

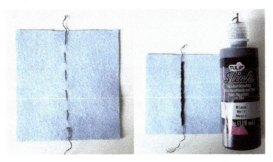

Figure 8.28 – Insulating conductive thread

Now, it's your turn. Make notes, drawings, collections, and find inspiration around you for ways you might like to connect components and electronics. Thinking back to the sensors and outputs we learned about, how would you like to integrate them with fabrics and conductive fabrics? What colors, shapes, or sensations motivate you? Remember that we can use existing items and repurpose them too. For example, the armbands for phones that people wear around their upper arms for jogging – they could make a great case for electronics. Could we use existing items to make new unique ones?

Take some time to think through the materials and prototyping, and start to sketch your inspiration. Allowing yourself the freedom to explore ideas and make a record of them is a huge part of the learning process. It's also so helpful when you are mid-project, but you might need some additional ideas, so you'll already have some jotted down. Getting comfortable with pencil and paper to record when ideas come to you is great practice. I've got a notebook filled with ideas I've never done, but who knows? One day, I may get another one finished!

Activity 8.6 – hunting for materials

There are many places you might be looking for fabrics. This includes local stores, online retailers, or marketplaces such as eBay. These are all good options. When you're starting out, I would really recommend trying to go in person a few times to fabric shops, or larger stores that might also have fabrics, so that you can start to observe and learn the way fabrics feel and move. As we've seen by following the selvage edge and the grain, we can see the strength of the fabric. We can also start to learn through touch the different weights a fabric can have.

It will be more difficult to feel and learn about conductive fabrics. If possible, due to the cost and often the amounts sold, you can find packs of multiple types of conductive fabrics. This can be a great way to learn about these fabrics and their properties. It will give you a chance to experiment with them. There is a multi-pack and other varieties on `http://tinkertailor.tech`, so you can play and get a feel for where these different fabrics might be used. You can bring your multimeter to test conductivity (remember to use the setting that looks like a speaker, and it will emit a noise if it is conductive) to a fabric shop, as sometimes you get lucky and find fabrics with metal stitched through them.

Also, don't forget local charity shops and friends and family. You can often get a few clothing items cheaply, allowing you the freedom to upcycle and experiment. This can be a great way to start out. I often buy gloves; this is a quick way to start prototyping a hand piece. Even better, I ask my local charities if people hand in any, or if they have single gloves! They often do, and they get discarded or sent elsewhere. I visit and ask whether they can keep them to one side so that I can come and pick them up to use them.

Many of my hand-based wearable prototypes only need one hand, or I sometimes cut off the fingers of the gloves to use the main hand part as a base. It's also a good way to experiment with different textures and materials without a huge commitment, or a type of clothing item without having to starting from scratch.

Keeping open-minded about where you can source your fabrics, especially for prototyping, can save you a lot of time and money. That brings us to the end of this chapter.

Summary

Prototyping is an essential part of good wearable design. It often helps to spark ideas, conversations, and ways of improving what we've made. This chapter explored different types of prototypes and how they can contribute to creating the iterations of our wearables to make them successful.

We looked at how we can make wearables usable, considering the placement and ease of use. Alongside that, we considered usability, the user's ability, and learnability. There are memorability and environmental factors too. We learned about making our wearable function effectively to allow a wearer to achieve their goals, and also how the system needs to be acceptable and comfortable. The chapter finished with a look at materials. We learned about fabrics and that starting with a denim or felt type of fabric, because of its stability and durability, might be a good first choice. We also saw that although neoprene is very movable, it also makes for a great near-body system.

Have you considered what makes for a satisfying experience for the wearer? We want the wearable to be a part of someone's life experience, and we don't want it to invade their space. The best way to find out is for you to test every wearable you make. Use it and learn from and with it. You'll learn a lot more in a shorter space of time by wearing it daily.

I hope you enjoyed this chapter; there was more theory than in other chapters, but these are important concepts. Looking ahead, we'll begin our journey to learn about and make a hyper-body system, so I hope you're as excited as I am!

References

Excerpts in this chapter section are from some of my research – Farion, Christine (`http://radar.gsa.ac.uk/view/creators/1393.html`). *(2018) Investigating the design of Smart Objects in the domain of forgetfulness. PhD thesis, Queen Mary University of London.*

Figure 8.11 features work by the following students, published with kind permission: Lisa Nikelowski, Drew Ewen, Arvind Prasad, Sayandanha Nayar, and Jiwon Lee.

Figure 8.12 and *Figure 8.13* features work by the following students, published with kind permission: Guilia Preponis, Ruoying Zhu, Yue Hu, Elisabeth Seidel, Meera Haridas, and Yingnan Weng.

Houde, S., and Hill, C. (1997). *What do prototypes prototype?*. In the handbook of *human-computer interaction (pp. 367-381). Helander, T. Landauer, and P. Prabhu (eds.): Elsevier Science B. V: Amsterdam, North-Holland.*

Lim, Y. K., Stolterman, E., and Tenenberg, J. (2008). *The anatomy of prototypes: Prototypes as filters, prototypes as manifestations of design ideas. ACM Transactions on Computer-Human Interaction (TOCHI), 15(2), 1–27*: `https://www.researchgate.net/publication/277527546_The_anatomy_of_prototypes`.

Gómez, G., and Lopez-Leon, R. (2019). *Impossible Design: fostering creativity by quick and dirty prototyping*: `https://www.researchgate.net/publication/337402794_Impossible_Design_Fostering_Creativity_by_Quick_and_Dirty_Prototyping`.

Virzi, R. A. (1989, October). *What can you learn from a low-fidelity prototype?*. In the proceedings of *Human Factors Society Annual Meeting (Vol. 33, No. 4, pp. 224–228). Sage CA: Los Angeles, CA: SAGE Publications*: `https://citeseerx.ist.psu.edu/viewdoc/download?doi=10.1.1.944.3572andrep=rep1andtype=pdf`.

Lauff, C. A., Kotys-Schwartz, D., and Rentschler, M. E. (2018). *What is a Prototype? What are the Roles of Prototypes in Companies?*. Journal of *Mechanical Design, 140(6)*: `https://www.researchgate.net/profile/Carlye-Lauff/publication/323198004_What_is_a_Prototype_What_are_the_Roles_of_Prototypes_in_Companies/links/5bd023bfa6fdcc204a0366c6/What-is-a-Prototype-What-are-the-Roles-of-Prototypes-in-Companies.pdf`.

Gopinaath Kannabiran and Susanne Bødker. (2020). *Prototypes as Objects of Desire*. In the proceedings of *2020 ACM Designing Interactive Systems Conference. Association for Computing Machinery, New York, NY, USA, 1619–1631*. DOI: `https://doi.org/10.1145/3357236.3395487`.

Schmidt, A., Gellersen, H. W., and Merz, C. (2000, October). *Enabling implicit human computer interaction: a wearable RFID-tag reader*. In Digest of Papers. *Fourth International Symposium on Wearable Computers (pp. 193–194). IEEE*: `https://www.teco.edu/~albrecht/publication/iswc00/wearable-rfid-tag-reader.pdf`.

Schmidt, A. (2000). *Implicit human computer interaction through context. Personal technologies, 4(2), 191–199*: `https://citeseerx.ist.psu.edu/viewdoc/download?doi=10.1.1.449.5726andrep=rep1andtype=pdf`.

Review questions

1. What are the three main areas of prototyping questions, as proposed by the Houde and Hill model?

2. What is an integration prototype?

3. What is a low-fidelity prototype?

4. How does a domain affect the design of a wearable?

5. What is the best way to get an understanding of the domain we are designing in? Do you *just make it up* – and not consider others?

6. What are the differences between knitted, woven, and bonded fabrics?

7. Describe the three ways we check the structure of a fabric, based on the selvedge.

8. How do we remember the differences between the types of fabrics?

9. How do we check the structure or elasticity and stretch of the fabric?

9

Designing and Prototyping Your Own Hyper-Body System

What is a hyper-body system and how can we make one? We will focus on designing and building low-fidelity and proof-of-concept prototypes for your hyper-body system, using components and microcontrollers suitable for your fashion tech item. This chapter will help you to choose the appropriate components for your purpose and to test your circuits. These are essential skills for creating working wearables and fashion tech pieces.

In this chapter, you will be consolidating the knowledge you've acquired in previous chapters to create a wearable technology project that is ambitious and exciting. We will learn about hyper-body systems and how to design one. Then, we'll do some project planning and jump into an ambitious wearable using the **Internet of Things (IoT)**.

By the end of this chapter, you will have completed a project that can be controlled by friends or family through the internet, and you will have your circuit ready for sewing into a wearable. You'll have learned many exciting new concepts that will help you to continue to advance your skills and create projects with wearable interactions that go beyond our desktops.

In this chapter, we're going to cover the following topics:

- What is a hyper-body system?
- How to design your hyper-body system, choosing materials, components, and purpose
- Building up your prototype – function by function
- Connecting the QT Py to the internet

Technical requirements

This chapter is about learning how to make more use of the ESP32-based boards we looked at in the previous chapter. We will continue our journey using a small but capable board for our project in this chapter. We will need the following:

- Arduino software as the IDE and access to `https://io.adafruit.com/`.

- An Adafruit QT Py ESP32-S2 (you can use -S3 or the Feather HUZZAH from previous activities).

- NeoPixels of your choice, a heating pad, and a vibration motor.

- You will also need a 1N4001 diode, a 270 resistor, and a PN2222 transistor, breadboard, and hook-up wires.

What is a hyper-body system?

Connecting three or more of the five basic senses would be considered hyper-body. We connect senses and materials by enhancing these senses or substituting them. The basic human senses are considered to be **touch**, **sight**, **hearing**, **smell**, and **taste**. Our body senses these and sends information to our brain to process the messages to help us perceive the world around us. Some sources consider some additional senses to be spatial awareness (proprioception and body awareness) and balance (equilibrioception) because we also couldn't live without them. You may see these terms referred to slightly differently, such as the vestibular sense or movement. Acceleration, time, pain, temperature, and kinesthetic senses are also sometimes discussed. Humans are complicated systems!

Touch is considered important not only for survival, for example, knowing to not get burned by fire, but also for communication. Compassion from others that we can sense through touch can contribute to our positive mental wellbeing. Our sense of touch can be described as different sensations registered through the skin. These include pressure, temperature, and touch variance – incorporating the sensation of air or wind, vibration, and pain. Textures sensed through our touch can help us to understand concepts and tactile sensations can alter the products we buy, based on how they feel. When I make wearables, I am aware of the wires I choose so that they are not only very flexible if I use silicone-covered wire but they also feel soft to the touch and don't restrict movement. I enjoy working with this material because of its specific physical properties.

Sight is very complex, so I won't go through how our eyes process sight – that is beyond the scope of this book. However, our sense of sight is very important to us for understanding information including color, color variance, the brightness of lights, and sensing motions or dangers. We interpret an enormous amount of information continuously and so it can also be important not to overwhelm this sense with unnecessary information. Also, for people with a visual impairment, it is essential to consider how our designs and wearables can be altered to be inclusive.

Hearing involves sounds being sent to the inside of our ears through an auditory canal to reach the eardrum, which is a thin sheet of tissue that vibrates with sound waves. Further through the eardrum, eventually, there are tiny hair cells that turn the sound waves into electrical impulses that travel to the brain. We also retain our sense of balance because the ear equalizes the pressure in the middle of the ear with the pressure in the atmosphere. Again, this is all overly simplified just for the purposes of a basic understanding. What we are concerned with is the auditory cues that we can get through beeps and tones as affirmations of events happening or that have happened. Sometimes, we may send a sound to confirm that something has been activated or turned on, or an action completed. These cues are all important to the understanding of our wearable system. Again, it is essential we make our wearables accessible and inclusive and be mindful of someone with a hearing impairment and how they might interact with a system. This can also be seen as an opportunity. *The Quietude Project* (*Wilde, D., Marti, P., 2018*) develops wearables with this in mind, "*using experimental participatory design methods, and the value of considering disability as an opportunity for wearables design, rather than as an issue that needs to be addressed or solved.*"

Smell happens through the olfactory cleft, which translates smells to our brain. We can detect 1 trillion odors using 400 smelling receptors. Smell is the quickest of the senses and is closely linked with our memories. It can be a trigger to our childhoods or an emotional experience. It can also be used for relaxation purposes or pleasant experiences via perfumes and other smells – or make us feel hungry when we smell fresh foods. It can also be a personal, emotional response in terms of personal body odors when we are near family, friends, and other loved ones. Smells can also alert us of dangers, such as fires, rotten foods, or chemicals.

Taste can often be combined with sight in terms of seeing the things we eat, as well as with touch, given the way that food feels in our mouths – the texture. Taste helps people identify what could be poisonous due to bitter or unpleasant tastes. The smell of our food also affects the brain's perception of taste. Some people also test whether a 9V battery has charge in it by touching it with their tongue. I'm not recommending it, but there is a buzz sensation on the tongue that tells us there is still charge remaining.

Other senses mentioned include awareness of where we are in space, as well as balance. We have a sense of movement and the positions parts of our body are in and where they are located. Can you touch your nose with your fingertip while your eyes are closed? This is the understanding of where we are spatially. Exploring existing technologies in creative ways to capture movements was the focus of Hedy Hurban's research in 2021. Focusing on cultural performance wearables, she focused on "*a wearable device that can be attached to clothing or held in the palm of the performers hand and used as an extension of the body or a wearable musical instrument.*" The Sound Drop device was created to augment a body for movement in performances (see *Figure 9.1*):

Figure 9.1 – The Sound Drop augmenting the human body in cultural performance

Whatever senses we focus on, it is the body that plays an important role. How can we connect our senses and materials using technologies and ourselves in this hyper-system?

Flex-N-Feel are emotive gloves for couples that support touch over distance. Singhal, S., Neustaedter, C., Ooi, Y. L., et al. examine the challenges of long-distance relationships in their work from 2017. They consider not only personal or intimate relationships but also work and educational systems as well. Earlier research also looks at this issue – Gooch, D., and Watts, L. authored *It's neat to feel the heat: How can we hold hands at a distance?* in 2012 for investigating communication technologies that support long-distance relationships. Even earlier than that, *Hug over a Distance* was a study regarding close relationships who are separated by distance and how can they express intimacy (*Mueller, F. F., Vetere, F.,2005*). Other mood, emotion, or wellbeing works include sweaters that interpret excitement levels and illuminate a collar in response (a GER mood sweater) and using a soft sensor that reads electrodermal activity (similar to a lie detector test). Also, keep in mind the wrist-worn devices that monitor everything from motion to sleep and stress metrics that record our everyday activities.

Now that we've had a look at some of the senses and thought about how they might inform design, let's learn more about designing our own hyper-body wearable.

How to design your hyper-body system – choosing materials, components, and purpose

We've completed several activities throughout the book and they have become increasingly complex. In this section, we'll look at designing your own hyper-body system and what you should consider as part of your wearable design process.

The many forms our wearables can take include socks, vests, underwear, scarves, wristbands, gloves, hats, belts, jewelry, and near-body items such as purses, handbags, and backpacks. How will you choose the form for your project? Making decisions about how to protect or secure your circuitry for a wearable is an important factor to think through as part of your planning. In a hyper-body system, we may have sensors or outputs in several locations. This has an impact on their placement too.

As the complexities of our circuits increase, you may decide to move from the typical placement of components on top of the fabric to a more incorporated and hidden design. *Figure 9.2* shows one on top of the surface and a more hidden placement design. This may move further away from a clunky circuit board to integrating it into the fabric as part of the design:

Figure 9.2 – Electronics on show and hidden

Our clothes have been designed from several pieces of fabric, which works out well for us. It means we can pick them apart to get access or add to them. We can use the clothing already created as our canvas, which we can modify, and doing this usually gives us a lot more time to prototype our circuits too. This is useful in the early stages of our wearable practice when we are creating a proof-of-concept piece or a low-fidelity prototype. Once you move beyond the first prototype and have specific requirements, then sewing the garment itself is also an exciting part of the process. For now, keep in mind hacking open those seams, zippers, pockets, and linings – rip it all!

> **Mini challenge**
>
> Spend a few minutes to look at some of the clothing in your home. Tops, jackets, boots, gloves, and more all provide opportunities for projects. Where could you place your components? Where would wires or electronics even enhance the item?

Try to look for thicker fabrics if you're at a secondhand shop. These can provide a little more stability, especially if we need to put a heavier component or battery pack in there. Hoodies, jackets, and jeans all provide a great base for your designs. Also, ripping the seam is a great way to get a wearable inside, but you can also add pockets or folds of fabric on top of the item of clothing. Maybe the clothing item is thin – could you add a lining to it that will give your wearable stability?

Keep an eye out for different types of textures, too. Is one faux leather or wool, and another canvas or denim? Having an open mind to creating with different materials can free up your designs. Don't forget sleeves on a top that you no longer wear can turn into two different forearm or full arm pieces, or even just bands of wearables that you then use a zipper or poppers to connect.

The purpose of your wearable will also dictate some of the fabrics or garments. Will it be for a child? Is this a wearable for a group of people – firefighters, for example, who will have very particular needs? Get to know who you are designing for and what the primary purpose will be. This will make your planning useful and accurate. Let's learn a little more about planning.

Understanding the importance of planning

Choosing components can affect your circuit's placement, comfort, and size – look for flat backs on components and how far things might stick out. Planning when making your wearable will save you time and errors. A few tips include gathering all your components together and really looking at each one to decide how it can be placed or accessed. What if there is a problem with the component or connection – will you be able to access it easily? Can you swap it out if something goes wrong?

Planning a back door

Do you have power needs or components that might need changing, and if so, can you get to them quickly and easily? Try to include a flap or a way to get to the components if you need to. I've had a wearable completely crushed, unfortunately – I had to open it up entirely and it created a lot more work for me than if I'd just sewn in a zipper or Velcro flap, for example, so I could get at the components more easily.

Place your components on the body part where you want to use it. Does it sit how you want it to? Make sure you don't restrict movement or make it awkward for the person wearing it. If it doesn't, before you change your plans or feel discouraged, most components are made by many different manufacturers, which means different form factors. You might swap out one component for another if it fits in better with your planning. If you do this, always check the data sheet! I accidentally swapped out a component for another before, but it needed 12V of power, which my circuit didn't have! Check that there are libraries and support for the new component you want to swap in.

Planning your layout before you sew or solder

If you plan everything out before you start to integrate it into the garment, it can highlight possible errors or difficult circuitry. You may realize that you need a lot more wire than you planned for if your design is on a cuff and your circuit board is on the opposite shoulder! You might want to plan it on paper in a notebook, or you might try tracing all your components on paper (or cardboard) and then placing it on top of the garment. This can really help to visualize how it would be made and what connections you might need. It can also help avoid awkward placements that may stop you from bending a knee or elbow. Mapping it out with chalk directly on the garment can be a good idea too.

If you're sewing all the traces and paths, make sure they won't cross and that you plan how they will be insulated. Some components also need to be placed in specific locations to be effective or work properly. For example, we saw with the UV sensor that it really needs to be placed upward facing the sky. This could be similar if you're using a distance sensor – it may have requirements in terms of placement.

Here are some things you might like to do:

- Draw sketches in a notebook.
- Look for inspiration in other fields, art, dance, and science, and look to nature.
- Create an inspiration board.
- Write ideas down, even when you don't have time for them. Don't dismiss anything – you may find a way, learn a new skill, or want to create a mix of one or more ideas at some point.
- Look at projects that inspire you.
- Dream hardware – is there a board or sensor that you'd just love to try one day? Make a list and see how it might be incorporated.
- What clothes are available in a charity shop? Use an existing garment as inspiration.

Lastly, as part of the planning, I'd make a note of some of the things that could go wrong. If you're inexperienced with a certain type of sensor, allow a little more time to learn more about it. This way you can avoid being disappointed if it does take a little longer to learn. Let's look at a checklist that might help formalize some of what we've learned about the planning and will help you plan your projects.

Activity 9.1 – Project Planning Checklist

Here are some things to consider when planning your projects:

- What are your inspirations?

  Planning your project goals is the most important part. Is there a purpose or an end goal for the wearer? How easily will they be able to reach this goal with your wearable design? Plan it and talk it through with someone who might be able to ask you questions about how it will work. This is a great way to eliminate problems quickly. Having someone say "*I don't get it*" might sound discouraging, but it's so much better coming from someone before you've spent every weekend for the last 4 months making your project!

- What is the fabric type?

  This will affect the way the components hang and how easy it will be for you to adapt this. Is it a delicate fabric you're using and how much will it stretch? Plan your materials.

- Project durability – who is using it and how durable will it need to be?

  Will this be a project for children who are playing outside or is this a jewelry item that is only worn infrequently? Consider the durability of the item and plan accordingly. Things may need to be reinforced or extra layers may need to be added.

- Access to batteries, components, and other circuit items

  How easy will access be to your circuit? Plan how it will be accessed – will you need to add a pocket, Velcro, or another way to get to the circuitry of your wearable? Does the person wearing it need to access anything in the circuit? If they need to access a button but it's on the back side of the garment, this is going to be very difficult!

- Does it need insulation?

  If there is a lot of movement, especially around joints in the body, will it be prone to short, creating a short circuit if a wire comes loose and touches a part of another wire or circuit connection? Would wires or connections crossing make it dangerous? Coat or protect any of the circuitry that a wearer might be exposed to.

- Visibility – can they see the circuit?

  I love being able to see the circuit, but not everyone else does. Do you want them to be aware of all the technology, or is it discreet and hidden so it works without them explicitly activating something? How will you plan this in? There needs to be an obvious way to use it.

Grab yourself a notebook and record what you are making and what components you've tried. Also, write what designs or body parts you'd like to design for. Maybe have a goal of creating one wearable for each area of the body! Plan your own hyper-body system – what senses are you most interested in working with and why?

Use it or do something else

At a conference several years ago, when asked his advice, Thad Starner said to me, "*use it or do something else*", and it was the most important message I can think of to share with you to. Once you've made the prototype, use it. This is so important. If you aren't convinced of the use or purpose, then why would anyone else? Wearing it or carrying it if it's a near-body system is the best way to get feedback. Often, there are things we didn't expect too. I made a handbag with the circuit on the outside, but it also had a large connector – and when I carried my bag, it was constantly rubbing under my arm and getting caught in my scarf. Not ideal. It was the first iteration of that version because it was so annoying and damaging my other clothing too. You will very quickly understand what's annoying about the wearable, uncomfortable, or not useful. Save a lot of time by fixing those things before someone else tries it. Take notes of everything and your designs will become more robust and easier to use.

Another important aspect of planning is building up our work step by step. *Figure 9.3* shows our final prototype build that we are working toward:

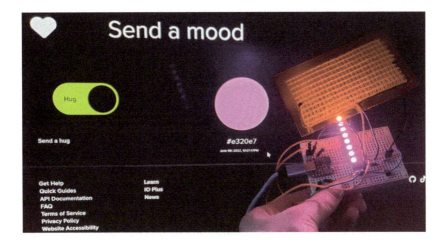

Figure 9.3 – The project we will be building

As shown in the preceding figure, the project will be first made on the breadboard. The photo shows me holding this breadboard up in front of my computer screen, where I have a web page open on my dashboard to alter the color of NeoPixels (and other exciting things too!).

Let's head to the next section now, where we look at implementing our prototype piece by piece.

Building up your prototype – function by function

It's finally time to get building. With our thoughts on planning done, there's just a few reminders of some of the techniques we've been learning along the way.

Here are some top tips for a successful project:

- Try to build your **projects in sections**. This also gives you a sense of accomplishment when something works. I've had the experience of trying to do too much at once and then there seems to be an insurmountable number of errors to fix.

- Prototype small and in a non-permanent way. All I mean by this is when you start the circuit, try to use **croc clips or breadboards**, and hook up wires so that you can easily fix, move, repair, and try things out.

- Don't forget to **check your board and port every time** you disconnect and connect the board to your computer and Arduino.

- It's a good idea to prototype and **test the connections as you finish them**. This might be checking for continuity or where a wire might be bridging or overlapping another.

- Check the **data sheets**, grab the library, and try the sample code to see it all working.

- **Never** leave your board powered on when you are swapping components.

Start with the easiest part or the part of the circuit you're most familiar with and have used before. It's a great feeling to get something working and it's motivating to help spur you on with the rest of your circuit design. Sometimes, a larger project can seem daunting or even insurmountable. All projects are possible if we take them in steps! I often work on a simpler version of a project and then as it's realized, I add extra interactions or components to it if it's needed (or just for fun).

Our project build – sending a mood

Can a heating pad be used as a communication device? What if when friends and family are thinking about us, they could send some warmth our way? That's what we're going to do in this system.

The wearable we are going to make is a prototype that will consist of an ESP32 board. It's a small board that I mentioned briefly in *Chapter 7, Moving Forward with Circuit Design Using ESP32*, the **Adafruit QT Py ESP32-S2**. We will also be using a few outputs (*Figure 9.4*) for the prototype, including the following:

- NeoPixels as a visual output

- A heating pad (`https://www.adafruit.com/product/1481`) as another feeling or sensation output, a 1N4001 diode, a 270-Ohm resistor, and a PN2222 transistor to enable the heating pad

- A small vibration motor

We will be sensing the heat, the colors visually, and the vibrations as well. Our hyper-body system will play with several of the senses but not necessarily with the *traditionally designated* senses:

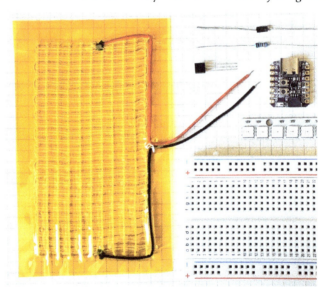

Figure 9.4 – The components for the circuit

The input will involve communication through the internet, straight to our QT Py ESP32-S2. Therefore, we will use the ESP32-based board because it has Wi-Fi capabilities. Our hyper-body wearable will use several of our senses within the wider definition, as we are using touch in terms of heating and the message it conveys. This is based on the importance of good mental health and well-being. Additionally, there will be vibration and visuals in terms of light.

About the QT Py ESP32-S2

Let's learn a little bit about the QT Py ESP32-S2 before we dive in. This board is tiny! It measures 21.8 mm x 17.9 mm x 5.7 mm, which is great for a wearable when we don't want any large circuit boards visible. It also has a **STEMMA QT** connector, which is a chainable I2C plug and play port so you can quickly and easily plug in many I2C devices to it – inputs and outputs. This is compatible with Seeed Grove I2C boards as well. It has a USB-C as a connector and uses an **ESP32-S2 240 MHz Tensilica** processor with a native USB – meaning it can operate as a keyboard or mouse, **musical instrument digital interface** (**MIDI**) device, and disk drive. The *Tensilica* processor has one core, not the two cores that we saw with the other ESP32 boards. When you see S2 in the ESP module name (many boards now use the S2), this is a mini-module that has reduced capabilities. However, this won't affect us, as we haven't needed to use the second core for any of our projects yet. There is also no Bluetooth on this board, but there is a lot of space for our files, with 4 MB of flash and 2 MB of PSRAM. There is also an RGB NeoPixel in place of the common pin 13 LED that we see on many boards.

Lastly, it has 13 GPIO pins, so we can use it for a lot of connections! For the full rundown on the features and specifications of this board, visit `https://www.adafruit.com/product/5325`. There are other versions of this board, so to see the latest releases and what features you find you need, it's best to get up-to-date information from the website.

Now that we know a little more about the board, we should get busy. We'll begin by making our first connection, NeoPixels to the QT Py ESP32-S2. Let's do this now.

Activity 9.2 – Making a connection (NeoPixels to the QT Py)

For this activity, we will connect the first output component to our board, the NeoPixel. I've chosen it first because we've hooked it up before (*Activity 6.1 - learning about NeoPixels - a hand HEX system*, specifically the third part of that activity, in *Chapter 6*, *Exploring Reactions Through Outputs*), so we will already have the NeoPixel library installed. If you haven't followed along with a NeoPixel example in the book yet, then please refer to the activity in *Chapter 6* and head back here to continue. For this activity, you'll need the following:

- NeoPixels (any size, for now). I'm using a row of 8 to test this prototype.
- The Adafruit QT Py ESP32-S2 (`https://www.tinkertailor.tech/product-page/esp32-s2-qt-py-wifi-dev-board-w-stemma-qt`).
- A breadboard and jumper wires.

Let's do this activity in two main steps.

Step 1 – Connecting and preparing to use a new board

We haven't used the QT Py yet, so we need to check the board is in the Arduino program's **Boards Manager** section. Let's look there now.

Open Arduino. Navigate to the **Tools** menu | **Board** | **esp32** and look for **Adafruit QT Py ESP32-S2**. See *Figure 9.5* for a reminder on where to find the boards:

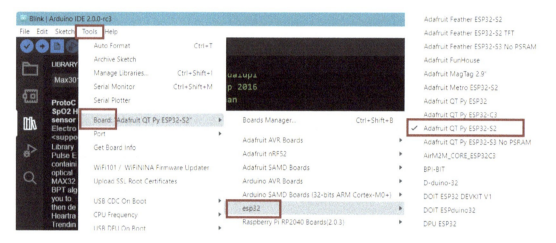

Figure 9.5 – Finding the QT Py board

If the board isn't there, you'll need to check in your **Preferences** that you have both board URLs in the boards manager section (see *Figure 9.6* as a reminder). Pop open the bigger window (marked with an arrow) so you can see what URLs are already there – the little icon on the right-hand side of the text field.

For current URLs and information, always check https://github.com/espressif/arduino-esp32, the official site for the ESP32 boards:

Figure 9.6 – Preferences and additional boards manager URLs

Then, in *Figure 9.7*, you can see the expanded manager with the URLs. For the Adafruit boards (`https://adafruit.github.io/arduino-board-index/package_adafruit_index.json`) and the ESP32 boards (`https://dl.espressif.com/dl/package_esp32_index.json`), if yours don't look similar to mine, then copy in the URLs to match what I have and paste them in. Then, click **OK**. Click **OK** again to confirm in the **Preferences** window and you will be back to your main Arduino sketch window:

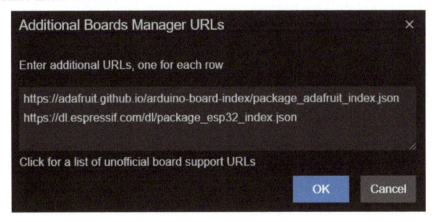

Figure 9.7 – The expanded boards manager URL window with the URLs shown

In the main Arduino window, click the Boards Manager icon in the left-hand side menu, the second icon down. Search for ESP32 (see *Figure 9.8*) and you'll see our QT Py board is listed there. We installed these boards previously in *Chapter 7, Moving Forward with Circuit Design Using ESP32*. However, if you don't have the QT Py listed in your set of boards (also see *Figure 9.8*), then I would click **Install** again and wait for it to install. Once it has finished, close Arduino and then open it again. Now, check again, as in *Figure 9.5*, to check the QT Py is listed for you in the **esp32** menu:

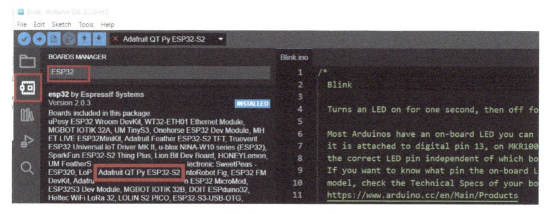

Figure 9.8 – Adding the ESP32 boards to Arduino

Now that the board is added, do you remember what our next step should be?

If you said "*test the board and our connection to it*," you'd be right! So, go ahead and plug your board into your computer and choose **board** and **port** in the Arduino **Tools** menu.

We usually check the board, port, and connection to our computer by uploading a sample blink sketch. However, the QT Py board doesn't have an LED on pin 13 – it has a NeoPixel, which is an RGB LED on a different pin. This is good news for us because we will be adding NeoPixels to our QT Py after our board setup. This way, we will already know that we can successfully program a NeoPixel with the QT Py. Let's test the board now. You'll need the following code, which you can download here: https://github.com/cmoz/Ultimate/tree/main/C9/9.2_Blink. In the code, we start by including the NeoPixel library in our sketch, and then defining the number of pixels:

```
#include <Adafruit_NeoPixel.h>
#define NUMPIXELS        1
Adafruit_NeoPixel pixels(NUMPIXELS, PIN_NEOPIXEL, NEO_GRB +
NEO_KHZ800);
```

```
void setup() {
  Serial.begin(115200);
#if defined(NEOPIXEL_POWER)
  pinMode(NEOPIXEL_POWER, OUTPUT);
  digitalWrite(NEOPIXEL_POWER, HIGH);
#endif
  pixels.begin();
  pixels.setBrightness(20);
}

void loop() {
  Serial.println("Hello!");
  pixels.fill(0x0225DD);
  pixels.show();
  delay(500);
  pixels.fill(0x000000);
  pixels.show();
  delay(500);
}
```

In the `setup()` section of code, we can see after initializing the **Serial Monitor** that there is an `#if` defined section. This code will only execute **if** the board has a power control pin. If it does, it will get set to `HIGH`, which enables the NeoPixel. If the code is written as an `#if` defined statement, it won't execute if the board doesn't have the power control pin, or whatever feature you're writing your statement for. It's a way of including code that won't get executed and will produce errors – for example, if the board didn't have a power pin.

After this, the NeoPixels are initialized, and we set the brightness to a low level. In the `loop()` function, we are printing to the Serial Monitor so we can do an extra check with our board, and then we are setting the pixel color to blue. The pixel lights up for half a second, and then goes off – a blink! **Upload the code** to your QT Py. You might need to press the **reset** button to see your changes after the code has been uploaded and have a look at the serial monitor to see the board saying "hello" to you too.

Quick challenge: Let's be fancy and make use of the pixel – add red or another color to this blink so that it blinks two different (or three) colors. I've added this color to mine: `0xFF00FF`. You'll have to try it to see the color:

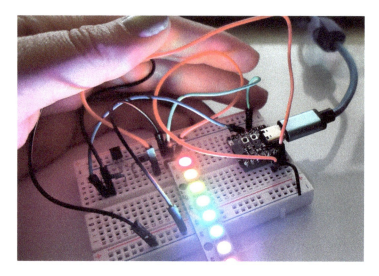

Figure 9.9 – Adding our NeoPixels to the QT Py ESP32-S2

Now that we have prepared Arduino to work with our board, we can proceed to the second step.

Step 2 – Hooking up the NeoPixels to the QT Py

Unplug your QT Py from your computer to connect the NeoPixel component. Then, hook up the ground and power lines of your NeoPixel to your QT Py, and the **Data-In (DI)** pin will hook up to pin **A2 – note this is GPIO 8** for the code – so it looks as follows:

- **GND** on the NeoPixel > **GND** on the QT Py

- **PWR** on the NeoPixel > **3V** on the QT Py

- **DI** on the NeoPixel > **A2** on the QT Py

Plug your QT Py back into your computer. Let's add code to see it working. Starting with the NeoPixel library, we will implement a rainbow effect along the strip or circle NeoPixel that you have chosen. We will declare the pin our pixels are on, **A2**, and I've also put the number 8 in the code line, `Adafruit_NeoPixel strip = Adafruit_NeoPixel(8, neoLine, NEO_GRB + NEO_KHZ800);`, because the strip I'm using has eight NeoPixels on it. Change this value to match what you have chosen. The completed code can be downloaded here: `https://github.com/cmoz/Ultimate/tree/main/C9/9.2bNeoPx`. In `void loop()`, we are calling one function, `rainbowEffect(20);` – this runs the code inside the `rainbowEffect` function:

```
void loop() {
  rainbowEffect(20);
}
```

The function, `rainbowEffect()`, cycles through color variations and five cycles of all the colors complete with `for (y = 0; y < 256 * 5; y++)`. This is a color transition of red to green to blue and back to red again:

```
void rainbowEffect(uint8_t wait) {
  uint16_t x, y;
  strip.setBrightness(45);
  for (y = 0; y < 256 * 5; y++) {
    for (x = 0; x < strip.numPixels(); x++) {
      strip.setPixelColor(x, Wheel(((x * 256 / strip.
numPixels()) + y) & 255));
    }
    strip.show();
    delay(wait);
  }
}
```

Upload the code to your QT Py. Once you see the success message after it is uploaded, press **reset** on the board, and you should have the NeoPixels in a rainbow color formation.

Now that we have our working NeoPixels with the QT Py board, we should hook up another component and repeat this process to increase the complexity of our wearable – with the heating pad!

Activity 9.3 – Adding the warmth of a heating pad

A heating pad can be used as a communication device. What if when friends and family were thinking about us they could send some warmth our way? That's what we're going to do for this wearable system. The heating pad component for Arduino typically comes in two sizes, and I'm using one that is 10 cm x 15 cm. We looked at the connection for this component when we used an axial fan in *Chapter 6, Exploring Reactions Through Outputs*, and there is a circuit diagram for it in *Figure 6.32, Figure 6.33*, and *Figure 6.34*. Please refer to those images for a reminder and a clear diagram. To make the circuit we need the **heating pad**, a **1N4001 diode**, a **270 Ohm resistor**, and a **PN2222 transistor**.

Using the breadboard from the NeoPixel connection earlier, add the diode, resistor, and transistor to start with. Double-check your connections and the orientation of your transistor and diode. As a reminder for the transistor, diode, and resistor setup, you can look to *Figure 9.10* for three views moving closer to the circuit. Note that I've hooked the heating pad to **5V** (via the diode silver side), not 3.3V:

Figure 9.10 – Views of the circuit (use 5V on the QT Py)

The heating pad is connected to **pin A3** on the QT Py, which is **GPIO 8** in our code. If you are ever uncertain of what the pin numbers are, search for a pinout diagram for the circuit board you are using. I do this often because there are a lot of circuit boards with many variations. It's the only way to be accurate with your pin names.

In *Figure 9.11*, we can see a figure from the PDF that has all the information about the board. The product PDF (`https://cdn-learn.adafruit.com/downloads/pdf/adafruit-qt-py-esp32-s2.pdf`) and similar ones are usually available for most circuit boards. It will list the pin outs for the microcontroller board and what they can be used for – for example, SPI and **pulse width modulation** (**PWM**). Look at pin **A3/8** in the following diagram:

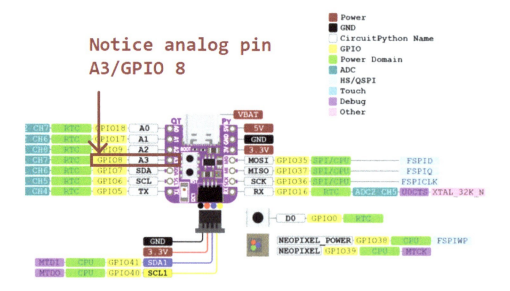

Figure 9.11 – An Adafruit pinout diagram for the QT Py ESP32-S2

I usually have the pin diagrams for my favorite boards printed out and nearby so I can quickly check which pins are SDA or SCL or the SPI pins of MISO, MOSI, SCL, or CLK. You might do the same when you've discovered which boards are your favorites.

After you've hooked the heating pad up, plug your board in and upload the code to test your connections – there is nothing in our `loop()` function for this code:

```
int heatPin = 8;

void setup() {
pinMode(heatPin, OUTPUT);
digitalWrite(heatPin, HIGH);
}
```

Once uploaded, the heating pad should slowly and gently be getting hotter – or warmer, rather. It won't get very hot. We could add to the circuit and incorporate a second heating pad in the future. One last comment about the heating pad – you don't need to be too gentle. I've seen people fold it in half for projects or curve it around a surface, for example. It isn't as delicate as it looks, so you can be creative but mindful.

That's another activity successfully completed. If your heating pad isn't getting warm, check that the transistor is pointing in the correct direct, and triple-check your connections.

Connecting the QT Py to the internet

We've chosen to use the Adafruit QT Py ESP32-S2 board for a few reasons, such as its small form factor, the huge number of accessible pins, the ability to expand our circuits easily and quickly with STEMMA QT connections, but also because it is an internet-capable board. A STEMMA connection is a three- or four-pin JST PH connector that manufacturers have been putting on boards over the last few years to make connecting components quicker. The four-pin version is for I2C use.

We will create a way for our friends and families to send colorful feelings to us, or if we give the wearable to a loved one, for us to send colors to them. This will be done using an IoT service. To do this, we will have to follow a few steps to create and use an online service, `https://io.adafruit.com/`, to make a connection. There are other services available – however, this service has a lot of support and users, so it is a good place to start. Let's go to *Activity 9.4* and set up our account and connection now.

Activity 9.4 – Getting connected to an IoT service

Adding IoT capabilities to our wearable will allow others to interact with the system. I find this an exciting prospect! However, there are a few steps to follow to set this up initially. Once you have done this process once, it will get easier and you won't have to do all the account setup again:

1. If you don't have an Adafruit account, we'll set it up now. Head over to `https://io.adafruit.com/` in your browser and click on **Get Started for Free** in the top-right-hand corner.

2. Once you're signed up and are logged into the site, look for **your key** in the **IO** navigation window (see *Figure 9.12*). You'll notice the key symbol. Click this to open your key area. This is where you'll access your username and active key that we need for a `config.h` file when we connect to Arduino:

Figure 9.12 – Accessing your username and key for the io platform

3. Copy your `username` and `active key` to Notepad or somewhere similar so you have them handy. Then, let's paste them into the `config.h` file:

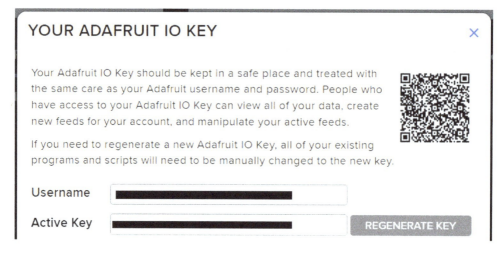

Figure 9.13 – The IO Key

4. Let's open Arduino and we will install the **Adafruit IO** Arduino library. Open the **LIBRARY MANAGER** and search for **Adafruit IO**. When you click **Install all**, there will be a message window that asks about installing dependencies (see *Figure 9.14*). These include important ones, which are the server files:

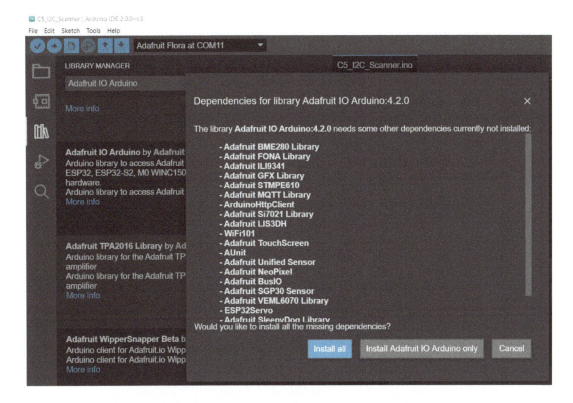

Figure 9.14 – The associated libraries with Adafruit IO

5. Once the libraries have all been installed, you can open the sample file from **File | Examples | Adafruit IO Arduino | adafruitio_14_neopixel** in the Arduino IDE (see *Figure 9.15*). If you don't see it, close Arduino and open it up again. If you still don't see it, go back and try to install the library again. This should fix any issues if you didn't see it. When you open this file, you might notice something a little different about it:

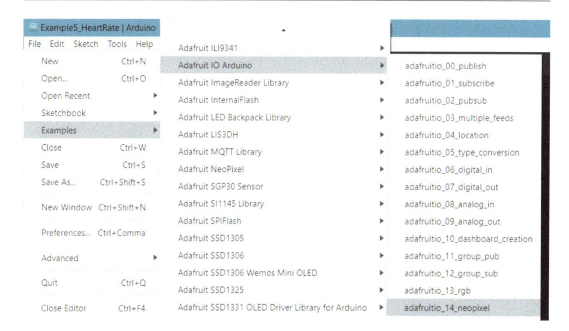

Figure 9.15 – Opening an example file in Arduino

6. This file has two tabs (see *Figure 9.16*), one that is the file name, `adafruitio_14_neopixel`, and another that is a `config.h` file. This has opened as a tab because if you look at the `adafruitio_14_neopixel.ino` file, it includes the `config` file. We need the information in the `config` file to load for this sketch to work:

Figure 9.16 – Showing the tabs in this Arduino file

The `config.h` file is where all the connection information is – let's edit it now.

7. Click on the `config.h` tab and we will change a few values. Starting with the first values, we need to input `IO_USERNAME` and `IO_KEY`, which we got from our account at `https://io.adafruit.com/` and which we copied earlier (see *Figure 9.12* and *Figure 9.13*).

The code to alter is the following:

```
#define IO_USERNAME "your_username"
#define IO_KEY "your_key"
```

8. Next, you'll need to enter your current Wi-Fi details for the network that you want to connect to in the following code:

```
#define WIFI_SSID "your_ssid"
#define WIFI_PASS "your_pass"
```

Change **your_ssid** to the name of your Wi-Fi network and then also change **your_pass** to your Wi-Fi network password. Click **Save** for this file so you don't lose your progress, and change it to `mod_adafruitio_14_neopixel` or something similar so you can find it again.

Now, we need to create the data service to connect to. Let's return to **io.adafruit**.

9. When you are back on **io.adafruit**, click on the **Feeds** tab (see *Figure 9.17*) so we can see our feeds. We don't have any feeds yet, so we will create a new feed:

Figure 9.17 – Opening your Feeds view

To create a new feed, click on the + **New Feed** button (*Figure 9.18*). This will open a window with two fields – one for a feed name and one for the description. I've called mine `send_a_thought` and I didn't enter a description, but this is a good idea, especially when you start to create many projects:

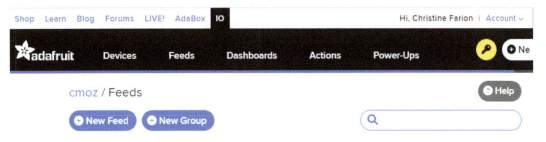

Figure 9.18 – Creating a new feed

Once the feed has been created, you will see it in your feed list along with the **Welcome Feed** that is there by default when you set up your account. The next thing we need to do is add a new **Dashboard**.

What is a feed?

A feed contains the data values that get pushed to your device. It also contains the metadata information about the data you use for your IoT connections. This includes information on whether your data is private or public, the general description of the data, if you've written one, the date and time, and if there are any license settings for it. One feed needs to be created for each form of data you want to send. For example, if you want to use a toggle to control something, that takes one feed, and if you want to add data from a distance sensor, that will need a feed too.

When you plan your wearable, be aware of how many data feeds you might need in your project and how often you call (or access) them. The free plan has limitations – at the time of writing, it was 10 feeds with 30 data points per minute. You can create five dashboards on the free plan too. Now, let's create a dashboard.

10. In the navigation bar, click on the **Dashboards** tab to open your Dashboards. This will open your **Dashboards** area:

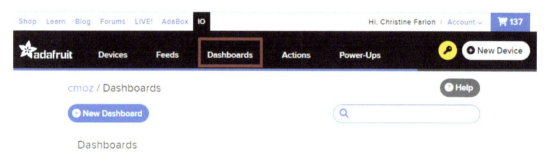

Figure 9.19 – Creating a new Dashboard

11. Once there, click the **+ New Dashboard** button (see *Figure 9.19*). This will open a new window for you to create your dashboard. Type the name of your dashboard and a description.

12. The Dashboard will be the interface part of your IoT connection. It allows you to visualize the data generated and received. I've called mine `SendingThoughts` so that I'll recognize my project. After you have created your dashboard, it will show you all your dashboards. Click on the one that you just made:

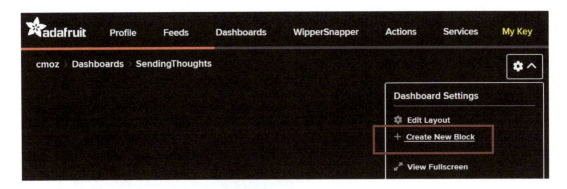

Figure 9.20 – The Dashboard for our project

This will open that dashboard (see *Figure 9.20*) and now we can create the application visuals and controls that we want people to interact with.

13. Navigate to the settings-style icon on the right-hand side of this screen and click the drop-down arrow. You will now have several options available to you. We want to choose + **Create New Block**:

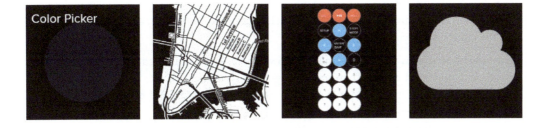

Figure 9.21 – Choosing our IoT elements on our dashboard (Color Picker)

14. Creating a new block opens a new menu. This has all the elements available to us for our IoT wearable. I'm choosing **Color Picker**, which is shown in *Figure 9.21*. When you select this item, a new window opens, **Connect a Feed**, shown in *Figure 9.22*:

Figure 9.22 – Connecting the dashboard elements to a feed

Create a new feed name called `color`, click **Create** to make it, and then click **Next step**:

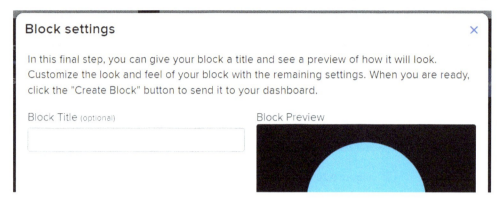

Figure 9.23 – Block settings

15. The **Next Step** button launches the settings and customization for the element we've chosen. When you have a chance, I would recommend coming back to the settings and customization window and trying each connecting element, looking at the settings, and getting a feel for what might be possible to create.

There isn't much to change with this **Color Picker** component. You can also change the settings for the components you made at any time.

Your dashboard with your component is now visible; I'm going to add text as a title for the dashboard that will be seen when someone goes to it online, `"Send a color"`, so people know what to do when they get here. The last step here is to change the privacy setting of this dashboard. Let's finish this in our last step:

Figure 9.24 – The Dashboard Privacy setting tab in Dashboard Settings

16. Click the settings icon and navigate down to the **Dashboard Privacy** tab (see *Figure 9.24*). Click it to slide it and a **Warning** popup will appear (see *Figure 9.25*). This is to confirm that you want to make this dashboard public. We do want it to be public – otherwise, no one would be able to use it, and that's not very interactive:

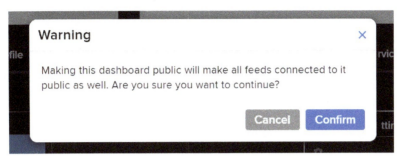

Figure 9.25 – The privacy warning

Click **Confirm** to the warning message. You can turn off the privacy again if you want to make changes.

You've done it – you've made your IoT dashboard and interactive area for people to visit. Now, we need to program our Adafruit QT Py ESP32-S2 board, so let's head back to Arduino, open it, and I'll see you there!

Activity 9.5 – Coding our ESP32 to access the IoT connection

Earlier, we opened an example file and entered our credentials. Go to that file again now – we saved it as mod_adafruitio_14_neopixel. There are only a few things we need to change. First, define your PIXEL_PIN variable as A2, which is what we used in our circuit. Change PIXEL_COUNT to the number of pixels you are using. Those lines of your code should look as follows:

```
#define PIXEL_PIN A2
#define PIXEL_COUNT 8
```

Further down in the setup() function, in the very last few lines, between pixel.begin(); and pixels.show();, I added a line of code for the brightness. I found that without it, the pixels were too bright. So, my code looks as follows just before the closing curly brackets of the setup() function:

```
pixels.begin();
pixels.setBrightness(64);
pixels.show();
```

If your `config.h` file has been altered with your credentials and Wi-Fi information, you should upload the code to your board. After it is uploaded, open the serial monitor. Press **reset** on your board, and you should see connection information in the monitor – connection to the Wi-Fi and the Adafruit IO service. Mine is shown in *Figure 9.26* as it's finding and checking credentials:

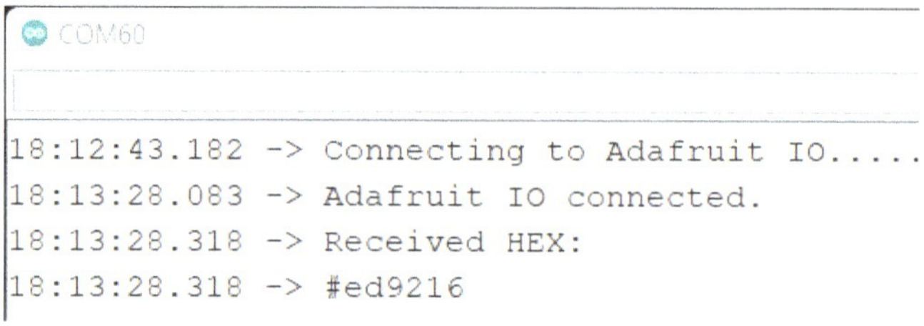

```
COM60

18:12:43.182 -> Connecting to Adafruit IO.....
18:13:28.083 -> Adafruit IO connected.
18:13:28.318 -> Received HEX:
18:13:28.318 -> #ed9216
```

Figure 9.26 – Checking the output after upload and pressing reset

Now, for the fun part – go back to the Adafruit dashboard that you made earlier. Click on the color picker and you can choose another color. Your NeoPixels will have changed color according to the color you chose:

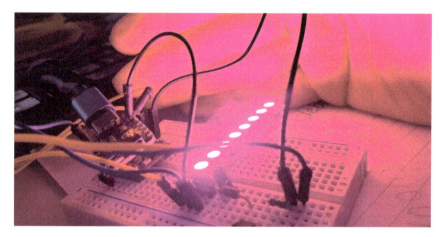

Figure 9.27 – A bold pink color to test my connection

Now that we've connected and tested this by looking at the colors of our NeoPixels, we should take a closer look at what the code is doing. This will help us to write code to add other objects and make changes.

What's the code doing?

If we have a look through the code, the feed we set up is configured in the code:

```
AdafruitIO_Feed *color = io.feed("color");
```

If we created a feed called `temp`, to take a temperature reading, we would write `AdafruitIO_Feed *temp = io.feed("temp");`, for example. We also have to make a connection to connect to the IO service and there is a function, `io.connect();`, that does this for us. Our program then accepts any messages that it might be receiving from the IO platform. This is the message handler. In this example, this `color->onMessage(handleMessage);` function is called when there is a message received. Next, in the code, we wait for the connection to be initiated. We can see in the serial monitor that a `.` symbol is generated for every half-second that we wait:

```
while(io.status() < AIO_CONNECTED) {
    Serial.print(".");
    delay(500);
}
```

While still in `setup()`, we call the `color->get();` instance method that checks whether there is a feed – `true` if successful or it will return `false`. In `loop()`, we maintain the connection to IO with `io.run();` and will process the data. It needs to be called often to keep the connection to the service.

The `handleMessage()` function that we called earlier pulls in the data from the calling feed – in our example, this is from `color->onMessage(handleMessage)`, and every time a message from the `color` feed is received, this function is executed. It will use the color information received and set the color of our NeoPixels with it:

```
void handleMessage(AdafruitIO_Data *data) {
    Serial.println("Received HEX: ");
    Serial.println(data->value());
    long color = data->toNeoPixel();
    for(int i=0; i<PIXEL_COUNT; ++i) {
        pixels.setPixelColor(i, color);
    }
    pixels.show();
}
```

For all the information on the classes and methods that we can use with the Adafruit IO library, you can visit `https://adafruit.github.io/Adafruit_IO_Arduino/html/index.html`.

Now that we've got the NeoPixel and QT Py ESP32-S2 connected to an IoT service, and we have a heating pad that we know works, let's put them together in one sketch before we take a break!

Activity 9.6 – Putting it all together

We've followed good practice and managed to get the parts working. This is great because it means we know where any errors were and we were able to fix them as we went along. All that remains, for now, is to add some interaction with our heating pad.

I returned to Adafruit IO to create a **slide-toggle** switch:

- I went back to my dashboard
- I selected + **Create New Block**
- I chose **Toggle**
- I connected it to a new feed, which I called **button**
- The entries were 0 for **Button On Value** and 1 for **Button Off Value** (see *Figure 9.28*):

Figure 9.28 – Adding a toggle to the dashboard

Click **Save** for your layout once you've added the button, and then we need to connect to it to get it to interact with our QT Py ESP32-S2 board. To see how I've altered my dashboard, *Figure 9.29* shows the added text and toggle:

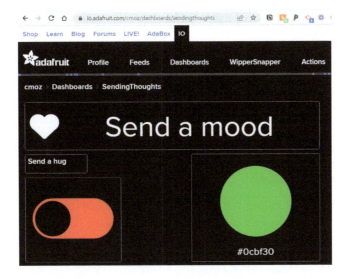

Figure 9.29 – My toggle added to the dashboard

We will amend our code to add in the toggle, which will be the remote input to activate our heating pad. Make sure your circuit is all connected (the NeoPixels and heating pad to the QT Py) and the complete code can be downloaded from `https://github.com/cmoz/Ultimate/tree/main/C9/9.3HeatNeoIo`.

If you remember from earlier, we need to set up the feed, so if you look in the completed code, we added this line, `AdafruitIO_Feed *button = io.feed("button");`, just after our color feed setup code line. In the `setup()` function, we also add the message handler for this toggle – for the color feed, we had `color->onMessage(handleMessage)`, so? what could we write to add a message handler for our new feed?

```
button->onMessage(handleHeatMessage);
```

I wrote a function called `handleHeatMessage`, so I know which data it is handling. Inside this function is the following code:

```
void handleHeatMessage(AdafruitIO_Data *data) {
   Serial.print("received <- ");
   if(data->toPinLevel() == HIGH)
      Serial.println("Heat On");
   else
      Serial.println("Heat Off");
   digitalWrite(heatPin, data->toPinLevel());
}
```

This will control the pin that our heating pad is connected to and turn it on or off with the toggle.

Lastly, I added a small vibration motor to pin **A1** and set it to vibrate when it receives a new color change. For this, I added a few lines of code that you can see in the completed version you have, but it includes the following in the `handleMessage()` function:

```
digitalWrite(vibrationPin, HIGH);
delay(500);
digitalWrite(vibrationPin, LOW);
```

Also, the pin number is declared and in `setup()`, we define it as an output.

Hopefully, you've got this all connected and working. Remember, once you've uploaded the code, you need to open the serial monitor to see it connecting and accessing the IO service. Typically, you'll see an output similar to *Figure 9.30*:

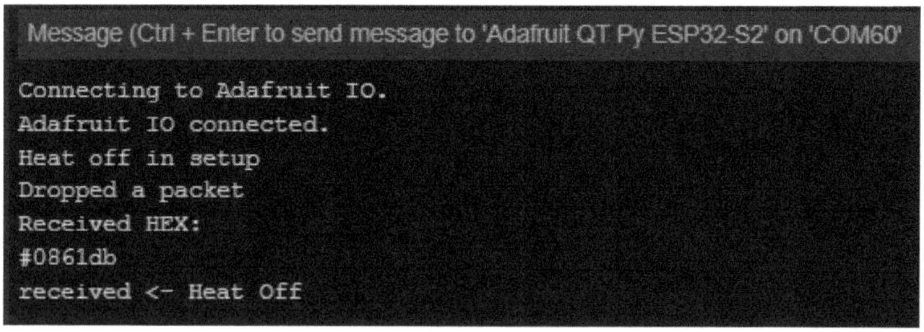

Figure 9.30 – The output in the serial monitor connecting to the IO service

I hope you enjoyed working with this little board and internet service. There were many steps to follow and it will take a few tries at implementing feeds and making dashboards to really understand it all. When you have time, head back to IO and look through some of the possibilities for creating more IoT wearables.

At the moment, we've created a prototype on a breadboard, and you may be wondering how will we be wearing this. Well, in the next chapter, *Chapter 10, Soldering and Sewing to Complete Your Project*, we will be learning to sew, solder, and complete this working prototype. We'll be making it a wearable one. So, there is a lot of fun coming up!

Troubleshooting

If you have any issues while connecting, then you might start by checking that you have altered the information correctly in the `config.h` file. Make sure you've got the username and the key copied exactly. Also, make sure you've got the correct Wi-Fi credentials.

To verify that you don't have internet issues, you can alter the `Serial.println(.);` code to `Serial.println(io.statusText());` – this will print to the serial monitor what the possible errors are:

```
// wait for a connection
while(io.status() < AIO_CONNECTED) {
Serial.println(io.statusText());
delay(500);
}
```

Check for a network disconnect message, which indicates that there is an issue with the internet connection. For other messages, try searching for them and going to the forums for IO.

I also had difficulties with my board dropping out or not being found on the port and other similar issues. I found I had to close Arduino and then relaunch it. Version 2.0 of the IDE is new and there are still glitches, so if you are finding it's being a little buggy, then closing and reopening should help with many errors. I've mentioned before that I've also had to reinstall libraries sometimes.

Don't forget there is a wealth of good information on the Arduino forums if you get stuck.

Summary

This has been another exciting chapter with a big learning curve – but so rewarding! I hope you find time to go back over some of the concepts and techniques and run through the project again, adding other data feeds or making a new dashboard. We looked at what a hyper-body system is and what the senses we can try to incorporate are. We looked at how to design, choose materials and components, and the importance of placement and planning. We then discussed building our projects up function by function – which we then put into practice. We started by adding the Adafruit QT Py ESP32-S2 board to Arduino, we added NeoPixels, then a heating pad, and then connected to an IoT service! It really was a busy chapter.

We've got the makings of an exciting wearable, and we will take our breadboarded work and turn it into a wearable garment in the next chapter as we learn techniques for how to sew and solder. This will bring our project to an exciting close and you will be equipped to make wearables, from the early stages of the prototyping process, through to creating high-fidelity prototypes. I'm excited to put it all together.

References

Some of the information in this chapter mentioned projects or research from the following papers:

Singhal, S., Neustaedter, C., Ooi, Y. L., Antle, A. N., & Matkin, B. (2017, February). *Flex-n-feel: The design and evaluation of emotive gloves for couples to support touch over distance.* In the proceedings of the *2017 ACM Conference on Computer Supported Cooperative Work and Social Computing (pp. 98-110)*. `https://www.researchgate.net/publication/313736576_Flex-N-Feel_The_Design_and_Evaluation_of_Emotive_Gloves_for_Couples_to_Support_Touch_Over_Distance`.

Gooch, D., & Watts, L. (2012). *It's neat to feel the heat: how can we hold hands at a distance?*. In *CHI'12 Extended Abstracts on Human Factors in Computing Systems (pp. 1535-1540)*.

Mueller, F. F., Vetere, F., Gibbs, M. R., Kjeldskov, J., Pedell, S., & Howard, S. (2005, April). *Hug over a distance*. In *CHI'05 extended abstracts on Human factors in computing systems (pp. 1673-1676)*.

Wilde, D., & Marti, P. (2018, June). *Exploring aesthetic enhancement of wearable technologies for deaf women*. In the proceedings of the *2018 designing interactive systems conference (pp. 201-213)*. `https://www.researchgate.net/publication/324361454_Exploring_Aesthetic_Enhancement_of_Wearable_Technologies_for_Deaf_Women`.

Hurban, H. *Exploring the Intersections of Cultural Performance Practices and Wearable Technology*. `https://www.researchgate.net/publication/357811279_Exploring_the_Intersections_of_Cultural_Performance_Practices_and_Wearable_Technology`.

Review questions

1. What are some of the alternative senses that are discussed?

2. What are some of the advantages of using clothing that already exists (how can we add wearables?)

3. Can you describe the importance of planning ideas and thoughts?

4. What are the two things we always need to check when we plug in our board and open Arduino?

5. What is the limit of the ESP32 S2 chip?

6. Why would we connect to a service such as **io.adafruit**?

7. What is a feed for?

8. Why do we have a Dashboard in io.Adafruit?

10

Soldering and Sewing to Complete Your Project

Learning soldering and sewing techniques to complete a project will provide you with a valuable skillset. This chapter teaches you the basics of soldering to help you to make your circuits more durable and permanent. These skills will help you to take your projects to the next level, from a low-fidelity prototype to a high-fidelity prototype, and ready for wearing.

In this chapter, you will try soldering! We will explore the tools and items we should have, learn some ways to improve our soldering practice, and try a few activities so we can learn this skill. After soldering, we will focus on sewing to make wearables. We will try some activities to put these techniques into practice. Once we have a foundation for soldering, we'll revisit our project from *Chapter 9, Designing and Prototyping Your Own Hyper-Body System*. This will provide the practical element as we turn it into a wearable system. Now is the time to take this **implementation** prototype and to consider the **look and feel** and the **role** of the prototype.

By the end of this chapter, you will have transformed your breadboard prototype from the previous chapter into a wearable! You'll also have practiced your soldering and sewing skills and picked up some hints and tips for a better maker practice.

In this chapter, we're going to cover the following main topics:

- Soldering
- Sewing
- Putting your wearable together

Technical requirements

This chapter is all about learning how to solder and sew your hyper-body wearable from the last chapter. These items are suggested, but we'll go through how to use them as we work through the chapter. Items can be found on various supplier websites (see `https://cpc.farnell.com/`, `https://www.digikey.co.uk/`, `https://uk.rs-online.com/web/`, `https://www.mouser.co.uk/`, or `https://www.tinkertailor.tech/`). You'll need your **prototype from the last chapter** and **a switch** to use as an on/off switch, as well as the following:

- Items for soldering:

    - A soldering iron, stand, and lead-free solder

    - Brass wire sponge solder iron cleaner and tip tinner

    - Wire cutters and tools for soldering

    - Resistors of any value and a protoboard/perfboard

    - Wires: 22 AWG or 24, an LED, a 220 Ohm resistor, and heat shrink tubing

    - Flux, helping hands, a solder mat, and masking tape

- Items for sewing:

    - A sewing needle, needle threader, and thread

    - Fabric, a hoodie, jumper, sweater, or similar

- Optional items: nail varnish, fabric glue, a glue gun, and glue sticks

Soldering

Soldering is a way to join metal (wires, for example) by adding another metal (fusible alloy) that melts (solders) at a lower temperature than the two metal pieces we want to be joined. The solder is the *glue* holding it together. The purpose is to form a permanent conductive connection between the two connections. It needs to be a good enough connection to survive a *pull test*. When we've soldered our items, we will try the pull test to be sure our connections hold. Welding melts all the metal items together using higher temperatures, and we won't be doing that with our soldering process. Solder is a mix of tin, lead, and sometimes flux. We can buy lead-free solder, and this is what I would recommend as lead-based solder is too dangerous, not environmentally friendly, and not worth the risk.

You'll need skill and dexterity to solder. This challenge is something I thoroughly enjoy doing! Practice using old components or buy resistors that are inexpensive and good for practicing with. Let's have a look at the different items we can use, or need, to solder.

Items used for soldering

These are some of the items we need for soldering. *Figure 10.1* is the base station that I use and take with me everywhere:

Figure 10.1 – My portable solder station items

On the left are the items: solder, a brass cleaning sponge with tip cleaner, tip cleaner, small 24 AWG silicone wires, my *Miniware* portable solder iron, and spare tips in different styles. On the right, is everything packed into a portable box. There's also a mini solder fan that I use that is USB-powered and it pulls the fumes away as I solder. The items in this list will provide you with a foundation of knowledge so you can then research what items you would like to work with. Let's set up your solder station!

Solder

You'll often see this sold as 60/40, which means it has a mix of 60 tin and 40 lead. This is called **soft solder** and melts around 180–190 degrees Celsius. There is **lead-free solder** that is ecologically responsible, which started appearing when rules banning lead in products started happening. Lead-free has a higher melting point. You'll also come across flux core solder. This is a spool that has a reducing agent in its center. This flux is released as you solder, and you get a cleaner connection because it improves the flow. Flux is typically made from rosin. When shopping for solder, you might also come across terms such as **SAC (Sn-Ag-Cu)**; this details the constituents in the solder, which can be silver, antimony, bismuth, copper, nickel, or others. SAC solder is a lead-free version that melts really well:

Figure 10.2 – Different types of solder in tubes and on a spool

You can buy solder in large spools, and in different widths (*Figure 10.2*). A solder with a diameter of **0.75 mm** to **1.0 mm** is good for the component sizes we are working with for wearables. If your solder is too thick, you're liable to get a big gloop of it that might **bridge** the connections. To bridge a connection means it might create a connection between two pins that we don't want to be connected. It can cause a short, or stop our component from working correctly, and is generally the way to break our components.

You can use your multimeter to test whether you have bridged your solder joins, and we'll learn how in the upcoming *Activity 10.3 – Using a multimeter to check connections*. Also, if you buy solder in tubes, don't throw away your tubes. Buy a spool of solder that you like and then, using a marker such as this sharpie (*Figure 10.3*), wrap your solder around it. Then, cut it and refill your tube:

Figure 10.3 – Making a refill of solder for solder tubes

I recommend getting 0.75 mm thickness, lead-free solder, in the handy solder tube format. Look out for *Antex*, *Duratool*, *Draper*, and other brand names that are good.

Flux

Flux is a chemical used for soldering (*Figure 10.4*). You can use it before you solder for preparing the surface of the item we are soldering. It prepares the surface by removing oxides that could prevent a good solder joint from forming. It helps the soldering process and I find it helps the **flow and transfer** of solder to the items I'm soldering together. Flux comes in different forms, which can be solid, pasty, or liquid. You can get it in tins or pen formats too, which makes it easy to apply straight to the parts you want to solder. I've found that soldering with lead-free solder can benefit from using flux to help the solder flow:

Figure 10.4 – Flux pen

The tin or jars can be good for dipping a wire in to coat it. Some flux varieties will need cleaning off the surfaces, so look for no-clean as a preferred type – though it is still recommended that you wipe your board off after using flux. You can use isopropyl alcohol to clean a circuit board. There is a flux pen made by *Chip Quik* that is lead-free and it's a reliable brand. This pen-style flux should last you a long time, depending on how often you solder.

Wires

A wire carries the current to the components in our circuit. There are a few types of wire that we can use that have different purposes. **Solid core** wire is a single piece of metal, called a **strand**. These wires are great for breadboards because we can easily bend them to fit into the breadboard holes and because the single wire is thick, it is easy to push through the hole and stays in place:

Figure 10.5 – Multicore (stranded) wire (left) versus solid core in a breadboard

Multicore (stranded) has many wires inside. This makes it easier to flex and bend than solid core wire. If you want to push it into a breadboard, you'll need to hold all the strands together and twist. This way the strands will stay together before you press them into the breadboard hole. Even then, it can be difficult to push the strands all through, and often a few strands sit on top of the breadboard. Also, after twisting the ends together to hold all the strands, you might want to tin them with solder. **Tinning** means covering it with a thin layer of solder to give it a light coating. In *Figure 10.5,* we can see the difference with a stranded wire; there is a chance that it may connect to the wrong area.

If you have moving circuit parts, then a stranded wire is better suited for the job due to its flexibility. The silicone variety of wires is great to work with for wearables. It has a soft super-flexible surface and comes in a variety of colors too. You can usually buy these in small packs with five or six color spools.

Wires are measured in **gauges**, and the gauge also determines the amount of current that can safely go through it. I've mentioned the **American Wire Gauge (AWG)** of the wires we've been using, around 22 AWG (0.644 mm) and 24 AWG (0.511 mm). I would recommend getting a variety of 22 and 24 AWG wire, in both solid core for your breadboarding, and silicone for when you want to solder your circuits and put them into wearables.

Headers

Headers are needed to solder different components. You can find colored headers, though the most common is black. It's a good idea to get a multipack with varieties to suit different needs depending on your components:

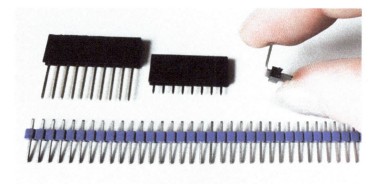

Figure 10.6 – Different headers; I'm holding the right-angle header

Figure 10.6 shows breakaway male headers on the bottom and a stackable header above. Stackable headers are useful when you want to put one board on top of another to save space, provided the pin numbers match up. When buying pin headers, be sure to search for Arduino pin headers or sized at **2.54 mm pitch**.

Heat shrink tubing

Heat shrink is a plastic tube that we place over our soldered connection and wires so we can insulate them. The tube is larger than the wires/component. You slide it over the connection and then apply heat. This can be done with a hot air gun. Some people use a lighter, but this can burn and melt it unevenly. *Figure 10.7* shows a NeoPixel end that has wires soldered to it, covered with heat shrink, and then heated so you can see the before and after of this process. This will add stability to our soldered wires and be less fragile:

Figure 10.7 – Heat shrink on the end of NeoPixels, covering our soldered wire end

You can buy single and dual wall heat shrink tubing; dual has adhesive inside and it will provide waterproofing when it is shrunk into place. Heat shrink tubing shrinks around the wires but it typically doesn't shrink in length. I would recommend getting a variety pack to start, with different sizes and colors. I mostly use black and red, and my preference is clear. It can be useful to be able to see the soldered connection just in case it has come apart. We will be looking at using heat shrink in the activities in this chapter.

Removing solder – desoldering braid

If you put too much solder on by accident or need to remove solder to swap a component, you can use **solder wick** (desoldering braid). Pictured in *Figure 10.8* is a selection of the forms that desoldering braid is available as. It's made from thin copper wire that is braided together:

Figure 10.8 – Desoldering braid

If you need to remove some solder, place the braid over the solder you want to remove and then place the solder iron tip on top. The heat will allow the solder to flow from the board to the braid as if the solder is being soaked up. It comes in different wick sizes, and it might be a good idea to grab one thin and one thick. For larger amounts of solder to be removed, you can use a solder pump. These are used by hand and there are also powered versions.

Tools

There are a few tools that will make soldering and component work much easier. For example, to cut wire, you'll need cutters, and to manipulate components and wire, you'll need pliers. I use **flush side cutters** for cutting wire and for cutting the ends of wire after I've soldered. This gets right up close against the circuit board and allows for a clean cut. **Needle nose pliers** are great for getting into small areas and doing small jobs. The pair from *Engineer* (see *Figure 10.9*, left) has a rounded tip so you can use these for winding your component legs into circles so you can sew them:

Figure 10.9 – Needle nose, flat nose, flush cutters, scissors, and wire strippers

The **flat nose pliers** have flat edges so are great for creating square bends in components and I often use them to hold components. I've also included *Engineer* **scissors** because they are multipurpose and make a great addition to a maker's toolkit. They have different blade areas and wire cutters between the handles. Also, a pair of **wire strippers** is a good idea to make stripping wires easier. You can use cutters, but it takes practice, and you won't want to do that long-term.

For soldering and electronics, try to find a pair of the following:

- Cutters

- Pliers (flat nose and needle nose)

- Wire strippers

I'll also mention that a **multimeter** is an essential tool too – but I'm hoping you'll already have one of those in your toolkit as we've been using it throughout the book. Have a look at the start of this chapter for links to where you can purchase these tools; good brands include *Engineer*, *RS Pro Tools*, and *Weller*, and the top of the range is often considered *Lindstrom*.

Helper tools

You'll find you need to be ambidextrous to hold your component, wires, solder, iron, and so on, and your hands fill up quickly. Having a stand such as a **helping hands stand** (shown in *Figure 10.10*) can make things easier. The one shown has a magnifier so you can see up close too. Some helping hands or multihand holders have lights, larger magnifiers, and more than two clips to hold multiple parts:

Figure 10.10 – Helping hands to hold your components

It helps to keep the component you're soldering steady. Sometimes, if we move too much when soldering, the solder starts to turn a dark color and the solder has a glaze to it. Using a tool such as helping hands will help to avoid these issues.

Cleaning – brass sponge, tip tinner, and sponges

Cleaning your solder iron tip will prolong its use. It keeps it efficient too. You can push your solder tip into the brass wool and twist it a few times, and then dip the tip in a tip tinner. I highly recommend using brass wool and Chip Quik tip tinner. It will last you well over a year (depending on your soldering amount) and it will keep the solder iron tip healthy for prolonged use. I don't use the wet sponge method, although others do. I've read on forums that the shock of the temperature change is bad for a tip. I find cleaning and tinning to be a useful process to protect my iron.

Solder iron stand (cradle)

You'll need somewhere to put your solder iron while you're soldering. For my portable kit, I have a minimal black tray with a metal stand for the iron to rest on. Do some searches on parts/supplier websites (listed at the start of this chapter) for the type of stand you want. Some solder stands have a roll holder for your solder or a sponge for cleaning. Always keep your iron in the stand when you are not using it. It's a safe place to put your iron when you aren't soldering.

Perfboard, stripboard, and flexible breadboard

When you want to make your circuit more durable and are looking to solder it, it's a good idea to use a surface; this can be a **perfboard** (*Figure 10.11*), **stripboard**, or **flexible breadboard**. Perfboard is a board that has holes in it and it's up to you to place your components through the holes. You then solder your components to each other and to the wires as needed. The board provides stability. The perfboard holes are independent of each other:

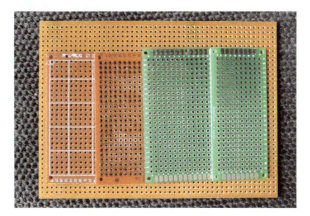

Figure 10.11 – Perfboard examples

Stripboard has strips of conductive traces along it; these copper tracks are on one side of the board. If you aren't using the whole strip (for example, for a ground trace), you would cut the trace so you can use it for other connections. This can be done with a blade, cutting knife, or similar. You can get all colors and shapes of perfboard and stripboard so look around for ones that suit your project. Larger boards can be cut with a small hacksaw or placed against a table edge so you can carefully break them into pieces. I've also seen people using a drill bit to enlarge the holes and then snap the board. Be careful with the copper plating. Sweat from your fingers can cause corrosion on the board.

Lastly, there is also a flexible breadboard that you can buy for your wearable projects. These are interesting but do come at a higher price. It's usually a good idea to have a few sizes, shapes, and colors to hand to suit all types of projects.

Solder iron

The section you've been waiting for! The most important part of soldering is choosing your soldering iron. There are a lot of choices and if you're a beginner, you don't need to buy the most expensive iron available. When I started out, I bought an Antex (`https://www.antex.co.uk/home/`) pencil-style solder iron (they have been in business for over 70 years). It felt great in the hand and did the jobs I needed easily. They have the choice of a burn-proof silicone plug and a variety of tips to choose from:

Figure 10.12 – A basic solder iron from Antex and a Miniware solder iron - very portable

For most of the components we are using for wearables, you'll want to look for a pencil-style with 15 watts or more for your first solder iron. I still use the Antex solder iron (*Figure 10.12*) if I'm at my electronics desk area. However, my solder iron of choice is my MiniWare TS80 (now TS80P) (`https://www.miniware.com.cn/`). This is a USB-C (needs 9V power) soldering iron with hot-swappable tips and it heats up fast. I made a video of the tips being swapped out at 400°C temperatures (`https://www.youtube.com/watch?v=WnVHVfRakTc&t=1s`), and you can see, in *Figure 10.13*, I'm swapping the tip out from the hot solder iron. You can control the temperature, and other settings are configurable. Most solder irons have tips that can be replaced and are of different styles. I have a chisel tip, for example, that has an angle that makes soldering certain types of components easier. We each have our preferred types, so you'll have to try different tips to get a feel for them:

Figure 10.13 – Hot-swappable tips, changing the tip at 400ºC

The MiniWare is a top-range portable solder iron and there is also a mid-range that is highly rated in maker communities: Pine64 Pinecil (`https://pine64.com/product-category/pinecil/`), which heats up in 12 seconds and is powered through USB-C or a DC5525 jack. If you enjoy soldering, it is worth investing in a good iron that you'll keep for years. Other brands that are highly recommended include RS Pro (`https://uk.rs-online.com/`) and Weller (`https://www.weller-tools.com/index.html`), who make good-quality tools and solder irons.

I would recommend getting a starter soldering iron, pencil-style, such as the Antex XS25 model, to learn and use your new soldering skills. For an iron you'll love and look forward to using, you might want to invest in one of the portable types. At `https://www.tinkertailor.tech/tools`, you can find a soldering range.

Now that we have learned about the items that help us to solder, let's get ready to solder our first items. Please always work slowly and be mindful. Almost everyone I know who has soldered has burnt themselves at some point over a silly mistake, myself included.

Activity 10.1 – Resistor practice

After prototyping your project, if you want to keep it, you might want to try soldering. Soldering components adds durability and reliability to connections. Using a breadboard is a temporary solution to test our circuit. Often, and you may have already discovered this, the wires fall out or bend, or components get disconnected. It can be very frustrating. Also, often it can end up looking like a bird's nest with a mess of connections and wires everywhere.

We can use conductive thread to sew connections to fabric, which will also allow for a more permanent solution; however, if your circuit needs to travel down a leg or other large distance, there can be signal strength issues. The resistance of the threads increases over length, and remember that resistance is a current-limiting property. We can use conductive fabrics though as these will carry the current over much longer distances and they allow for a lot of creativity too.

For learning to solder we'll need the following:

- Resistors, bulk of any value, LEDs, and a 220 Ohm resistor.

- Protoboard or perfboard, 22 AWG wire in red and black, heat shrink larger than a resistor.

- A solder iron, solder, wire strippers, side cutters, and helping hands are useful.

Practice first – grab some resistors and perfboard so we can practice. Practicing is the best way to learn and build up confidence. After looking at the photos in the figure, let's follow a few steps to practice. Remember, we all started with a similar activity, and it takes a little time to get a feel for it. *Figure 10.14* shows the process we will follow. You should **wear safety goggles, and work somewhere with good ventilation** when soldering:

Figure 10.14 – Pushing resistors into a protoboard and opening the legs so it stays in place

Here are the steps to make our first solder connection:

1. Holding your perfboard, push each leg of the resistor through one hole. After the resistor is through, pull the legs apart slightly to anchor the resistor in place. Feed through several resistors.

2. Heat your solder iron. When it is at temperature (320°–420° depending on the solder you are using; the solder packaging will tell you), tap the solder to the tip of your soldering iron. The solder should just coat your soldering iron tip slightly. This won't be used to solder with, but it helps the conductivity of our soldering.

3. Hold the iron tip against the two areas you want to solder. Hold the solder iron tip so it touches both the leg of the resistor and the metal of the perfboard surface. Hold the tip against these two surfaces for a few moments so it heats up (*Figure 10.15*). There shouldn't be any bubbling. If it bubbles, it's too hot – remove the tip to let the surface cool:

Figure 10.15 – Holding the solder iron in place and gently adding solder

4. When both surfaces are heated, touch a solder strand to them. You want this to melt and flow; if it is flux core solder, there will now be some bubbling as it melts and heats. This is normal. Keep pushing in solder until there is a small mound forming.

5. When you can see a small mound of solder, remove both the solder and the iron tip.

6. Let the joint cool for a moment. This should harden into our solid solder connection between the resistor leg and perfboard. It will take time to be able to correctly judge how to get a feel for the amount of solder and the time to heat the components.

7. When you have finished, clip the ends of the wires that are sticking out (*Figure 10.16*). Hold your cutters against the ends and clip – be sure to hold your hand over as you cut as they tend to ping off:

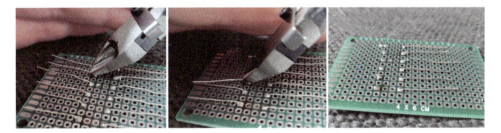

Figure 10.16 – Cutting the ends of our soldered wires

Keep practicing until you feel confident to try our next activity: soldering an LED with its resistor.

I love soldering so I hope you have a good experience too. Soldering will open a lot of possibilities for your wearables. There is no rush to move on so take your time and enjoy this learning process!

Activity 10.2 – Soldering an LED, resistor, and wires

Practice over… now that you've had a chance to practice, let's try a challenge. This time, we will be soldering a resistor to an LED, then soldering two wires, one to each leg, and lastly, putting heat shrink on to protect our work.

I would read through this section in its entirety first and then go through it again as you solder.

To do this activity, you'll need, as shown in *Figure 10.17*, an LED, a 220 Ohm resistor, heat shrink, and two wires. Also, you'll need a coin cell battery to test that it works:

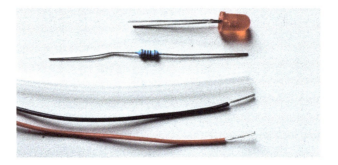

Figure 10.17 – Items needed for this activity

Don't forget, you can use other resistor values if you don't have a 220 Ohm; if you use a 330 Ohm, the LED won't be as bright, but it will still work. Now that you've collected the items, let's start:

1. Strip the wires. The wire stripping tool looks like a pair of scissors with channels on the side. There are different types and sizes. Match the channel size with the size of your wire. If it is too small, you can break the wire and pull part of it out. If it's too big, it just won't strip the wire. Put the end of your wire into the jaws, squeeze the handle, twist the wire slightly, and then pull it out (*Figure 10.18*). The insulation should come away from the wire as you pull:

Figure 10.18 – Using wire strippers

You don't need a wire stripper; you can do this gently with a pair of cutters. Just apply light pressure so you can feel the wire plastic covering cutting through, rotate your cutters, and then pull. You only need a small amount of wire exposed; don't over-strip the wire.

Now that we have our wire prepped, we will try soldering an LED so that it has a resistor on it and wires to connect it to our wearable.

Silicone Wire

You might notice how soft silicone wire is. With this wire, you can usually just pinch off the amount needed. With your nails pressed into the end of your wire, pinch and then pull.

Now that the wires are prepped, let's wrap the resistor on the LED leg.

2. Wrap the resistor around the ground leg. This is the shorter leg of the LED. Don't worry if it moves around, as the solder will hold it in place. *Figure 10.19* shows the wrapping of the resistor in the photo on the left:

Figure 10.19 – Wrapping the LED leg and resistor for soldering

3. After the leg and resistor are wrapped together, tape the component to a soldering mat with masking tape to hold it in place. Apply heat from your solder iron to both the leg of the LED and the leg of the wrapped resistor at the same time. You'll have to maneuver the iron to touch both items. Once they have heated up, apply solder to this area so it flows between the gaps. It's satisfying to watch.

4. Move your solder iron and solder along these gaps between the resistor and LED leg. Watch as the solder fills this area and coats it; this is shown in the middle photo in *Figure 10.19*.

5. Once soldered, do **the pull test**. Pull your resistor and LED to make sure your soldering holds.

6. Looking at the photo in *Figure 10.19* on the right, wrap the black wire (stripped end) around this same leg with the resistor. Wrap it at the end of the existing wire. After you have wrapped it, solder it using the same process. Hold the solder tip to heat the wire, then add solder to cover the connection of both the exposed wire and LED leg.

7. Cut the resistor leg that extends beyond the black wire.

8. Wrap the red wire around the power leg of your LED (*Figure 10.20*). Solder this wire in place, just as we have done for the previous two soldered connections. Cut the LED leg that extends beyond your red wire. The wrapping, trimmed, and soldered legs are shown in *Figure 10.20 (right)*:

Figure 10.20 – Wrapping the red wire and soldering it

9. After both legs are soldered, and you've done the pull test, put heat shrink around each leg. Slide the heat shrink around one leg and then the other. Make sure it covers the entire area you soldered. See *Figure 10.21* showing the clear heat shrink added:

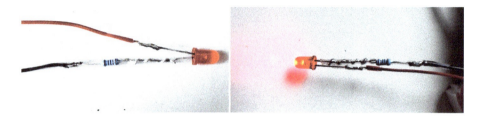

Figure 10.21 – Heat shrink added to each leg (left) and the working LED

10. Once the heat shrink is in place, use a hot blow dryer, or a heat gun (a lighter can be used but hold it far away from the heat shrink!), and heat it slowly. You'll see it get tighter and smaller around the circumference in size. It will start to fit tightly around this soldered area.

After the heat shrink has shrunk to fit snugly, using a coin cell battery, test your circuit works! (Reminder **power** + on the battery to the red wire, and **negative** – to the black one.) You now have a working LED with an integrated resistor; that's amazing!

Now that you've done a more complex solder job, let's look at something that you will find yourself doing often: soldering in headers. It is often the case that when we purchase a new component, it can come pre-soldered, or we can choose to solder it ourselves. This is a good option for wearables because soldering in wires is usually the better choice so that we can integrate them into clothing.

Soldering in plain headers

An important soldering skill to have is to solder pin headers on your components. If you can add this skillset to your soldering knowledge, then you'll be able to create a variety of projects.

To start with, prepare the header strip by cutting it to the length you need. Some components come with the headers, so they are already the correct size. In *Figure 10.22*, the top left shows the breadboard with header pins pressed into it. Be sure to press long pins down:

Figure 10.22 – Soldering plain headers on a QT Py

Now that the pins are in, place your component on top, as in *Figure 10.22 (bottom left)*. I used a flux pen to go over the top of the header pins that are exposed, as in *Figure 10.22 (middle)*. When soldering, be careful not to touch the breadboard with your soldering iron, because it will melt your breadboard immediately! Then, as previously, hold the solder iron tip against the pin and circuit board; think of it as holding the side of the solder tip against it. Make sure they get hot and then hold the solder to it as well.

You'll want to do a **tack solder**.

> **Tacking Solder**
>
> Tack solder is a solder point to help hold the pins you are soldering, in place. Solder one of the pins on one side of the board – I chose the top right – and then solder a pin on the opposite side of the board, say bottom left, for example, tacking it in place.

Solder all the pins, then check them to see that they all have good coverage, but not too much, and that none have solder overlapping to the pin next to them. This is called a **bridged join**. We can check for bridges with our multimeter.

Checking for bridged joins

Using your multimeter's continuity setting (the symbol that looks like a speaker as it will make a noise), we will check whether the soldered pins are connected where they shouldn't be. *Figure 10.23 (left)* shows holding the two ends of the multimeter touching so it is a connected circuit that it registers a value and will make a sound:

Figure 10.23 – Checking for bridged connections using a multimeter

When there is no connection, the reading is **open loop** (**OL**), as we've seen previously in *Chapter 2, Understanding and Building Electronic Sewable Circuits*. Let's check whether we have bridged our connection:

- Hold one probe to one pin on the circuit board that you've soldered.
- Hold the other probe to the pin next to it.

- Does your multimeter make a sound?

  - No? Great! There's no bridge.

  - Yes? Oh-oh, you'll need to remove the solder to fix that pin so it doesn't touch the one next to it.

Do this for all pins that you think might be bridged. You're done!

Activity 10.3 – Other activities

The last thought on soldering: first, protection from helping hands for your board or components. I've added some protection to the crocodile clips of the helping hands that I have. You can do this too:

Figure 10.24 – Adding heat shrink to the crocodile clip on helping hands

You'll need two pieces of heat shrink that are large enough to fit over the crocodile clips on your helping hands. I've used these black pieces (shown in *Figure 10.24*). Place one over one of the clips (*Figure 10.24*) and then place the other heat shrink tubing over the other clip. Then, using a heat source, hot air gun, hot hair dryer, and so on, warm the heat shrink consistently and evenly. Don't hold the heat for too long in one place:

Figure 10.25 – Adding heat shrink tubing to a set of helping hands

See *Figure 10.25*, which has the heat shrink over both clips and is then shrunk over it. This will provide protection from physical damage when your components are held by the clips. Now that we've added protection for our components, let's have a look at alternative ways we can connect our components.

Alternative ideas for connections

The ideas here are to show you that we can use other ways to connect. You can look at things you find that are conductive to see how they could form part of your circuit. For example, you can use the ends of your wires to create loops, similar to when we looped our LED legs. This time, loop the wire end and solder a connection to make the loop solid. *Figure 10.26* shows a wire end (top) that has then been looped (middle) and has a solder applied to the loop (bottom):

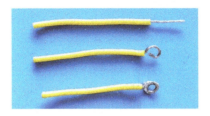

Figure 10.26 – Wire with a soldered sewable end

This will create a stable connection that is easy to sew. Another possible solution is to use a safety pin in place of a crocodile clip. When we are working with fabrics, crocodile clips can cause damage to the fabric. They can mark it, or even cause small rips. If we get inventive and use a safety pin – which is made for fabrics – then we can use this as a connection for our components. In *Figure 10.27*, we see a safety pin that has been soldered with wire:

Figure 10.27 – A soldered safety pin with silicone wire

We could have soldered one side and left it as a wire or soldered it to a crocodile clip to connect to our circuit board. What I'm saying is, be creative with the connections that you need for your circuits. You don't always have to buy something off-the-shelf if it isn't suitable for your purpose. You can make it with your soldering skills! For further inspiration, Irene Posch explains needlework tools that have been adapted for electronic making here: http://www.ireneposch.net/tooling/.

Now that we've seen alternative uses for our soldering skills, let's have a brief look into what to look for when we are soldering – how to spot errors, for example, and fix them.

What to look for when you're soldering

Soldering takes practice and, over time, you'll learn to recognize when you have the perfect solder joint. There are a few types of joints that you'll see as you're learning, and you may need to fix something you've soldered. Typically, it is too much heat, too little heat, or the wrong amount of solder that causes the most problems. Look through *Figure 10.28*, which demonstrates the way your solder might look and why. Most of the problems with soldering can be fixed.

In *Figure 10.28*, we see the following:

- **A**, which is the type of solder joint we want. There is an even distribution of solder that fills the hole around the component pin or wire.

- In **B**, the solder hasn't stuck to the joint of our circuit board, so it has formed a ball and almost floats around the leg of what we are soldering. If you add flux to the pad and reheat, the solder will flow to that area as well and this will be fixed. This also looks typical of what might be called a **cold solder joint**. A cold joint means the solder didn't completely melt. If not enough heat has been applied, the solder looks dull, has no shine, and the joint will be weak. Sometimes, when people fix this type of joint with additional heat, they add more solder. This can lead to too much solder on the joint and so you might have to also use the desoldering braid to just remove a little of it.

- Error **C** results in a bad connection; there isn't enough solder applied. This can easily be fixed. Reheat the area and apply more solder so it flows and you get the volcano shape in **A**. This is sometimes called a **starved joint**.

- **D** is also a bad connection that will need reheating, and it also looks a bit like what's called a **disturbed joint**. If, as you're soldering, there is a lot of movement, especially when you are removing the solder and soldering iron tip, it can appear frosted or have darker color areas. Make sure you apply enough heat and only remove the solder iron and solder when you have let enough solder flow. Don't hover around or move the iron tip for no purpose.

- Lastly, **E** is how a **bridged connection** will look, as was described earlier. The connection is across more than one pin, which will cause a lot of problems. You will need to remove the excess solder so there is no connection between them and then test it with your multimeter to be sure there is no connectivity.

Use *Figure 10.28* as a quick go-to reference for checking your solder joints and what types of quick fixes you can do:

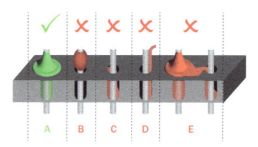

Figure 10.28 – Types of solder joint formations

There can also be **discoloration** of your solder if you've used too much heat. Sometimes, we hold our iron on the joint for too long because we just aren't sure how much heat is needed. This can sometimes damage the pads we are soldering to. Also, sometimes as we solder, small **solder spatters** happen. These are little flecks of solder that flick and then stick to the board. If they come off while we are using our circuit, it could cause a short circuit. Always remove (with tweezers or a knife) any spatters that can occur.

If the soldering isn't going how you're expecting it, take a break, let the joint/leg/header and solder iron cool, and try again.

> **Clean!**
> Don't forget, many soldering issues can be avoided if we keep our solder tip clean and tinned. Always brush your tip in the brass wool and then use a little solder or tinner to tin the end of your soldering iron.

I hope you've enjoyed our work with soldering. As a reminder, when soldering, follow these steps:

1. Heat the iron; when at temperature, clean the iron and tin the tip.
2. Steady the parts you want to solder using helping hands, or similar.
3. Heat the joint – both the parts that you want to be connected together.
4. Apply the solder and let it flow into the joint and circuit.
5. Allow time to cool, undisturbed.
6. Then, trim any wires or pins that need to be cut.

There are many reasons for varying results; it could be the temperature of your solder iron tip, the type of solder you are using, the wire thickness, or the surface of the circuit board. These variables will alter the time it takes for the solder join to form and it is only through practice that you will get a feel for it.

Now we will learn about sewing so we can continue our project from the previous chapter.

Sewing

After learning more about soldering and the advantages of soldering our circuits, to allow for durability and reliability, we will look at another *making* skill: sewing. As mentioned earlier, conductive thread isn't great over long distances due to the resistance. However. we can sew conductive textiles that we have cut in shapes to suit our designs. This allows a larger current to be sent through the material, and we can use this for creativity in our circuits too!

We are going to learn more about sewing through practice. We'll use our wearable technology project from the hyper-body system we started to prototype in the previous chapter. First, let's take a look at recommended items for sewing.

Sample items used for sewing

There are a few essential items you need for sewing, and many other optional items too. See what items you already have, and then you can build up slowly all the sewing supplies:

Figure 10.29 – Sewing supplies

If you want to give sewing a miss altogether, you can glue-gun fabric together, or repurpose old clothes. Then, you'll mostly just need the seam ripper.

Cutting

Although sewing is connecting fabrics and items together, you'll spend a lot of time cutting in various ways. **Seam rippers** are great for when you make a mistake, as you can quickly pull the seam back up again. Also, when we are modifying existing garments, the seam ripper will help us get into sewn areas such as hems, pockets, seams, and more. For cutting close to the thread ends and with a sharp edge, you might want a pair of **thread snips**. These are two sharp, pointy blades that cross over each other in a rapid scissor action. They are great for close thread cutting.

Fabric scissors/shears are a great idea if you will be making things often. Don't use them for anything else! They will cut neatly and accurately without puckering or ripping parts of the fabric. Usually, these have a flat edge to place on a table and cut through the fabrics. You can also buy them with a slightly blunt nose, so they don't catch or snag your fabrics. **Pinking shears** are an ideal tool to keep your fabric edges from fraying. Cut along the edges and you can achieve a neat finish. Lastly, **rotary cutters** are so quick to cut through several layers of fabrics against a metal ruler, and the edges will be the straightest of all the other methods. If you have a **self-healing mat**, the cutter will be fast and accurate and last for many years. The mat will also protect your surfaces.

Threads and fabrics

I've put threads and fabrics together, as the general rule is to use the same thread type to match your fabric. For example, if you have a cotton-based fabric, then use a cotton-based thread. You don't have to follow this, and polyester threads can be stronger than cotton. I use *Gütermann* threads as I've had no quality issues with them. You can also buy clear or invisible thread for areas where you don't want the thread to be noticeable. Conversely, you can buy threads that are for embellishment, top stitching, and to add a highlight or interest to the stitches that you make.

Fabric for wearables was previously discussed in *Chapter 8, Learning How to Prototype and Make Electronics Wearable*, so I will iterate that denim, scuba or neoprene style, and felt are my fabrics of choice. They have durability and curve well with the bends of the body.

Needles, pins, and clips

You'll need a **sewing needle** for sewing by hand, and a **needle threader** will revolutionize your life. Don't waste your time struggling to thread a needle. The conductive threads are notoriously bad for having tiny wisps of metal coming off them, making threading even more difficult. Use a threader and it will end all frustrations. If you haven't used a needle threader before, it's a great (almost essential tool when sewing with conductive thread) way to make needle threading pain-free. *Figure 10.30* illustrates how to use it. Holding your needle and the threader, push the metal wire of the threader through the needle eye:

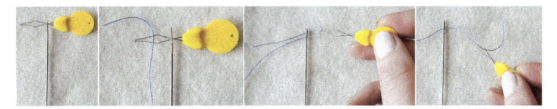

Figure 10.30 – Using a needle threader

Once the threader is pushed through, put the thread through the threader. Then, pull the threader out of the needle eye. The thread follows and your needle is now threaded.

You'll also need a selection of **pins** to pin or hold your fabric together while you sew, but I also use **wonder clips** when the fabric is likely to mark, such as neoprene. You may also want to get or make a pin cushion or have a magnetic tray to keep your pins in. Lastly, an **awl** can be handy for poking holes in fabrics so you can thread wires through.

Other tools

Other various items you may need include a **tape measure** that is very flexible and has metal ends. These tape measures for sewing are handy when measuring, especially when used around body parts for making. **Chalk** is very useful for marking your circuit on the fabric. Placement is very important so making chalk markups on the fabric is a great idea. It will easily rub off. You can buy chalk specifically made for pattern cutting, and chalk in pencil form with a brush on the end to help it to rub off. A **seam gauge** with an adjustable notch can be helpful for accurate measurements. You can create an adjustment and slide the notch to where it represents the area we are focused on. You can then use the ruler with the correct distances mapped out with the notch. To keep your fabric looking great, you should have an **iron** handy. Using an iron to press interfacing, press a conductive fabric with lining in place, or flatten seams will improve your wearable. You can iron sticky backings onto conductive fabrics. You can purchase a special mat that sits under and around a sewing machine, so you can use the surface for ironing. I have a mini-iron that looks like a small travel iron (no bigger than my hand) and works great for wearable projects, which can often be small. There are also small desk stands for an iron, which allow you to continue ironing on your desk area. This includes mini quilting irons for fusing and spot ironing; you can add small patches of fusible materials and it's a great way to iron very small places often inaccessible by any other means. Lastly, you can also get various filled shapes (a tailor's pressing ham) that you can use to iron where the fabric might curve.

A **glue gun** is a useful tool. It can cover wire that is exposed or help stick our components in place so they don't move when we sew. You can also buy glue sticks in different colors. Also, a **sewing machine** is a great item to have if you do continue with sewing. This will help to speed up the process of sewing and allows for professional results. No more wonky stitches! There are many types of sewing machines and this falls outside the scope of the book, but I have a few *Brother* machines (`https://global.brother/en`). *TYSEW* (`https://www.tysew.co.uk/sewing-machines`) has a huge selection and offers demos, and they are great with advice too.

Now that we have our sewing supplies, let's start putting our wearable together.

Putting your wearable together

We have our electronic components and we know they are working because we made a low-fidelity prototype with them and the code. Now, we can transfer this prototype to a more stable version by sewing and soldering it in place. Let's make our wearable in a few steps.

Activity 10.4 – Sewing a pocket for the heat pad

For the heat pad, I'm making a pocket for it to sit in. Because we want the wearer to feel the warmth, I'm using a thin linen fabric. You'll want to choose a fabric that has stability but that is thin enough to allow the heat to transfer to their back. Measure out the amount of fabric needed and cut wider and longer than the heat pad to allow extra fabric for a folded seam for the edges. *Figure 10.31* shows the measuring with the heat pad. Linen can fray, so we want to turn the edge of our fabric inside to create a nice edge that doesn't come apart:

Figure 10.31 – Measuring out fabric for a pocket

This can be ironed flat (*Figure 10.32*) to allow it to stay neatly in place when we pin and sew it:

Figure 10.32 – Ironing the fabric for crisp edges

In *Figure 10.33*, we see the jumper on the left, and then placing our components where they will fit nicely for this purpose in the middle and left:

Figure 10.33 – The jumper and placing components for planning the wearable

Pin the material in place and before we sew it with our heat pad inside, let's solder longer wires onto our heat pad. Measure out the wire length needed for the heat pad to the area where the other components will be. Then, strip the ends of the wires. Once they have been stripped, twist them with the exposed wire ends of the heat pad (*Figure 10.34*), and solder them together:

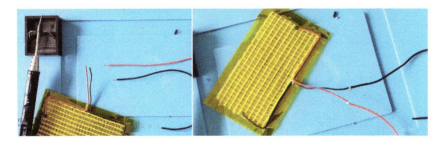

Figure 10.34 – Stripping the wire ends, twisting them together, and soldering

You'll notice there is a potential issue with how we've left our soldering. Can you tell what it is? If you noticed that there is a potential for a short – you are correct! The black wire and red wire both have exposed conductive areas right where they would meet if the wires were moved together.

How can we fix this? Using heat shrink, we can cover each wire, and shrink it. Then, both wires will be insulated, and they don't have the potential to touch anymore. After you have added the heat shrink to each wire, let's solder the parts needed to make the heat pad work – the transistor, resistor, and diode. In *Figure 10.35*, I've mapped my circuit out again in my notebook because I don't want to make any errors. It's also handy to refer back to in the future:

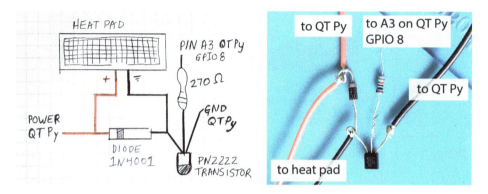

Figure 10.35 – Mapping out and making the circuit

Curl the ends of the diode, transistor, resistor, and wires so you can connect them together. After connecting these parts, solder them together. You'll want to add heat shrink on these as well.

We could have soldered these to perfboard but it is a hard surface and we want this to be in the hood part of our clothing. This wouldn't be comfortable, so I opted to use the same technique that we did with the LED soldering in *Activity 10.2*. Now that we have everything we need for the heat pad, let's sew it into place. With your needle threaded, let's sew the heat pad pocket – with the heat pad inside and wires outside – to our garment:

Figure 10.36 – Stitching the pocket

I'm using a wide stitch on the inside of the jumper and a very small stitch on the outside to hide it. We've done this before, and it's called a **hidden stitch**. You can stitch for whatever suits the jumper you are working with.

After our pocket is stitched all the way around and the heat pad is fully enclosed, with wires sticking out, we can move on to soldering our circuit before we put it in the hood of our garment.

Activity 10.5 – Soldering the QT Py ESP32-S2

Now that we've completed the first part of our wearable, we will finish soldering the connections to the QT Py, and then we can place it all inside the hood. Strip the ends of the wires that you've soldered to your diode and resistor for the heat pad circuit. You'll also need a ground, power, and pin wire for your NeoPixel. Strip the ends of these wires too.

With your QT Py board secured in helping hands, push the wire ends through the pin number you are soldering. See *Figure 10.37* for an example on pin A3. I've pushed the wire through, folded it over, and then soldered it into place. Do the same for pin A2:

Figure 10.37 – Soldering wires to the QT Py

Adding a second wire is shown in *Figure 10.38*. Repeat this process for all the wires you need in your circuit, such as power and ground. I trim the connections after they have been soldered:

Figure 10.38 – Soldering a second wire

Add the connections for your NeoPixel too. Now that we've soldered the connections, I'm going to add power to our circuit. So, let's do another activity!

Activity 10.6 – Adding power

There are power pads on the bottom of the QT Py board. They are marked as + for power and – for ground (*Figure 10.39*). We need to add solder to these pads so that we can then add a wire. First, add flux to these pads to help the flow of solder to them. Heat your solder iron, and when it's at temperature, touch the pad with the iron, and wait a moment while it heats up:

Figure 10.39 – Applying solder to battery pads

When it is hot, touch the solder to the pad, and watch as it melts onto the pad surface. When it is covered, remove the solder and your iron. Do the same for the other pad. You want enough power pads solder so you can heat it up and put the wire on to it. Now that both pads are coated, touch the black ground wire of your battery to the ground connection. Heat this up very steadily. The wire will start to sink into this space. When it has melted in, remove the iron carefully so you don't disturb the wire at all. This will take some practice.

Adding an on/off switch

We will need a switch added to our circuit. Without it, as soon as we solder our power to the QT Py, it will turn it on. Using a switch of your choice (I've gone for a sewable type), solder the wire from the QT Py **power** + tab on the underside of the board to one end of the switch. See *Figure 10.40* showing the switch with a soldered wire on a sew tab connection. Try to keep the hole so we can sew this to our jumper:

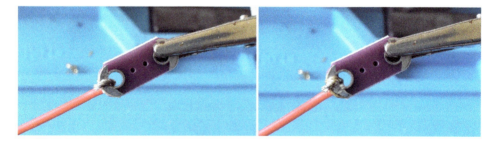

Figure 10.40 – Soldered switch with wires

We need to complete the circuit. **Check that your switch is off before soldering!** Think of the switch being placed between our wires that will carry the power. With that in mind, solder the battery power wire to the other side of this switch to complete the circuit, as in *Figure 10.41*:

Figure 10.41 – Soldering the other wire, and the complete switch with battery and QT Py

We now have a working power connection, so let's sew this circuit board and our electronics into our item of clothing.

Activity 10.7 – Sewing the Adafruit ESP32-S2 QT Py into your garment

We've been very busy soldering and preparing our circuit so that we can add it to our clothes. The completed wearable is shown in *Figure 10.42*. So, what last steps do we need to do to finish our wearable? We need a seam ripper to gently pull apart a seam in the jumper so we can slide in the circuit. We can then sew this in place:

Figure 10.42 – Our completed send a mood wearable

It can be a good idea to first sew the circuit to a piece of soft fabric, such as felt, for example (*Figure 10.43*). Then, you only need to sew the felt in place. Let's start by sewing our circuit to a piece of felt. When you've finished, start to pull apart the seam in the hood of your hoodie, or create a cut to place the electronics inside:

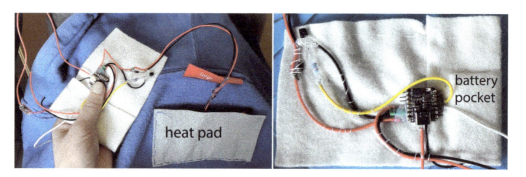

Figure 10.43 – Sewing your electronics to a felt base

After you've made an opening, push the electronics on the felt inside (*Figure 10.44*). Sew them into place. You can sew all the way around your microprocessor, or just structurally where it needs support. Sew the hole you made closed:

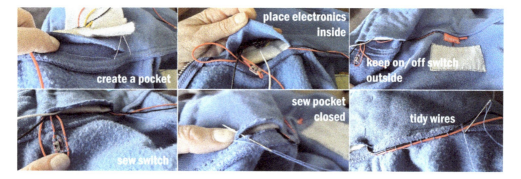

Figure 10.44 – Creating an opening, and hiding the electronics inside

Lastly, measure, place, and sew your NeoPixels. I'm using a leather holder for them so they don't move, but you could use sewable NeoPixels, or sew other types of NeoPixels to the jumper:

Figure 10.45 – Deciding the placement of NeoPixels

When you have finished, turn it on, making sure you have the Wi-Fi network working so your QT Py can connect to the internet, and go online to the URL you set up at `io.adafruit` in the previous chapter. You can control the heat pad and NeoPixel colors from your browser. You can see multiple photos of the completed jumper in *Figure 10.46*:

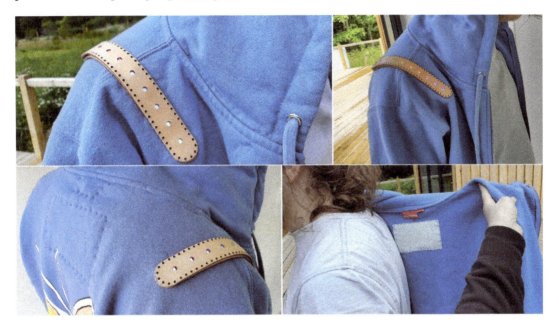

Figure 10.46 – The completed jumper outside and the heat pad against the back

You can build upon this circuit. Maybe add vibration, sound, or more lights too. You might also want to create a backdoor to access the electronics. You can do this by creating a flap with a snap so you can open and close it when you need access.

The last step is to give this jumper away to a friend or family member and send them a hug!

Summary

This chapter has covered a lot of new techniques and skills. We learned about and practiced soldering, and then we looked at sewing in more detail. These two skills were then used to complete our previous project. The practical nature of the learning should give you a much better understanding of some of the techniques. We completed a wearable that we can use with our family and friends, and we finished an IoT project wearable. This was an exciting chapter, and you will hopefully have time for more practice before jumping into the next chapter.

In the next chapter, we get into the theory behind our informed wearables, and this is by looking at Design Innovation as a process. Another exciting chapter is ahead!

Review questions

1. What advantages are there for soldering a circuit?

2. Why shouldn't we sew all our circuits?

3. What is a bridged connection?

4. How can we tell whether we have a bridged connection? What tool can we use?

5. Can we remove solder from our wire/connection?

6. What are some good fabrics for making wearables, and why?

7. Why would we use a seam ripper?

8. What is the advantage of using IoT in a wearable?

Part 4:
Getting the Taste of Designing Your Own Culture-Driven Wearable and Beyond

By understanding the Design Innovation process, you'll create a culture-driven wearable. We can use this process to improve quality of life, interpersonal communication, and community well-being.

This part of the book comprises the following chapters:

- *Chapter 11, Innovating with a Human-Centered Design Process*
- *Chapter 12, Designing for Forgetfulness: a Case Study of Message Bag*
- *Chapter 13, Implementing the Best Solutions for Creating Your Own Wearable*
- *Chapter 14, Delving into Best Practices and the Future of Wearable Technology*
- *Chapter 15, Appendix: Answers and Additional Information*

11
Innovating, with a Human-Centered Design Process

The Design Innovation process can be used to create relevant and socially conscious wearables that can highlight gaps in our thinking. Through a human-centered design process, we seek depth and meaning through the interactions we create. Using insights from listening to people, we can appreciate the benefits of human-centered design practice. This chapter explains some Design Innovation processes we can take and repeat in our own projects and designs. The chapter provides frameworks and guidance on how to conduct research for wearable projects so that humans are respected and considered.

In this chapter, you will explore Design Innovation to work toward creating an informed wearable. We will learn about scoping a project, getting to know the problem, stakeholder mapping, engagement, gaps in the field, human-centered design, **co-design** (or codesign) and **participatory design**, sense-making, prototyping, testing, and iterating. That looks like a lot of content, but once you recognize the information you need to make your wearable valuable, it will come naturally to you. Hopefully, this will stimulate innovative thinking.

By the end of this chapter, you will have the knowledge to plan an informed wearable and understand how to create your own steps as part of a Design Innovation process. You will have the skills to understand the context of social, economic, environmental, or technological impacts and how there is potential to enhance experiences or improve daily life for those concerned.

In this chapter, we're going to cover the following main topics:

- Getting to know the problem
- Engagement—Stakeholder mapping and speaking with people
- Gap—What's in the field and context research
- Human-centered design
- Sense-making
- Prototype, test, and iterate

Technical requirements

This chapter is all about learning the theory that will take your wearable projects to a deeper, more meaningful, and more engaged level. We won't be directly building any projects, but you'll be exploring the process you can take to develop meaningful wearables. Remember—designing with empathy and purpose will lead to a wearable that will be needed and used.

Getting to know the problem

Our journey starts with getting to know the problem. Although this is written as the start of this chapter, it might not be the start of your project. The next few sections that describe a Design Innovation process are interchangeable and are rarely done in isolation. So, dip in, move around, and learn in a way that suits you.

When creating wearables that have a purpose, a need, or satisfy some desire, it is important to know the scope of the area you are designing for. This is where researching the problem area is significant.

What is your topic choice? This is where a scoping phase happens.

Scoping

Understanding what the current situation is in the area of your choice provides a good base for when you engage with people, experts, or stakeholders. When I was researching forgetfulness, it was important that I understood why it was important, what research was done already, and some understanding of memory. This type of research, because it already exists, is called secondary research. We are using resources that aren't ours.

Part of scoping should involve reading journal articles, newspapers and magazines, and books. Fortunately, some resources can help with this process. Using credible resources or being critical of sources that might not be evidenced or contain only personal opinions is important. Using evidence-based insights and informed opinions will add credibility and can help you to avoid designing something that there is no need for. If you come across an article or paper that is behind a paywall, you can try searching on `https://sci-hub.se/`.

Google Scholar is a great search tool to find sources `https://scholar.google.com/`. You can filter articles published anytime or select a specific range of years. You can see an illustration of this in the following screenshot. Saving articles to different library lists is done by clicking the **Start** icon under the listing, which launches the saving dialog:

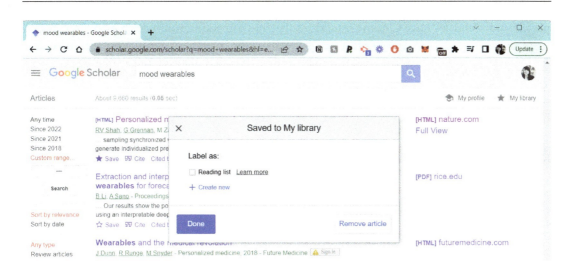

Figure 11.1 – Using Google Scholar: library feature

Using this dialog, you can save and organize your finds. Another tool I find useful is *Mendeley* (*Figure 11.2*). There is an online version or an app for devices or computers. You can access Mendeley at `https://www.mendeley.com/`. Mendeley is a tool to organize the papers you download. It's helpful for organizing, and you can annotate the papers or write notes about what you're reading.

There is also *Paperpile* (*Figure 11.3*), which has similar features to Mendeley. You can save papers and organize and annotate them. Paperpile is accessible online. See `https://paperpile.com/app`.

Here's an overview of Mendeley:

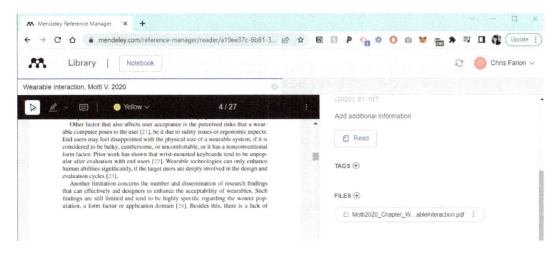

Figure 11.2 – Mendeley online to organize papers and more

Paperpile and Mendeley have Chrome extensions that you can add to your Chrome browser. This will add an icon that you can click to add a paper directly to the application. Reading a paper or book and looking at their references is a great way to find other references that you might want to read.

You can see an overview of Paperpile here:

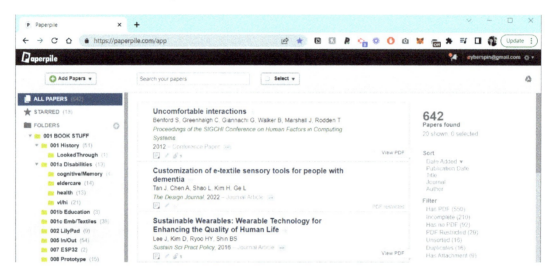

Figure 11.3 – Paperpile reference manager system

There are other ways to learn about a topic. We can find other sources of information such as online videos, blogs, newsletters, and podcasts too. Be sure to think about the different ways you can collect information. Finding many sources in different formats can be an effective way to build your knowledge on a particular topic. Don't forget to keep notes about what you discover. This is an exploring phase, and the goal is to learn about a topic so that you can confidently speak to people about it. You can also ask better questions if you have a base knowledge. For our first activity, we will do some desk research.

Activity 11.1 – Let's do desk research!

Don't bother having a conversation until you know what you need to know!

Spend some time learning about a chosen topic area. Document your findings. Compare and contrast. What are similar researchers, scientists, and artists exploring in this field? Choosing a topic you're invested in or concerned about will always make it more interesting for you. If you're looking for motivation, there could be an interesting article in the news that you'd like to explore further. Why is it like this? Use more than one source stream. This includes seeing which ideas are moving to start-up or commercialization phases.

After you have made your notes and learned more about your topic from several sources, you'll know more about who you should talk to for collecting primary research.

Engagement – Stakeholder mapping and speaking with people

Speaking with people is the most important part of a wearable interactive project. Looking at the human experience through listening and understanding someone's personal experiences is what provides the stories that will bring your wearables to life.

"When stakeholders and their interests shape and contribute to the design process, the quality of the design increases" (Fletcher, 2013).

Part of this process involves the following:

- Gaining an understanding of local context. Give attention to your geographic context and the specific technological, cultural, and economical needs and habits.

- Talk with local experts to enhance your knowledge.

- Delve into the problem through the eyes of the people it affects.

- Looking at the problem you are trying to solve, what impact could solving the issue or reducing some of the pain points have?

It is through engaging with people that we make engaging wearables!

> **Important when engaging with people**
>
> Always remember that you are asking for people's most valuable assets: their **time** and their **knowledge**. It is important to be respectful, and you should be reaching out to people you are really interested in talking to. Keep initial communication short and to the point—until you build a rapport.

Revisiting ethics

Beginning this process requires an understanding of ethics. We looked at ethics briefly in *Chapter 1, Introduction to the World of Wearables*, and you should revisit it when starting a wearable project. You should have **informed participant consent** and voluntary participants should understand if there is any potential for harm. Also, you must assure confidentiality and anonymity, and communicate your outcomes with participants. It is essential we speak with people to find out the current state of play of a topic, and to also find out what are the real issues—the issues that affect people about this topic. Be mindful of cultural identities such as age, race, ethnicity, disability, family status, occupation, and education. Some topics may be more sensitive than others.

Another thing concerning ethics is to honor someone's time. What if the person we are speaking with doesn't directly benefit from our design? Be aware that time is a valuable commodity and be appreciative of the time people give you. Also, before you speak with people, check your assumptions of the topic and your potential biases. How does your background or experience affect the topic or how you interpret their answers? Give the person you are speaking with space to speak. Don't interrogate someone—let their stories flow naturally; pauses are OK. Ethics should be integral to a wearable project and throughout all phases of development for it.

Asking better questions

Knowing how to speak with people is a skill that will help to get useful and interesting information. For example, if you are doing a project with a theme of recycling or waste, and you want to find out how often people donate to charity shops, you might ask someone: *How often do you donate to a charity shop?* They may answer: *Pretty often.* That might seem like the obvious question to ask, and a reasonable answer. However, if you were to ask someone: *When was the last time you donated to a charity shop?* their answer suddenly gets real, and you have a clearer picture of the truth about their donations—or not, as may be the case. People don't want to look bad, so admitting you don't donate often to charity—for example—might make someone believe that you think they are a bad person. They aren't, but we can't help how they might feel. We can ask better questions to get answers that are useful to our projects. We'll have a clearer context for our projects if we have collected useful information.

Understanding how to ask better questions is essentially the focus of *The Mom Test*, by Rob Fitzpatrick. This book can help you to understand how you can structure questions so that even your mom can't lie to you. He illustrates this process with useful examples. Talk about their life instead of your idea, and you will be rewarded with meaningful stories that will contribute to you creating a wearable that is truly useful. You don't want to focus on any questions that discuss generic opinions about the future, and you want to dig for specifics in the past. *The Mom Test* is a short book and a useful tool that I use with my students to help them to ask better questions. It's worth a read if you can pick one up. I heard a student the other day saying they were *only getting terrible answers* to their questions. I couldn't help but think: terrible answers come from terrible questions. Asking a boring series of *yes/no* questions is the quickest way to get someone to lose interest and want to stop talking to you. It's easy to fix!

Lastly, it isn't only about what people say. What are they doing? Observations can answer many questions. If you are curious about how they use their mobile phone, for example, rather than asking them: *How do you use your phone?* ask them to do a task and observe. Watching where they stumble or where they excel can answer a thousand questions! Now, we need to find people to speak with.

Finding experts, stakeholders, and people

Speaking to a variety of people will offer a balanced picture of the topic. They may have a direct interest in what you are working on or are affected by it; they may have privileged information; they may be opposed to it. They could be a policymaker, a researcher, or a patient's family member. So, we need to find people to have conversations with. It can be good practice to make a mapping of possible areas of interest for your topic.

Using paper and pencil, or an online tool such as Miro (`https://miro.com/`), Bubbl.us (`https://bubbl.us/`), or MURAL (`https://www.mural.co/`), create your stakeholder map.

Activity 11.2 – Stakeholder mapping

This involves identifying who has a stake in the outcome. If you start a project and identify these people early, it can make a project have a well-rounded view. You should consider who is involved in the project and invested in the outcome, as well as who are the decision-makers, researchers, creatives, opposed, and similar.

First, start by gathering stakeholders. Using post-it notes on a wall can be an involved way of doing this exercise. Write a potential stakeholder on a sticky note. You might want to consider people from different perspectives, including the following:

- Educational, research organizations, and researchers
- Government or policymakers
- Employers/workers/patrons
- Professional associations/advocacy organizations
- Standard setting and technological assistance organizations
- Companies/commerce/charities
- Directly involved/affected by/age groups

Secondly, create an organizational structure to place the stakeholders in. It could be that they are clustered by their group affiliations, or you could use a bullseye-style diagram where the people with the most vested interest in the topic are central and concentric circles go out, depending on the importance of the topic, as illustrated here:

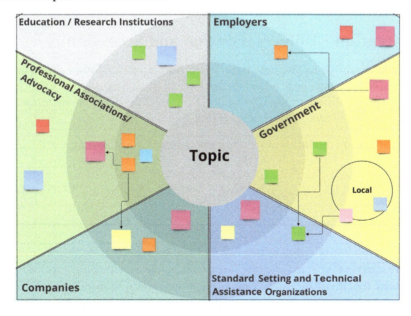

Figure 11.4 – An example stakeholder map I made using Miro

How you organize your stakeholder map is for you to decide. *Figure 11.4* illustrates an example; you will have different categories from me. In each of the sections, for example, you might add more categories. This was created using `https://miro.com/`. For **Government**, you could add international governments, federal governments, local governments, and so on. Each of those headings has potential stakeholders. Identify anyone involved with or impacted by the project. Use actual and not imaginary people. Include their title, name, organization, and contact details if you have them. As you identify them, use connecting lines to describe their relationship—how do they depend on each other and how do they interact? Cluster and label groupings. As your project progresses, you will now have a variety of people to contact and speak to, adding richness and balance to your wearable design.

> **How many people do I need to speak to?**
> Generally, you should keep having conversations with people about your project until you stop hearing new information.

I'm asked a lot by my students: *How many people do I need to speak to?* Or, I'm asked: *How many people should I test it with?* Often when testing, you can usually get away with six or seven people, and they will generally find the things that can obviously go wrong with it—meaning, after two or three people have said they can't find the on/off switch or they thought the sound was too loud, you can make amendments to your design. You don't need to hear this from 25 people. You'll already have enough information to start to iterate your wearable designs. For more information about speaking with five-seven people initially, and how it will catch 80% of errors, you can read the research from the **Nielsen Norman Group** (**NN**), as it did the research that established this: `https://www.nngroup.com/articles/why-you-only-need-to-test-with-5-users/`.

Inclusive intention – Universal design and accessibility

By carefully considering the people we design for—their norms, conventions, cultural backgrounds, and personality aspects—we can create wearables that have an inclusive intention. An inclusive design recognizes that we are all different. Designs should be usable, flexible, and customizable. Create wearables that can accommodate and include everyone.

Accessibility and inclusivity should consider impairment that is the following:

- Sensory
- Physical
- Cognitive

Sensory impairment is a loss of vision or hearing. Physical impairment affects one or more parts of the body that have a loss of function. Cognitive impairment could be a learning impairment, or loss of memory or cognitive function. This can be from old age but can also be from brain injury or trauma. The general rule is to **make wearables as accessible as possible for as many people as possible**! Keep in mind that impairment has three possibilities too. This can be a permanent or **long-term** impairment—for example, in a wheelchair due to physical impairment. However, impairment can also be **temporary**. This can happen after an accident or illness—if you've ever had a body part in a cast, for example. Lastly, the impairment could be **situational**. You might be in a noisy environment; maybe the wearable you're making is for people working in a machinery factory and they cannot hear above the noise of the machinery.

Fewer than 20% of people are born with a disability, and 80% of people have a disability after 85 years old.

Additional to the accessibility mentioned, new technologies are highlighting cultural and ethnic considerations. Here are some examples of this:

- Face recognition that cannot see faces of a darker complexion
- Auto faces/photo selections that cannot detect dark skin
- People from different socioeconomic backgrounds affect what is a priority
- Postcode/ZIP code dictates your access

It is important to remember that not everyone has an equal voice. This often creates imbalances in discussions you may have when creating wearable technology; it may result in oversimplification of a problem or skewed perspectives about what accessible and inclusive design really means. This section only offers a sliver of considerations, and I highly recommend researching more into this essential topic. A starting read could be https://uxdesign.cc/why-can-inequalities-appear-in-digital-accessibility-c66fbe414a7b or https://www.un.org/en/.

Engagement tools

It can be difficult to speak with people. A lot of people aren't sure how to approach someone, and an engagement tool can help this process. A good engagement results in you having **qualitative** data to inform the wearable. It's OK to collect **quantitative** data too—for example, *How many people have a mobile phone?* gives very different answers from *What did you use your mobile phone to do yesterday?* Quantitative is a numerical indicator, but qualitative offers the stories behind the data—it gives you the *why*. These tools can be categorized as a **boundary object** (*Star, S. L. & Griesemer, J. R. (1989)*) or a **bridging concept**. The classifications shown in the following diagram help to elicit different responses:

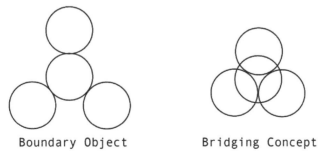

Boundary Object   Bridging Concept

Figure 11.5 – Engagement tool categories

The boundary object engagement tool helps the meaning to be found and expressed by people around a central question or a theme. The bridging concept tool takes the information discovered and it is a way to confirm the information and understanding of a topic. Creating these objects offers an opportunity for many people from different stakeholder groups to interact with them, build on them, and speak about their thoughts, experiences, and memories. The engagement tools will all look and work differently because they are made for your topic. I won't be able to describe your engagement tool. It comes from the needs of the research you are doing and the questions you need answering. Some examples of tools that my students have made for their projects are illustrated in the following photos. These tools allow for collaborative work and engagement with stakeholders:

Figure 11.6 – Sample engagement tools

In *Figure 11.6*, frame *1* shows a tool that was used to find out which social media platforms were used during certain types of activities. Activities were sectioned out, and small icon pieces for social media were created. These were then placed in the sections of the activities. Frame *2* shows an object created offering respondents the chance to rate on a scale, while frame *3* shows small tokens and sections used so people could offer their thoughts on the topic. Lastly, frame *4* shows several boards with locations and activities in these locations. The respondent is given string pieces of different colors, and they wrap the string according to the activities they do and the frequency of these activities.

Another interesting engagement tool designed, shown in the following photo, was a tool that had different travel methods and destinations, and people were asked to show how far they would travel with each transport method. What was interesting about this tool was that after using it, they realized that bicycle travel was predominantly used, when their assumption was that using a car would have been the most frequent travel method. Their project had been about encouraging cycle usage, but they discovered this was not a problem in the city they were researching:

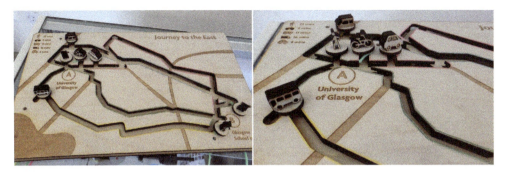

Figure 11.7 – Engagement tool for generating conversations

One tool that uses color as a primary way to communicate, and was a successful tool for recording time allocation in a person's day, is the tool shown here, made by Leixi Chen:

Figure 11.8 – Engagement tool showing the use of a person's daily time

On the left is a box that has *time*, with color paper, designed to fan out when opened. These fans of color are then slotted into place during the day so that we can quickly build up an accurate view of the activities someone is doing, or how much time is allocated for the activities. It is a very simple yet effective tool.

Throughout the use of all these tools, the goal is to have meaningful conversations. They allow a respondent to speak about their experiences. Another way to offer an engaging tool experience is to **gamify** it, adding fun elements such as rules, timings, turns, goals, and end can make for a fun experience for the people using it.

A **generative tool** can be a unique way to offer more conversational opportunities. This is a tool with several stages. The responses from the participant in one section provide the elements in the next section. For example, you might be interested in food, so in one section the participant draws their favorite food items, and these drawings are used in the next section to break down food content from some of the foods they drew. You can see an example of output from a generative tool here:

Figure 11.9 – Generative tool, using content from a previous section

This new drawing can be used again to discuss just the sugar content or similar, opening up conversations regarding lifestyle or nutrition (*Figure 11.9*).

An engagement tool does the following:

- Helps us to have conversations in an engaging way
- Encourages conversations
- Is typically fun for the participants
- Allows us to record data

Be a good listener, and record what people are saying. Take photos of the tools in use and after use. Tools can help with time management and focus. You can read more about bridging concepts and engagement tools through the work of *Dalsgaard, P. & Dindler, C. (2014)* and the research of *Islind, A. S., Lindroth, T., et al. (2019)*, and *Groot, B., & Abma, T. (2021)*. References including the 1989 work on boundary objects and reflections on the origin of that concept are provided at the end of the chapter. Don't forget to get informed consent before documenting participants. Lastly, when interviewing people with physical or cognitive impairments, or other accessibility needs, the interviewer (you) may need to adapt their tools to engage with people. Tools with different colors, sounds, raised areas, other touch abilities, or context-aware wording are all ways that can help make your tools more accessible.

Activity 11.3 – Engagement tools

Think about what type of engagement tool you can design to help get the stories you need for creating your wearable. Typically, a boundary object is created first, to explore a theme in a wider context, and then a bridging concept looks closer to confirm the information you've obtained.

Plan the following:

- What information you want to collect
- How to record and process that information
- What this information can teach you

Decide on the conversation you want to have and how can you extract themes and symbols to help people understand what your topic is about. Often, using **nostalgia** can be a good idea—do you have images of old-style ice cream carts to start conversations? Or, do you use crayons to allow more freedom for drawing as people aren't worried about creating a perfect drawing that they will be judged for? Do you allow a more temporary feeling—creating their comments with chalk so that they can be rubbed out? Build a tool that can interact to help people through the process of understanding and contributing to your topic. Use paper, sticky notes, cardboard, physical objects, wood, fabrics, and any other materials you have to hand.

Spend time on the planning and goals, and then the creation. Once your tool is made and you've taken photos, test it by speaking with people! You will use the data collected to help picture the insights that are important. These ultimately can lead to your designs. Part of these insights may also go toward the requirements planning—there may be certain necessities that have been highlighted. For example, does someone have the dexterity to use certain clips or fasteners?

Now that we've learned more about speaking with people, it would be a good idea to find what gaps, pain points, or opportunities exist in our topic.

Gaps – What's in the field and context research

Finding gaps happens when we research what has been done in the field. Researching with a variety of sources will help you to identify current solutions. What has worked in this field and what has not been as successful? Make notes of the technologies that have been used, and how you might integrate these into your work. Are there techniques or ways of working that have been explored in this problem space that you want to adapt for your topic?

Finding gaps can create opportunities. You might want to understand a range of products that have been created, but that people aren't using. Explore the reasons behind this. Is it an overly complicated design? Are there too many features? Once you have done additional desk research on what exists in your chosen field, it is important to start creating a list of requirements. This planning can help shape the work you do.

Activity 11.4 – Requirements planning

Requirements can drive your wearable project, so it's important to work through these at the start of a project and revisit it as you progress. You might want to create an initial list of requirements as mentioned by people you've spoken with. Or, you may want to list requirements that you've learned about from your first round of desk research when you were exploring the topic area. Create a list of the important issues that people are affected by. This might be as small as two or three items. You might want to set up a document with your planning mapped out similarly to what's shown here, where I have separated some information:

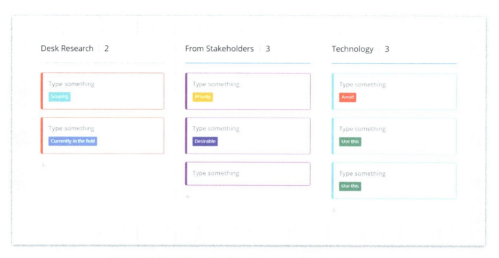

Figure 11.10 – Planning for your wearable requirements

I added tags to organize the information—for example, what was part of the scoping desk research and what was the field survey. This is a document that you should update as the project progresses and as you speak to people. It can help you keep focus.

Remember to include the needs of the people using your design too. This may vary from: easy to charge washable, how easy is it to put on, and similar. Now that we've looked at our requirements, let's explore human-centered design.

Human-centered design

This is an important approach to empower you to design a wearable that will address the needs of the people and stakeholders we've identified in our stakeholder mapping session. On a basic level, this process involves observing people, then ideation, and finally implementation. The overarching theme is that we can help people to live better, easier lives through our designs and design improvements. These phases involve what we've been discussing so far in the chapter, speaking to people to better understand them and their needs. Then, ideation, or making sense of what people are saying, which we will examine in the *Sense-making* section. This involves identifying opportunities for design and generating ideas, followed by the implementation, bringing the wearable to life.

Observing people and keeping notes on these observations provides valuable information that can help inform the design. Often when observing, we think we will remember, so we rely on memory. Observations might be of people in a general context, going about their daily lives, or this might be in the context of using the wearable that you have made. This is part of usability testing that you can do when you have made and given your wearable to someone to use in their own environment. I would highly suggest taking photographs, videos, and writing notes—an example of which is shown here; that may include drawings too:

Figure 11.11 – Journal keeping: written observations

This is an example from my observation journals. It isn't important to read what the notes describe for this purpose—it is just to show you that note keeping doesn't need to be super tidy; it can be a quick format with the use of multiple colors and symbols. Notes provide you with an accurate picture compared to what we think we saw. Include comments on the environment in which the observation took place, the weather conditions, time of day, key incidents, and what your impressions are. I would note the tip that notes from observation should be reviewed and tagged, highlighted within 24 hours as memory fades quickly.

All of this is part of **ethnographic research**, and it is a great way to uncover the insights you need. Some example research that you may want to read includes the following: *Prototyping wearables for supporting cognitive mapping by the blind, Ugulino, W. C. & Fuks, H. (2015)*; *Empathetic iteration of a SnuggleTime garment system for kangaroo care of mothers and babies in a neonatal intensive care unit, Cobb, K. A. & Clarke-Sather, A. R. (2020)*; *Spheres of practice for the co-design of wearables, Fairburn, S., Steed, J. & Coulter, J. (2016)*; and *Imagining future technologies: eTextile weaving workshops with blind and visually impaired people, Giles, E. & Van Der Linden, J. (2015)*.

Allowing meaningful engagement begins with a co-design or participatory design process, so let's have a look at that next.

Co-design and participatory design

Co-design and **participatory design** are often used at the same time or one in place of the other, but they aren't the same. Though they are both **user-centered design** processes, there are differences. For both, users are consulted not only at the start and end of a project but are also spoken with as the process develops. In a co-design process, the wearer is directly involved in the wearables design, with the designer. This allows a deeper understanding of the problem area and helps guarantee that there is a result that is useful to this group of people. With co-design, the participants are active throughout the entire project at each step, and the researchers, designers, and participants all contribute equally. All involved should not have any ideas at the start of this process or be able to foresee the outcome. Typically, it is the same participants throughout this process. With participatory design, participants join in at certain steps of the process. It may be different participants who are involved. When these processes are done successfully, all involved are valued and treated as equals, and it usually produces mutual learning and transformative outcomes.

If these methods are not done correctly or with sensitivity, they can lead to undesirable outcomes, as noted here:

> *"Done badly, they can serve to exploit labour, invalidate local knowledge, neutralize voices, and silence dissent" (McCarthy and Wright 2015).*

After speaking with people and collecting large amounts of data, we need to do something to it so that we can establish what are the useful aspects and insights and what will help form our wearable designs. In addition to that, it's important to remember that the point is not to be harvesting people for their data, but in some way, we are providing value and leaving the community better or offering them a way to continue the work on their own. The next activity is about sense-making, and this is where we turn our data into useful information.

Sense-making

Sense-making gives meaning to the information and stories that we have collected. It allows us to come up with an understanding of the situation and—possibly—the reasons why there are pain points. We analyze the data by looking for patterns and themes. Were there any challenges that you observed, and can this help to inform your designs? You can add hierarchy to this so that the most pressing or important problems become clearer. Let the data tell you the story—which themes are emerging, and which keywords or codes show themselves? We want to cluster similar information, and the quotes and stories provide evidence for these codes. One example from my own projects is shown here:

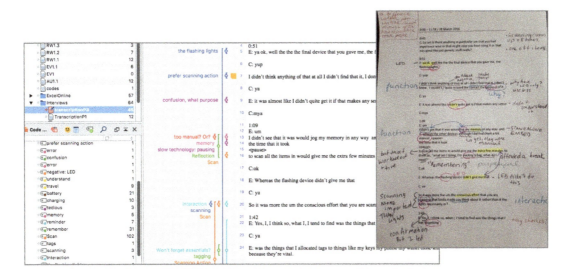

Figure 11.12 – Creating codes to group the data you collected

If you use sticky notes again, you might want to color-code them—maybe yellow for a theme, and blue for direct quotes for evidence. Add a color for the insights that emerge. What you are trying to establish is what you found out, what information is missing, how effective it was, and what flaws there were. You might want to use Miro again or similar to cluster sticky notes on a board and arrange them according to themes. While doing this process, ask yourself the following:

- What surprised you?
- How might what you learned affect what you design?
- What ideas might these learnings inspire?

When you have collected your answers and understand the problem space, you should prototype some solutions for testing. This could be a co-design process, where the people you are speaking with design with you, or it could be ideas you've generated from the information you've gathered. Typically, we can create an **affinity diagram** to highlight commonalities, any themes, and what scope exists for this problem. There are templates for online affinity diagrams, such as this free version from InVision that has sections noted (`https://www.invisionapp.com/freehand/templates/detail/affinity-diagram-template`):

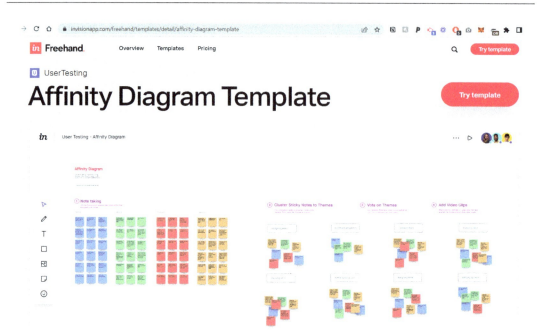

Figure 11.13 – Creating an affinity diagram can help you

You might want to create an **empathy map** based on your discoveries about the people you spoke with. An empathy map has four areas defined where you can get an overall image of a person at a glance. It includes the following:

- Says

- Thinks

- Does

- Feels

The person is at the center of this. The information in *says* would be direct quotes from the person, while *thinks* captures thoughts such as what matters to them or whether they are unsure about something. The *does* section has actions that they do physically—how they use something or interact with it, and how that might ultimately inform your design. Lastly, *feels* is their emotional state. This could be something that the person finds worrying or confusing. Creating an empathy map might be something you do at the start and later in the design process. You might start with a quick one based on a persona, and then fill in an actual one representing someone you have spoken to.

You can add to your empathy map additional sections, such as goals, or pains and gains. Design it to suit your wearable-design needs. There are also examples of alternative areas, such as in this worksheet from Game Storming: `https://gamestorming.com/wp-content/uploads/2017/07/Empathy-Map-Canvas-006.pdf`.

Remember—this chapter should be used as a reference. Reading through and working on the activities gives options and considerations for your projects, but you don't have to do everything. It is likely that if you do an affinity diagram or an empathy map, you will want to follow up with scoping again. This will be continuing desk research following on from the insights these processes discovered.

Prototype, test, iterate

The prototyping process has been well documented in *Chapter 8, Learning How to Prototype and Make Electronics Wearable*. The prototype you make will be designed with the analysis of the interviews and engagements you carried out with stakeholders. The prototype you make will be tested with the stakeholders you identified earlier in the Design Innovation process. Ideally, you want to decide how well the prototype responds to stakeholder needs. They will tell you very quickly if it is too confusing to use or not fit for purpose! Remember earlier in the chapter, we looked at how observations can be valuable in discovering issues with your prototypes. Keep detailed notes of your observations.

It's extremely important to get the prototype to the wearer and create a feedback loop —a way for them to offer you feedback on what you are prototyping. It could be you give them a journal to write their thoughts as they use it, or you make a mini-website of a page or two for them to fill in responses as they use it. A Google form can capture basic information from them, but be sure to try to interview them again or have a workshop or forum where several people trying your wearable can chat about how it worked (or didn't!) for them.

Now that we've come to the end of this chapter, it's time to do it all again! That's a process of Design Innovation, to do these slices of a process in the order that suits your projects. It isn't a step-by-step process that becomes immovable. Be iterative, follow the research, and enjoy finding out where the research takes you!

Summary

This chapter focused on learning parts of a Design Innovation process so that we can create an informed wearable of value. Remember—these are not done in isolation but are overlapping and often repeated stages. We looked at several elements, including desk research, which we started with. This was about finding secondary information to help us learn about the topic. We followed up with speaking with people, which involved a revisit of ethics, learning how to ask better questions, and finding stakeholders and people to have conversations with. You did this by designing a stakeholder map. An inclusive intention was highlighted as an essential part of today's design. Considering accessibility and inclusivity should happen throughout all phases of a project. Gaps were identified through researching what is currently done in the field. This helps us to identify opportunities for design. Following on from that was a look at human-centered design. This included understanding co-design and participatory design so that we could include them in our own practice. Creating wearables with the people who will wear them can create a far richer experience for all involved. It's also a valuable learning experience and improves our skillset.

Lastly, we analyzed the data that was produced from speaking to people in our design process. This is an essential step to understand not only the stories but to also provide substance to our wearables. We know what our wearers want because they told us, and we listened.

Having meaningful engagements will always improve the wearables we create. We should set our goals of creating an experience that will enhance or augment our ways of working, communicating, and living.

Now that we've learned more about the Design Innovation process and wearable interaction, we will create the first iteration of an informed wearable in the next chapter. So, grab your sewing supplies and your soldering tools, and let's get making!

References

Fletcher, K. (2013). *Sustainable fashion and textiles: design journeys. Routledge.*

Fitzpatrick, R. (2013). *The Mom Test: How to talk to customers & learn if your business is a good idea when everyone is lying to you. Robfitz Ltd.*

Star, S. L. & Griesemer, J. R. (1989). *Institutional ecology, 'translations' and boundary objects: Amateurs and professionals in Berkeley's Museum of Vertebrate Zoology, 1907-39. Social studies of science, 19(3), 387-420.*

Leigh Star, S. (2010). *This is not a boundary object: Reflections on the origin of a concept. Science, Technology, & Human Values, 35(5), 601-617.*

Dalsgaard, P. & Dindler, C. (2014, April). *Between theory and practice: bridging concepts in HCI research.* In Proceedings of the *SIGCHI conference on Human Factors in Computing Systems (pp. 1635-1644).*

Islind, A. S., Lindroth, T., Lundin, J. & Steineck, G. (2019). *Co-designing a digital platform with boundary objects: bringing together heterogeneous users in healthcare. Health and Technology, 9(4), 425-438.*

Groot, B. & Abma, T. (2021). *Boundary objects: Engaging and bridging needs of people in participatory research by arts-based methods. International Journal of Environmental Research and Public Health, 18(15), 7903.*

Ugulino, W. C. & Fuks, H. (2015, May). *Prototyping wearables for supporting cognitive mapping by the blind: Lessons from co-creation workshops.* In Proceedings of the *2015 workshop on Wearable Systems and Applications (pp. 39-44).*

Cobb, K. A. & Clarke-Sather, A. R. (2020). *Empathetic iteration of a snuggletime garment system for kangaroo care of mothers and babies in the neonatal intensive care unit. Journal of Textile and Apparel, Technology and Management.*

Fairburn, S., Steed, J. & Coulter, J. (2016). *Spheres of Practice for the Co-design of Wearables. Journal of Textile Design Research and Practice, 4(1), 85-109.*

Wright, P. & McCarthy, J. (2015). *The politics and aesthetics of participatory HCI. Interactions, 22(6),* 26-31.

Giles, E. & Van Der Linden, J. (2015, June). *Imagining future technologies: eTextile weaving workshops with blind and visually impaired people.* In Proceedings of the *2015 ACM SIGCHI Conference on Creativity and Cognition (pp. 3-12).*

Review questions

This is a chapter for reflection and action. See if you can answer the following questions:

1. What can scoping out a project allow us to accomplish and why is it important?
2. Why should we speak to people in the context of creating our wearables?
3. When creating a stakeholder map, what are some of the broad categories that we can consider?
4. What are the three categories of impairment?
5. Regarding accessibility, what three aspects are important to consider?
6. What is the difference between a co-design project and a participatory design project?
7. What is an important part of the prototyping process?

12

Designing for Forgetfulness: A Case Study of Message Bag

In the previous chapter, we looked at a Design Innovation process. This chapter is looking at that process and considers the case study of Message Bag to understand the Design Innovation development in practice. What is Message Bag? Message Bag is a purpose-built object-based memory aid that emerged as a result of investigating forgetfulness and speaking with people. To create it, extensive autobiographical research and design-led inquiries were used, alongside testing investigative prototypes and field testing high-fidelity prototypes. Creating a wearable through understanding the context of a chosen topic, and focusing on a need, is how we can design a **culture-driven wearable**. These wearables with a purpose, specifically, to make something better for a person or group of people, are at the forefront of the design.

By following along and building a Message Bag, the near-body wearable provides a concrete example of using the Design Innovation process. In this chapter, we're going to cover the following topics:

- Following a Design Innovation process
- Creating your prototype
- Testing your prototype
- The future of Message Bag

Technical requirements

For this chapter, we will be creating a prototype of Message Bag. We will need the following:

- The Adafruit QT Py - SAMD21 Dev Board with STEMMA QT
- An **RFID (Radio Frequency Identification)** reader, Mifare RC522, and the corresponding tags
- Sewable Flora NeoPixels and a sewable Flora Sewable 3-Pin JST Wiring Adapter

- An Adafruit LiIon or LiPoly charger BFF add-on for the QT Py and a rechargeable battery, with 3.7 V and a 2-pin JST-PH connector

- Conductive thread, a breadboard, and hookup wires

Following a Design Innovation process

This chapter focuses on a case study that follows parts of a Design Innovation process to help illustrate how we can design an informed wearable. The case study of Message Bag starts by scoping your wearable project. In this example, the problem area is forgetfulness and involves cognition and memory as the research topic. Scoping encompasses looking at the problem, so part of the research is for object-based memory aids. This ultimately led me to RFID systems. My original **proof-of-concept** prototype is shown here, photographed by Toby Harris (see *Figure 12.1*):

Figure 12.1 – Message Bag

When scoping the topic, I read papers on forgetfulness and discovered that forgetfulness can impact an individual's life negatively. It also has ongoing consequences. These consequences include stress, anxiety, embarrassment, shame, and feeling *off* or *unsettled* throughout the day (*Ponds et al., 1997*). When forgetfulness concerns someone younger, say, below 50 years old, forgetfulness is blamed on tension, emotional problems, and poor concentration (*Imhof et al., 2006*). Feeling this way daily leads to overall negative feelings and changes to a person's lifestyle. This includes creating coping mechanisms. A coping mechanism is a way to help deal with the problem. For forgetfulness, this ranged from waking up earlier to ensure nothing was forgotten – packing items for the day, for example – to constantly checking that items were packed. It is important, as we learned in the previous chapter, to read a variety of peer-reviewed papers to fully understand the scope of the problem area.

My research looked at the ways a smart object (in this instance, an augmented bag) could reduce someone's negativity and therefore enhance their overall quality of life. This involved embedding technology to support the user when they use a bag, backpack, or purse. This bag would have the ability to communicate with the wearer using **Arduino technology**. It would notify them of the things that are packed after being scanned. This is done with an RFID system. This system is chosen because RFID tags don't need a direct line of sight – it is a contactless system. It is relatively low-cost, especially in comparison with other memory aid systems. Also, reading the tags doesn't depend on the area being lit well, as with barcode scanning or QR code scanning. It can be used at any time and in any position or lighting. The RFID system, which is what we will use for our prototype in this chapter, consists of a reader and tags with unique IDs. The tags are **passive**, making batteries unnecessary. There are integrated circuits with a small antenna that is sealed inside the different shaped tags. The energy to register the tag in the system comes from the RFID reader. When you place the tag near the reader, it is powered through electromagnetic induction.

RFID technology has many useful applications, including in retail (for store operations and managing inventory), asset management in healthcare, and in heavy industry, which uses RFID for oil and gas equipment, container, and vehicle tracking. *Schmidt, Gellersen, & Merz (2000)* pioneered a **wearable RFID** system that was integrated into a glove. The glove had an embedded reader that detected tags that were on objects. The glove would touch the objects and could register the tags. At the time, an additional computing unit needed to be worn on the hip to provide the computing power for data processing. However, the prototype helped to establish miniature RFID systems. This led the way for smaller power supplies and processing power and resulted in RFID systems being implemented in surgical gloves and bracelets. The *iGlove* presented by *Fishkin et al. (2005)* is a modified glove that contains small, inexpensive hardware. It was a prototype for testing daily household tasks. This was improved and redeveloped for medical use. There was also a bracelet prototyped for in-home care. There are many more examples, including uses for surgery – so that surgical equipment doesn't get left in patients – and in the aviation industry, so tools don't go missing.

Gaps – what's in the field and the context of research

After conducting research to scope out the topic area, there is a need to understand where a gap might be. Was there a gap for electronic bags? I decided to conduct observations because my research told me that it would need to be a device with the person daily. This was done during the daytime at several locations, including parks, museums, shopping areas, and cafes. To get a cross-section of people, I thought these locations would include locals, tourists, and people working and doing other activities. I wanted to observe what objects people had on them to find out which are used every day. This is how I came to the realization that bags of some description were used universally by most people. This was based on documented observations over several days of what items people used daily. Also, after conducting another round of desk research, it was apparent that there were not many electronic bag devices.

Requirements planning

One understanding of providing an experience that is useful to the wearer is recalling what Houde and Hill call the *look and feel* of a product or system. They describe it as *"the concrete sensory experience of using an artifact — what the user looks at, feels and hears while using it"* (*Houde & Hill, 1997*). The planning includes consideration for a near-body system includes an easy setup, would match the wearer's style and social setting, and is durable, comfortable, and easily understood. This follows the ideals of creating a culture-driven wearable. To create a wearable system suited to a person who feels forgetful, we would consider this context and incorporate that into the system:

- Requires no additional cognitive load – they don't need to learn anything new

- Has a minimal learning curve – they can easily use the wearable

- Information about packed items has visible feedback

- A contactless system for ease of use

- Aligns with the wearer's existing behavior

The system will use five lights to communicate the state to the wearer. It will be our challenge to use these in the most effective way. This is an advantage of using NeoPixels because we can make them any color we want to and call each LED individually, all while only using 1 GPIO.

Engagement and insights

Although I won't cover the process I followed in detail due to space constraints, as well because it is already published online in my PhD thesis (`https://qmro.qmul.ac.uk/xmlui/handle/123456789/39747`), it is important to highlight that testing and engaging with people took place. Engagement allows our designs to be iterated in response to what people have told us. Speaking to people also helps us empathize with the issues they face. For example, hearing a story about how someone is impacted by forgetting things they need for their day helps us to understand the importance of the issue and the impact we can have. These are the insights that create a more effective, usable, durable, aesthetically pleasing, and useful wearable.

In the early development stages of Message Bag, there were many iterations. We learned about prototyping in *Chapter 8, Learning How to Prototype and Make Electronics Wearable* – specifically, the Houde and Hill model. This was the basis for many of the prototypes I created. The experience prototype was a way to explore and evaluate design ideas. I also used autoethnography, which involves keeping research and design journals for documenting all aspects of the use and observations of Message Bag. This enhances the prototypes we create. Experience Prototyping allows the designer to experience it themselves, rather than *"witnessing a demonstration or someone else's experience"* (*Bucheanu & Suri, 2000*).

The prototype we are creating today resembles the one I made for my studies in its function and goals. However, the technology I initially used and what I created wasn't as small or as magical as, say, using

NeoPixels are. I'm making this new iteration along with you and I hope the delight I witnessed in the past use of Message Bag carries forward for you now in the prototype you make.

Creating your prototype

We will create our prototype in stages, as we've done with past projects. The RFID system we are designing consists of processing power for control, an RFID reader, RFID corresponding tags, and communication with the wearer in the form of lights. My research showed that people prefer to learn through doing. By using RFID as a system to enable quick recall, it should be beneficial to the wearer. Scanning a tag is also an easy action, so it should not overload someone's memory.

Why this system? The purpose of the system is to track your items. The RFID reader and tags create a *scan-in-and-scan-out* system. The external LEDs allow the wearer to *see* which items are contained within the bag. The LEDs are bright and easily visible across a room. This allows an individual to determine whether all their items are packed. They don't need to stop whatever other activities they are doing. It is this communication that the bag provides, which, in typical circumstances, never happens and this makes the device unique. Essentially, it tells us what is inside.

Collect the components for making this circuit (see *Figure 12.2*) consisting of the following:

- The Adafruit QT Py - SAMD21 dev board with STEMMA QT
- An RFID reader: 13.56 MHz Mifare RC522, and five corresponding tags
- Five sewable FLORA NeoPixels and the sewable FLORA sewable 3-pin JST wiring adapter
- An Adafruit LiIon or LiPoly charger BFF add-on for the QT Py and a rechargeable battery (3.7 V with a 2-pin JST-PH connector and long leg (15 mm or longer) header pins)
- Conductive thread, a needle and threader, wires, and soldering items

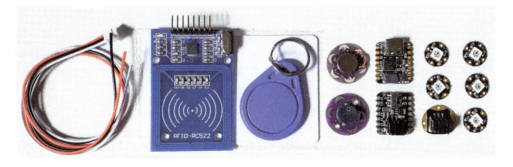

Figure 12.2 – The components for the Message Bag circuit

All of the supplies for this circuit can be purchased from component retailers, as noted in the appendix. Because this circuit is on the outside of a bag, try to use **steel-based conductive thread**. It will last a lot longer and not be affected by the weather. Silver thread can tarnish, losing conductivity, so for circuits that we want to be more durable, it isn't a good choice. Lithium batteries (rechargeable batteries) can also be difficult to get delivered to certain areas, so you may need to check different stockists. I've found 110 mAh batteries at Proto-PIC (`https://proto-pic.co.uk/product/polymer-lithium-ion-battery-3-7v-110mah/`), Cool Components (`https://coolcomponents.co.uk/products/lithium-polymer-battery-110mah?variant=45222884686`), and Adafruit (`https://www.adafruit.com/product/258` has `1200mAh` batteries).

To connect to both the QT Py SAMD and the charging board (the BFF add-on for the QT Py), you'll also need longer header pins if you want to use it in a breadboard to test your circuit. In *Figure 12.3*, the longer header pins are shown on the right of the header pins that come with many components for size comparison. The longer legs are needed because we will solder these boards back to back:

Figure 12.3 – Header pins and the two boards we are using

You'll also need a handbag, backpack, or another bag of some description to put your circuit onto. You can reuse an existing bag that you already have or go to a charity or thrift shop to get something secondhand to repurpose or upcycle!

We haven't used the QT Py SAMD board. It has SPI and I²C connections and it is very, very small, which is great for hiding it in our wearables. It's the same form factor as the QT PY ESP32-S2 that we used previously. So, if you use these boards, the choice of sensors with STEMMA connections (chainable I²C ports) is plentiful. It also has capacitive touch pins on A0, A1, A2, A3, A6, and A7. It has a USB Type-C connector and 11 GPIO pins. Lastly, it's a good price – around $8 or £7 at the time of print. To see the pins and capabilities of the SAMD21, look at and refer to the pin-out diagram in *Figure 12.4*, courtesy of Adafruit (`https://learn.adafruit.com/assets/110643`):

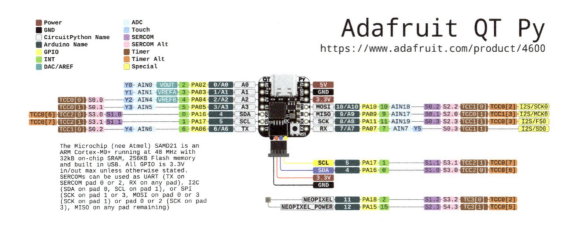

Figure 12.4 – An Adafruit pin-out diagram of the QT Py SAMD21 (Eva Herrada, Share Alike Creative commons http://creativecommons.org/licenses/by-sa/3.0/)

Now that we've gathered the supplies we need, let's begin planning our circuit and soldering some of the connections to prepare our board.

Activity 12.1 – Planning and first steps

To start our project, we'll make some decisions on how we will mount it to our bag. Because we have learned how to solder and sew in *Chapter 10, Soldering and Sewing to Complete Your Project*, we could begin with sewing the Flora sewable NeoPixels:

1. Place the Flora NeoPixels where you want them (see *Figure 12.5*). I'd like the NeoPixels prominent on the front of the bag, visible. I'm using the sewable JST connector, so the wiring is minimal on the front. **Double-check that the white arrows on the NeoPixels are all pointing in the same direction**. This indicates the **data in** (**DI**) and **data out** (**DO**) pins. Once in place, glue them so they are easier to sew:

Figure 12.5 – Placing and gluing the components before sewing, and check the data-in connections face in the same direction

2. Start sewing the common connections with conductive thread. I'm starting with the + power connection for all the NeoPixels. Sew from + on the last NeoPixel, all the way up to the right-hand side of the JST connection sew tab where the red wire is when the connector is plugged in (on the left in *Figure 12.6*). Then, sew the – ground connection on the last NeoPixel, all the way to the middle of the JST connection sew tab (in the middle of *Figure 12.6*), where the black wire is on the connector.

3. You'll notice that our next connection to sew is the **DI** pin. If we sew it, there will be an overlap with the ground thread that we've just sewn. What does this mean? It will cause a short, so our connections won't work, and it could damage our components. We need to provide **insulation** to the conductive thread:

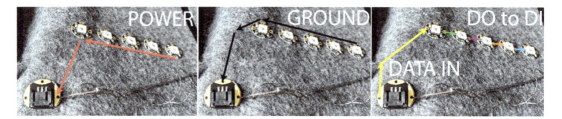

Figure 12.6 – Sewing the three connections

To insulate it, use a piece of fabric but you can use dimensional fabric paint or similar. If you use one of the puffy paint methods, you'll need to leave it to dry.

4. Place the fabric on top of the portion of the conductive thread that will overlap (see *Figure 12.7*). Glue in place. With the thread covered, sew over where the ground thread is. You can also place another piece of fabric on top and sew that on:

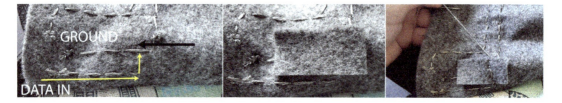

Figure 12.7 – Covering a conductive thread overlap with a fabric piece

5. Sew from the left-hand sew tab on the JST connector up to and around the sew tab for **DI** on the NeoPixel, securing it in place. Cut the thread after you've tied a knot.

6. Now, we need to sew all the connections between the NeoPixels. Sew from the DO to the next NeoPixel DI pin. Replicate this for all the NeoPixels. On the right in *Figure 12.6*, we can see the NeoPixels and each arrow is a different color to indicate the DO to DI connections. The back of your completed sewing will resemble where there are short conductive thread stitches sewn between each NeoPixel on the right in *Figure 12.8*:

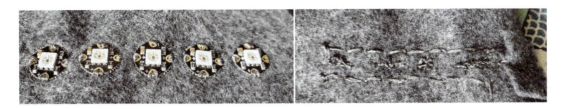

Figure 12.8 – Sewable NeoPixels (front view) and underside stitches

Be sure to seal your knotted cut ends with Fray Check (see *Figure 12.9*), or clear nail varnish. Conductive thread can fray and this can cause problems in your circuit:

Figure 12.9 – Using Fray Check to finish the thread ends

Now that we've finished sewing the NeoPixels of the circuit, we'll have to solder the long header pins to the QT Py SAMD. Let's do that now.

Activity 12.2 – Soldering headers on components

Did your **RFID board** come pre-soldered? If so, you won't need to do this step. If not, then let's solder headers on the RFID reader. Following the same steps you learned about in *Chapter 10, Soldering and Sewing to Complete Your Project*, solder the header pins that came with your RFID board to the board. When that's finished, we can solder the QT Py SAMD and power board.

We are soldering the power board (the charger BFF add-on for the QT Py) directly to the back of it. Using longer header pins (that are over 11 mm), we are going to put our two boards onto it. Let's put the charge board on first. We want to access the power switch, so this will be at the top. See *Figure 12.10*, which shows the headers being put into the circuit board holes and then the placed in the breadboard:

Figure 12.10 – The charger board on header pins in a breadboard for soldering

Solder these pins. We will do a **solder tack** by soldering one pin on one side of the board, then soldering a pin on the opposite side. This anchors our board for us to complete the soldering. Solder all the pins. *Figure 12.11* shows flux being applied to the pins, then one pin being soldered, and another pin being soldered on the opposite side. It also shows the completed soldered charge board in the breadboard:

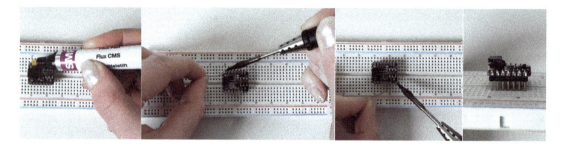

Figure 12.11 – Soldering the charge board, solder tack, and finished solder

With the power board soldering complete, carefully remove it from the breadboard (so we don't bend the pins). Let's solder our QT Py SAMD. In *Figure 12.12*, look for the two pins marked **5V** on both boards. These pins will be connected by the header pin, so when you've located them, slide the boards together so that they connect. Double-check and check again before soldering!

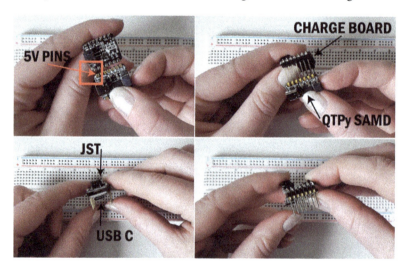

Figure 12.12 – Aligning the 5 V pins for soldering

Solder this board in place and, as a reminder, clean your solder tip and tin it (see *Figure 12.13*). One thing to note is that the **power board uses the A2 pin** as a simple voltage divider on the cathode side of the diode. This is so the firmware can detect the voltage. If it is higher than 4.3 V, it means you're likely to be plugged into the USB for charging instead of using the battery power. Because of this, you can't use the **A2 pin** when using this power board:

Figure 12.13 – Soldering the QT Py SAMD and the charge board (right), caring for your solder iron

Once all the pins have been soldered and both the RFID reader and QT Py SAMD are in the breadboard, we can start testing our circuit. Let's breadboard our components now.

Activity 12.3 – Breadboard the circuit

Because our QT Py SAMD is facing upside down, we can't see the names of the pins. It can help to sketch out the board and connections so you don't make errors. You'll notice the RFID board is using an **SPI** connection. We've used I²C in our circuits so far but we need some practice with SPI. As a reminder, we need to hook up ground and power and the SPI interface – **Serial Data (SDA)**, **Serial Clock (SCK)**, **Microcontroller Out Signal In (MOSI)**, and **Microcontroller In Signal Out (MISO)** pins. On the QT Py SAMD board, the SPI interface uses these pins:

- SDA / A3 / D4
- SCK / A8 / D8 – The hardware SPI clock pin
- MI / A9 / D9 – The hardware SPI MISO pin
- MO / A10 / D10 – The hardware SPI MOSI pin

SDA is the serial data that is being transferred, **SCK** is the serial clock that controls the timing of the messages or data, **MOSI**, is the microcontroller out and signal in, and **MISO** is the microcontroller in and signal out. The QT Py SAMD is clearly marked with these connections too. Using six wires, connect the circuit according to the SPI pins and the labels on the RFID board (see *Figure 12.14*):

Figure 12.14 – Connecting the RFID board and the QT Py SAMD21

A few points to note – place the QT Py SAMD so that the USB is facing left to match the orientation of the pins, and the reset pin can be set to any pin. I've chosen **pin 3**, as the charge board is using **pin 2**.

Activity 12.4 – Checking the board and blink sketch

The Adafruit QT Py SAMD21 board should be installed through the Boards Manager, as we installed the Adafruit boards in *Chapter 3, Exploring e-textile Toolkits: LilyPad, Flora, Circuit Playground, and More*. Check the board is available by heading to the menu and selecting **Tools | Board: "Adafruit QT Py M0 (SAMD21) | Adafruit SAMD (32-bits ARM Cortex-M0+ and Cortex-M-4) Boards | Adafruit QT Py M0 (SAMD21)**. This is shown in *Figure 12.15* as a reminder:

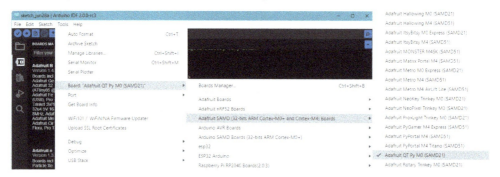

Figure 12.15 – Checking for the QT Py SAMD board

If you don't have this board in the menu, check that the board is installed through the **Boards Manager** (see *Figure 12.16*). Install **Adafruit Boards** and **Adafruit SAMD (32-bits ARM Cortex-M0+ and Cortex-M-4) Boards** if it's not there. You'll need the URL `https://adafruit.github.io/arduino-board-index/package_adafruit_index.json` as part of your additional Boards Manager URLs under Arduino **Preferences**:

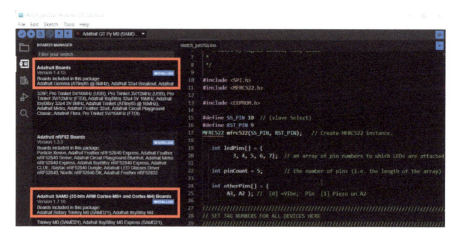

Figure 12.16 – Checking board packages installed

When you have found the board, upload the test code to check that the connection, port, and board are all communicating. Plug in your board, choose the correct board and port information from the **Tools** menu, and let's use a blink sketch. The QT Py SAMD board has an RGB NeoPixel on it in place of an LED – it's on **digital pin 11**. We did this previously in *Chapter 9, Designing and Prototyping Your Own Hyper-Body System*, with the following code: `https://github.com/cmoz/Ultimate/tree/main/C9/9.2_Blink`. Upload the blink code that will blink a NeoPixel to check that your connection and board are working now (see *Figure 12.17*):

Figure 12.17 – The working blink sketch

You can see the NeoPixel changing colors under your board. Now that you have a blinking QT Py SAMD board, we can program the RFID reader to read the corresponding RFID tags.

Activity 12.5 – The code to test the RFID reader

Our board is blinking and it's breadboarded with the RFID reader. The next steps are to add an RFID library so we can use RFID. For this example, I'll install the **MFRC522** library, so search for it in the Library Manager.

After installing the library, navigate to the examples so we can load a sketch. Go to **File** | **Examples** | **MFRC522** | **DumpInfo**, as shown in *Figure 12.18*:

Figure 12.18 – Opening the DumpInfo example sketch

We can run the code after changing the pin numbers for **SDA** and **RST** (reset). The only variables we alter in this code are the following lines:

```
#define RST_PIN         9
#define SS_PIN          10
```

We should amend it to this:

```
#define RST_PIN         3
#define SS_PIN          4
```

Upload the code. After receiving confirmation that the code has been uploaded, open the Serial Monitor. You will see the RFID reader is waiting for a tag to scan, so hold your tag up to the reader now. There will be a *dump* of the card contents. While we are here, grab the **Card UID** value and save it:

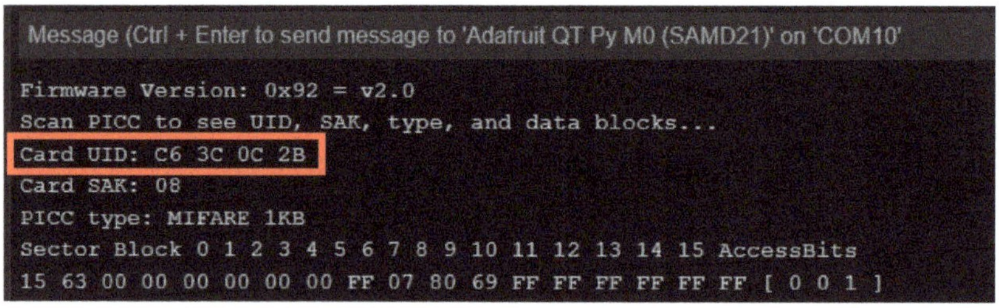

Figure 12.19 – Displaying the tag contents

Scan all five tags and make a note of their **unique identifiers** (**UIDs**) – we'll need them for the RFID code later. With the RFID reader working, it's a good idea to look through the examples provided and run a few more so you can start to understand what is happening in the code. Don't forget to change the pin numbers in your code for the SDA pins and reset pin. Try a few before jumping into the next activity.

Activity 12.6 – The code for the NeoPixels and QT Py SAMD

Now that the RFID board is working with the example code, we can add NeoPixels to our circuit and try the NeoPixel code. Then, we will combine the requirements of our project so we can create the final code. Working in a modular way, as we've done with previous projects, helps to avoid errors and makes troubleshooting easier because we only have to fix one component.

Add the three wires from your sewn NeoPixel circuit, or I'm using a NeoTester, which is handy for when I'm testing neo code with a circuit board. It's a strip of eight NeoPixel lights with a header pin. You can make these yourself or https://www.tinkertailor.tech/product-page/breadboard-rgb-leds provides them pre-soldered with heat shrink versions. Wire your QT Py SAMD in the following ways:

- The ground on the QT Py -> the ground on the NeoPixel

- The power on the QT Py -> the power on the NeoPixel

- A1 on the QT Py which is digital 1 -> the DI pin on the NeoPixel

With our NeoPixel connected, open an example sketch from the NeoPixel library. I usually use **strandtest**. Edit the pin number for your pixels and the number of pixels:

```
#define LED_PIN     1
#define LED_COUNT 8
```

Now **upload** the code. You should see your NeoPixels lighting up in rainbow compilations (see *Figure 12.20*):

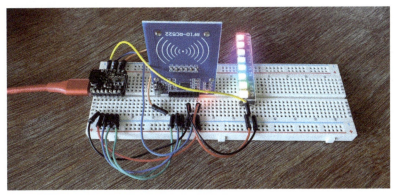

Figure 12.20 – A sample sketch working with the NeoPixels

On to our next steps! We've got the RFID board correctly connected and the NeoPixels working too. Now, we need to define the code and purpose of Message Bag.

Activity 12.7 – Code for Message Bag's RFID and NeoPixel functionality

I usually have written down in my notebook the pins I'm using as a reminder for when I'm editing code. We have decided the following:

- **pin 1** = NeoPixels

- **pin 3** = RST reset

- **pin 4** = SDA

The other pins are part of the SPI protocol that has already been written into the library for us, so we don't need to define them.

What's the code going to do?

Often when developers are creating new code, they write it in **pseudocode**. This is a form of human-readable code that describes how the **algorithm** works. Think of it as a step-by-step outline of the process. It helps us with planning and understanding the problem and then turning it into code line by line. This is good practice. Typically, writing pseudocode starts with the overall **purpose** of the code you will write. Thinking of Message Bag, we know we want someone to place an RFID card, fob, or something similar up to the reader to scan their item. This registers on the system. The goal of the bag is to let you know whether you have or have not packed an item. The lights are on or off as indicators, Typically off indicates that your item is missing. When you *scan* an item, the light goes off. To define the purpose of the code, the **program will wait** for an RFID card to be presented; when presented, it will **record the card** in the system and **output a response** based on the card. It will also check whether there was a **previous scan** of that card to determine whether it was a scan in or a scan out.

Requirements planning for the use of Message Bag

How will this be used? Our understanding is that if someone has items to pack (car keys or a wallet, for example), these items have RFID tags on them. To use the system, they would do the following:

1.   Turn on the system – there is an initial sequence of lights. This is positive feedback from the system to communicate to the person that the system is functioning.

2.   Scan in or scan out. Hold the item tag to the RFID reader.

3.   Has the tag been scanned already?

   I.   No? Turn on the light.

   II.   Yes? Turn off the light.

4.   Light on/off responds to the tag being scanned in or out of the system.

The list of four steps for the system should be broken down into bite-sized chunks that we can program. I know that we want an initial confirmation sequence for Message Bag, so the wearer knows that it is turned on and working. We only need this to happen once, so where should this code go – in the `setup()` section? Correct!

There is a version of the code without the modifications so you can see the differences, here: `https://github.com/cmoz/Ultimate/tree/main/C12/Activity12_7Unmodified`.

In the **strandtest** code example that we've been using, the `rainbowEffect(20);` code calls the function, which has the code for the effects. We want this to light up as the bag is turned on, but we also need it to stop. We can control the number of cycles by amending the code and function. Open the completed code example at `https://github.com/cmoz/Ultimate/tree/main/C12/Activity12_7` and you can see the code in `setup()`. We amended how we call the `rainbowEffect()` function. Now, we **pass 2 arguments** – the **delay** for each light and the **number** of cycles. Using `rainbowEffect(1, 3);`, we have a 1-second delay for each light effect and 3 cycles. We need to amend the function now too to take this second argument:

```
    rainbowEffect(1, 3);
    strip.fill((0,0,0), 0, 10);
    strip.show();
}
```

At the bottom of the code, after `loop()` is finished, are the function definitions. We see that `void rainbowEffect(uint8_t wait)` was defined in the example code with only the delay time. I've added another integer variable, `int cycles`, which will take our new argument to let it loop three times. So, in the sample code, the declaration is now `void rainbowEffect(uint8_t wait, int cycles)`. We then need to swap the value of 5, which was in the initial code, for the `cycles` variable, which holds the value of how many cycles we want. That is in this line:

```
    for (y = 0; y < 256 * 5; y++)
```

We changed it to the following:

```
    for (y = 0; y < 256 * cycles; y++)
```

The `strip.fill()` function fills the NeoPixel strip with one color. First, defined with `(0,0,0)` are the RGB color values. Second, we define which NeoPixel we want to start from – 0 is the first one. The third is the pixel number to finish with. I choose pixel 10 because we want the entire strip to have no color. We have a functioning RFID reader and working NeoPixels, so now we need to combine them and make our RFID reader useful!

Activity 12.8 – Adding the NeoPixels and RFID code to scan tags

Using the code provided, let's look at what it's doing and then we can upload and test it: https://github.com/cmoz/Ultimate/tree/main/C12/Activity12_8. The libraries we need to include to run the code are the **SPI, MFRC522**, and **Adafruit_NeoPixel** libraries, so these are declared at the start, followed by the pin numbers for the RFID reader, which are **SS_PIN 4** and **RST_PIN 3**. We then initialize the RFID reader by creating an instance of it – this is where we allocate the pins:

```
 MFRC522 rfid(SS_PIN, RST_PIN);
```

After declaring the pin that our NeoPixels are using, **int neoPin = 1**, we initialize the NeoPixel strip as we have done in previous code. The next part of the code is how we will identify our tags. This is the only part of the code you will need to edit:

```
 byte readCard[4];
 String redTagUID = "7A6CA21A";
 String purpleTagUID = "8C4CFF4";
 String yellowTagUID = "B6E0972B";
```

```
String greenTagUID = "DBC24335";
String blueTagUID = "399DA1A3";
```

We can see it is a variable declaration. To create this variable, see the following:

1. We **declare the type**, which is a **String** data type.

2. We **allocate a name** for it, which is different for each tag. So, we've used names that describe the information that we can easily recognize. In this code we have used `redTagUID` and so on.

3. We then assigned a value for `redTagUID`, which is in " " marks because it is a **String** data type. A **String** data type is reserved for data values that are ordered sequences of characters. We've used strings a lot when we have written to the Serial Monitor.

Remember the values you copied earlier in *Activity 12.5 – The code to test the RFID reader*, when we ran the RFID code from the MFRC522 library, **DumpInfo**? Swap out the values I've written for the values of your tags. Then, save the file.

We have also allocated an empty **String** variable to hold the **value of the scanned tag**. The variable is called `tagID`:

```
String tagID = "";
bool redTag = false;
bool purpleTag = false;
bool yellowTag = false;
bool greenTag = false;
bool blueTag = false;
```

Following that are declarations of `bool` variables. A `bool` variable holds a value of `true` or `false`. We need this variable to hold information about whether a tag has been scanned, `true`, or scanned out, `false`. We set the value to start with as `false` for all our tags and the lights are all off. This way, when we scan our tag, it will register `true`, and the light will turn on.

Looking through the code in setup()

Now, let's jump to `setup()`. It follows the conventions we've been observing for most of the code examples so far. We open the Serial Monitor through `Serial.begin(9600);` – we do the same for the SPI protocol with `SPI.begin();` and we also set a timeout. The timeout allows the reader to wait for up to 20 seconds to read the tag. We then initialize the RFID reader, `rfid.PCD_Init()`. Following that is the code we worked out earlier for lighting the NeoPixels. Showing the details of the RFID reader when we start the program is handled by the following line of code:

```
rfid.PCD_DumpVersionToSerial();
```

This finishes the `setup()` code.

Looking through the code in loop()

Now, let's look through `loop()`. `loop()` is where the RFID reader is waiting for a tag to be presented. This is done by the `while (getID())` function:

```
while (getID())
{
  Serial.println(tagID);
  if (tagID == redTagUID)
  {
    tagActions('1');
  }
  else if (tagID == purpleTagUID)
  {
    tagActions('2');
  }
```

It starts by printing the ID that it has scanned from the tag to the Serial Monitor. This is how we see the *TAG UID* numbers. We then use this number to perform comparisons. Five checks happen. The checks confirm whether the `tagID` String matches one of the stored ID numbers (in `String redTagUID = "7A6CA21A"`, which was declared at the start of the code) that is associated with the different tags. If the tag ID matches, it calls the `tagActions()` function and sends a *char*, which is a single character. It uses this single character to understand which part of the code to execute next. That is the only purpose of the code in `loop()`. Let's look through the functions that we call in the code.

Looking through the three functions for this code

The first function we will look at is `boolean getID()`. This is the first function that was called in `void loop()`. It is checking whether there is a tag present. If a tag is placed at a distance to read, it will continue. It will pull the card's UID number:

```
if ( ! rfid.PICC_IsNewCardPresent()) {
  return false;
}
if ( ! rfid.PICC_ReadCardSerial()) {
  return false;
}
```

Then, we see that because there is a 4-byte UID, the code is executed four times in a `for loop()` to get all the numbers from the card:

```
for ( uint8_t i = 0; i < 4; i++) {
```

```
        tagID.concat(String(rfid.uid.uidByte[i], HEX));
    }
    tagID.toUpperCase();
    rfid.PICC_HaltA(); // Stop reading
    return true;
}
```

The 4 collected bytes are then concatenated (joined together) into a single string variable, tagID. This is done using the tagID.concat(String(rfid.uid.uidByte[i], HEX)) code line. These bytes are then all changed into uppercase (if they aren't uppercase already) using the tagID. toUpperCase() code, which takes the value stored in the tagID variable and appends it with the .toUpperCase() function, which will turn a String variable into all uppercase digits.

Now, let's look at the tagActions(char tag) function. This was called in void loop() when a tag has been read and identified. This is a **switch case** control structure. The char variable that was sent when the function was called now plays an important role. It is used in the **switch** to identify which **case** it should execute. For the example of a red tag being identified, tagActions('1') called the function with a value of 1 being sent. The switch looks for 1, and to start with, the code will print to the Serial Monitor red tag, text so we know a red tag was scanned. This is for troubleshooting the code. I wanted to check that the correct tag was working:

```
void tagActions(char tag) {
  switch (tag) {
    case ('1'):
      Serial.println("red tag");
      redTag ^= true;
      if (redTag == true) {
        strip.setPixelColor(0, 255, 0, 10);
        strip.show();
        Serial.println("scan in R");
        delay(100);
      } else {
        Serial.println("scan out R");
        strip.setPixelColor(0, 0, 0, 0);
        strip.show();
      }
      break;
```

We flip the variable from true to false in redTag ^= true so we know that we have scanned it, and next time, it will do the opposite when we scan the item out. This line of code can also be written:

```
redTag = !redTag;
```

It can also be written this way

```
redTag = redTag ? false : true;
```

This means *not* redTag, as in the opposite. The second example is also that if the value is false, return true, and if it's true, return false. It is a matter of preference. For me, I find it more readable to write true in the expression. Our if (redTag == true) statement is checking that redTag is true and if it is, executing the code that follows between the { } curly braces.

The point of a **switch case** control structure is that there are many **cases** to evaluate. Therefore, the code continues with the next case, 2, and so on:

```
case ('2'):
      Serial.println("purple tag");
      purpleTag ^= true;
      if (purpleTag == true) {
         strip.setPixelColor(1, 245, 0, 255);
```

If you look closely at the code, each **case** is completed with a break; statement. This allows the program to jump out of the **switch case** as soon as it is reached. It's an exit point and the remaining code won't get executed.

The last two functions we have are the functions for the NeoPixels, so I won't go through those again.

There are many ways to write code that will have the same outcome. My example here is just one of many solutions. You could set yourself the task of writing some parts of the code to see how it might be written another way.

Troubleshooting

Some errors can happen.

I had an issue where **the tag was not recognized**, even though I had the correct tag ID written in the code. If this happens to you, run the *Activity12_8* code and when you scan a tag, look at what the output is in the Serial Monitor. When I scanned it with the **DumpInfo** sketch, it registered **8C 4C FF 04** as the tag UID. However, when I ran the code from *Activity12_8* and looked at the output, it was registering as, 8C4CFF4. Notice the missing **0** from the UID. Copy the UID that is in the serial monitor output from *Activity12_8*, because it's the tagID variable our program is using. Paste it in place of the one that isn't registering as a tag. That should fix any errors with tags not being recognized.

There was also an issue at times that Arduino seemed to have **lost connection** with the board or that it just wasn't registering in the program. If this happens, you may need to unplug your board from the computer and plug it in again. Arduino should find your board and port for you and list it without you having to find it.

If the **code doesn't compile**, always check your pin numbers and that you've changed them to match what you are using on the board.

Also, if you are having issues uploading, general problems, or you're sure the code is correct, but it doesn't refresh your code, close the program and then open it again. This helped to resolve some issues. If I wasn't too sure why the program wasn't uploading the code, as a failsafe, I also have the older version of Arduino on my computer, version 1.8.16. It can be useful to check your code in another version. Be sure to close the other version of Arduino first, as there is usually a port conflict.

Testing your prototype

With the code explanations done and errors resolved, it's important to test your prototype for how it works. This includes asking others to try it. We've been testing it as we added components, and tried code, and if we look at the model presented in *Chapter 8, Learning How to Prototype and Make Electronics Wearable*, it will probably sit between an implementation and role prototype. We have worked on the implementation and when we test the function, that will help us see how the role of the prototype might be iterated. We could plot our prototype back on the model from Houde and Hill. *Figure 12.21* shows how it might be situated:

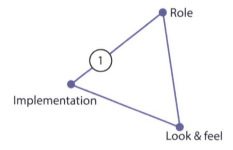

Figure 12.21 – Where our prototype sits on the Houde and Hill model

To better understand how the prototype works, test it with someone who hasn't seen or used it. Explain your concept and watch them use it. Do they understand it?

Some observations

I used a similar version of Message Bag – it wasn't exactly the same as the one we've created here because we've updated the bag to reflect current technologies. However, I did get a lot of feedback about the system, including the following:

- Many people were excited by the colored lights on the bag. They said that this made them feel like they had a special or unique bag. They liked the feature so much that they reversed my initial intention of use – that the lights would all be off when all items were packed. This had to be reversed so that when items are packed, the lights were on instead.

- People noted that scanning the items formed part of the way they remembered their items. Having to scan in an item triggered the fact that there must be items to remember. This scanning action became an important part of their daily activity.

- They liked being able to look across the room, see the lights, and know immediately what was packed and what needed to be packed. People commented that it was *nice to have feedback on the outside* of the bag.

- They thought it would be complicated to use when they heard the word *technology* but were surprised at how easy it was to use. This was important because the research on forgetfulness showed that people found it difficult to learn new ways of doing things if they did feel forgetful.

- Some were curious as to whether this system could be made and attached to any bag.

- Some wanted a way to monitor the battery levels and when to charge the bag.

- A few people were unsure of what the light signified – which light was for which item?

- Some wanted the technology on show while others preferred it to be hidden.

- Some people commented about the weather and whether this might have an effect on the prototype, including for use in the rain or extreme cold or heat.

- Overall, people enjoyed using the bag and felt confident that they wouldn't forget their essential items.

- People mentioned that they knew of someone who could use the device.

- My observations of people using the bag were that they found it easy and fun to use. This was due to the smiles, emotional responses, and excited nature of people who tried it.

When testing your wearables, find out whether there are things the people using it would alter for ease of use. Did they have any feedback for you? Make notes of what you've observed and what they have told you. Ask them specific questions about their usage and ask them to give examples of when they experienced the thing they are discussing. For example, if they say *"it didn't work,"* ask them to talk you through what actually happened when it didn't work. What were they trying to do – when did this happen? You want to find out using real examples and not get their opinions on things that haven't happened. This data is far more valuable to you for being able to fix any issues. I've also used Google Maps to map out a journey taken and to make notes about the usage of the wearable. A typical mapping could be similar to *Figure 12.22*:

Figure 12.22 – Mapping a journey as part of testing

We can use the information we learn from people testing our wearables to improve upon our design and make a wearable even better suited to the person using it. With that said, what's the future of Message Bag?

The future of Message Bag

Hopefully, after getting some feedback and using this prototype yourself, a few points might have been raised. You may want to make a list of the features or improvements you could try. This could include some of the ways the wearable works, what it could be better at, or how it communicates with the wearer. One example is in the instances when there is a delay in the tag scanning – I'm left confused if the tag is actually being recognized or scanned. Having some feedback to communicate when an item is being scanned would be a good improvement.

Additionally, you'll have noticed that when the system is turned off and on again, if we were packing items, this information is lost. We should look at implementing code to use the memory on the circuit board to store the values of the tag being scanned in or out. It won't be as useful if the bag can't remember what tags are in the bag!

Lastly, we need to sew and solder the completed circuit so it becomes an **integration prototype** that we can use for testing. We've also done some work with `https://io.adafruit.com/`, so it's worth a look at how this service could benefit our Message Bag.

Summary

This chapter focused on creating a prototype for Message Bag, an informed wearable that follows a Design Innovation process. It aimed to help guide you in the process and create a near-body system. We started by revisiting our sewing skills and sewed the NeoPixels onto a bag with conductive thread. We used a new circuit board, the QT Py SAMD21, and it was chosen based on its capabilities, versatility, size, and price. We soldered the board to a charge board and then breadboarded it. We worked iteratively on the circuit (by adding one function and component at a time) to test it. We learned about the RFID reader and its capabilities. After completing this wearable implementation prototype, when we test and evaluate it, we see there are improvements and iterations that could be made. This is part of the process that should happen with all wearables you make.

As we look ahead to the next chapter, it is these iterations that we will focus on, and we will have another chance to put our sewing and soldering skills into practice. How will we create a Message Bag for the future?

References

References found in this chapter include a portion of the work from my PhD thesis, as previously referenced, and the following:

Imhof, L., Wallhagen, M. I., Mahrer-Imhof, R., & Monsch, A. U. (2006). *Becoming forgetful: How elderly people deal with forgetfulness in everyday life.* In *American Journal of Alzheimer's Disease & Other Dementias®, 21(5), 347-353.Ponds et al., 1997).*

Schmidt, A., Gellersen, H. W., & Merz, C. (2000, October). *Enabling implicit human computer interaction: a wearable RFID-tag reader.* In *Digest of Papers. Fourth International Symposium on Wearable Computers (pp. 193-194). IEEE.Fishkin et al., 2005.*

Houde, S., & Hill, C. (1997). *What do prototypes prototype?.* In *Handbook of human-computer interaction (pp. 367-381). North-Holland.*

Farion, Christine (2018). *Investigating the design of Smart Objects in the domain of forgetfulness. PhD thesis, Queen Mary University of London.* https://qmro.qmul.ac.uk/xmlui/bitstream/handle/123456789/39747/FARION_Christine_PhD_final_010618.pdf.

Buchenau, M., & Suri, J. F. (2000, August). *Experience prototyping.* In Proceedings of the *3rd conference on Designing interactive systems: processes, practices, methods, and techniques (pp. 424-433).*

Blythe, M., Wright, P., McCarthy, J., & Bertelsen, O. W. (2006, April). *Theory and method for experience centered design.* In *CHI'06 Extended Abstracts on Human Factors in Computing Systems (pp. 1691-1694).*

Review questions

1. Why couldn't we sew over the top of our ground thread with the data thread?

2. What does the tack solder do?

3. After soldering, what good practice should we always do with our soldering iron?

4. Why shouldn't we use **pin 2** if we are using the charge board with the QTPy SAMD 21?

5. What does the `strip.fill()` function do and how do we configure it?

6. How would `case ('2'):` get called in our code?

13

Implementing the Best Solutions for Creating Your Own Wearable

The skills that you've been practicing throughout the book feel like pieces of knowledge you've earned and this chapter is a little like the final piece in the puzzle. You've worked through a journey of activities (over 50) to get to this point and as you work through the iterations of Message Bag, it will provide you with a complete skill set to create your own wearables. Although you are continuing your wearable journey using Message Bag, you should start to think about parallels in how you will implement these techniques into your own future wearable designs.

In this chapter, you will look at making decisions for iterations in an early prototype version of a wearable, and we will upcycle and complete the Message Bag prototype we started in the previous chapter. We'll also take a sneak peek at even more potential upgrades, which we don't necessarily have to implement, but it's important to learn to push and iterate your designs. I feel like I'm always pushing to learn more in this exciting field and you will see how the wearables we create can be improved, revised, and upgraded over time.

By the end of this chapter, you will have come full circle on your journey and created a wearable near-body system with iterations, soldered and sewn it into place, and started planning for your own wearable design.

In this chapter, we're going to cover the following topics:

- A template for design
- Upcycling your own Message Bag
- Upgrades for the ambitious using IoT
- Use it or do something else

Technical requirements

In this chapter, we will create an iterated prototype of Message Bag – therefore, we need the prototype created from the previous chapter. We will also look at activities that use the following:

- Arduino software as the IDE and access to `https://io.adafruit.com/`
- The Adafruit QT Py ESP32-S2 or the Adafruit QT Py ESP32-C3

You will need your prototype from the previous chapter, which was made with the following:

- Adafruit QT Py - SAMD21 Dev Board with STEMMA QT
- An RFID reader: Mifare RC522 with five corresponding tags
- Sewable Flora NeoPixels and a Flora Sewable 3-Pin JST Wiring Adapter
- Adafruit LiPoly Charger BFF Add-On for QT Py and a rechargeable battery, with 3.7V and a 2-pin JST-PH connector

A template for design

Working through this chapter, we will create iterations to improve on our Message Bag design from the previous chapter. To be able to do this, we'll look at what observations we made and how those affect the use of the system. This is an essential step in the process of *creating a wearable*. Before we do that, let's create our template for design based on some of what we have learned throughout the book. You will be able to use this template to help form the ideas for the wearable you want to create and the purpose behind it.

Activity 13.1 – Creating the road map for your wearable Project

Making wearables is fun! There are often many approaches to creating a wearable and through the activities in the book, we've taken a very hands-on, learning-through-doing style, and learned about a Design Innovation way of making a wearable. We can create a road map for the wearable we want to make for our different goals. If you're looking to continue your learning and exploring, then you might want to do your project planning based on the components you have.

A component-based project plan

Your planning may look similar to the following:

- What components or microcontroller do I want to use in my wearable?

  I have a Gemma M0, an OLED screen, NeoPixels, and a motor. I'll decide on a sensor to buy to have input for the system.

- What part of the body do I want to prototype for?

  The ankle and foot area (choose a new body part to learn different skill sets to be able to make a wearable comfortable to fit that body part, jewelry style, or off-body shape.)

- What features make this wearable a useful item and who is it useful for?

  I'll research topics related to mobility and health. There could be an application in relation to gait and walking.

You can refer to *Chapter 1, Introduction to the World of Wearables*, for an illustration (see *Figure 1.17*) of possible body placement locations. Additionally, *Chapter 8, Learning How to Prototype and Make Electronics Wearable*, has the information you should refer to for planning out your wearable. In particular, we talked about **comfort**, **usability**, and **style universe**. These questions can help you form a starting position for your wearable. Planning is an exciting process. Put these ideas in a notebook – or a page on Notion, for example, (`https://www.notion.so/`) – so you can add links to resources that you find or even sample code to help you get started.

A topic-based project plan

Your planning may look similar to the following:

- What topics interest me?

  I'm interested in exploring nature as a theme. Maybe more about awareness of our environment. This might have sensors or communicate about environmental issues.

- What goals would I like the wearable to have?

  I'd like the wearable to let people experience nature in alternative ways – to highlight what they might not have noticed before, or the unseen. This might be information about our air quality, for example. How can I make it visible?

- How could this be implemented and what components would I need?

  This could use light as the output and maybe an air quality sensor for the input to get data from the air around us. I'd need a circuit board with I2C connection and at least 1 pin for NeoPixels.

For either of these two starting project positions, you'll need to read about the **domain** – what the context for your wearable is. With research and information about that area, you'll be able to create a more effective and interesting item. Additionally, find people to speak with about this topic to discover how they are affected, and what their stories or usage are. Often, learning useful information can be carried out by making observations. After collecting this information, think about what this data and information tells us. What are the **insights** from speaking with people?

Looking into what solutions have been tried or made previously, what worked what was successful, or what is missing in this area is an important step for consideration. Now that we've had a brief look at setting our road maps, let's return to our previous case study of Message Bag.

Upcycling your own Message Bag

When we ended the previous chapter, you may have collected some information for improvements to the use of Message Bag. What it currently does is follow a process with four stages, including an initial sequence of lights to communicate that it is on, a scan-in or scan-out of a tag, checking the state of the tag and whether it is scanned or not, and then a response based on the state of the tag.

When using this prototype, although it functions well, there are a few issues you may have noticed. These iterations are related to the function or role of the prototype, not the aesthetics or look and feel. We can implement these iterations while it is still breadboarded.

For example, in the instances when there is a slight delay in the tag scanning process, I'm left confused. Is the tag recognized? Is it still scanning? Secondly, when the system is powered off and back on again, the tags I scanned are not recorded.

Did you also make these observations? Feedback to communicate when an item is being scanned would be a good improvement, as would using non-volatile memory to store the state of the tags. Non-volatile memory is retained even if the system is powered down.

A new plan for the functionality of Message Bag could be described in the following steps:

1. Turn on the system.
2. There should be an initial sequence of lights to inform the wearer it is working. This is positive feedback from the system to communicate to the person that the system is functioning.
3. The lights will illuminate according to the last use scenario. The circuit reads the stored tags from the last time it was used.
4. Depending on the tag information stored in memory, it will light the corresponding lights.
5. Scan in or scan out. Hold the item tag to the RFID reader.
6. Lights confirm that it is scanning.
7. The tag state is encoded to memory to scan in or out. If the item is not yet scanned, this means the item is being put in a bag. So, it will scan it in. If the item has been scanned, it means they are removing the item.
8. The on/off light responds to the tag being scanned in or out of the system.

Now that we have a plan of what we would like to implement to make this a more effective prototype, let's implement the first change.

Activity 13.2 – Iterations on Message Bag for communication

This activity involves implementing a light sequence that will happen when the tag is scanned, to allow for **positive feedback** from the system. This way, the wearer knows that their tag is being scanned. I've posted the code for this exercise here: `https://github.com/cmoz/Ultimate/tree/main/C13/Activity13_2Iterations`.

Open and look at the code. In `loop()`, as it waits for tags to be scanned, the `while (getID())` function runs. We'll add the following:

```
rainbowEffect(1, 1);
```

This will run the `rainbowEffect()` function once. This will improve our circuit because the rainbow sequence displays when a tag is scanned in or out. Look a little further into the code. In the function definition that sets the color for our scanned NeoPixels, `void setNeoColor()`, at the end of this function, we call `checkAllOn()`. Let's look through this function's declaration.

The purpose of this is so that if **all the tags** were scanned in, this indicates to the wearer that all the corresponding items have been packed. We want to reward this with a positive light sequence. The rainbow sequence plays several times after the last tag is scanned and this happens because of the `rainbowEffect(3,5)` code.

Continue to look at `void checkAllOn()` – we use `&&` as a **Boolean operator** to evaluate conditions. This **logical AND** decides that only if *this* condition is true (`&&`) and *this* condition is true, then we play the rainbow effect.

The Boolean operator, `&&`, returns `true` if all the conditions are true. In this code, that is possible with this line of code – `if ((redTag == true) && (purpleTag == true) && ( yellowTag == true):`

```
void checkAllOn() {
  if ((redTag == true) && (purpleTag == true) && (
        yellowTag == true) && (greenTag == true) && (blueTag ==
true)) {
    rainbowEffect(3, 5);
  }
  if ((redTag == false) && (purpleTag == false) && (
        yellowTag == false) && (greenTag == false) && (blueTag
== false)) {
    theaterChase(strip.Color(  0,   110, 127), 100);
  }
}
```

We've also added another `if` statement, so that if all the tags have not been scanned in, there is a pale blue light sequence to communicate to the person that there are no scanned tags, or all tags are out of the bag. This plays a sequence that is called `theaterChase()` and we added a `strip.fill((0, 110, 255), 0)` line of code at the end of the function because we want the lights to stay on, as pale blue, so the wearer knows that the bag is working and it's waiting for a tag to be scanned.

Our aim as makers of wearables is to help the wearer as much as possible. We want them to achieve their goals in as easy a way as possible. These changes should help us with that! Now that we've amended the code for the light responses, we should look at storing the tag state in memory so that they keep the same state as when they last scanned it. This is the next activity.

Activity 13.3 – Storing variables in non-volatile memory

The QT Py SAMD21 board has 256 KB of flash for storage. If your sketches need more, there is an additional chip you can buy to solder more memory – it's similar to adding a 2MB SSD drive. After soldering this memory, it is accessible through SPI flash using Arduino on SPI1 and a chip select pin (CS) 17 – there is sample code as part of the Adafruit SPIFlash library. However, 256 KB flash is enough for us.

Storing data on the microcontrollers that we've been using is done through a version of **EEPROM** memory. EEPROM is electrically erasable, programmable, read-only memory. Flash is an offshoot of EEPROM and the differences are in the way they access and erase the memory – byte-wise for EEPROM or block-wise for Flash. We can erase the bytes and reprogram them. It's used for small amounts of data. We don't need to go into too much detail here about memory, but we do need to use a library to help us to write to it. Because the board we are using isn't compatible with the Arduino ATMEL-based library to store using EEPROM, we can use a different library to store data into flash memory on the ATSAMD21 and ATSAMD51 processor families that our QT Py SAMD21 uses. There is a `FlashAsEEPROM.h` library that can be used if you are familiar with the EEPROM library and have used it for Arduino boards. This is also an EEPROM emulation library for these processors.

We will be using the **FlashStorage** library. It provides us with the implementation to store and retrieve data, and in this case, it's the tag state we want to record. We will write to the non-volatile flash memory on the QT Py SAMD21. Using the Library Manager in Arduino, search for `FlashStorage` by Arduino. It might already be installed, but if it isn't – install it.

> **Using Flash Memory**
>
> One note about flash memory is that it has a **limited** number of cycles on the same flash block for writing, which is around 10,000 write calls. After that, it may start to degrade.

Let's look through how to implement the code after we have added the FlashStorage library. The code is here: `https://github.com/cmoz/Ultimate/tree/main/C13/Activity13_3FlashStorage`.

First, as you'll have seen in several examples already, we **include** the library in a declaration at the start of our code – this is done with `#include <FlashStorage.h>`. Then, we declare a **global object**, called **FlashStorage**, for each data item we want to store in memory. Because we've used versions of variables for the color tags already, I opted for naming the variable `my_flash_store` with an appending initial – R for red, P for purple, and so on – for the color of the tag and NeoPixel.

A **global object** or **global variable** is declared before `setup()`, which allows it to be used throughout our program. The `FlashStorage(my_flash_storeR, bool);` code snippet is telling the program to create `FlashStorage` with a `bool` variable called `my_flash_storeR`. We create one of these storage areas for each of our RFID tags:

```
FlashStorage(my_flash_storeR, bool);
FlashStorage(my_flash_storeP, bool);
FlashStorage(my_flash_storeY, bool);
FlashStorage(my_flash_storeG, bool);
FlashStorage(my_flash_storeB, bool);
```

Once the program loads and runs `void setup()`, we want the program to retrieve the values stored in the memory. We can read and retrieve the tag state using the `redTag = my_flash_storeR.read()` code. This allocates the values held in that memory space to each bool variable – for example, `bool redTag` is created. I've then added `Serial.println(redTag)` for each tag so I can see the values in the serial monitor to troubleshoot if these aren't correct. The `setNeoColor()` function will then run and depending on the bool values from the flash storage, the corresponding light for that tag will be on or off:

```
redTag = my_flash_storeR.read();
purpleTag = my_flash_storeP.read();
yellowTag = my_flash_storeY.read();
greenTag = my_flash_storeG.read();
blueTag = my_flash_storeB.read();
```

This all happens as we start our program. The setup is complete and the system is ready for use. We need to write the tag state as we scan the tags. The `tagActions()` function is called when the tag has been scanned and the UID of the tag is known. After, we flip the bool for the tag to `true` or `false` depending on whether it has been scanned already. That's when we write the value or state of the tag to memory using `my_flash_storeR.write(redTag)`:

```
void tagActions(char tag) {
  switch (tag) {
    case ('0'):
      Serial.println("red tag");
      redTag ^= true;
      my_flash_storeR.write(redTag);
      Serial.println(redTag);
      break;
    case ('1'):
```

```
Serial.println("yellow tag");
yellowTag ^= true;
my_flash_storeY.write(yellowTag);
Serial.println(yellowTag);
break;
```

The code snippet is a portion of our `switch case` control structure and we have included the code to write the tag value for all five of our tags. Now that we have had a look through the code, **upload** it to your QT Py SAMD and try it for yourself.

You'll see that when you turn off the power for your board, when you turn it back on again, the lights will light up the same way you left them. This is now a useful circuit for the wearer. With the code explained and uploaded, we should fully integrate it into our bag. Before integrating it (and committing it to solder and sewing), do a final check that your connections work (see *Figure 13.1*):

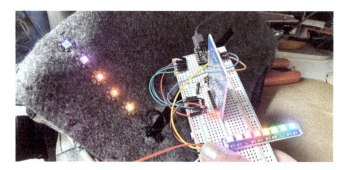

Figure 13.1 – The final test of our connections

All the lights should be working and although we can edit the code after we've soldered it, it's better to check that we are correct now to avoid a mistake.

Activity 13.4 – Integrating your circuit

Earlier, we created a prototype on a breadboard, essentially making an **implementation** with some aspects of a **role** prototype. This activity will transform that prototype into an **integration** prototype because it will involve the **role**, **implementation**, and **look-and-feel** aspects. Let's start by soldering the circuit to make it more permanent.

Soldering the components for placement

Now that we know our code and components are tested and working, we will make it permanent, durable, and wearable! We're going to start by soldering the wires to our RFID reader. We're starting here because it will be the easiest step:

Figure 13.2 – Planning the RFID reader placement

To start with, hold your RFID board in place – mine is going inside the bag (see *Figure 13.2*) – and measure wire lengths to reach your circuit board. I'm taking advantage of the pocket inside the bag and I'll cut through it carefully so I can put the RFID reader behind the fabric. Do you have a feature such as a seam or pocket that you can use to modify the bag?

After you've planned where the RFID board will go, we need one wire for each of the following connections:

- Ground and power

- The SPI interface: SDA, SCK, MOSI, and MISO (and reset)

That makes seven connections. Add a little more wire to your measurements just in case. Cut seven wires. Sometimes, with folds of fabric, it can make our measurements slightly off when we come to sew or solder the connection:

1. I'll start by soldering the RFID board wires. I always solder with the easiest-to-identify connections, so in this case, I'm soldering the ground and then the power wires. Strip the end of one side of your wires and make sure the wire won't fray by giving them a little twist. Push them through the circuit board, one wire into the **GND** and one wire into the **3.3V** hole. Solder in place (see *Figure 13.3*):

Figure 13.3 – Soldering the ground and power connections on the RFID reader

2. Continue soldering the other wires (for the SPI connections) to your RFID board. If you look at *Figure 13.4*, at the top of the photo is a small USB-powered fan. This is helpful for soldering, as it pulls the fumes away from you. This can be a really good idea if you're soldering at your desk!

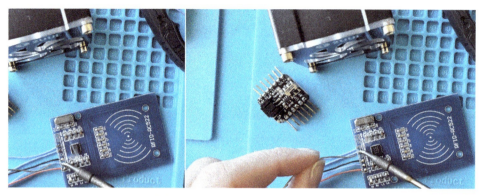

Figure 13.4 – Soldering the other wires (SPI) to the RFID board

3. After all the wires are soldered to the RFID board, strip the ends off them in preparation for soldering our connections to the QT Py SAMD board.

4. Straighten the pin legs as we've done previously (see *Figure 13.5*). Once straightened out, we will solder the wires to them. To do that, we need to prepare the wires and board:

Figure 13.5 – Straightening the pin legs

5. To start, let's **tin** the wire ends that we stripped. To **tin** them means that we are going to add a little solder to the wires to coat them (see *Figure 13.6*). This will make it easier to solder to the pin legs on the QT Py SAMD. Also, add solder (**tin**) to the legs on your circuit board. Only apply a thin amount. By applying a thin layer of solder to both surfaces we want to join, it helps the solder to flow more easily between them, creating a good connection:

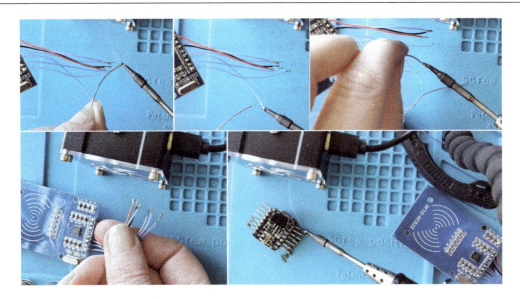

Figure 13.6 – Tinning the wires and circuit board pin legs

6. Don't solder power and ground just yet, as these pins need more than one wire! We have power and ground going to the RFID reader and to the NeoPixels, so we'll do them a little later.

    With the wires and circuit board tinned and ready for soldering, solder one wire at a time and double-check the connection is correct. After you solder, do the **pull test** to check whether it is a solid connection. I've also added heat shrink on the wire that I'll slide over the top of the leg once it is soldered. See *Figure 13.7*, which details this process:

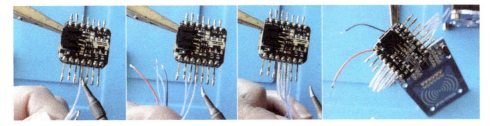

Figure 13.7 – Soldering to the circuit board and using shrink wrap on the connections

7. Because ground and power will have two connections, it can be easier to solder a wire to the board first, then connect the other two wires to that connection. Let's start by soldering a wire to the circuit board, one for ground and one for power.

    Start by **stripping** the two wires, then **tin** them. Solder each (power and then ground) to the circuit board legs (3.3 V and ground) and put shrink wrap over the connections. Then, we need to solder the wires for the NeoPixels that we've sewn on the bag.

8.   Make a hole in your bag – if it has a pocket, that works well for hiding the circuit (see *Figure 13.8*). Using seam rippers, gently push them between where there is a seam edge. Break a few of the threads with seam rippers to create a hole large enough to push your RFID reader into:

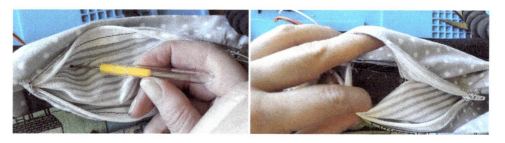

Figure 13.8 – Using seam rippers to create an opening for the RFID reader

9.   With the components in place, slide the heat shrink over the ground and power wire. Then, take the three power wires (one from the circuit board, one from the NeoPixels, and one from the RFID reader) and twist them together. Solder these together. *Figure 13.9* shows the crocodile clip part of my helping-hand solder station holding the three wires together for me so I can solder them. It is a lot easier if you can clamp the three wires together and then twist them. Make sure the solder gets through all three wires so that you make a solid connection. It will help a lot if you use **flux** for this join. Pull the heat shrink over the soldered joint. Be sure to let it cool first or it will start shrinking:

Figure 13.9 – Clamping the three wires for the power together to
solder them and doing the same for the ground

10. Now, do the same for the ground wires – slide the heat shrink over the ground wire coming from the circuit board and twist all three ground wires together. Solder the three ground wires together. Then, slide the heat shrink up over the solder joint. Heat it to shrink in place.

11. Lastly, solder the NeoPixel data wire to **pin A1**.

You should now have a soldered circuit board, NeoPixels, and the RFID reader. Plug it in and test it before we sew it in place and close the hole we made. If it works, we can start to sew it in place. Put the RFID board into the hole you made earlier and place the QT Py SAMD outside of this.

We need access to our charge board – it has an on/off switch. A future improvement could be that you add a switch outside the bag somewhere and hide all the technology (see *Figure 13.10*):

Figure 13.10 – Placing your soldered circuit in the bag

If it isn't working, see the following:

- Check each connection that you soldered. Wires might have come loose or maybe it doesn't have a solid connection. You can resolder it.

- Make sure you don't have any frayed wires touching the wire next to it – that can cause a short.

- Check your pins and wires are going to the correct circuit parts. For example, the MISO pin on the RFID board connects to the MISO pin on your circuit board.

- You can also check for loose threads on your sewable NeoPixels.

- Have you powered your circuit and does your battery have enough power for it?

Once it's working, thread a needle, and with your board in position, sew the legs to the bag to secure it in place. I've added some neoprene fabric to hide the legs that are showing. I cut a square and then cut a + shape in the center of the neoprene, folding the + part back to push the circuit board through the gap this made. Then, I stitched around the board (see *Figure 13.11*):

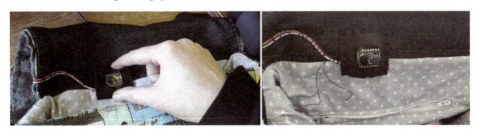

Figure 13.11 – Stitching neoprene (or fabric) around the board to hide the legs and our soldering

12. Finished (see *Figure 13.12*)! You should plug your battery in and make a small pocket for it. Plug it in and try your new wearable! If it's all working, you just need to close the holes we created when we were putting the components in place. So, I'll sew up the pocket and you might have a seam or pocket to sew back together:

Figure 13.12 – A completed Message Bag with NeoPixels, an RFID reader, and the QT Py SAMD21

Well done, you've completed the process from Design Innovation to the creation of a wearable with a purpose! Hopefully, this meets the wearer's goals and needs. Through testing is when you would be able to find out more information about iterating our design. I have a few ideas on ways this could become even more interesting – you might want to look at upgrades using the **Internet of Things** (**IoT**).

Upgrades for the ambitious using IoT

Now that we've implemented the best solutions for creating this wearable and iterated to a prototype that has more features, including giving the wearer better information on the system state, we can look at features we may want to bring to future devices.

Often when I make a project that I really like, there are ways to improve or future-proof it, and this can involve switching to a different circuit board. Some of my earliest projects started on an **Arduino Uno** board, which is a lot larger than the boards we've been using. This meant that the wearable projects I made had a more cumbersome implementation or used more space than I would want for a prototype. When creating a proof-of-concept prototype, a larger board such as the Arduino Uno is perfectly acceptable, and we've seen in *Chapter 8, Learning How to Prototype and Make Electronic Wearable*, that using this board alongside 3D printer pens and TPU is a fun, inexpensive, and quick way to prototype initial ideas. Keep in mind that you can't solder to an Uno and it is a prototyping board, not a final implementation one. When I want to start to refine and iterate a prototype, it often involves choosing a more appropriate microcontroller board for the purpose. This is part of implementing the best solutions.

Modifying the prototype with the QT Py ESP32-S2

There may be instances of using Message Bag when we want a record of all the scanning in and out that we've done. This is where involving IoT integration can help us out. We did some activities with ESP32 development boards in *Chapter 7, Moving Forward With Circuit Design Using ESP32*, where we learned about its Wi-Fi capabilities. We also looked at a tiny-sized board, the QT Py ESP32-S2, in *Chapter 9, Designing and Prototyping Your Own Hyper-Body System*, which is the board we will use for the next activity. Before we can add the IoT capabilities, we should upload our current code – with modifications. So, let's grab our QT Py ESP32 and dive in.

Activity 13.5 – Using EEPROM.h for memory access

Time to experiment with extending implementations with a board that has more capabilities than the one we were using. Open Arduino, plug in the QT Py ESP32-S2, and select your board and port. When we compile our code using the **verify** button, you'll see that there is an error message:

```
WARNING: library FlashStorage claims to run on samd
architecture(s) and may be incompatible with your current board
which runs on esp32 architecture(s).
```

Reading this message tells us that it won't compile for the ESP32, so we need to change our **FlashStorage** library, because that library is made for the SAMD architecture. If we look up this error online, you'll see that the ESP32 can use the EEPROM library, so we can implement code that performs the same functionality after making a few modifications.

> **EEPROM Limits**
> EEPROM memory has a life of around 100,000 to 1,000,000 write and erase cycles before it degrades. This is higher than the flash memory.

The QT Py ESP32-S2 has 4 MB of flash that we can use, which is also a lot more than we saw in the QT Py SAMD board. Having said that, the board was still suitable for the purpose at the time.

Wiring up and pin name changes

Before adding the library code, we need to alter a few pin numbers so that our RFID reader works with this board. When we look at our pinout diagram, my **SDA** on the RFID reader goes to the **SDA** on the QT Py ESP32-S2, this is the **SS pin** in the code, and we will define it as follows:

```
#define SS_PIN 7
#define RST_PIN 17
```

Also, the **reset** pin, on **A1** on my board, is defined as **GPIO 17** for Arduino, so change that pin number. The **A3** pin on the QT Py ESP32-S2 is defined as Arduino **GPIO 8**, so I've modified that too for the NeoPixels:

```
Int neoPin = 8;
```

You can use a different pin but be sure to change it in the code too. All the other pins are the same.

Using the EEPROM library

With the EEPROM library, we can use 512 bytes of flash memory, which means 512 different addresses. We can save a value between 0 and 255 in each of those addresses.

We need to change the library we are currently using to the EEPROM library, which is a preinstalled library in Arduino, so we don't need to install it. If you open the code that we've been using, we want to change the library. We can do this by changing the current `#include <FlashStorage.h>` library that we have been using to the following:

```
#include <EEPROM.h>
```

We need to allocate an **address** for each piece of information we want to store. Because we have five tags that we want to keep track of, we will allocate five places in memory. For the EEPROM library, we use `define` to allocate the number of memory places we need:

```
#define EEPROM_SIZE 5
```

Lastly, we need to establish that we are using the EEPROM, so we add the `begin()` initializer with the size of memory we want to allocate:

```
EEPROM.begin(EEPROM_SIZE);
```

I put it at the beginning of my `setup()` function because we will be accessing EEPROM in `setup()`, so we need to initialize it. My code looks as follows:

```
void setup() {
  Serial.begin(9600);
  EEPROM.begin(EEPROM_SIZE);
  SPI.begin();
  Serial.setTimeout(20000);
```

We can remove `FlashStorage(my_flash_storeR, bool)` declarations for memory space because they are from our previous library. Delete all five of those.

The functions we'll use to access memory are similar to our previous implementation. We use `read()` and `write()` and the implementation for both is as follows:

```
EEPROM.read(address)
EEPROM.write(address, value)
```

You can always find the implementation information for libraries by reading the documentation that comes with the library. Usually, a library has a link that will take you to a GitHub page where all the information is defined, along with sample code.

Lastly, to save it to memory, the EEPROM library uses a commit call, this is written with the following:

```
EEPROM.commit();
```

The `commit()` code needs to be written after every `write()` function.

Using these functions, we can now look through the code and modify where we have the `read()` and `write()` functions for our previous library.

Challenge!

Take a moment now and search through the code. Alter the `read()` and `write()` functions in the correct places and then come back here to check whether we have the same results.

Currently, the `read` function is written in `setup()` as follows:

```
redTag = my_flash_storeR.read();
purpleTag = my_flash_storeP.read();
yellowTag = my_flash_storeY.read();
greenTag = my_flash_storeG.read();
blueTag = my_flash_storeB.read();
```

This should be altered for the EEPROM library as follows:

```
redTag = EEPROM.read(0);
purpleTag = EEPROM.read(1);
yellowTag = EEPROM.read(2);
greenTag = EEPROM.read(3);
blueTag = EEPROM.read(4);
```

Did you have this change in your code?

If we look at the function definition of `read()`, it tells us that we need to send the address location, `EEPROM.read(address)`, when we call the function. Let's look at where else in our code we need to alter it. Currently, the `write()` function for **FlashMemory** is in the `switch case` part of our code:

```
void tagActions(char tag) {
  switch (tag) {
    case ('0'):
      Serial.println("red tag");
      redTag ^= true;
      my_flash_storeR.write(redTag);
      Serial.println(redTag);
      break;
    case ('1'):
```

If we modify it to use the EEPROM library, our code should look as follows:

```
void tagActions(char tag) {
  switch (tag) {
    case ('0'):
      Serial.println("red tag");
      redTag ^= true;
      EEPROM.write(0, redTag);
      EEPROM.commit();
      break;
    case ('1'):
      Serial.println("yellow tag");
      yellowTag ^= true;
      EEPROM.write(1, yellowTag);
      EEPROM.commit();
      break;
```

When we write to EEPROM, we needed to define the **address** and the **value** that we are sending. Again, that was defined when we looked at the syntax, `EEPROM.write(address, value)`. For more information and other implementations of the EEPROM library, you can visit the official Arduino documentation: `https://docs.arduino.cc/learn/built-in-libraries/eeprom`.

Upload your code and test out your new implementation with our improvements! Now, when you scan a tag, remember what tags were scanned and unplug your device. You'll see that when you plug it back in, the same tags will stay lit. This means these values have been stored in memory. The full code that you've followed along can be downloaded from here: `https://github.com/cmoz/ Ultimate/blob/main/C13/Activity13_5ESP32/Activity13_5ESP32.ino`. This is now a more valuable device for everyone using it and we've modified the code for the QT Py ESP 32-S2 board. With that finished, we can now look at connecting it to an IoT service.

Activity 13.6 – Connecting with Wi-Fi to an IoT service

You may want to revisit some of the work we did in *Chapter 9, Designing and Prototyping Your Own Hyper-Body System*, because we connected to a service at `https://io.adafruit.com/` and we are going to connect to it again:

1. Open the **io** service to access your feeds. We'll need to create a new feed that we can connect to for Message Bag. As a reminder, *Figure 13.13* shows where we create a feed by clicking on **New Feed**:

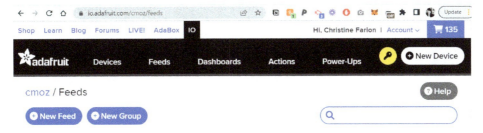

Figure 13.13 – The Feeds window

I'm calling my feed **tags**, as this will store the tag information that we scan. After you've created the feed, it will appear in your **Feeds** list.

2. To use the service, you'll need to connect to both your Wi-Fi and the **io** service online. We do this using a `config.h` file. We can use the contents of that file again for this activity, so if you have saved the code previously, open the example from *Activity 9.3*, which is the code we will use. The `config.h` file contents is here if you need a copy of it: `https://github. com/cmoz/Ultimate/blob/main/C9/9.3HeatNeoIoT/config.h`. **Copy** the contents of the file.

3. In Arduino, there down arrowhead in the top-right-hand corner of the interface (see *Figure 13.14*). Click on that and you'll have some options. We want to create a **New Tab**:

Figure 13.14 – Creating a new tab

There will be a popup asking for you to name this new tab, which is a file. Call it `config.h` and then click **OK** (see *Figure 13.15*). Make sure to save it once you've done that:

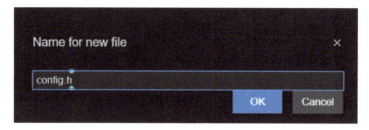

Figure 13.15 – Naming the file

Now, there is a tab called **config.h** and when you click it, you can **paste** in the code from the `config.h` file we looked at earlier. If you copied it from the file that you made previously, your details may already be stored in it – however, if you copied it from the online version, you'll need to enter in your credentials again.

4. In the code, you need to define your **username** and **IO key** details, as well as your **Wi-Fi ID** and **Wi-Fi password** details. Fill in the information for the following:

    ```
    #define IO_USERNAME "change"
    #define IO_KEY "change"

    #define WIFI_SSID "change"
    #define WIFI_PASS "change"
    ```

That's all we'll have to do with this file. Now, we need to modify the main code file that we completed in the previous activity, *Activity 13.5 – Using EEPROM.h for memory access*.

5. Check you are in the correct tab for the main program file (not the `config.h` file). To start, include the file we just created and added in a tab:

    ```
    #include "config.h"
    ```

This should be added with the other `include` files at the top of the code. We then need to set up the feed that we created on the **io** site.

6. We set up the feed by declaring it before `setup()`:

    ```
    AdafruitIO_Feed *scannedTags = io.feed("tags");
    ```

Make sure this matches with what you have called your feed if it is different from mine.

7. In `setup()`, we want to connect to the Adafruit **io** service, so I'm going to add this after I've initialized the Serial Monitor. I'm also adding a message to print to the serial monitor so I know that it is connecting:

```
Serial.print("Connecting to Adafruit IO");
io.connect();
```

I'll wait for everything else to initialize and for the lights to come on so the wearer knows something is happening. Then, we wait for a connection to **io**:

```
while(io.status() < AIO_CONNECTED) {
Serial.print(".");
delay(500);
}
Serial.println();
Serial.println(io.statusText());
```

Once it has made a connection, we want the status of our connection printed to the serial monitor. Printing it to the serial monitor when we are writing code and checking it is a great way to see what is going on in our program. I use it a lot as I'm writing code.

8. Lastly, we add the code to keep the connection open – this goes at the top of the `loop()` function and should look as follows:

```
void loop() {
io.run();
while (getID()) {
```

9. Now that we have all the groundwork done for the connection, we want the tag to be saved and uploaded to the **io** service every time we scan it. So, we will add the code:

```
scannedTags ->save(redTag);
```

This code will go after the memory save has been done and you'll add one of these for each tag. The completed `tagActions()` code will now look as follows:

```
void tagActions(char tag) {
switch (tag) {
case ('0'):
Serial.println("red tag");
redTag ^= true;
EEPROM.write(0, redTag);
EEPROM.commit();
```

```
scannedTags->save(redTag);
break;
```

Now that we have modified the code, we will create a new **Dashboard**. We've created a Dashboard before and it is the same process. Click on the **Dashboard** link in the top navigation area, and then click the **New Dashboard** button. This opens a window where you will type in the name of your Dashboard. I'm calling mine `Message Bag` (see *Figure 13.16*). Once you've typed in the name, click **Create**:

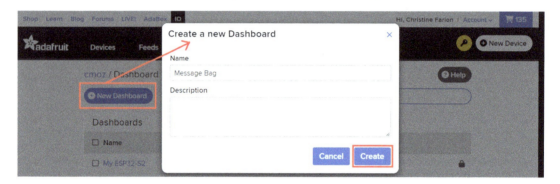

Figure 13.16 – Creating a new Dashboard

After your Message Bag Dashboard is made, we go to **Create New Block** – click on the settings icon on the right-hand side and choose **Create New Block**, which opens the window with all the blocks for the dashboard. We want an indicator so we can see whether the tag is scanned or not scanned. Choose the **Indicator** block (see *Figure 13.17*):

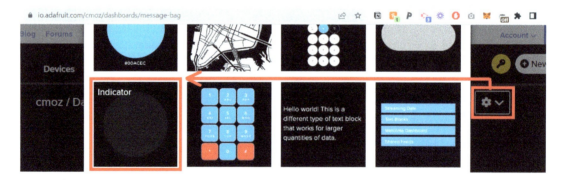

Figure 13.17 – Click the settings symbol on the right-hand side and choosing the Indicator block

There are options we can configure for this block. First, you will need to choose the feed, so check the **tags** checkbox, and then click **Next step** (see *Figure 13.18*):

Figure 13.18 – Selecting your feed

Then, you can alter the settings. See the image in *Figure 13.19*, which shows how you can edit it, including changing the **condition**. We want it to display the following:

- One color when the value is equal to one, meaning the tag is scanned or the value is `true`.

- Display a different color when the value is zero, meaning no tag scanned and the value is `false`.

You can edit these settings and try out sample data to see the change:

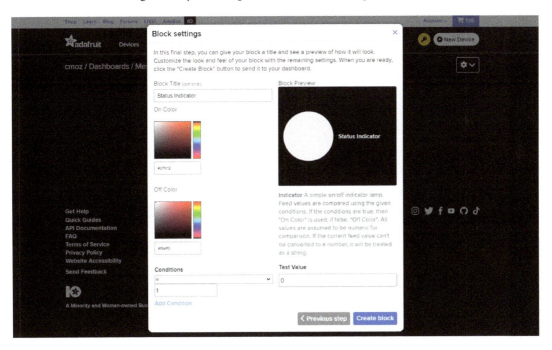

Figure 13.19 – Settings for the Status Indicator Block

I've chosen red as the primary color and white as the off color. Once you have finished modifying, I have altered the speed of the serial monitor because this board can handle a fast connection and it's typical for the ESP32 to use a **115200 baud** rate. When you open the serial monitor, don't forget to alter the **baud** rate there too.

Now, **upload** your code. The complete code is here if you want to check it against yours: `https://github.com/cmoz/Ultimate/tree/main/C13/Activity13_6_IoT`. When you scan a tag, watch what happens on your Message Bag Dashboard.

What are your observations?

You'll notice it kind of works. It does what we asked it to – when there is a tag present, it is one for true and the **Status Indicator** changes, but it changes our one indicator for all the tags, so it is getting confused. This could be implemented in a better way – we want to know which tag is scanned.

How would you implement it? Think about the problem and when you think you've got a solution, jump to the next activity!

Activity 13.7 – Iterations to the IoT connection

After looking at the behavior of the tags when scanned, I want to have one status indicator for each tag that I have. We need to add more feeds for this information. Click on your **Feed** tab back in `io.adafruit.com`, and let's add a feed for each tag (see *Figure 13.20*):

Figure 13.20 – The feeds for all the tags

I added my feeds to a group called Message Bag to organize them, so my key for these has changed slightly. Instead of referring to them as **blueTag**, it would be **messagebag.bluetag**.

Let's edit our **Dashboard** now.

Open the **Settings** tab and choose **Create New Block** on the Message Bag Dashboard. I'll create a **Status Indicator** for *each* tag. This time, I'm also going to name the Status Indicator to whatever the red tag will represent. For example, I'll have the red tag in my wallet – so I'll call it wallet packed. I'll do this for all five items. I'll change the scanned color to match the color of the NeoPixel and I'll choose white for the color when the item isn't scanned in.

After you have finished creating and you've saved your dashboard, we need to modify the code.

At the very start of our code, we have a declaration for the feed we are using:

```
AdafruitIO_Feed *scannedTags = io.feed("tags");
```

We need to modify this and add the other tags too for the new feeds we've created. My code looks as follows:

```
AdafruitIO_Feed *scannedRedTag = io.feed("messagebag.redtag");
AdafruitIO_Feed *scannedBlueTag = io.feed("messagebag.bluetag");
AdafruitIO_Feed *scannedGreenTag = io.feed("messagebag.greentag");
AdafruitIO_Feed *scannedYellowTag = io.feed("messagebag.yellowtag");
AdafruitIO_Feed *scannedPurpleTag = io.feed("messagebag.purpletag");
```

The portions that have messagebag in them are there because I put them in a **MessageBag** group. Delete that part of the tag identifier if you didn't make a group.

We also need to update where we are sending the tag state, which is reflected in this line:

```
scannedTags->save(redTag);
```

This will need to be amended to the following:

```
scannedRedTag->save(redTag);
```

Change all the code instances where this code appears in the tagActions() function. After you have finished, **upload** the code and try out your Message Bag Dashboard now. My completed code for this activity is here for you to check your code against: https://github.com/cmoz/Ultimate/tree/main/C13/Activity13_7_IoTImproved. *Figure 13.21* shows three views of my dashboard, with the first showing all tags are not scanned. The middle view shows that some of the tags have been scanned – the red, blue, and yellow and the objects they represent – and lastly, all tags are scanned in the final part of the diagram:

Figure 13.21 – Message Bag Dashboard online reflecting the scanning of tags in real time

Hopefully, you'll notice that it's surprisingly fast! We can see the changes in real time, with a slight delay but it's very accurate. If you make the Dashboard public and send yourself the link, you'll be able to see the tag scanning on your phone (see *Figure 13.22*):

Figure 13.22 – The IoT service on my mobile phone as I scan tags

I hope you've enjoyed adding IoT capabilities to this circuit. You might look at adding other functionality too. You could connect a screen or other peripherals through the STEMMA connection. The STEMMA I²C connection is broken out and separated from the pins on the board so you can chain other devices. A screen could display the Wi-Fi connection information or similar. There is also a sewable Flora GPS component that you could add. You could perhaps track where the items were scanned and this location could be displayed on an IoT service privately. How about sound or vibration as another confirmation for the wearer? Adding other ways that wearers can interact with your system, or including ways to make it more accessible, should always be a goal or part of the subtext in a system we design for people. Additionally, although our circuit board is tiny, there are smaller RFID readers that you can try too.

Always remember to think about the purpose, use, and how it affects someone's goals before adding it. Let's finish up by adding a reminder to use what we make as the first round of important testing for our wearables.

Use it or do something else

This concept is one that is so important when designing with people for people. When we create our prototypes, it's essential that we take the important step of trying them ourselves. It doesn't matter if it is larger than what you'd like or if your soldering is wonky – it's about using it to discover how we can make it more seamless with our goals.

Activity 13.8 – The importance of using your wearable and observing what's around you

When you've completed a prototype, regardless of the implementation, test it. Wear it. Bring it with you. Everywhere.

Now that we've created Message Bag, we should be using it over the course of several days in the first instance. Bring a notebook with you and write down observations of it in use. I've done this for extended periods of time and used a similar version in many situations. Try to use your device in the shops, when traveling, visiting friends, and at work. Take it with you in as many situations as you can to test the use. One example of valuable feedback was when I'd made a version with a tone that confirmed every scan. I quickly realized it was too loud or that it should have a volume control when I visited a quiet café!

This activity is about making notes and drawings to document how you can make your wearable more suited for your purpose. After you've made your observations over many days, iterate the prototype. Then, repeat this cycle. You should use what you make if you want others to use it.

Summary

This chapter focused on iterations of Message Bag, alongside putting into practice several of the skills that we've been working on throughout the book. We looked at a template for designs, how to start our projects, and whether we want to focus primarily on the technology we have to skill up or whether we want to focus on a certain context. We discussed our observations when using the proof-of-concept prototype that we created on a breadboard and the ways that this could be improved. This gave us the content to make iterations and finish off the wearable design to create an integration prototype. We soldered and sewed it into place too, completing the project nicely.

After completing Message Bag, we learned that all prototypes have opportunities for improvement. Often, we can swap out a component for a smaller one, or something with more functionality. In this chapter, we looked at adding memory, used to store our tag scanning, and adding IoT capabilities so we could even see on our phones what tag we had scanned. We finished with a reminder to always use what we make so we can improve our wearables and make them more suited for our purpose.

I'm sad to say that the next chapter is the last chapter, but we have some exciting concepts to look forward to. We take a sneak peek at what the future of wearables might look like. We'll learn some top tips and tricks for creating durable and interesting wearables, as well as pushing your prototyping further using new and unusual techniques!

References

As a final note, I wanted to highlight some research and projects where RFID technology has been used. This could provide a springboard for your own wearables and possible applications for this type of interesting and useful technology. These research papers are a good start with differing applications for RFID technologies:

Sedighi, P., Norouzi, M. H., & Delrobaei, M. (2021). *An RFID-Based Assistive Glove to Help the Visually Impaired. IEEE Transactions on Instrumentation and Measurement, 70, 1-9.* `https://wp.kntu.ac.ir/delrobaei/files/TIM_2021_Delrobaei.pdf`.

Dang, Q. H., Chen, S. J., Ranasinghe, D. C., & Fumeaux, C. (2020). *Modular integration of a passive RFID sensor with wearable textile antennas for patient monitoring. IEEE Transactions on Components, Packaging and Manufacturing Technology, 10(12), 1979-1988.* `https://ieeexplore.ieee.org/abstract/document/9249015`.

Zhong, T., Jin, N., Yuan, W., Zhou, C., Gu, W., & Cui, Z. (2019). *Printable stretchable silver ink and application to printed RFID tags for wearable electronics. Materials, 12(18), 3036.* `https://www.mdpi.com/1996-1944/12/18/3036`.

Wang, C., Liu, J., Chen, Y., Xie, L., Liu, H. B., & Lu, S. (2018). *RF-kinect: A wearable RFID-based approach towards 3D body movement tracking.* Proceedings of the *ACM on Interactive, Mobile, Wearable and Ubiquitous Technologies, 2(1), 1-28.* `https://dl.acm.org/doi/abs/10.1145/3191773`.

Jiang, Y., Xu, L., Pan, K., Leng, T., Li, Y., Danoon, L., & Hu, Z. (2019). *e-Textile embroidered wearable near-field communication RFID antennas. IET Microwaves, Antennas & Propagation, 13(1), 99-104.* `https://ietresearch.onlinelibrary.wiley.com/doi/full/10.1049/iet-map.2018.5435`.

Tajin, M. A. S., Amanatides, C. E., Dion, G., & Dandekar, K. R. (2021). *Passive UHF RFID-based knitted wearable compression sensor. IEEE internet of things journal, 8(17), 13763-13773.* `https://ieeexplore.ieee.org/abstract/document/9383785`.

Chen, Y. L., Liu, D., Wang, S., Li, Y. F., & Zhang, X. S. (2019). *Self-powered smart active RFID tag integrated with wearable hybrid nanogenerator. Nano Energy, 64, 103911.* `https://www.sciencedirect.com/science/article/abs/pii/S2211285519306184`.

Luo, C., Gil, I., & Fernández-García, R. (2020). *Wearable textile UHF-RFID sensors: A systematic review. Materials, 13(15), 3292.* `https://www.mdpi.com/1996-1944/13/15/3292`.

Review questions

1. What does setting our road map involve? How might you plan your wearable project?
2. Why is it important to iterate our designs?
3. What is **non-volatile** memory?
4. Describe positive feedback and give one example of it.
5. What is EEPROM?
6. What do we always need to be aware of when using flash memory?
7. What is a **global object** or **global variable**?
8. What is an **integration** prototype?
9. Why do we **tin** our wire?

14

Delving into Best Practices and the Future of Wearable Technology

This chapter will provide information on the steps to take to help find solutions for common errors or issues that can happen when we prototype. We will look at a few handy tips to help us with our wearable journey, as well as understand how to set up our circuits so that they last. We will also have a look at batteries and power solutions.

We will look at troubleshooting and some of the common ways you can take a step-by-step approach to finding the problem. We will finish up with a look at the future and what the world of wearables may hold! What are scientists, technologists, engineers, and designers exploring in these intersections? For example, designers and engineers are creating medical devices worn on the body and collecting essential information for healthcare. We look toward the possible future directions for wearables, on-body systems, and creative circuits. We discuss *"What does the future hold?"* through learning about where this exciting research is taking us.

In this chapter, you will consolidate your learning using my tips and tricks to help you continue with your wearable practice.

By the end of this chapter, you will have additional resources to continue with your own learning journey. You will understand the essential information about providing power to your circuits and ways to find the errors that are preventing your wearables from working. You will have thoughts about where the future of wearables may be heading, and hopefully, you'll be planning your own first project!

In this chapter, we're going to cover the following topics:

- Best practices
- Additional techniques
- Taking your prototypes further

- Power considerations
- How to troubleshoot
- What's in the future?

Technical requirements

This chapter includes new techniques and explores ways to move your circuits from prototypes to even more ambitious projects, so we don't have a specific requirement list.

Best practices

I hope you've had an exciting journey with me from our first steps in learning about electronic circuits to using conductive threads and fabrics and exploring e-textile toolkits. We've whizzed by several Arduino systems and explored some of the functions of ESP32-based boards. Throughout all the learning, we also had time for theory, the important consideration of *why* we want to make wearables, and what was made before us. We looked to a Design Innovation method to help create wearables with purpose. Hopefully, you're now equipped to bring your wearables to life through recreating that process, from early concept prototyping to making and using your wearable.

This chapter is a place for some of the extras that can help to improve or bring your wearables to the next level or just simplify the process for you – some of which I've learned over the years of making and teaching, and all of which I've found useful.

Let's start with a few pointers that can help make a project all the more successful!

A few handy tips

There are many things you can do to make your wearable journey a more enjoyable and active experience – let's start with storage.

Storage

It's all about small parts! Creating wearable systems means there's a world of small parts. You'll probably find as you progress that you start collecting many different resistor values, fabric samples, and wire thicknesses. Sometimes, getting a delivery of new items feels so exciting that it's easy to lose or misplace some of these small items. The best idea is to invest in some good storage containers of various sizes. Separate your items by type or categories – for example, I group the sewable items. *Figure 14.1* shows one example of storage I found at Christmas time and used to store baubles (on the left), or these Muji (https://www.muji.eu/) drawers (on the right), the perfect size for components:

Figure 14.1 – Storage options for components

The best thing to do when unboxing all your parts is to separate them by type. It's nice to have all your resistors in a separate place from your LEDs, or even to have separate places for different LED colors and resistors of different values. Most hardware or craft supply stores sell plastic boxes that will make this easy and fun to sort out.

I also have a toolbox that I use if I want to bring my tools with me to work on projects. As shown in *Figure 14.2*, there are many options for toolboxes that suit your size requirements. I love **Trusco** toolboxes because they have a great range to choose from and they are well made. Suppliers for Trusco that I've found include `https://www.labourandwait.co.uk/collections/trusco` and `https://tinkerandfix.co.uk/collections/trusco`. They may seem expensive, but I've had mine for well over a decade and there's no sign of even a dent in it. They are great quality and will last a lifetime:

Figure 14.2 – My Trusco toolbox and the tools I store in it

I also have a little yellow plastic toolbox that I carry around too depending on where I'm going and what components or tools I need. These can be very handy and a good low-cost solution. This one (see *Figure 14.3*) has a lot of storage areas with a pull-out tray:

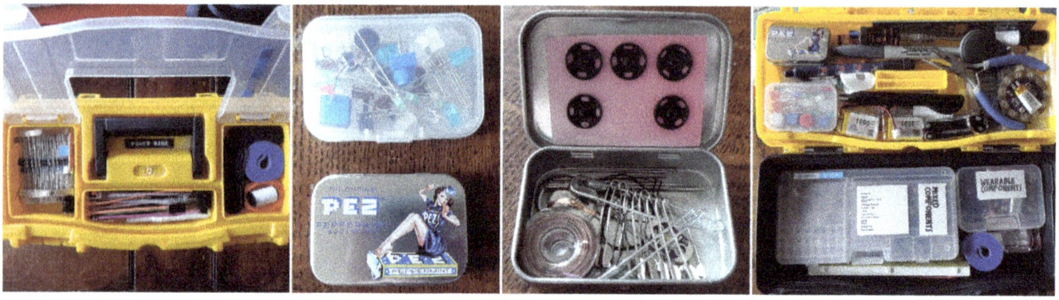

Figure 14.3 – A small plastic toolbox solution

Also, when ordering components or kits, they sometimes come in a plastic box. Here are some examples (see *Figure 14.4*) of boxes I got from Proto-Pic (`https://proto-pic.co.uk/`), which I turned into storage for projects I'm working on, and a container that a kit once came in, which is a great size for storing loose components or active projects that I'm moving or carrying around:

Figure 14.4 – Using storage solutions from Proto-Pic packaging (right) and another component box (left)

I also usually separate my soldering items for taking them with me. These items all fit nicely in a component box and the boxes make great solutions for carrying all you need. Shown in *Figure 14.5* is one that I've been carrying with me for a very long time:

Figure 14.5 – My portable solder iron box made from a reused plastic box I had

You can find small portable-sized solder, tinning flux, and solder irons so that you can bring your practice with you!

Lastly, it's a good idea to get storage boxes for fabrics, conductive materials, and threads, so that you don't lose small sewing parts. I have sealed storage, so everything is kept organized and tidy, as well as sewing boxed so I know where to find what I need when I'm sewing.

> **Storage of Conductive Materials**
>
> A little tip to remember is that many conductive materials and threads can oxidize over time. They often need to be stored in sealed bags to prevent discoloration. Also, try not to handle these materials unnecessarily. Sometimes, the oils from our fingertips can leave marks on these materials.

Having quick access to the materials and tools you need makes a big difference when you're working on a project. If things are handy, you'll be much more likely to get on with it when the inspiration strikes!

Documentation

Document your project, then share it! One way to encourage you to make and build projects is to share what you're doing. When you share on a site (see *Figure 14.6*) such as **Instructables** (`https://www.instructables.com/member/CMoz/`), you also can see what other people have been making. **Hackaday** (`https://hackaday.com/`) has fresh hacks that are interesting for the engineering community every day. I also document a lot of projects on my personal website, `https://christinefarion.com/`, so it doesn't matter what projects you document or where you do it – just do it! Here are some examples of documenting your work:

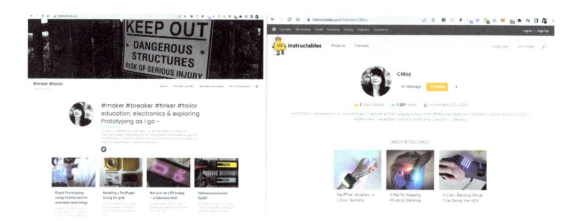

Figure 14.6 – Sharing your wearable projects, either on a personal site (left) or Instructables (right)

Seeing what others make can be very motivating and inspirational. Also, documenting your projects is a great way to remember what you did and how you did it. Forgetting how to connect components or code elements of your wearables is easily done, so having a record of it with good photos and diagrams is helpful for you to also remember how you did it or what aspects you want to fix or improve. When taking photos, try to be sure your wires are clearly visible, color-coded, and there's not too much of a spaghetti junction happening.

Sites to help your prototyping

There are many sites that can help support your project planning. One of these sites is **Circuito**, available at https://www.circuito.io/, where you can make schematic diagrams of the components (see *Figure 14.7*). You can drag components into the main work area and it has sample code you can use to test your components too:

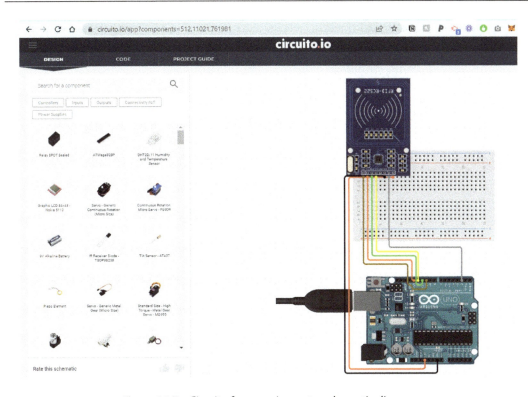

Figure 14.7 – Circuito for mapping out a schematic diagram

It can be a good way to try an idea without buying the boards and components. Similar to Circuito is a service on **DigiKey** (https://www.digikey.co.uk/schemeit/project/) for mapping out your projects. There are components for you to drag into the project area (see *Figure 14.8*). They have a huge range of components in their catalog, so it's worth a try:

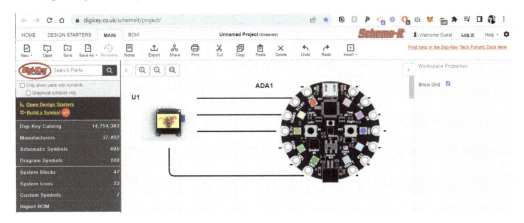

Figure 14.8 – Using the resource at Digikey

Another popular site is **TinkerCad** (`https://www.tinkercad.com/`), which you can use for circuits and designs. These sites can be useful to try out your ideas before you've bought the components. I use **Fritzing** for creating schematics (`www.fritzing.org`), which I've used in this book, as well as for tutorials I make online (see *Figure 14.9*):

Figure 14.9 – Fritzing for schematics

Fritzing now has a donation fee of €8 to download and keep the software. If you are going to make many diagrams, then I find it is worth the small fee.

Identifying opportunities

When making wearables, it is important to find what interests you for your inspiration. Sometimes I look to sites such as the UN's Sustainable Development Goals (`https://sdgs.un.org/goals`), of which there are seventeen. This could be a great starting point for an informed wearable. Similarly, think of *cross-fertilization*, meaning looking to other fields. These are fields that are different from ones you might be directly involved in. This could be architecture, science, arts, industry, fashion, or nature.

The following are suggested possibilities for creating new and exciting wearables:

- You might look at increasing your wearable's **complexity** – adding more outputs and inputs just to test your coding skills and circuit design.

- This might develop into designing with a **theme**, so maybe one that is all sound-based, or only light-based.

- You could base a project around one **microcontroller** so that you try it and use the features – for example, trying an ESP32 circuit or Flora-based wearable if you haven't before.

- Challenging yourself to a £20 or $20 build, or a build with some **cost** limit, can also be a fun challenging way to build up a project. This could inspire you to use as many recycled or reused parts as possible – a challenge for building with only a fiver!

- Maybe you want to limit yourself in terms of the amount of **time**. Could you make three projects in three days? Or follow a seven-day build? How much could you accomplish with a finite amount of time – say, 30 minutes? Go!

- **Expand** a current project you've made. Could you take a project you've made, perhaps from following along in this book, and expand it or add to its capabilities?

- Choose a different **body part** to create a wearable. This one I love. You might take an existing project and make it for a different body part. How would you need to adapt it? Or you can simply try making a wearable design for a part of the body you haven't yet designed for. Designing for the neck or ankle requires different challenges and skills and can help advance your skill set in a fun way.

- Make things *wrong* or *opposite*. Use a unique or different component – meaning use a sound output where you might typically have a screen or use a button in place of a typical slider component – or the opposite body part or function. Shaking things up can spark new ideas for your creations or ways to solve a problem. It's important to find the fun when *hacking your own design*.

Through identifying new opportunities, you will have an endless stock of wearable ideas. Don't forget to record ideas in your notebook as you go.

Additional techniques

The techniques in this section are ways you can make your wearables more durable or construct them in different ways. If a circuit I'm working on is particularly fragile or has very thin wires that could break off from where they are soldered, I like to make it more durable. I use a more permanent solution than what covering ends with fray check or clear nail varnish can accommodate.

Using **resin** will give a very sturdy bond and covering for your wires. You can buy epoxy resin, which comes in two bottles typically – one is a hardener and when you mix it with the other, they will cure (harden or set) over a specific period of time. This can often be 24 hours. However, many **gel nail polish** systems are made from a resin, which cures with UV lights in a minute or so. You can be very specific about where you want the resin to go and you don't need to mix large quantities – you don't need to mix anything! This can be a great way to add the amount you want to the specific part of the system that needs it. One of the gels I have used in the past is the **NYK1** brand, which has resin in a pot (see *Figure 14.10*) as shown:

Figure 14.10 – Resin nail gel in a pot

The pot of resin allows you to use a small brush to apply it to where it is needed. You will need to keep your resin out of sunlight or it will start to cure! I made the mistake once of leaving the lid half off while I accessed the resin and one side of it is now hard and unusable.

I made a ring with NeoPixels and it had a join that was very fragile where the wires met the solder pads. I applied the UV nail resin to this seam and then put it under a UV LED light. In *Figure 14.11*, we can see the ring under a UV LED lamp:

Figure 14.11 – Curing gel polish under a UV lamp

It cures in the UV lamp for around 60 seconds. The lamp is made for curing nail polish and can be purchased from online retailers for around £20 or $20 at the time of writing. I have seen tutorials for making your own UV lamp Arduino system using UV LEDs with a timer, so you could make one.

Look out for UV-activated gel nail polish – you can get colors such as black for a particular project, though I usually go with clear.

Similar to that system is a product called **Bondic**®. This is a liquid plastic system that comes with the resin in refillable tubes, as well as a UV LED that you press against the battery and aim at the resin. It only takes a few seconds for it to harden. You can use it to create a durable connection, as shown in *Figure 14.12*. I used it on wires on a NeoPixel ring because they kept pulling off. I added the Bondic, cured it, did one more layer to build it up, and cured it again:

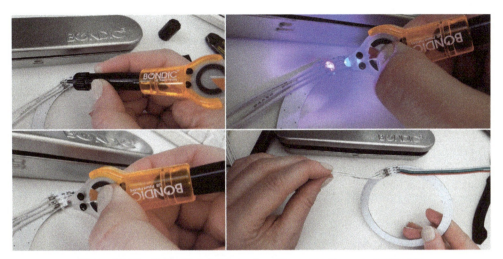

Figure 14.12 – Using Bondic® to make wire connections more durable

Use a layer-by-layer approach, use a thin amount then cure it, then apply again and cure it. In the final image (on the bottom right), you can see I'm now pulling at the wires, and they do not move away from the NeoPixel ring solder pads at all. It's very durable. More information about Bondic is available on their site: `https://bondicuk.co.uk/`.

It is worth mentioning **3D printing** as a technique that can be used to add to your wearables. We saw the beautiful wearables created by Anouk Wipprecht in *Chapter 1*, *Introduction to the World of Wearables*, and there is an interesting article online that features some of her 3D-printed creations: `https://parametric-architecture.com/3d-printed-interactive-wearable-designs-by-anouk-wipprecht/`. Another mesmerizing work using a variety of tools and skill sets is the work created by Behnaz Farahi, *Returning the Gaze, 2022*, shown in *Figure 14.13*:

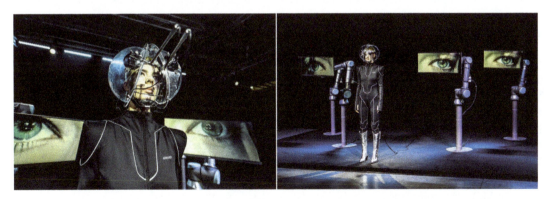

Figure 14.13 – Returning the Gaze by Behnaz Farahi, 2022 (photographer: Nick Soland)

Returning the Gaze is a cyber-physical robotic installation by Behnaz Farahi supported by Universal Robots for ANNAKIKI's Milan Fashion Week. More information can be read at: `https://behnazfarahi.com/`. The project is described as a wearable that "*... brings together robotics, fashion, design, feminism and critical thinking in order to critique the asymmetry of social and political power relations between men and women.*" What is important to note as well is that this is a wearable that also uses the space and place around the wearable itself. It bridges the environment through the monitors that are projecting the wearer's eyes to the audience.

Using 3D printing can be elaborate, as we've read in the previous examples, but it can also be a way to test out a prototype idea. This 3D-printed part (see *Figure 14.14*) allows me to incorporate an 8 LED NeoPixel stick and two buttons:

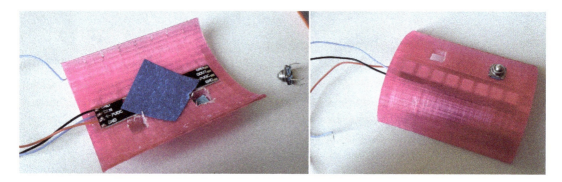

Figure 14.14 – 3D printing for prototyping

This piece will give rigidity to a circuit that is then added to a soft cloth wristband. It allows me to test it with a quick structure. To 3D print, you may be able to go to a local hackspace, maker space, or library to borrow their equipment. They would usually also help someone to learn how to use the tools. There is free software such as **Cura** (`https://ultimaker.com/software/ultimaker-cura`) and **Prusa 3D** (`https://www.prusa3d.com/`) to help you make and send files to a 3D printer.

3D print technology has been around since around 1981 with documents supporting research in Japan. Hideo Kodama was looking for prototyping solutions. Around the 1990s, startups began to experiment with 3D printing technologies for prototyping and machines were expensive and not user-friendly. Around 2005, **Open Source** allowed a more rapid spread of innovation and interest by launching an initiative to create a 3D printer – that could build a 3D printer! In 2008, we saw the first prosthetic leg printed, which helped to bring attention to this technology to the public. Also, in 2015, cat owner Fergus Fullarton Pegg created an orthosis, which is a temporary support brace, for his cat. Working with a vet after his cat was badly injured, Fergus decided to design a leg support with a Form 1+ SLA 3D printer (see *Figure 14.15*). Using a cast from the vet, he designed an orthosis that would allow movement in the joint and release the front paw naturally:

Figure 14.15 – An orthosis for a cat, Sprocket

Prices for 3D printers over time began to decline and the printers got smaller and more portable, which allowed them to be easier to access. 3D printers are now being used in industry to print hearing aids and other medical aids, but also for creating rapid prototypes. New technologies have led to resin printers using UV technology to harden layers, as it prints from liquid, as well as mill style (see *Figure 14.16*) so that they can continue printing. I've seen photos of these hung on walls so that the printing falls into a basket below:

Figure 14.16 – Creality CR-30: The 3DPrintMill, Infinite-Z, Belt 3D Printer

Creality have a range of 3D printers (`https://www.crealityofficial.co.uk/`), so it's worth heading to their website to see the different types and possibilities. Lastly, you can experiment with conductive, recycled, medical-grade, and flexible filaments, so there are materials that should be suitable for your needs. If you're unsure where to start, there is **Thingiverse**, which has user-submitted printable designs (`https://www.thingiverse.com/`). You can download the files and print them yourself. There are also 3D printing services, so if you have a design that you need printing, you can usually email a file to a printing company.

Another prototyping material that can be used for creative wearables is a product called **Worbla**. This is a non-toxic thermoplastic that comes in sheets that can be molded to different shapes using heat. You can get sheets in natural, black, white, red, and clear. When you heat it, it can be manipulated into shapes, but it's also sticky, so you can build up what you are trying to make to give a prototype depth. Worbla can be heated with a heat gun – the same that we could use for our heat shrink. You may need heat-proof gloves to make this a safe activity, although if you make a mold first and apply the Worbla to the mold, you should be okay. You can find more information about Worbla here: `https://www.worbla.com/`. They have tutorials and sample uses (see *Figure 14.17*):

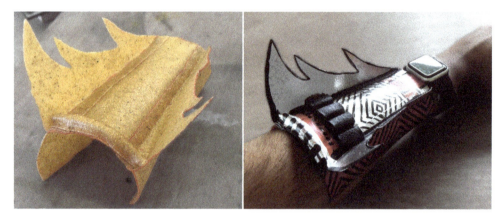

Figure 14.17 – A Worbla project created by Ahmed Zia

The ease of using Worbla allows for rapid prototyping that can help you achieve unusual and durable results. In *Figure 14.17*, we can see the Worbla in its raw state after being heated up and molded into shape. This is also layered up, as it becomes tacky when heated, so you can glue it to itself. You can build up layers this way and integrate electronics.

Laser cutting is another method that you can use for rapid prototyping. A laser cutting machine can cut a variety of materials, such as thin wood, fabric, leather, and plastics. You will need to check what chemicals are in your materials before you use the laser cutter with them so that they do not release toxic fumes. The laser cutter can cut and etch and is efficient if you need multiple items. Conductive materials can be laser-cut to allow for crisp and precise shapes. You can use the ScanNCut machines too.

There are also programmable **embroidery machines** that can sew many designs or shapes. Using conductive thread, you can start to build up conductive designs. Alternatively, you could use it to create your patterns and designs, and then sew with conductive thread and fabrics into it for stunning visual effects. Shown in *Figure 14.18* is a starting point for a conductive project and the thread is made of steel woven with fibers:

Figure 14.18 – An embroidery machine using conductive thread

One thing to note when using conductive threads is that it often involves some trial and error. Certain threads may be too thick (or thin) for your sewing machine and so may need to be used by hand. You may need to try different thread thicknesses or try conductive thread in the bobbin and not the main thread spool area.

One little trick I will share for anyone who hasn't enjoyed soldering or finds it too time-consuming – there is another solution when soldering two wires together. You can buy heat shrink sleeves with solder (for example, `https://uk.rs-online.com/web/c/cables-wires/cable-joints-cable-sleeving/solder-sleeves`). These come in different sizes to suit your wires and they will heat down to fit your wires. I've shown the process in *Figure 14.19*, which uses the shrink sleeves with solder, and then using stripped wires, they go inside the tubes:

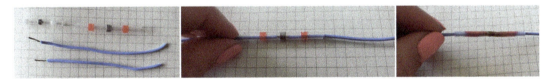

Figure 14.19 – Using heat shrink tubes with solder

Align the tube solder section in the center with the wire ends so that you will melt this center part and the solder will go through the wires and connect them. I would add a little flux on the wire ends to help the conductivity and solder flow. Then, when you heat it with a heat gun, it will melt the solder. Allow it to cool for a moment and then try the pull test. If it comes apart, check that you have applied enough heat and for long enough.

Now that we've looked at other techniques we can use for making wearables, let's explore how you might want to take your wearable designs from an integration prototype to your own circuit board.

Taking your prototypes further

If you've made a prototype on a breadboard and then moved it to a garment, it's likely you're testing it. This will help you to iterate it and discover improvements. Once these have been worked through, it might be time for you to move it to a circuit board. A **printed circuit board** (**PCB**) is the unique design that you've taken to a manufacturer to build according to your custom designs and then you can make unlimited copies. One of the boards I've made (see *Figure 14.20*) has slits in the sides so you can attach it to a strap for attaching to clothing or bags:

Figure 14.20 – A PCB manufactured from my design made in Eagle

The circuit board has the traces, the connections between the components, and you would solder on the actual components. You can also get **flexible circuits** now, but they cost a lot more than traditional circuit boards. I usually go for the thinnest board they offer so that you do get some flex in it. You might want to look at the cost and specifications of what you can buy for low-print runs for your designs at places such as **Seeed**, (https://www.seeedstudio.com/fusion_pcb.html). They can create small batches of around 10 to 12 circuit boards for you at a very low cost. I've also bought PCBs that I've designed from **Dirty PCB** (https://dirtypcbs.com/store/pcbs). Again, these were also low-print run numbers of around ten.

Circuit design software includes **Fritzing**, as seen earlier in this chapter, and **Eagle CAD**, which has a limited version for hobbyists (https://www.autodesk.co.uk/products/eagle/free-download), the **Easy EDA** online PCB design tool (https://easyeda.com/), and **KiCAD** (https://www.kicad.org/). Using manufacturing services, costs vary, so reducing the risk of errors can be done through several rounds of prototyping and testing. It is very important to make sure all your connections and sensors work.

Typically, some process elements that some wearable designers follow include the following:

- Decide your wearable's **purpose**, what question are you trying to answer, and for whom.

- What is your **minimum viable product**? Understanding what the minimum functionality or features are to satisfy what the wearer wants.

- Work **iteratively** – make one part of your circuit at a time, get it to work, and then move on to the next part. We've been following this process throughout the book too.

- How to make it **safe** for prototyping? Understanding how to make your wearable safe for the people you want to test it is a priority. This includes power requirements and checking your wiring, as well as how it is used.

- Sourcing **parts** for your wearable that are cost-effective, available, and standard in case your designs are made by a manufacturer.

- Creating your **look-and-feel** prototypes – a lookalike prototype so people can see what your idea is going to be like and a **role** prototype, or a works-like prototype, so people can test the function. Using two prototypes together in this way can help someone understand the overall picture of your wearable. As you make iterations, be sure the changes that you make are a direct result of speaking to people.

- If you are finding it difficult to complete a prototype or work out the code or circuit issues, there is nothing wrong with putting it aside and working on a different project.

- Once prototypes have been tested, build in **cost engineering**. Don't do this part too soon because you'll find you limit yourself. This is about managing the costs involved in making your wearable. You might remove essential features or not make parts of your design. You might want to swap out a circuit board if costs for it have gone up. For example, I was using the ATMEGA48P microchip for a lot of projects, but I soon realized that costs have gone up a lot with chip shortages. An ESP32 chip now is a lot less expensive with a lot more functionality, so I work with that one more. However, it's important to also realize that you don't have to stick with a design if it's just not working. Maybe you need more experience with a component or code, or sometimes, having a rest can refresh you and you may see the problem differently or in a new light. You may want to try different components.

- Don't forget you can ask for help. There are forums for Arduino-based help – some good forums are on the Arduino website itself (`https://forum.arduino.cc/`) at Adafruit, where they too have forums (`https://forums.adafruit.com/`), or you can head to a local hackspace or maker space if there is one near you.

- If you are bringing your design to a circuit board, you don't have to make one huge feature-packed board – you can **make it modular**. Make parts of the circuit and check they work. Doing this is a good way to check your designs, part by part. If parts break or need replacing, it is a lot easier to do if it's only a module or a single part that needs changing and not the entire design.

A Tip for Making: Simplify!

Consider making more designs with fewer features instead of one design with every feature. Sometimes, it's easy to get distracted by building something that is over-complicated and confusing, instead of creating one thing that works very well.

Creating a PCB is a very exciting process. Using software such as Eagle to create something that doesn't yet exist is also a very rewarding process. If you are using software such as Eagle, you can download the libraries that companies have created so you can add their components. Two libraries that I add include the Adafruit parts library for Eagle (`https://github.com/adafruit/Adafruit-Eagle-Library`) and Sparkfun has an extensive parts library that is very useful too (`https://github.com/sparkfun/SparkFun-Eagle-Libraries`). Using Eagle is beyond the scope of this book, but the libraries should help you on your way. There is also a component search site (`https://componentsearchengine.com/part-view/ATMEGA328P-PU/Microchip`), so you can search for the parts that you need for your circuits. In *Figure 14.21* is a schematic diagram for (left) and the corresponding circuit board (right) of a board I made in Eagle:

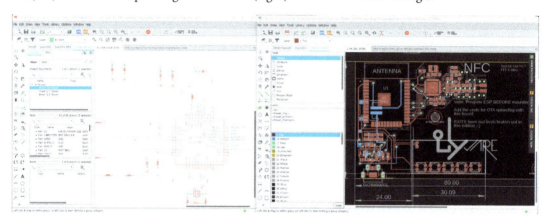

Figure 14.21 – Using Eagle to make a circuit board

If you start small with a project that only has a few components, you can work your way up to more complex circuitry. This guide from **Autodesk** explains how to install libraries: `https://www.autodesk.com/products/eagle/blog/library-basics-install-use-sparkfun-adafruit-libraries-autodesk-eagle/`. Additionally, I bought the book *Make Your Own PCBs with EAGLE: From Schematic Designs to Finished Boards*, by *Simon Monk*, which was great for getting me up and running. There's no rush or requirement for you to ever move to that stage of prototyping your own circuit boards, but it is important to let you know this is an option. Take your time enjoying making wearables and making a PCB might be something you explore in the future.

Power considerations

Powering the wearables you make is an important part of the overall circuit. Using a **Lithium Polymer (LiPo)** battery means that it is rechargeable. We need ones rated at **3.7 V** for our projects because the circuit boards we are using are 3.3 V-rated, as shown in *Figure 14.22*:

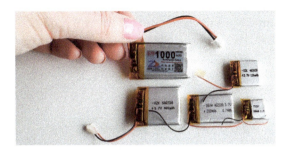

Figure 14.22 – Varieties of LiPo batteries

The battery's capacity is measured in amp hours – you'll see **mAh** for milliamp hours on the LiPo batteries that we use for wearables. We can use a capacity in the range of 150 to 2000 mAh for our projects. They will be flat and different rectangular shapes. They typically have a foil-type case and don't weigh a lot, which makes them good for wearable designs. It can be a good idea to provide information for the wearer to know how much charge is left. You can buy a battery capacity indicator (see *Figure 14.23*) that you can integrate with your circuit:

Figure 14.23 – A battery capacity indicator

A battery that is rated at 1 Ah discharges 1 amp for 1 hour, or 0.5 amps for 2 hours, and so on. You might see some batteries with a C rating; this is for describing a maximum discharge rate. If a battery has a 1C rating, it will charge at a maximum of 1 amp over an hour, or a rating of 10C tells us that the battery will charge at a maximum of 10 amps over 0.1 hours, or 6 minutes. Most of the batteries we use will have a 1C charge rate, meaning that the current will charge the whole battery in one hour. Pulling a large current often makes a battery get hot and this can also shorten the life span of a battery.

> **LiPo Safety**
>
> If your battery gets puffy, **stop using it immediately**. This is from gas escaping and building up inside the battery. They can be prone to self-ignite, so dispose of these batteries very carefully. If it does catch fire, you must wait for the fire to burn out, as water is ineffective and may react with it. Alternatively, you can use a fire extinguisher for electrical fires (a Class D L2 powder fire extinguisher).

You can buy safe bags for storage of LiPo batteries that are explosion-proof. Although even with these bags, don't overpack them. We should handle batteries carefully to avoid them being crushed or penetrated. Always use the correct charger made for a LiPo battery. Shown in *Figure 14.24* are some of the LiPo battery chargers that are good sizes for wearables:

Figure 14.24 – A sample of LiPo battery chargers

These chargers can be soldered into your circuits and then charge your battery using USB-C, mini, or micro cables. Some of the circuit boards we have been using have a built-in charger too and we used a special charge board, the Adafruit LiPoly Charger BFF Add-On, for QT Py. The batteries from the wearable websites recommended in this book all have circuit protection and it is highly unlikely you will come across any of the issues mentioned. I have only had a few batteries go puffy over the course of many years, but I just disposed of them safely at a purpose-specific dump site. The temperature can also affect your battery – if it is cold, the battery may not last as long.

> **A Note on Alternative Power Sources**
>
> Another way to power your wearables is to use **small power banks**, which are easier to handle and are useful beyond building the wearable. I have seen a lot of people making the shift from unpacked LiPos to power banks in recent years. You can get these power banks with solar cells on the top, so they recharge in an environmentally friendly way too. These banks can often fit into pockets or other areas of your wearable.

You can also use **alkaline** batteries, which are not rechargeable. These are usually AA or AAA for wearables because of their size. Using these batteries can be a cheap way to add power and you can buy battery holders (see *Figure 14.25*) that have switches:

Figure 14.25 – Switched battery holders

If you use these, you'll also have to plan for replacing the batteries. Because they need replacing, they are less friendly to the environment and will end up costing you more. You should also build an easy way to access where you have put the batteries into your wearable.

There are also many more options for **solar panels** to be integrated into wearables. For these, it's good to make a battery charger circuit that will consist of your batteries, a solar panel, and a power diode. This is the **1N4001 diode** we used in *Chapter 6, Exploring Reactions Through Outputs*, that has polarity. Electricity will only flow in one direction – toward the silver line. Think of this line as the exit line. This is placed so that the power never goes back to the solar panel.

Choose a solar panel based on the voltage and output – if it has a maximum of 100 mAh, this tells us that in good lighting conditions, the panel will output 100 mAh per hour at 6 V. If we have a battery connected to the solar panel that has a 1,100 mAh capacity, it will take 11 hours for this solar panel to charge up our battery. There are a variety of solar panels (see *Figure 14.26*) to choose from and here are some examples:

Figure 14.26 – Various solar panels (flexible)

Some of these are very rigid, so would suit a wearable that has a stable, large flat surface. There are flexible panels see (*Figure 14.26*) that would suit curved areas of the body.

To hook up a solar panel, we would connect the ground wire from the solar panel to the ground of our battery. Then, we would connect (or solder) the power side to one side of the diode. Ensure that the diode with the silver end is facing *toward* your battery. Solder the end of the diode to the positive wire on your battery, as shown in *Figure 14.27*:

Figure 14.27 – Soldering the battery and solar panel circuit

I usually like to run mine through a charge board first (as shown earlier in *Figure 14.23*) to handle the charge current, as well as allow me to charge my battery with a cable during less sunny months.

Some of the solar panels come with a thin film on top to protect them, so be sure to remove this first or it won't work. If your panel isn't marked with + and –, then use your multimeter to check which connection is correct before you solder wires. Using a solar-powered circuit is a great way to be more ecological in your practice. Lastly, for small wearables and interesting solutions, you can find these ultra-mini solar panels (see *Figure 14.28*):

Figure 14.28 – A mini solar cell

The single solar can be purchased at `https://www.mouser.co.uk/ProductDetail/SparkFun/PRT-09541?qs=WyAARYrbSnbrhplj7dcHPA%3D%3D`. You could plan an interesting wearable where these mini solar panels become a feature of the design.

There is interesting work in the field of power and *Jianliang Xiao* (*2021*) et al. at CU Boulder have developed a low-cost wearable biological battery device. Pictured in *Figure 14.29* is a thermoelectric ring:

Figure 14.29 – A thermoelectric ring (Credit: Xiao Lab)

It is stretchy, so it could be worn as a ring or a bracelet that touches the skin, using a person's natural heat to convert that heat into electricity. It is also fully recyclable.

Lastly, you could look to add **wireless induction charging** capabilities to your wearable. You can buy the compatible Qi charge coils (see *Figure 14.30*) that you add to your power circuit to charge your battery:

Figure 14.30 – A wireless induction coil to charge your battery

They can be expensive, so make sure it has a purpose in your project. You'll need to plan exactly how the wearable would fit onto the base unit to charge, which the wearer would need as well. With many mobile phones now charging wirelessly, many people do prefer this way to charge their electronics, so it could be an interesting upgrade to a wearable.

After seeing some of the ways we can add power to our wearables, learning about some of the ways to troubleshoot can help you to solve some issues when making wearables.

How to troubleshoot

Sometimes, things go wrong when we are connecting our circuit hardware or programming it. As we've worked through the exercises, I've noted some things you can try to help with issues. I usually turn to forums to see whether someone has had a similar problem or issue to what I am experiencing. You'll find that this is one of the really positive things about using the boards we've chosen throughout the book – they are all very well-supported. You'll find many help documents, tutorials, resources, and support from the community.

Issues with the QT Py ESP32-S2 board

One of the ways to help solve issues with the QT Py ESP32-S2 board that I came across was that you can factory reset this board. I also didn't realize that you can use this board as a drive, and when you press the reset button on it twice, if it's plugged into your computer, it will appear as a drive. *Figure 14.31* shows the drive when it is opened on my computer:

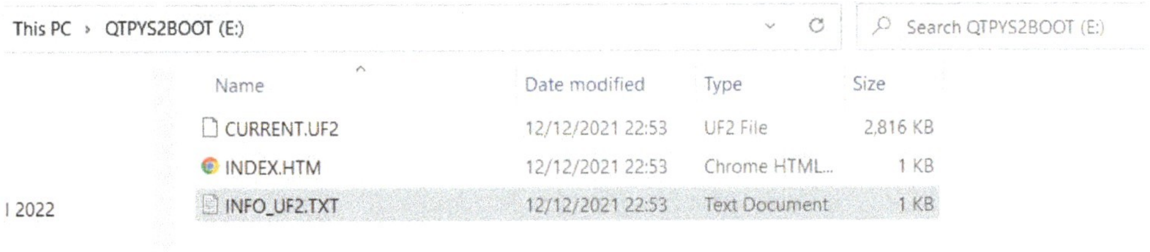

This PC › QTPYS2BOOT (E:)				
Name	^	Date modified	Type	Size
□ CURRENT.UF2		12/12/2021 22:53	UF2 File	2,816 KB
● INDEX.HTM		12/12/2021 22:53	Chrome HTML...	1 KB
▫ INFO_UF2.TXT		12/12/2021 22:53	Text Document	1 KB

Figure 14.31 – Bootloader files on the QT Py ESP32-S2

If your board isn't working how you are expecting it to, then you can upload a new bootloader. The short tutorial is available on the Adafruit site: `https://learn.adafruit.com/adafruit-qt-py-esp32-s2/factory-reset#factory-reset-and-bootloader-repair-3107941-7`.

The Arduino IDE

Another way we can make programming a little easier is to take advantage of some of the features in the Arduino software. Sometimes, we need to make a change in the code – maybe change a variable name or pin number:

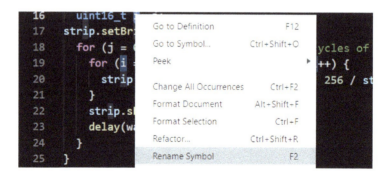

Figure 14.32 – Selecting the x variable to change it

In this example, I needed to rename the x variable. There is a built-in feature to make this quick and accurate. If I were to miss one of the x variables in my code, then I would get an error message and the code wouldn't work. Highlight x (see *Figure 14.32*) or whatever variable you want to change.

Right-click your mouse to bring up the menu (see *Figure 14.33*) and choose **Rename Symbol** from the pop-up menu:

Figure 14.33 – Renaming all the variables at once with Rename Symbol

When you've selected **Rename Symbol**, it will open a little popup where you enter what you want to change it to. I've entered i for the new variable name, as in *Figure 14.34*:

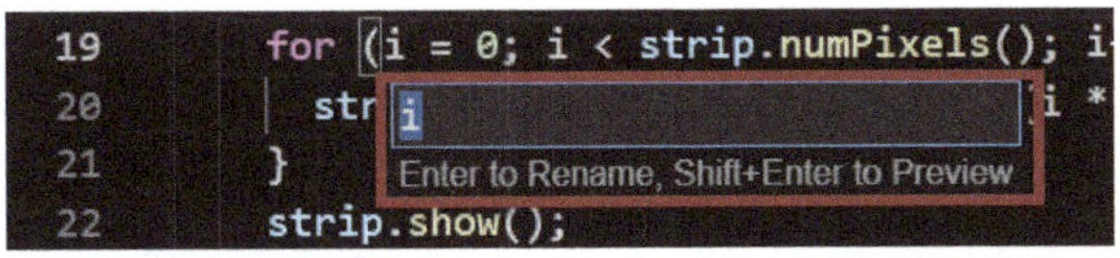

Figure 14.34 – Renaming the symbol by typing in the new symbol name

Then, hit *Enter* on your keyboard, and it will change the occurrence of your x variable to i throughout the code.

Recognizing errors is also important so that you know how to search for help. In *Figure 14.35*, it shows an error message in the console:

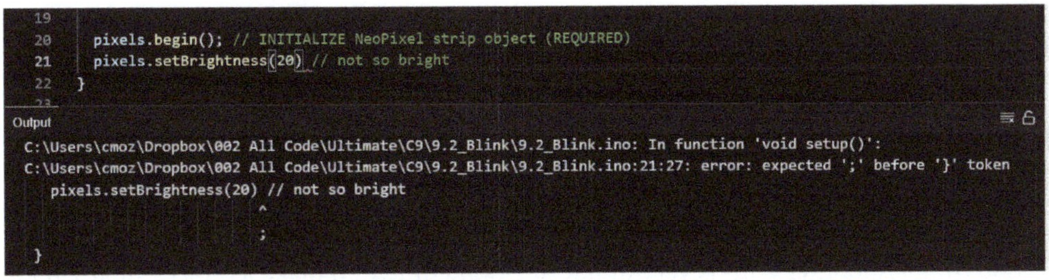

Figure 14.35 – The Output window showing an error

The code won't compile and it tells us in the **Output** message that there is an error:

expected ; before the } token

This tells us where to look in our code. So, I will look through the code for the line:

`pixels.setBrightness(20)`

I can see that there is a ; symbol missing from the end of the code line, so this is the problem. In *Figure 14.36*, when we hover over the code line with the error, it also has a popup for how we can fix this line:

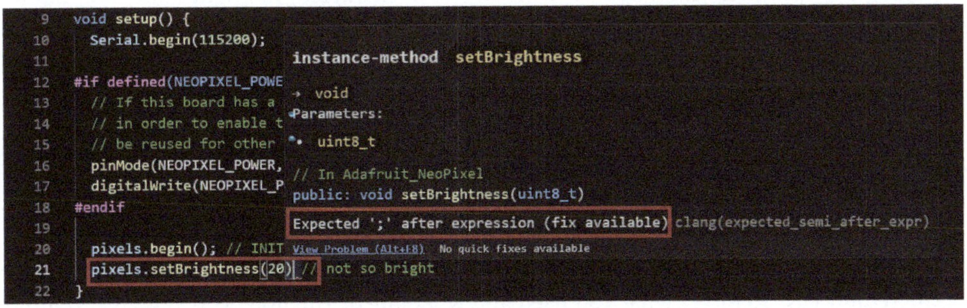

Figure 14.36 – Finding the errors in our code

Make the fix and then upload the code again. Always look to **Output** and check what the errors are. It's important to be able to interpret the error messages and over time, you will become familiar with certain errors and how to fix them. A lot of this will come with experience.

Sometimes with Arduino, I also open previous versions of Arduino. Trying it in another version sometimes fixes errors I may have had with libraries or installs. There are also other platforms to program Arduino, including **Platform.io**, which is an IDE that has a lot of extra tools such as code snippets and debugging (`https://platformio.org/`) and which is built on top of **Visual Studio Code** (`https://marketplace.visualstudio.com/items?itemName=platformio.platformio-ide`). This will take a little time to read through in order to get it up and running, so I wouldn't recommend it for beginners. Once you have Arduino IDE under your belt though, it's a platform to which many people migrate. There is also **Codebender** (`https://codebender.cc/`), which is an online editor that allows you to share code online. This does require a monthly subscription though, so you will need to evaluate the pros and cons for yourself. Lastly, **Arduino** itself has an online editor that you might want to try: `https://create.arduino.cc/editor`. You can save sketches online and you won't need to update libraries because they will be maintained for you.

Documentation

Having good troubleshooting skills is very important. Sometimes, I'll make a project and then I find myself saying, "*that shouldn't happen*," "*why is that doing it this way?*", or "*darn, it's not working.*" Sometimes, the wearable might work differently from what you intended, and sometimes, you'll need to figure out whether it is the hardware connections or the code that has gone wrong. For all these issues, try to follow a *step-by-step process*.

If you can **document** what you did to fix the error or document what you are trying so you don't repeat yourself, that can be a good process to do. Record your error, describe exactly what is happening and what is affected, record the results, record the data or what the output is from the code, and record what steps you've taken to try to solve the issue. This is also important when you are asking for help. You'll be able to describe the issue or problem and its outputs.

Take this to a formal level – you could get a **Lab Notebook**, or create a page in Notion for each project you are working on. Be formal with it and write the story. For example, you might write, "*this morning, the sensor still wasn't putting out values that made sense, so I tried changing the baud rate from 9,600 to 115,200, and this didn't fix the error. I checked that I had the correct library installed, which was DHT11, and I tried a new library, DHT11_Test. I've since loaded a new example file that was included with the library, test_sketch_temp.ino, and after changing the pin number to A3, I uploaded the code. This has worked. So, I need to figure out what the differences are between the code and libraries so the error won't happen again.*" It's so easy to go in circles if you haven't written it down. If you're lucky enough to have a friend who also makes things, they might read it and ask you, "*Why didn't you try the DHT12 library?*", which may help you solve the issue. Lastly, if you are away from your computer or project for a few days, it is incredibly easy to forget what you tried and what failed. The notebook is a great reminder.

There are usually a few things that can fix some problems – following this list may help:

- Check your **power** is on.
- Check the **battery** is charged.
- Are there any **wires** touching that shouldn't be?
- Have wires become **disconnected**? Check for any open circuits.
- Check that the wires are hooked up correctly. Double-check.
- The pull test – if it's a soldered circuit, tug at the wires to be sure they aren't only barely connected but that they have a strong connection.
- Check the **polarity** of components – don't forget the diodes we've used need to be the correct way around.
- Does the board need a driver, library, or a board installed to work?
- Have you chosen the board and port from the **Tools** menu?
- Check if your USB cable is a data/sync cable and not just a charge cable.
- Is anything on the board hot?
- Check your resistor values and whether they need replacing with different values.
- Try this: **upload a basic blink** sketch to check your board and connections all work.
- Try resetting the board.
- Check your component **datasheets**, particularly the power requirements, and the pin connections.
- Check the **pinout diagram** of the board you are using – what are the SPI connection pin numbers?
- Start by removing one of the sensors – check whether it works with fewer components to try to eliminate the part that could be causing the issue. Add the parts back together one by one.
- Try to focus on the hardware or software individually.
- Try one then the other. If you do both at the same time (which I have done in a panic before), it is extremely difficult to find problems, and you generally make more.
- Have you tried swapping out one component for a similar one or the same one? For example, swap out an OLED for another OLED to see whether it was the one you were using.
- Is it just the **environment** that is making your circuit appear that it isn't working? For example, I've programmed UV sensors, and they won't work indoors where there isn't UV, or perhaps your temperature sensor has been set for temperatures that don't exist where you are testing your circuit.

- Lastly, take a break and come back to it with fresh eyes. You'd be surprised how often this works. Also, try telling a duck. So, I have a little toy duck, but you can use anything – when you say the problem out loud and what you've tried to do to fix it, it can sometimes trigger you to think of another solution or something else to try.

I used to keep a similar list printed in the front of my notebook as a process to go through in case I've not been able to solve a problem I'm experiencing. Over time, checking these issues will become second nature to you.

After looking through a lot of the ways we can troubleshoot our circuits, let's change gear a little and think about the future!

What's in the future?

You are now part of the future of wearables too! With your new making skills, you'll join the wearable field and be able to contribute informed wearables, wearables with a purpose, to the wearable community. Hopefully, you'll also explore alternative ways of making or using and mixing up components from other fields – for example, I've mashed together one of my QT Py circuit boards with these little **ring terminals** to create a version of the board (see *Figure 14.37*) that I can quickly get connected with croc clips:

Figure 14.37 – Adding your own inventive connections to the circuit boards you use

I started by soldering wires to the circuit board. Then, I stripped the wire ends and folded them over to create good connections. I pushed heat shrink onto the wire before pushing the wire end inside the ring terminal. There, I applied a small amount of flux to help the solder flow through, and I soldered the wires to the ring terminal. I gave it a little tug to be sure there was a good connection. Then, when it has cooled (if you don't wait for the ring end to cool, your heat shrink shrinks), slide the heat shrink over the end. Shrink into place and enjoy!

Get inventive and explore – there is no right or wrong way to do things.

We've seen many projects and research outputs throughout this book, as examples of how sensors are used, what creations people are making, or topics that are being explored to create a wider dialog – but where is the field of wearables headed? Some of the key themes I've been seeing in the wearable field include work on sourcing power for wearables and a continued effort in medical wearables, but what else is there?

Current literature discusses the benefits of wearable technology. We see themes of social benefits, medical purposes, increased self-awareness, and sometimes behavior change. These positive aspects I see continuing, and hopefully, future materials and techniques will reinforce the current good practice being done. One final note – you might find a fair in your area where you can try and sample new materials. Here's one example of an event that showcases new and exciting materials: `https://techtextil.messefrankfurt.com/frankfurt/en.html`.

Materials

I find stretchy electronics very fascinating. New and unusual materials are becoming available to produce sensors such as this wireless tag (see *Figure 14.38*) with a stretchable sensor and antenna:

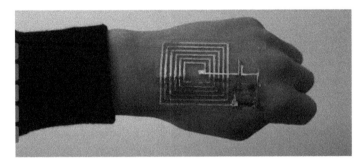

Figure 14.38 – A stretchy tag on skin

This is a collaboration of a team of engineers from **Stanford University** and **Keio University** in Tokyo and their research is presented in their paper: `https://www.nature.com/articles/nature25494`. Because it is soft, it behaves similarly to skin. These types of wearables will likely become more common as their usefulness increases. There are possible applications in the fields of medicine or caring for the elderly, but I could see an application for any place where scanning was needed, for work or safety scenarios. There is also research for clothing for personal thermoregulation, which involves bendable smart clothes that adapt how they use thermal insulation functionality. It mimics pores in human skin – see *Zhong, Y., Zhang, et al. (2017)*. Would this technology become widely used and applied for other wearables?

Along with new materials, there are possibilities with coatings. Purdue engineers have developed a new spray-coating or sewing method that can alter conventional fabric items into battery-free wearables that can be washed in a washing machine. "*By spray-coating smart clothes with highly hydrophobic molecules, we are able to render them repellent to water, oil and mud*", said Ramses Martinez. "*These smart clothes are almost impossible to stain and can be used underwater and washed in conventional washing machines without damaging the electronic components sewn on their surface.*" You can see and hear more at `https://youtu.be/gQ0TCLXZ6Q8`.

The material aspects could also move us toward researching and working with protective gear and body enhancements. Do these wearables become a **second skin**, and if so, what would the requirements be for this? There could be medical applications and uses for this, as well as support for certain occupations. Room for a hybrid design of spray and thin material that can be applied directly to the skin could be an interesting direction – provided the context and purpose are clearly defined.

Lastly, materials could also involve the way we **make materials**. Experimenting with reuse, recycling, and repurposing should play an essential role in the fashion and electronics industries moving forward. How do we incorporate these principles into our own prototypes? Harvesting components should also be a skill we try to learn as e-waste becomes prolific in our landscapes. Does reusing components and elements of other circuits play an essential role in developing innovative wearables?

The body

I hope we see new takes on **body-centered wearable technologies**, particularly ones that aim to improve the wearers' quality of life. We are starting to see themes of *Fashion takes Care*, and I hope this theme continues through to the wearable community. This could include more research and experimentation with e-tattoos – electronic ink being printed on someone's skin or embedded within it. This could be to create integrated circuits. How would this be a seamless embedding with their skin? What purpose could this have? Creating **e-tattoos** could offer a low-maintenance solution to wearables too. Could these solutions coordinate with the research on generating power through movement, so these wearables would require no external power sources? Creating a device that was printed on the skin would also allow for immediate responses through the electronics – could it be implemented for safety features?

Is the body-centered theme carried to **injectable** devices? These are devices that are inserted into a person's body, usually for an extended amount of time. They usually remain at the skin surface level. If we continue to make technology smaller, we might see more implant technology being used. These miniature devices are currently used particularly as RFID devices, but can we continue to push this further? Possible issues could be the comfort in terms of placement and size and also security issues – would this be used to track wearers and would we feel comfortable with technology on us all day and night? Similar to the injectable are **digestible** wearables. These include pills with electronics that are used to diagnose issues internally. This could help with medical diagnosis, as they are currently being used, but what could the future hold for these types of devices? They need to be made from biocompatible materials so there is no harm to the person.

This leads me to think about natural interfaces and ways of communicating. Combining e-tattoos with ways of sensing our gestures could be a way forward with wearables. Using less obtrusive designs could mean that exploring implicit interaction, or passive interfaces, becomes a natural progression within wearable technology.

Environments

A leap into interesting technology could be **bio-culture** – do we grow wearables? Do we see organic materials, renewable sources, or wearables growing with us as a step to more environmentally conscious designs of systems? Research on mycelium has been conducted into the uses of this incredible root communication structure. Mycelium, with its massive branching underground structures, has been used to create furniture prototypes, hats, and packaging from this same structure. Can we combine electronics with it to create new and exciting materials and purposes?

A **mix of real and virtual environments** is likely to be a direction that wearables take us in. I had an email from a company describing a new suit they had developed. It was a full-body suit that they were testing for gamers. It responded to the virtual environment through sensors and motors. After reading this, it was revealed that it was an April Fool's Day joke – however, these are not such futuristic or far-off technologies. The only surprising thing is that this is not already a current product. Some interesting artistic projects pushing these boundaries include Janne Kummer working on `https://www.jannenorakummer.de/projects-8` and `https://www.jannenorakummer.de/leakingbody`; a current research project at HAW Hamburg, `https://www.haw-hamburg.de/en/research/research-projects/project/project/show/klima-act/`; and lastly, the student Anastasia Almosova who has built impressive 3D virtual journeys that are guided by wearables – `https://anastasiaalmosova.com/Interface`.

Even taking one step removed from this, the prospect of creating a wearable that allows the wearer to interact in a meaningful way with their environment is an interesting direction. Are there sensors, monitors, or technology in an environment, inside or out, that respond and interact with an item we are wearing? Is the garment controlling our environment – for example, is it monitoring the air quality in our offices and adjusting it if our clothing monitors that pollution levels are too high? It's worth noting how **artificial intelligence (AI)** might also have a role in the future of wearables. We are already seeing shops that track us when we simply take what we want from the shelves and leave – how would certain wearables be used in the context of AI? Does a relationship with technology alter our perception of wearables? Is it a luxury or does it become more ubiquitous and necessary in daily life? Does it all just become about consumer habits and what happens with our data? Who will own it? Do the wearables revolt and become beacons that break technology nearby, stopping or scrambling cameras, circuits, and signals? Do we use the wearables to notify us of these surveillance activities?

We've touched on the essence of **culture-driven** wearables and **hyper-body** systems and these are areas that warrant further exploration. Integrating our culture, innovation, and ethos into the wearables we make to support and enhance society or societal living should be a focus for wearable designers. Through learning about society, we can use this to inform the designs, creating far more useful and valuable wearable technologies. Alongside this, creating wearables that focus on and use more than one part of the body could give us a better understanding of the value that wearables can have for the wearer. We can create a sensual, meaningful, involved experience for wearers.

Lastly, I want to end on a **fun** note! Often people use wearables, for example, as step counters, because they consider it fun to meet challenges, even if they are set by themselves. Fun, enjoyment, and pleasure are important parts of the human spirit. There is a lot of research in the field of **Funology**, (*Monk, A., Hassenzahl, M., Blythe, M., & Reed, D., 2002*), and the enjoyment of designing should never be discounted.

Even when designing *serious* wearables, it is important to give the wearer moments of delight and little sparks of magic and make their experiences enjoyable. Not only that but innovative wearables should also be fun, creative, and exploratory to make. Ideas, exploring, creativity, and imagination are all important parts of the development phase.

Summary

Congratulations! You have now finished the book.

I hope you have found it an inspiring and, at times, challenging journey. You will be equipped to design sewable circuits using conductive fabrics and threads, as well as create circuits with sensors and outputs. You also worked to create a smart wearable using IoT for connecting to an online service with an ESP32-based board. Hopefully, you'll be carrying around a small multimeter with you as you hunt for metallic fabrics.

You have followed a Design Innovation process and now have the tools to design your projects. There are templates and guides, along with questions to ask yourself when creating in this field.

This final chapter has links and references to other programs and applications you might want to try. It could be that you start to create your schematics in Fritzing or that you look at circuit design in Eagle. Whatever direction you decide to head in, remember that there are many support forums, tutorials, and guides online. The wearable community is welcoming and helpful, so hopefully, you will become someone who can help and guide those new to the field too. Thanks for following along on this journey and I hope you've had as much fun as I have.

References

The following references were referred to in this chapter or are suggested for further knowledge about the topics presented:

Ren, W., Sun, Y., Zhao, D., Aili, A., Zhang, S., Shi, C., ... & Yang, R. (2021). *High-performance wearable thermoelectric generator with self-healing, recycling, and Lego-like reconfiguring capabilities*. In *Science advances, 7(7), eabe0586*. https://www.science.org/doi/10.1126/sciadv.abe0586

Matsuhisa, N., Niu, S., O'Neill, S. J., Kang, J., Ochiai, Y., Katsumata, T., ... & Bao, Z. (2021). *High-frequency and intrinsically stretchable polymer diodes*. In *Nature, 600(7888), 246-252*.

de Medeiros, M. S., Goswami, D., Chanci, D., Moreno, C., & Martinez, R. V. (2021). *Washable, breathable, and stretchable e-textiles wirelessly powered by omniphobic silk-based coils*. In *Nano Energy, 87, 106155.* https://www.researchgate.net/profile/Debkalpa-Goswami/publication/351824432_Supporting_Information_Washable_Breathable_and_Stretchable_e-Textiles_Wirelessly_Powered_by_Omniphobic_Silk-based_Coils/data/60ac00f592851ca9dce1d6a2/2021-OSC-Supporting-Information.pdf

Zhong, Y., Zhang, F., Wang, M., Gardner, C. J., Kim, G., Liu, Y., ... & Chen, R. (2017). *Reversible Humidity Sensitive Clothing for Personal Thermoregulation*. In *Scientific reports, 7(1), 1-8.* https://www.nature.com/articles/srep44208

Monk, A., Hassenzahl, M., Blythe, M., & Reed, D. (2002, April). *Funology: designing enjoyment*. In *CHI'02 extended abstracts on human factors in computing systems, (pp. 924-925).*

Blythe, M. A., Overbeeke, K., Monk, A. F., & Wright, P. C. (Eds.). (2004). *Funology: from usability to enjoyment. Dordrecht: Springer Netherlands.*

Wright, P., McCarthy, J., & Meekison, L. (2003). *Making sense of experience*. In *Funology (pp. 43-53). Springer, Dordrecht.*

McCarthy, J., & Wright, P. (2004). *Technology as experience. interactions, 11(5), 42-43.*

McCarthy, J., & Wright, P. (2018). *The enchantments of technology*. In *Funology 2 (pp. 359-373). Springer, Cham.*

Dodgson, M., Gann, D., & Salter, A. (2005). *Think, play, do: Technology, innovation, and organization. OUP Oxford.*

Review questions

1. What are the benefits of documenting our projects?

2. Name three possible good ways you can troubleshoot your circuits.

3. What are some of the techniques we can use to bring other dimensions into our wearable designs?

4. Reflect on your learning throughout the book. What activities did you find the most helpful or useful for your wearable designs?

5. What next steps will you take to create wearable technology?

6. What does the future of wearables look like to you?

Appendix: Answers and Additional Information

This chapter has useful links for your wearable practice, as well as lists some of the suppliers that I would recommend. There are also the answers to the review questions that have been asked throughout the book.

In this chapter, we provide information on the following topics:

- Useful links
- Suppliers
- Answers to chapter questions

Useful links

The links are for online services and tools that can help with your wearable designs:

- Resistor Calculator: `https://www.calculator.net/resistor-calculator.html`
- Voltage divider calculator: `https://ohmslawcalculator.com/voltage-divider-calculator`
- Ohm's Law calculator: `https://ohmslawcalculator.com/ohms-law-calculator`
- All about circuits: `https://www.allaboutcircuits.com/`
- Electronics Club: `https://electronicsclub.info/`
- Maker Pro: `https://maker.pro/`
- The EasyEDA online PCB design tool: `https://easyeda.com/`
- Circuito for mapping out your circuit: `https://www.circuito.io/`
- The Digi-Key Schematics editor: `https://www.digikey.co.uk/schemeit/project/`
- Tinkercad for circuit design: `https://www.tinkercad.com`
- Fritzing for creating schematics: `www.fritzing.org`
- Documentation of your projects, competitions, and sharing: `https://www.instructables.com/`

- Projects listed daily: `https://hackaday.com/`
- Projects, documentation, and competitions: `https://www.hackster.io/`
- Free 3D printable designs: `https://www.thingiverse.com/`

Also, as a reminder, the tools that I use are mostly all **Engineer** tools. My preferred soldering iron and other electronics items are **Miniware**. For sewing supplies, I usually choose **Gütermann** or **Prym** items.

Suppliers

The suppliers listed are suppliers I have personally purchased from in the past and have had good experiences with.

US-based suppliers

There are many suppliers in the US that provide components – however, these are ones that I have experience with:

- `https://www.adafruit.com/`: Many of the wearable items in this book have come from Adafruit – they have great forums for seeking help and many fun project tutorials. They also have Wearable Wednesday, where you can submit your wearable projects for a chance to be featured.
- `https://www.digikey.com/`: They are Europe- and UK-based as well.
- `https://www.mouser.com/`: They are Europe- and UK-based as well.
- `https://www.sparkfun.com`: The Lilypad suite of wearable items can be purchased here.
- `https://www.newark.com/`: This is the counterpart to Farnell in the UK and a huge distributor worldwide.

UK- and Europe-based suppliers

These are suppliers I have purchased from in the past and have had a good experience with:

- `https://www.tinkertailor.tech/`: This is new to the scene but is the place to go for all conductive materials and all wearable items, from the electronics to the sewing items needed too. All wearable-focused.
- `https://proto-pic.co.uk/`: A great site where I got a lot of my first ever components.
- `https://kitronik.co.uk/`: They do a lot of school projects and have kits, as well as inexpensive wearable items. They also have a lot of supplies for laser cutters and prototyping.
- `https://coolcomponents.co.uk/`: Another good supplier that I've placed many orders with. Often, they have items that are out of stock elsewhere.

- `https://thepihut.com/`: I've always had super quick delivery and good prices from here. I realize it's called PiHut and we didn't cover any of the Pi technology, but they have a range of wearables, circuit boards, sensors, and outputs.

- `https://www.bitsbox.co.uk/`: This is a good site for general hardware that you might need.

- `https://uk.farnell.com/`: Farnell has everything you could ever need, but it can be difficult to find through their search, as there is so much choice.

Answers to chapter questions

Throughout the book you have been challenged with review questions – here are answers to the questions.

Chapter 1

1. Sometimes, they are defined by augmenting people in some way, such as memory, communication, or in a physical sense.

2. Typically, wearables have embedded electronics, a power source, and inputs/outputs of some description.

3. Some exciting intersections exist between wearables and science, fashion, medical, and art. Take inspiration from other fields or plan projects with others who are involved in these areas for interesting and inspired results.

4. Informed wearables are wearables that consider and focus on uses that will improve someone's life or help them in some way. They can be designed with the thoughts and feelings of people to understand an issue better.

5. Wearables can be made for the upper body or lower body and be head-mounted, held, or worn on the wrist.

6. Ethical considerations when designing wearables include data security, what data we are recording, and privacy. When testing our prototypes, we need to be sure to provide information about what we are doing and get consent.

7. You should have some sketches and planning for some future projects!

Chapter 2

1. Swapping out the resistors resists the current and alters the amount of electricity going to that component. It will make our light brighter if we reduce the resistance, and if we add a higher resistance, it will make our light not as bright.

2. We looked at series and parallel circuits.

3. A closed circuit has a flow of current through it, so it will work. When it is open, electricity will not flow. This can be an error or done with a switch or button, for example.

4. A parallel circuit has both ends of the component wired to its power source and ground. These all will work at the same time, as electricity is given to all the parallel components equally.

5. A soft circuit is a great way to take advantage of fabric and material properties. We can have very flexible circuits that move easily and comfortably compared to rigid breadboards and other structured components.

6. Conductive materials allow the flow of electricity through them. We can use a multimeter to check whether current is flowing through and whether we can use them in our circuit. We can also check if it is an insulator – so electricity won't pass. Then, we can use this to cover parts of our wiring.

7. A practical activity – to create two circuits.

8. A drawing task to sketch ideas out – I hope you managed it!

Chapter 3

1. Sensors include temperature and light sensors and accelerometers. There are also speakers, buzzers, and vibration boards.

2. These kits provide a way to connect a microcontroller easier because most of them have sew tabs and a smaller or flatter shape to integrate into a garment better.

3. The I/O pins are very important because they mean we can connect the sensors to our circuit through the microcontroller. The number of pins will dictate how many things we can connect to the board. There are digital and analog pins.

4. The difference between digital and analog pins, is that digital has two states, ON/OFF or 1/0 for example. An analog pin is often used to read sensors so it uses data with values. For example it converts voltage ranges from 0 to 5 volts, to the digital value of 0 to 1023.

5. We need to check our board is plugged in, that we have selected the correct board from the **Tools** menu, and that we have the correct **Port** selected.

6. The `void setup()` function is the first code that is executed (**one** time) if the board is started up or reset. It sets any parameters and initializes what we will be using in our sketch.

Chapter 4

1. We can test our flex sensor using a multimeter. This will give us a range of values from 0 to the `high` value. We know it is working because these values will change on the multimeter or in our code through the **Serial Monitor** window.

2. The Arduino IDE will give you an error message of `"unexpected unqualified id"`. The easiest way to fix this is to change your variable name to something else.

3. This is a good way to see whether our code is working as we expect. We looked at examples to show the position of our accelerometer and the flex sensor output.

4. We wanted to light the LED with varying intensities, so to do this, we need more control, not just a digital pin of HIGH and LOW. The PWM pin allows us to have a range.

5. These next questions were for you to sketch out ideas and inspiration.

Chapter 5

1. We learned about I²C and SPI protocols.

2. No! It's a great way to start, with the sensors we buy, but there is a whole world out there in terms of creating sensors, so we really should try that too.

3. Making our own sensors allows us to create the exact fit, style, and size to suit the wearable we are making.

4. Libraries add so much to our program. They have pre-written functions that allow us to quickly program the components we want to use.

5. We can use a digital pin.

6. Find out the power consumption – is it a 3V or 5V sensor? Also, look for the pinouts – where does ground connect? Find out where the ground, power, and any other connections should be connected.

Chapter 6

1. The Protocol uses two wires, and it is for **serial clock (SCL)** and **serial data (SDA)**.

2. Unplugging the board so you don't accidentally surge the power.

3. The line of code turns on pixel number 4 in a string of pixels and turns it blue.

4. We can add light and vision to our wearables using LEDs, EL wire, NeoPixels, OLED displays, TFT screens, and other screens too.

5. The switch can be used to select different programs to run on the board.

6. The additional components are a transistor, a diode, and a resistor.

7. This was a reflection question.

Chapter 7

1. We can use any circuit board, but we may need to adapt it to fit the type of wearable we are making. We looked at modifying a circuit board to sew it into our circuit with more ease.

2. The three main parts of the microcontroller are the processor, memory (volatile, temporarily lost at board reset, and nonvolatile, where the memory stays even when power is off), and I/O peripherals.

3. Most have Wi-Fi and Bluetooth.

4. It is a good idea to develop your wearables in parts, component by component, mapping out a circuit on paper, and then building that one part. For example, add the OLED, make sure it works, then move on to adding the second component, and so on. The steps we followed to add our code were the following:

    I.   Begin by adding the libraries that the OLED uses at the top of the sketch

    II.   Then, work towards the `setup()` function where what we are using is initialized

    III. Follow with the behavior you want the code to execute

5. An API allows us to connect to and get data or information from another source. We are using the weather API, for example, to get the current weather information.

6. We needed the key to connect to our account so the service knows who is accessing this data information. We may have a limited account, for example, with limited calls, so they want to check our rates.

7. Yes, we can edit variables all at once throughout the code. Right-click and select **edit all occurrences** from the menu. Now, it will edit them all at the same time.

Chapter 8

1. The three main areas of prototyping are role, implementation, and look and feel.

2. These integration prototypes answer several of the design questions. They represent *the complete user experience of an artifact*. These are time-consuming to build because all the parts should be working or be good representatives of the final prototype.

3. A low-fidelity prototype might not necessarily look like the final version and will likely use different materials and an altered configuration, but it encourages reflection.

4. Understanding that different domains will have very different outcomes in terms of the environment we design for, the use, the placement, and so on. There are so many possible variations that designing a wearable for one domain will result in a completely different wearable solution for another.

5. The best way is to speak with people. Listen to them, their experiences and stories, and they can contribute in a meaningful way.

6. Fibers and yarns form the structures by being knitted, woven, or non-woven. Fibers can be bonded together using heat or a mechanical or chemical process.

7. Knit fabrics are made through a machine that forms rows and loops, and then it continues to create rows and loops through the previous row. Woven fabric on a loom has one set of yarns lengthwise and one set crossways. These yarns cross each other. Non-woven fabrics are made when fibers are molded, bonded, or felted. Faux leather is made using this technique.

8. One way to remember these differences is that knits are made from a single yarn and woven fabrics use multiple yarns (or threads) that cross each other.

9.   Checking the structure can be done by pulling the grin of the fabric and checking the movement in the straight grain, cross-grain, and diagonal bias.

Chapter 9

1.   Other senses discussed include movement, balance, and the position of where our body is and where we are in space.

2.   If we use clothing we already have, we don't have to create the item to wear first, which can be time-consuming. For rapid prototyping, starting with clothes that we can upcycle is economical and a great solution.

3.   Planning will save you time and help to prevent errors. Planning can help avoid putting components into places that you'll end up moving because they may stick out too much or be uncomfortable for the wearer.

4.   Plugging in the board, we should always check both the correct board and port have been selected from the **Tools** menu.

5.   A limitation of the ESP32 S2 chip is there is no Bluetooth.

6.   We would connect to a service such as `io.adafruit` to create our IoT projects.

7.   A feed is for connecting to our wearable or circuit to read or send data.

8.   We have a dashboard in `io.adafruit` so we can make the frontend, or the part that someone sees and interacts with. This is where we can display our data from the ESP32 and also use items such as buttons and graphs.

Chapter 10

1.   Soldering will make our wearable more durable and it will last a lot longer than if we left it on a prototyping breadboard.

2.   Some circuits have components too far apart. As we increase the distance of the conductive thread, the resistance also increases. This will prevent electricity from getting through.

3.   A bridged connection means that wires or pins are connected that should not be connected.

4.   We can tell if we have a bridged connection by using a multimeter to check whether there is an **open loop** (**OL**) or whether our multimeter makes a sound and registers a connection. If we hear the beep, that means it is bridged.

5.   We can use a solder wick to remove the solder from our wire or connection if we have put too much or need to remove the connection we made.

6.   Some good fabrics for wearables are sturdy fabrics such as denim and felt.

7.   A seam ripper will help us to open up a seam so that we can put electronics in between the fabric. It makes this process easier and less likely to damage the fabric.

8.   Adding IoT to a wearable can increase its usefulness for the wearer if used correctly. We can use IoT to track our data or to interact with the garment.

Chapter 11

1.   It's important to understand the context and history of your subject area. If you speak with people and they don't understand the subject, you will likely be wasting their time by not asking the right questions.

2.   Speaking to people is the best way to find out the stories that will ultimately help to create a design that is much more suited to its purpose.

3.   Some of the broad categories that we can consider include educational and research organizations, and researchers, government or policymakers, employers, professional associations and advocacy organizations, standard-setting organizations and organizations that provide technical assistance, companies, and the people directly involved in or affected by the topic.

4.   The three categories of impairment are the following:

   •   Permanent (a long-term wheelchair user, for example)

   •   Temporary (after accident or illness)

   •   Situational (a noisy environment, for example)

5.   Three important aspects to consider are the following:

   •   Sensory impairment (loss of vision or hearing)

   •   Physical impairment (loss of function in one or more parts of the body)

   •   Cognitive (a learning impairment or loss of memory or cognitive function due to old age or conditions such as Alzheimer's)

6.   With codesign, you are designing with the people who will benefit from the thing that is being designed. This happens all the way through the process so that they are part of it and offer meaningful contributions. Participatory design is about people participating at certain points in the project, but not necessarily the same people, and the amount of contribution will differ.

7.   It's extremely important to get the prototype to the wearer and create a feedback loop – a way for them to offer you feedback on what you are prototyping.

Chapter 12

1.   If we sew it, there will be an overlap with the ground thread that we've just sewn. It will cause a short, so our connections won't work, and it could damage our components. We need to provide insulation to the conductive thread.

2. The tack solder is a way to start soldering the board so we get an even and secured solder. We start with soldering one pin on one side of our board and then continue to the opposite side. It's a way to *tack* or hold it in place.

3. Clean and tin your solder iron to protect and extend the life of your tips.

4. You shouldn't use **pin 2** if you are using the charge board with the QT Py SAMD because it is being used by the board. There is a simple voltage divider on the cathode side of the diode. This is so that the firmware can detect the voltage. If it is higher than 4.3 V, it means you're likely to be plugged into the USB, allowing charging versus using the battery power. Because of this, you can't use the **A2** pin when using this power board.

5. `strip.fill()` fills the NeoPixel strip with one color. First, defined with (0,0,0), are the RGB color values. Secondly, which NeoPixel we want to start from is defined. NeoPixel 0 is the first one, and the third number in `strip.fill()`, is the NeoPixel position number to finish with.

6. `Case ('2')` gets called in our code through being sent in the code. We would have to send the 2 value to the switch case when we call the function – in this example, `tagActions('2');` is how we would call it to then execute the code.

Chapter 13

1. Setting the road map means that we can plan projects in different ways, but we might start with a component-based plan or a topic-based plan. This helps to set up our plan. Overall, it's good to consider the domain – for example, forgetfulness, or whatever your topic is – and look at comfort, usability, and style universe.

2. Iterating the designs is very important because it would be very rare to get a project perfect the first time round. After trying our devices and testing them with people, issues may surface that we can use can improve what we have created.

3. Non-volatile memory is retained even if the system is powered down.

4. Positive feedback – and one example of it is an initial sequence of lights to inform the wearer it is working. This is positive feedback from the system to communicate to the person that the system is functioning.

5. **EEPROM** is electrically erasable programmable read-only memory.

6. One note about flash memory is that it has a **limited** number of cycles on the same flash block for writing, which is around 10,000 write calls. After that, it may start to degrade.

7. A **global object** or **global variable** is declared before `setup()`, which allows it to be used throughout our program.

8. An **integration** prototype will involve **role, implementation**, and **look and feel**.

9. Tin the wire and add solder to **tin** the legs on your circuit board. Only apply a thin amount. By applying a thin layer of solder to both surfaces we want to join, it helps the solder to flow more easily between them, creating a good connection.

Chapter 14

1. The benefits of documenting our projects are that we can share them with the community and remember what we did.

2. Three possible ways to troubleshoot our circuits are to run a blink sketch, to check the board, and check the port. There are a few different responses to this though, including checking you are using a data cable, checking the power, and checking there are no bridged connections.

3. Other techniques include using 3D printing and laser cutting as tools for prototyping.

4. This is a reflection question. If there are aspects you've enjoyed or have questions about, you can tweet @cmoz.

5. This was a personal question about your techniques.

6. This is about your personal thoughts on the future, as a reflection exercise.

Index

`Packt.com`

Subscribe to our online digital library for full access to over 7,000 books and videos, as well as industry leading tools to help you plan your personal development and advance your career. For more information, please visit our website.

Why subscribe?

- Spend less time learning and more time coding with practical eBooks and Videos from over 4,000 industry professionals

- Improve your learning with Skill Plans built especially for you

- Get a free eBook or video every month

- Fully searchable for easy access to vital information

- Copy and paste, print, and bookmark content

Did you know that Packt offers eBook versions of every book published, with PDF and ePub files available? You can upgrade to the eBook version at `packt.com` and as a print book customer, you are entitled to a discount on the eBook copy. Get in touch with us at `customercare@packtpub.com` for more details.

At `www.packt.com`, you can also read a collection of free technical articles, sign up for a range of free newsletters, and receive exclusive discounts and offers on Packt books and eBooks.

Other Books You May Enjoy

If you enjoyed this book, you may be interested in these other books by Packt:

Developing IoT Projects with ESP32

Vedat Ozan Oner

ISBN: 9781838641160

- Explore advanced use cases like UART communication, sound and camera features, low-energy scenarios, and scheduling with an RTOS
- Add different types of displays in your projects where immediate output to users is required
- Connect to Wi-Fi and Bluetooth for local network communication
- Connect cloud platforms through different IoT messaging protocols
- Integrate ESP32 with third-party services such as voice assistants and IFTTT
- Discover best practices for implementing IoT security features in a production-grade solution

Raspberry Pi Pico DIY Workshop

Sai Yamanoor, Srihari Yamanoor

ISBN: 9781801814812

- Understand the RP2040's peripherals and apply them in the real world
- Find out about the programming languages that can be used to program the RP2040
- Delve into the applications of serial interfaces available on the Pico
- Discover add-on hardware available for the RP2040
- Explore different development board variants for the Raspberry Pi Pico
- Discover tips and tricks for seamless product development with the Pico

Packt is searching for authors like you

If you're interested in becoming an author for Packt, please visit `authors.packtpub.com` and apply today. We have worked with thousands of developers and tech professionals, just like you, to help them share their insight with the global tech community. You can make a general application, apply for a specific hot topic that we are recruiting an author for, or submit your own idea.

Share Your Thoughts

Now you've finished *The Ultimate Guide to Informed Wearable Technology*, we'd love to hear your thoughts! Scan the QR code below to go straight to the Amazon review page for this book and share your feedback or leave a review on the site that you purchased it from.

https://packt.link/r/1803230592

Your review is important to us and the tech community and will help us make sure we're delivering excellent quality content.

Download a free PDF copy of this book

Thanks for purchasing this book!

Do you like to read on the go but are unable to carry your print books everywhere? Is your eBook purchase not compatible with the device of your choice?

Don't worry, now with every Packt book you get a DRM-free PDF version of that book at no cost.

Read anywhere, any place, on any device. Search, copy, and paste code from your favorite technical books directly into your application.

The perks don't stop there, you can get exclusive access to discounts, newsletters, and great free content in your inbox daily

Follow these simple steps to get the benefits:

1. Scan the QR code or visit the link below

https://packt.link/free-ebook/9781803230597

2. Submit your proof of purchase
3. That's it! We'll send your free PDF and other benefits to your email directly

Ingram Content Group UK Ltd.
Milton Keynes UK
UKHW052334310523
422672UK00004B/22